IEE Management of Technology Series 4

Series Editor: G.A. Montgomerie

C000140990

MARKETING FOR ENGINEERS

About the author

John Bayliss has a broad experience of engineering industry, having worked in many product areas, such as electronics, heating and ventilating, vehicle components and electromechanical equipment. Following a degree in mechanical engineering his early career concentrated on the technical side of business, but following a masters degree in business administration he moved into marketing. Specific engineering experience includes product development, production engineering, quality control and factory management, while his marketing experience encompasses marketing research, planning, new business analysis (including takeover analysis), product management and marketing management.

In 1982, John joined the University of Aston for two years as a (Royal Society/ Science and Engineering Research Council sponsored) fellow to teach and research marketing, and it was in the latter part of the fellowship that he completed most of the work for this book and its associated case histories. Since the beginning of 1984 he has worked at the British Gas National Management Centre.

MARKETING FOR ENGINEERS

J S Bayliss

Peter Peregrinus Ltd on behalf of the Institution of Electrical Engineers

Previous volumes in this series

Volume 1   Technologies and markets
            J.J. Verschuur
Volume 2   The business of electronic product development
            Fabian Monds
Volume 3   The marketing of technology
            C.G. Ryan

Published by: Peter Peregrinus Ltd., London, UK.

© **1985: Peter Peregrinus Ltd.**

All rights reserved. No part of this publication may be reproduced, stored in a retrieval system or transmitted in any form or by any means — electronic, mechanical, photocopying, recording or otherwise — without the prior written permission of the publisher.

While the author and the publishers believe that the information and guidance given in this work is correct, all parties must rely upon their own skill and judgment when making use of it. Neither the author nor the publishers assume any liability to anyone for any loss or damage caused by any error or omission in the work, whether such error or omission is the result of negligence or any other cause. Any and all such liability is disclaimed.

British Library Cataloguing in Publication Data

Bayliss, J.S.
    Marketing for engineers. — (IEE Management of
technology series; 4)
    1. Marketing
    I. Title   II. Series
    658.8'02462   HF 5415

ISBN 0-86341-035-9

Printed in England by Short Run Press Ltd., Exeter

Contents

Preface		xv
1	**The marketing concept**	1
	1.1 What is marketing?	1
	1.2 The marketing concept	2
	1.3 Definitions of marketing	3
	1.4 Marketing management	3
	1.5 Strategic marketing	4
	1.6 Operational marketing	5
	1.7 Customers do not choose between competing products purely on technical performance and price	5
	1.8 Marketing and engineering	6
	1.9 Historical reasons for companies being product orientated	7
	1.10 Selling versus marketing	7
	1.11 Product orientation was no longer the right road	8
	1.12 Resistance to marketing	10
	1.13 Summary	11
2	**The marketing environment**	12
	2.1 Why the environment is important	12
	2.2 Macro environment	13
	2.2.1 The economy	13
	2.2.2 Technology	14
	2.2.3 Society	14
	2.2.4 Public policy	14
	2.3 Market environment	15
	2.4 Organisational environment	15
	2.5 Industrial market environment	16
	2.6 Chain of derived demand	18
	2.7 Ratchet effect	21
	2.8 Marketing response to a changing market environment	21

3   **Organising for marketing**   24
     3.1   Principles of organisation   24
     3.2   The functional organisation   26
     3.3   Product group organisation   29
     3.4   The matrix organisation   31
     3.5   Project based structures   32
     3.6   Customer or industry based structures   33
     3.7   Geographic based structure   34

4   **Information**   36
     4.1   Information provides a factual basis for decisions   36
     4.2   Information provides early warning of change   36
     4.3   Information time horizons   37
            4.3.1   Long term   37
            4.3.2   Medium term   37
            4.3.3   Short term   39
     4.4   What information should be sought   39
            4.4.1   The environment   39
            4.4.2   The market   40
            4.4.3   The product   40
            4.4.4   Company performance   40
     4.5   Information sources: records of company performance 41
     4.6   Information sources: company contacts with the market 42
     4.7   Information sources: publications   43
     4.8   Information sources: formal marketing research   45
     4.9   The research brief   45
     4.10   General research methodology   47
     4.11   Choosing field data sources   47
     4.12   Choosing sources in industrial markets   48
     4.13   Postal questionnaires   50
     4.14   Personal interviews   53
     4.15   Telephone interviews   55
     4.16   Causes of incorrect information   55
     4.17   Marketing research summary   57
     4.18   Marketing information systems   58
     4.19   Using information   62

5   **Forecasting**   64
     5.1   Why and what to forecast   64
     5.2   Choice of forecasting method   65
     5.3   Technological forecasting   67
     5.4   Scenario building   69
     5.5   The Delphi technique   71
     5.6   Normative relevance analysis   73

5.7	Substitution forecasting	74
5.8	Forecasting market potential	75
5.9	Trend extension	76
5.10	The experience curve	80
5.11	Forecasting unit costs	82
5.12	Correlation	82
5.13	Models	83
5.14	The PIMS model	84
5.15	Bayesian analysis	86
5.16	Sales forecasting using probabilities	89
5.17	In conclusion	92

6 Market structure and segmentation — **94**
6.1	Structural elements of a market	94
6.2	Number and size of producers	95
6.3	Influence of economies of scale	96
6.4	Influence of technology	97
6.5	Influence of product differentiation	99
6.6	Number and size of distributors	101
6.7	Horizontal and vertical integration	101
6.8	Market segmentation	102
6.9	Methods of segmentation	103
6.10	Benefiting from segmentation	105

7 Product analysis — **107**
7.1	Introduction	107
7.2	Product life cycle	107
7.3	Using product life cycles to shape marketing strategy	110
	7.3.1 Introductory phase	110
	7.3.2 Growth phase	112
	7.3.3 Maturity phase	113
	7.3.4 Saturation phase	114
	7.3.5 Decline phase	115
	7.3.6 Abandonment	115
7.4	Using product life cycles to plan product succession	116
7.5	Technology life cycles	119
7.6	Life cycle expenditure and income	120
7.7	Portfolio analysis	122
	7.7.1 Boston matrix	123
	7.7.2 GEC/McKinsey matrix	127
7.8	Gap analysis	128

8 Planning — **131**
8.1	Why plan?	131

8.2	Planning alerts companies to gradual change		132
8.3	Planning is systematic and hierarchical		133
8.4	Planning is an iterative process		136
8.5	Elements of a plan		138
	8.5.1	Company purpose	138
	8.5.2	Business definition	138
	8.5.3	Objectives	139
	8.5.4	Strategy	140
	8.5.5	Action programmes	140
	8.5.6	Budgets	140
8.6	Preparing a plan – the logical approach		141
8.7	Why the logical approach is rarely followed		141
8.8	Preparing a plan – the normal approach		143
8.9	How the planning process can be improved		145
	8.9.1	Understanding how planning helps companies survive	145
	8.9.2	Helping managers in their daily activities	146
	8.9.3	Simplifying the planning process	147
	8.9.4	Introducing incentives to plan	147
8.10	Implementing plans		148
8.11	Planning – a summary		149
9	**Product market planning**		152
9.1	What is a product market strategy?		152
9.2	Evaluation of markets		153
9.3	Evaluation of product and market related risk		156
9.4	The buyer's risk premium		159
9.5	Towards a product market strategy		162
9.6	The problem of product abandonment		165
10	**Introducing new products**		168
10.1	The importance of new products		168
10.2	Methods of innovation		169
10.3	Unnecessary innovation		172
10.4	Organising for innovation		173
10.5	Scale of development effort needed		175
10.6	Product development risk		177
10.7	Idea generation		178
10.8	Screening		180
10.9	Business analysis		186
10.10	Development and testing		187
10.11	Product launch		191

11 Pricing   194
11.1   What is price?   194
11.2   Pricing goals   195
11.3   Price tends not to be used aggressively   197
11.4   Price–volume relationship   199
    11.4.1   Companies cannot systematically change prices   200
    11.4.2   A large number of interdependent variables affect
            price   201
    11.4.3   Influence of industry wide prices   202
    11.4.4   Existence of price bands   202
    11.4.5   Link between price and reputation   203
    11.4.6   Influence of discounts   203
11.5   Price–profit–volume relationship   203
11.6   Cost-plus pricing   204
11.7   Matching the competition   207
11.8   Price and market structure   208
11.9   Price and the economic cycle   210
11.10   Pricing products   211
11.11   Pricing product ranges   214
11.12   Competitive bidding   215
11.13   Pricing capital goods   220
11.14   Summary   221

12 Industrial buying   225
12.1   Why study buyer behaviour?   225
12.2   Consumers buy different types of goods differently   225
12.3   Basic consumer buying behaviour models   227
    12.3.1   Buying stages model   227
    12.3.2   Choice parameters model   228
    12.3.3   Learning model   228
    12.3.4   Psychoanalytic model   229
    12.3.5   Social psychological model   229
    12.3.6   Buying role model   229
    12.3.7   Logical model   231
12.4   Industrial buyers   231
12.5   Industrial purchasing is not necessarily logical or thorough   233
    12.5.1   Decisions are affected by previous experience   234
    12.5.2   Team decisions are often not logical   234
    12.5.3   Industrial purchasers are not necessarily well in-
            formed   235
    12.5.4   Industrial purchasers seek to reduce risk   235
    12.5.5   Industrial purchasers seek satisfactory purchases
            rather than best buys   237
12.6   Process used to search for alternative suppliers   238

12.7 Factors which inhibit a thorough search for and evaluation of suppliers   240
12.8 How purchasing decisions are arrived at   241
12.9 Different types of product are bought differently   243
12.10 Implications for marketing   247
    12.10.1 Buying team   247
    12.10.2 Different types of purchase   248
    12.10.3 Risk   251
    12.10.4 Established purchaser—supplier relationships   252
    12.10.5 Limited search   253
    12.10.6 Inability to properly compare competing products   253
    12.10.7 Post-purchase dissonance   254
12.11 Buying in the future   255

13 Promotion   256
13.1 Why promotion is needed   256
13.2 Popular image of advertising   257
13.3 Role of advertising   259
    13.3.1 Awareness   260
    13.3.2 Interest and image   260
    13.3.3 Credibility   261
    13.3.4 Distributor enthusiasm   261
    13.3.5 Enquiries   262
    13.3.6 Reinforcement   263
13.4 The advertising process   263
    13.4.1 Audience identification   264
    13.4.2 The message   264
    13.4.3 The medium   265
    13.4.4 Presentation   267
    13.4.5 Advertisement positioning, timing, size, coverage and frequency   268
13.5 Exhibitions   273
    13.5.1 Why exhibit?   273
    13.5.2 Types of exhibition   274
    13.5.3 International exhibitions   274
    13.5.4 National exhibitions   275
    13.5.5 Local exhibitions   276
    13.5.6 Single company exhibitions   276
13.6 Direct mail   277
13.7 Other promotion   278
    13.7.1 Brochures/catalogues   278
    13.7.2 Public relations   279
    13.7.3 Conferences and technical articles   280
    13.7.4 Posters   281

	13.7.5	Sponsorship	281
	13.7.6	Free trials	281
	13.7.7	Packaging	282
13.8	Promotional budgets		282
	13.8.1	Matching historic levels of expenditure	284
	13.8.2	Budgeting to spend a fixed percentage of forecast sales	284
	13.8.3	Matching the competition	286
	13.8.4	Residual money approach	286
	13.8.5	Task related method	287
	13.8.6	Budget setting recommendation	288
13.9	Looking ahead		288

14 Sales force decisions — 289

14.1	Introduction	289
14.2	Role of the sales force	289
14.3	Sales force size	290
	14.3.1 Sales forecast	290
	14.3.2 Number of sales visits required	291
	14.3.3 Call capacity and journey planning	293
	14.3.4 Calculation of sales force size	293
	14.3.5 Can this sales force size be afforded	294
14.4	Sales force structure	296
	14.4.1 Division by customer type	296
	14.4.2 Division by product type	296
	14.4.3 Division by geography	298
	14.4.4 Division by a combination of criteria	298
14.5	Territories and sales quotas	300
	14.5.1 Calculation of territory sales potential	300
	14.5.2 Practical problems	302
14.6	Sales force control	303
14.7	Recruitment	309
14.8	Training	310
14.9	Motivation	312
14.10	Payment schemes	312
14.11	Appraisal	314
14.12	Expenses	315
14.13	Key accounts	315
14.14	Technical applications advice	316
14.15	Customer training	316

15 Selling — 318

| 15.1 | Sales role | 318 |
| 15.2 | Identification of potential customers | 320 |

15.3	Assessment of customers and prospective customers	321
15.4	Preplanning sales visits	323
15.5	Selling	324
15.6	Time planning	328
15.7	Selling high value items	331
15.8	Selling to large organisations	333
15.9	In conclusion	334

16 Distribution — 336
16.1	Why distribution is important	336
16.2	Influence of the type of product	336
16.3	Elements of physical distribution systems	338
16.4	Some basic concepts pertinent to physical distribution	339
	16.4.1 Customer service level	339
	16.4.2 Influence of order processing delays	340
	16.4.3 Delivery reliability	341
	16.4.4 Cost effective stock levels	342
16.5	Factors influencing the choice of physical distribution method	343
	16.5.1 Value and physical size of orders	343
	16.5.2 Number and geographic spread of customers	344
	16.5.3 Delivery frequency	345
	16.5.4 Technical complexity of the product	346
	16.5.5 Installation and service help required	346
16.6	Types of industrial distribution channels	347
16.7	Choice of distribution channel and channel members	347
16.8	Controlling a channel	352
16.9	Influence of computers	354

17 Marketing control and audit — 356
17.1	Defining marketing control	356
17.2	Setting objectives: measurable parameters	357
	17.2.1 Numerical parameters	358
	17.2.2 Time parameters	359
	17.2.3 Non-numerical parameters	359
17.3	Setting objectives: typical examples	359
	17.3.1 Sales mix	359
	17.3.2 Customer service level	360
17.4	Reporting procedures	361
	17.4.1 Reporting numeric data	362
17.5	Tracing the cause of deviations from plan	363
17.6	Control response time	364
17.7	Link between control and motivation	365
17.8	Marketing audit	367

17.9   Independent plan   371
17.10   Auditing the system   371
        17.10.1 Objectives*   371
        17.10.2 Information   372
        17.10.3 Preparation   373
        17.10.4 Using the plan   373
17.11   In conclusion   374

References   375

Bibliography   379

Case histories   382

Preface

Few engineers start their career in marketing, but most become involved in some way as their career evolves; initially, perhaps, because of marketing constraints on their design freedom or their ability to produce at what seems to be maximum efficiency. However, as they move up the hierarchy and become more involved with planning and policy, marketing considerations begin to play a larger role in their jobs. Many engineers will actually take on marketing responsibilities at some stage in their career, possibly early on as sales engineers or as market planners, or perhaps later on as general managers. Nearly all of them will have had little or no formal training in marketing. Quite a few will rely on studying what their peers and superiors do, but unfortunately many of these people will themselves have had no formal training. Others will try to correct their lack of knowledge by studying a text book or attending a course. However, there is a good chance that the material will be more related to selling televisions, sausages or furniture than to control systems, machining centres or castings, and will be presented on the assumption of large resources, a large advertising budget, a large marketing research department and a large sales force. As a result, many a new student is 'turned off'; he simply cannot relate 'marketing' to what he sees around him at work.

This book tries to put that right, partly by setting marketing concepts in the context of the engineering industry, and partly by referring to examples of how engineering companies actually market their products. These examples have been published separately (see order form) in the form of case histories, with each case specifically written to expand points made in the relevant chapter of this book, and to provide the opportunity to apply the ideas to real life situations. Hopefully, working through case histories in this way will reduce the tendency for new converts to marketing to apply marketing concepts without thinking through the complications. Application without understanding usually does not furnish the desired results, and not only does this reduce the convert's enthusiasm, it also damages the image of marketing within his company.

This is damage that marketing needs to avoid if it is to be more widely applied in the engineering industry; and the evidence indicates that it does. There are still too many companies failing to plan a succession of products, preferring to wait for irrefutable signs of falling sales of existing models before commencing development of successors; or failing to develop new products based on researched customer needs rather than on engineering or production grounds; or failing to realise that a good product is only part, and sometimes a minor part, of sales success; or failing to study buyer behaviour and plan the promotion and sales strategy accordingly; or failing to adopt many of the other marketing principles dealt with in this book.

Marketing departments in engineering companies tend to be small — in many cases as small as one person — and therefore none of the methods described requires the resources of a large department to enable them to be properly applied. They are equally applicable to both products and services, and to home and overseas markets, and so no special reference to the marketing of engineering services or to export marketing has been necessary.

Although primarily aimed at engineers taking on marketing responsibilities, the book is suitable for other engineers, who need to appreciate the aims and methods of marketing if they are to fully contribute to their companies' commercial success. They will be better placed to understand otherwise inexplicable decisions, leading perhaps to less resentment of inputs from marketing which limit their freedom of action. Proper application of the marketing concept requires the co-operation of all departments, and this co-operation is more likely if everyone has an understanding of what is involved. Knowledge of marketing can also help engineers in more direct ways, such as winning support for a particular plan or development project, or ensuring that new products are enthusiastically taken up by operating units.

All engineers need to understand that even in high technology companies, technical superiority is not sufficient by itself to guarantee success. Non-technological factors such as a superior sales organisation, a strong image for service, efficient forecasting, or careful planning, can be more important. Perhaps it would help if the label 'excellent engineering' were not applied to technical excellence on its own, but only where the technical excellence leads to beneficial use; and beneficial in the eyes of users rather than producers.

J. Bayliss
August 1984

Chapter 1

The Marketing Concept

1.1. What is marketing

Without orders companies go out of business. In order to obtain orders companies have to continue to offer products and services at a price people are prepared to pay; but that is only half the story. The price people are prepared to pay has to yield sufficient profit to enable companies to cover their immediate operating costs, their development costs and their existing capital costs, as well as providing enough net profit to attract further investment. Marketing helps achieve this state of affairs by:

1 Finding out what people will buy, now and in the future (i.e. by marketing research and forecasting).
2 Assessing a company's strengths, be they in a particular manufacturing technique, design skill or distribution system, in order to determine which markets the company can efficiently operate in, and which products (or services*) it will offer for sale in those markets (i.e. by planning).
3 Selecting from the possibilities, products which can be sold in sufficient volume and at a sufficient price to generate an adequate profit (i.e. product planning).
4 Ensuring that the products which are developed do actually meet customer requirements (i.e. product testing and pricing).
5 Drawing attention to and presenting the chosen products in their best light (i.e. selling and promotion).
6 Making the products readily available to customers (i.e. distribution).
7 Ensuring that the product(s) continues to meet customers' requirements; in the short term via quality control, cost control and after-sales service; and in the long term by evaluating how customer requirements are changing (i.e. by control, marketing research and forecasting).

* For the sake of brevity from now on reference will normally be made to products only, but most of the ideas equally apply to services.

Item 7 brings us full circle, back to finding out what people will buy, and therefore the marketing process can be considered as a loop of activities (see Fig. 1.1) round which a company must continue to travel if it is to remain competitive.

information
gathering

ensuring that the
product continues to
meet customer requirements

information analysis
and forecasting

making the product
readily available

deciding what demand
the company can
profitably meet

influencing
demand

organising to meet
those requirements
including developing
and producing
products

Fig. 1.1   *The marketing loop*

1.2 The marketing concept

It can be seen from Section 1.1 that the marketing process focuses on identifying and meeting customer requirements. In other words 'organisations must learn to think of themselves not as producing goods or services, but as buying customers, as doing things that will make people want to do business with them' (Leavitt [1]). Marketing then is an approach to business which places the customer at the centre of company thinking. It recognises that the market is the final arbiter of success or failure, and that the requirements of the market are paramount.

These concepts led to the development of so-called 'marketing concept'. The concept embraces three key ideas, namely:

1 It is not sales volume alone that is important but profitable sales.
2 In today's climate it is often marketing and not technical or production problems which are most critical to the success of a company.
3 Potential customers must be offered what they (and not the suppliers) perceive as real value for money and this can only be achieved by identifying and understanding their requirements.

To quote Kotler [2], 'the marketing concept is the achievement of good profits by giving the customer genuine value and satisfaction'.

1.3 Definitions of marketing

These ideas have been encapsulated in numerous definitions of marketing. One of the better ones reads as follows:

> Marketing is the management function which organises and directs all those business activities involved in assessing and converting customer purchasing power into effective demand, for a specific product or service, and in moving the product or service to the final consumer or user so as to achieve the profit target or other objective set by a company. (Institute of Marketing)

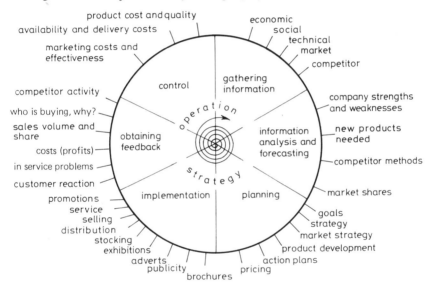

Fig. 1.2 *The marketing cycle*

1.4 Marketing management

Marketing management involves many different functions. To help understand how each function relates to the others, they can be fitted into the continuous loop or cycle referred to earlier (Fig. 1.1), as shown in Fig. 1.2. It is not necessary or sensible always to travel continuously right round the circle; it may be necessary to dodge from one part to another or to emphasise one function more than another, as circumstances demand. However, the overriding need to circulate the outer loop should not be forgotten.

The marketing management cycle divides naturally into two parts; the longer term or strategic part, and the shorter term or operational part.

1.5 Strategic marketing

Strategic marketing is concerned with the broad issues; with which markets a company should operate in; with whether a company should incorporate the latest technology in its products or adopt only what has been proven in service; and with whether a company should operate in Germany or Hong Kong or wherever. For example, if the industry is to be electronics, is it to be components, control panels, hi-fi or video games; is the main competitive weapon to be a superior product, low cost production, superior distribution, better promotion or some combination of all these? Is the operation to be limited to the UK, to Europe or is the company going to try to compete in other parts of the world?

Strategic marketing takes the objectives laid out in a company's corporate plan, such as target turnover, target profit margin and the specification of the industries in which the company wishes to operate, and interprets them into a marketing plan. The marketing plan specifies how the objectives are to be achieved, in the light of the forecast behavior of what have been termed (Kotler [2]) the non-controllable demand variables. The non-controllable demand variables are the factors which will affect industry as well as company sales, namely:

(a) Customer variables – the number of potential customers in the market and their rate of usage of the product.
(b) Environmental variables – technology, culture, public policy and the economy.
(c) Competitive variables – competitor actions including new entrants to the market.

The ability to forecast changes in these variables is one of the crucial factors of business success, and will be dealt with in more detail in later chapters.

Based on the forecast behaviour of these variables, the marketing plan will specify the settings of those variables that a company can control; that is, the variables which will influence its sales volume alone. These factors have been termed [2] marketing decision variables and they have been defined in terms of either:

(a) (i) the offering – the product, packaging, branding, price, service; and
    (ii) the methods and tools – distribution channels, advertising, promotion, publicity, personal selling (Frey [3]).
(b) the well known four Ps (McCarthy [4]) of the marketing mix (see Fig. 1.3).

The marketing mix contains the factors which a company can control in order to maximise profits and sales volume, namely:

Product	what it does, appearance, expected life
Place	getting the product to where the customer will buy it or use it
Promotion	drawing attention to the product
Price	including discounts, credit terms, free delivery or installation

Fig. 1.3 *The marketing mix*

Once the overall marketing plan has been agreed a more detailed operating plan will normally be prepared. Taken together the two plans will specify what is to be sold, in what quantities, at what price, when, where and how.

1.6 Operational marketing

Operational marketing is the area of most concern, at least in time terms, to marketing personnel. It is concerned with the day to day management of the marketing mix. That is, the management of the sales force, the development and placing of advertisements, the preparation for and attendance at exhibitions, the processing and delivery of orders and so on.

To summarise, strategic marketing involves appreciating what a company can do best and interpreting that in terms of current and predicted market requirements, in order to decide what product(s) will be offered to what groups of customers. Operational marketing involves maximising profitable sales of those products.

1.7 Customers do not choose between competing products purely on technical performance and price

It is worth emphasising that decisions about what products to offer for sale should not be made purely on the basis of the technical strengths of a company (see Section 1.1 [2]). This is because, when customers choose between similarly priced products, they do not just take into account product features and product performance. As a result, competitive advantage cannot be attained only by product related attributes, that is, by technical excellence alone. In fact customers take into account a whole range of benefits which may be on offer, such as quick reliable delivery, technical applications advice, installation help, users guides and training, after-sales service, compatibility with other equipment and supplier reputation. For example, as products become more complex, customers are less able to select individual components and package them together in a manner which provides the best system for them. Manufacturers increase the utility of what they offer by providing this packaging service, that is, by offering a system rather than a collection of products – perhaps an energy control system rather than individual flow meters, thermostats, temperature recorders, electronic control devices and so on.

Computers are an excellent example where customers clearly do not choose between makes entirely on the basis of the hardware, but take account of applications advice, programming services, standard software, training programmes and manuals, maintenance and extendability.

Obviously customers do not evaluate these benefits in a general way, but instead, in relation to how they can be of direct use to them. The more exactly their needs are satisfied, the more highly they will value any 'package of benefits' offered to them. To take a very simple example, if the prime need is to have a pump which works reliably, it is of no advantage to be shown a new pump which is quieter or is more efficient, but requires more maintenance. Therefore, although attaining improved performance is undoubtedly a technical achievement, it will not necessarily by itself increase customers' perceptions of the value offered. In fact it is possible to design products which can be readily sold at a higher price than other products that may have higher production costs and be technically brilliant, but which do not meet customer needs so exactly.

1.8 Marketing and engineering

How do these ideas affect engineering? Well, engineering companies generate wealth by adding value to raw materials. They generate profits by adding more value than the cost of their operations, as shown in Fig. 1.4.

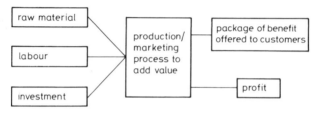

Fig. 1.4   *The value adding process*

Obviously profits can be increased either by reducing costs or by increasing customers' perceptions of the value of the package offered to them. The following are typical ways of reducing costs:

1 Increased volume
2 Improved utilisation of raw materials — by good product design, good buying or reduced process waste
3 Improved utilisation of labour — by good product and organisational design, efficient operation and good buying/training
4 Increased investment — in efficient development, efficient plant and equipment, efficient promotion and distribution, and efficient organisation and planning

and of increasing the perceived value:

5 Good product design — that is quality, performance, reliability, expected life, versatility, appearance, ease of use, life costs etc.
6 Efficient distribution
7 Effective promotion and pricing

Clearly, marketing has a vital role to play with respect to items 1, 3, 4, 6 and 7, but following from Section 1.7, marketing also has a crucial input into item 5, in the form of product specifications (see Section 10.10) which direct engineering efforts towards providing benefits that customers particularly value.

1.9 Historical reasons for companies being product orientated

While all this may sound obvious, it does not seem to be reflected in the actions of all engineering companies. Part of the reason may lie in the past. If one looks back to the beginning of industrial production, the ability to design and produce something that worked at all, and which actually kept on working in use, was a major achievement. Companies which were able to achieve in this way tended to find a ready sale for their products, because, on the whole, each new working product represented a significant improvement on what was previously available. The ability to sell was largely dependent on the ability to produce the product in the first place.

As time progressed more and more people learned how to produce satisfactory working products. However the obvious answer to this additional competition seemed to be to build a better product. The emphasis was still firmly on design and production.

Inevitably this situation gradually changed. Competition hotted up; more and more people became capable of producing a given product. In parallel, designs became more complicated and it became more difficult for customers to judge whether one product was really better than another. As a result, while technical superiority still supplied a significant answer to the increased competition, in order to ensure a healthy level of orders, it became necessary to actively persuade customers of the merits of one's products. The ability to sell had become crucial to commercial success.

1.10 Selling versus marketing

Although this was a significant step-forward, selling was not the complete answer. To understand why, it is necessary to examine the differences between marketing and selling. Marketing has developed out of selling. A good salesman does not attempt to close a sale until he has found out the reason the customer became interested in the product in the first place. Unless the salesman is aware of what will motivate the customer, he cannot be sure that he is using the right arguments to persuade the customer that his product is precisely the one that the customer wants. To take a simple example, it is no good trying to sell a house to someone who does not like walking upstairs. Marketing has taken this concept and enlarged it into a complete system for finding out about and fulfilling customer needs.

However, there is a major philosophical difference between selling and marketing. Selling enters the picture *after* products have been designed and produced. Selling concentrates on persuading as many people as possible to buy those products. Marketing, on the other hand, enters the picture *at the beginning* rather than at the end of the marketing cycle (see Fig. 1.5). It involves (refer to Section 1.1 and Fig. 1.5) identifying the requirements of the market, and then, in the light of company resources, highlighting those requirements that a company can organise itself to meet with the greatest competitive advantage. In that way marketing tries to prevent companies from designing and producing products which will be hard to sell because they do not meet customer requirements, and/or do not offer a significant competitive advantage.

To do this properly involves finding out exactly what the customer wants, not just in terms of product features, but in terms of items such as delivery availability, payment terms, installation help, and servicing; and liaising with the rest of the company or organisation to ensure that these wants are properly satisfied. The aim is to satisfy customers' needs more closely than one's competitors and for this approach to be successful all departments within a company whose actions affect the customer must be geared to the meeting of customer needs. It is surprising when you think about it how many departments are involved: research and development; buying; accounts; production; distribution; quality control; secretarial; telephonists, as well as sales, marketing and senior management.

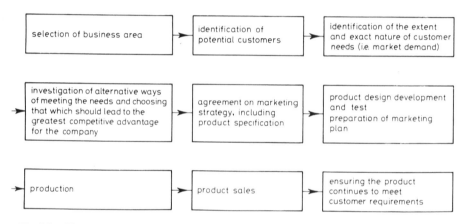

Fig. 1.5   *The activity flow in a marketing oriented company*

Marketing is only really of use when it forms part of a total approach to business and is integrated into the organisation and its decision making structure. It will not work if the concept is restricted to the activities of a single department: 'the difference between marketing and sales is the difference between seeding a field and harvesting the crops. Good marketing is tantamount to planting seeds; without planting there would be no future crops' (Kotler [5]). It is this difference that is at the heart of the marketing concept. It is not sufficient to sell what production can most efficiently make, instead it is necessary to adapt the production facility to produce what people wish to buy. A real change in the way of thinking is needed.

1.11 Product orientation was no longer the right road

The need to change the way of thinking became increasingly apparent in the 1950s and 60s, because companies which held to the traditional product orientation lost more and more market share to those which had adapted the marketing way of thinking. Engineering companies faced the following situation:

1 The world's technical ability had advanced so far that many companies in many countries were now able to design and produce acceptable reliable products.
2 Even when a better product was developed and launched, rivals were soon on the road to producing a copy, something similar, or often, something better.
3 The rate of technical change had increased, making it necessary to introduce new products more frequently, simply to keep up and to avoid being left with dated products.
4 Although many improvements in production technology had been aimed at improved product quality, most had been aimed at reduced unit costs – largely achieved by designing plant and equipment that could produce at higher rates. In order to be competitively efficient even small companies had to produce at increasingly high volumes. This meant that when new products were launched a much higher initial investment was required in order to provide plant of the required capacity, and a much larger sales potential was needed for that plant to be competitively utilised. It also meant that the world's capacity to produce had begun to outstrip its desire to consume, and more and more companies found themselves selling into a buyer's market.

Increased investment, shorter product lives, and increased worldwide competition, made it necessary to profit from new products more rapidly than previously. In other words, rapid sales growth was needed. Companies could not afford to launch products which might not sell well, and to avoid this possibility, they needed more exact information about the customer requirements that products were aimed at, about who the customers would be, about how they could be reached and about the volume they were likely to buy. Companies had to begin to think in marketing terms.

Increased competition also meant that customers were provided with a wider product choice, and as a result they became more selective, only buying products which met their requirements more or less exactly. Companies who did not take the trouble to find out what it was that people wanted to buy, and who did not organise themselves to provide it, found it hard to sell in sufficient volume to generate sufficient profit to keep up with technical change. Typical examples were the British machine tool and motor cycle industry.

In addition, buyers continued to find it increasingly difficult to directly compare the performance of competing industrial products, because as they became more complex, and there was more copying, the differences became less obvious to the non-specialist.

As product differences became less and less obvious, and product advantages increasingly short lived, companies had to look for non-product competitive advantages that might last longer and that might compensate for less product differentiation. Advantages such as product training, after-sales service, free consultancy, or, perhaps most important of all, a good reputation (see also Section 6.5).

Thus, there were two main reasons why marketing grew in importance. First there was the need to find out as much as possible about market requirements, and second there was the need to find and promote non-product competitive advantages.

1.12 Resistance to marketing

Unfortunately it took many companies far too long to recognise the changed business environment (and some companies still have not). They continued to concentrate on product superiority, sometimes with fatal results. This was partly due to the historic factors already outlined, but there were many other reasons (see, for example, Rodger [6]). Some of these reasons arose because engineering companies found it difficult to implement the marketing philosophy. For example:

1 In technically oriented companies engineers are often sent out to undertake marketing research. They seek out and talk to other engineers in customer companies and not surprisingly return with a list of technical parameters dominating their reports. As a result too much attention is paid to the technical aspects of product development, and too little attention to planning a succession of new products which closely meet customer requirements, to the method of launching these new products, and to obtaining rapid acceptance of them by the market. Concorde is perhaps a classic example of the results of this type of approach.
2 It is not easy to find out exactly what customers need. Often they do not know themselves. Almost certainly it will be different to what the manufacturer expects them to want. There is a temptation to dismiss the differences along the lines that customers cannot be expected to know any better; we will educate them. While this can be true of new technology it is rarely true of established technology.
3 The benefits are slow to show. It can be several years before a changed approach leads to a significantly improved sales position.
4 The first task often given to a new marketing department is to research and forecast next year's sales. Such first forecasts are notoriously inaccurate, leading to the reaction 'you cannot do any better than us'. It is forgotten that part of the marketing approach is to build up a sound information base in order to improve forecasting accuracy, precisely because forecasts made from poor information almost certainly will be poor themselves.
5 Many long term successful companies have never claimed to be marketing oriented but in reality are, whereas many who claim to be marketing oriented have simply changed managers and departmental titles and not their basic approach to business.

The situation was not helped by early overselling of marketing as a universal panacea (a common happening when people are trying to persuade others to adopt something new). Nor was it helped by some writers who suggested that because marketing was crucial to success, companies should be dominated by their marketing departments — with associated loss of authority and status by other departments; the very people who were being asked to introduce marketing.

1.13 Summary

In the past, formal marketing may not have been undertaken, but many successful businesses were founded on the entrepreneur's instinct for what the customer wanted. The proverbial high class mousetrap only sold because: (1) lots of people needed one; (2) lots of people came to hear it was superior, and (3) it was readily available. What has changed is that there are now 20 other companies who can make an equally good mousetrap, ten of them are very active at publicising the fact and seven of them can offer the mousetrap at a better price. Five of these offer immediate delivery and three attain superior profits.

What has also changed is that tastes and technology move on more rapidly than they used to and it is only the three more profitable companies who can generate sufficient resources to take advantage of new technology. Possibly only two of these are truly marketing orientated and recognise that customers now want better looking and easier to clean mousetraps. Gradually they introduce even better mousetraps and at a more competitive price, and attain market dominance. In other words, the faster tastes and technology change and the more competitive the market, the more important it is to offer a preferred product — preferred in the sense that more people are persuaded that they wish to buy it.

Much of the skill of marketing lies in an ability to understand the appeal of a product, not from a product oriented or manufacturers view, but from the would be purchasers' point of view. It has often been said that customers do not buy product features, they buy benefits — benefits to them as a result of using the product. Taking a real interest in the needs of the user helps manufacturers understand what those benefits are.

The marketing approach to business requires a marketing input from the beginning of the product development cycle. The emphasis should be on the anticipation of change and on the planned response to that change. The aim is to achieve the sale of a succession of profitable products and this will only become possible if customers are offered what they perceive to be real value for money.

Thus, marketing offers companies the following potential benefits (Rodger [6]):

1 A reduction in business risk, following the systematic gathering of information. A reliable data base reduces the uncertainty involved in taking decisions.
2 Improved planning, by concentrating on the early identification of changes in the non-controllable demand variables, and highlighting market trends and opportunities. Marketing particularly helps minimise the risk of mistiming the introduction of new technology and new products by concentrating on the applicability of technology to user needs.
3 Improved competitiveness through the practice of skills aimed at correctly identifying customer needs and aimed at skillfully presenting the resultant 'offering' in terms of those needs.

Chapter 2

The Marketing Environment

2.1 Why the environment is important

Businesses not only have to exist in their environment but they exist because of it. It is the environment that provides the customer need which businesses set out to meet. The environment provides the business opportunity. The environment is also

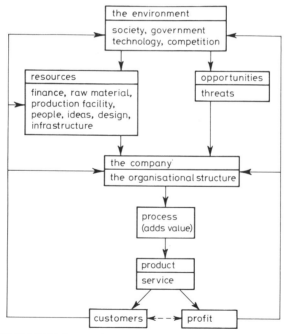

Fig. 2.1 *Business and its environment*

a source of threat to the ongoing health of a business because it limits and changes the resources available, limits and changes customer needs, and creates and changes the nature of competition. This interdependence of business with the environment is summarised in Fig. 2.1.

'Business strategy is a statement of how resources are to be acquired and used to take advantage of selected opportunities, and which will minimise recognised threats in order to achieve a stated result' (Michel [7]). Management's role is to select and implement strategy. To do this they must be aware of the environment in which they operate, of how it is changing, and of opportunities and threats which that changing environment creates.

At the broadest level the (macro) environment is influenced by the economy, technology, society and public policy. The macro environment influences and provides the setting for a number of micro or market environments, which in turn influence and provide the setting in which companies operate (see Fig. 2.2).

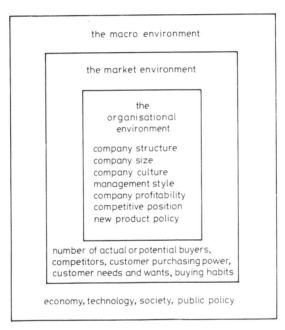

the macro environment

the market environment

the
organisational
environment

company structure
company size
company culture
management style
company profitability
competitive position
new product policy

number of actual or potential buyers,
competitors, customer purchasing power,
customer needs and wants, buying habits

economy, technology, society, public policy

Fig. 2.2   *The environment*

2.2 Macro environment

How then do each of the macro environmental factors affect the market environment.

2.2.1 The economy

The effect on markets of the economic cycle of recession and expansion is well known, and therefore need not be detailed here. Although there are still some inevitable leads and lags between the cycles of individual countries, particularly between countries which supply raw material and the rest of the world, the trade of the developed world is now so interlinked that the cycle is tending to occur more or less at the same time all around the world. As a result, it is no longer valid to assume that the worst effects of recession can be countered simply by exporting a larger percentage of one's output. Other action is needed.

One possibility is to attempt to increase market share, but quite obviously many of one's competitors will have the same thoughts. A second possibility is to try to ensure that one has a flexible manufacturing process; one which can be efficiently operated at low volumes as well as high volumes. The third possibility is to try to forecast the cycle so as to keep ahead of it, or at least to keep in tandem with it, rather than behind it. In other words, by the time a recession has begun, companies which look ahead will have begun to cut back production so as not to be left with high and depreciating stocks which tie up cash. For example, in mid-summer 1982 a well known car producer had fields full of unsold cars, built as long as eighteen months previously. In order to clear high stocks, production has to be cut back to even lower levels than the reduction in demand (see Section 2.6).

2.2.2 Technology

Technological progress not only affects what can be produced and how it can be produced but it also affects people's expectations of what they need. For example, improvements in technology made home central heating possible; the existence of central heating affected people's clothing habits and created a demand for double glazing and wall insulation. As indicated in Chapter 1, the faster technology changes and the faster customer needs change, the more vital it is for companies to plan and to market their products effectively. They have less time to recover an increased level of investment.

2.2.3 Society

People have different priorities about how they will spend their money, and these priorities are conditioned by the society in which they live. As a result society has an effect on economic and technical development, as well as influencing the customer requirements which businesses set out to meet. Society also sets the tone of what is and is not acceptable marketing practice in terms of promotion, pricing and distribution.

2.2.4 Public policy

Public policy has some effect on the economic cycle, the development of technology and on society. For example, tax and other financial policies will directly affect net company profits and hence the methods of undertaking business. The law will affect the demand for safety products, the level of safety to be built into products, minimum quality standards, minimum wage rates and salary scales. Government research programmes affect the rate of technological development. Inasmuch as the government is a very large purchaser of goods, its policies will directly affect the demand for a wide range of products. Grants to encourage companies to purchase capital equipment or to set up in particular areas, education and training schemes, rates of taxation and so on are all going to affect individual companies and their marketing strategies to a greater or lesser extent.

2.3 Market environment

The macro environment provides the setting in which demand (or a market) for a product or group of products can arise. Sometimes there may be an established customer need but no market because it is not possible to satisfy that need at a price customers – or at least a sufficient number of customers to make the enterprise worthwhile – are prepared to pay.

The market environment influences how sales volume responds to changes in the marketing mix. It determines exactly what the market buys, who buys, why they buy, how they buy, how much and when. The number of competitors who are encouraged to enter a market will be dependent on

1 the forecast size and duration of the demand
2 the level of variation in the nature of the demand (variation reduces economies of scale)
3 the nature of the production technology (which affects economies of scale).

2.4 Organisational environment

The organisational environment affects how individual companies can attempt to meet market demands. Clearly there is little to be gained by setting up a grand strategy and creating a detail operating plan, if that plan cannot be implemented by the organisation which currently exists or can be made to exist. Organisations are living things, they are formed from people and as such they adapt and can be made to adapt to circumstances. However the task which needs to be carried out is not the only factor which will affect the form of the organisation. Companies set their goals in the light of the current and forecast environment. They in effect decide what business they will be in, what market needs they will serve, the technology they will use to serve those needs, the products they will produce, the methods they will adopt to operate the business and the people they will need to undertake the task. The technology and business methods will affect the choice of people. However, the people once established in an organisation will inevitably begin to influence the technology and business methods.

This is because people who are brought together over a period of time form cultures. The nature of the culture will be related to the nature of the people themselves, the tasks they are faced with, and the environment in which they find themselves. Changes in company size and profitability will also affect that environment. Once established, the culture will then itself influence the subsequent choice of people, choice of goals, choice of technology, introduction of new products and so on in a continuous loop (see Fig. 2.3), and consequently will tend to be self perpetuating. Although every single interdependent effect cannot be predicted, it is important to understand that the organisational environment will exert a major influence on the effectiveness with which any chosen action programme can be undertaken.

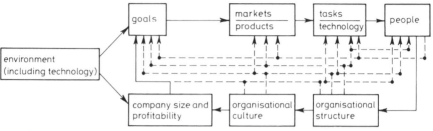

Fig. 2.3 *Organisational relationships*
——— main influence loops
———— sub-loops

2.5 Industrial market environment

The UK industrial market is a particular form of market environment that has been affected by the decline in importance of primary (agriculture, fishing, mining) and secondary industry (manufacture, construction, process) in favour of tertiary industry (service and distribution trades). While the decline of secondary industry makes life very difficult for manufacturers it also creates new opportunities for them to offer industrial services such as maintenance, drafting, design, development, raw materials stocking and so on.

Another important trend has been the growth of the public sector. The buying process in the public sector is significantly different to that of the private sector and in many cases political decisions can have a major impact on purchasing criteria. Similarly the differences between industrial and consumer markets have a major impact. Some of the more significant differences between consumer and industrial markets are summarised below:

(a) Buyer behaviour and distress purchases
Industrial goods are not bought for pleasure. They are only bought because businesses could not operate without them. Purchases made in these circumstances are sometimes called 'distress purchases' (like petrol and car insurance, you do not want to spend your money, but you have to).

The distress nature of much industrial buying provides one of the reasons (see also d, e, f, g, and Chapter 12) why industrial buyers go about their task differently from consumers.

(b) Customers are not equal
Within obvious limits, if one were selling soap powder or shampoo it would not be unreasonable to assume that each household would consume as much as any other.

However, if one was selling bulk conveyors, that is, conveyors that transport ore, gravel, slurry or coal, it would be foolish to make such an assumption. The National Coal Board represents about half of the UK market. Another example is portable compressors, where most sales are made to a small number of plant hire companies. Typically in industrial markets, a small number of companies will purchase a large proportion of the product, and a large number of companies will purchase relatively little. The well known Pareto curve can be applied to these markets, that is, 80% of a company's business will come from 20% of its customers.

(c) Small number of customers
An industrial market with under five thousand potential customers is normal. In many cases there will be as few as five hundred; in a few cases as few as fifty. For example, in the UK, industrial warm air heating is sold to installing companies which number some three thousand; vehicle braking systems to only about twenty vehicle manufacturers; and mining equipment largely to the National Coal Board. The danger of operating in a market with a small number of customers, especially where the 80–20 rule applies, is that inevitably producers become very dependent on one or two customers.

(d) Purchase value
If a key component within a product fails in service, or a key item of production equipment breaks down, the potential loss to the manufacturer may be many times the purchase price. For example, there might be three or four £1000 burners in a £1 000 000 amonia reformer. If one burner fails the whole reformer will be affected.

To take a more general example, a cooker out of action in a restaurant is much more serious than a similar failure in a private household. The cost to the restaurant is much more than the cost of the repair. The major cost is the loss of business and reputation.

As a result it is often necessary for low priced products to be bought with equal or more care than high priced products.

(e) The importance of technical parameters
Buying with care often involves specifying precisely what is required in terms of technical parameters as well as performance. Buyers can then undertake detail technical investigations to evaluate competitive products, and to ensure that the best choice is made.

The need to evaluate alternative products in depth means that many industrial sales are not completed in one short visit. Very often, for example, in the case of the incorporation of a material or component into a new design, or the purchase of new capital equipment, the buying process will extend over several months or even over several years. In such cases the selling company cannot rely only on salesmen to provide the breadth and depth of contact needed to ensure sales success. Buyers expect inputs from many different areas – design, quality control, production control, service – and the seller will need to contact many different personnel within the buying company. Industrial buying and selling is often a team process.

(f) *Systems*

There is an increasing tendency to buy complete systems; a production control system rather than assorted planning boards and cards; a mechanical handling system rather than assorted conveyors, control boxes and pick and place arms; a packaging system rather than assorted boxes, fillings and wrappers. It is akin to the difference between buying a music centre and buying individual hi-fi units and trying to match them for oneself. Increasingly industry cannot afford to employ specialist staff capable of evaluating individual parts and putting them together to make a whole. It is often preferable for suppliers to perform this role, as they can spread their costs over many systems rather than just one, and accept responsibility for system operating performance.

(g) *Made to order products*

While few consumers can afford to have products made to suit their exact individual requirements, this is quite common in the case of industrial purchases, even when suppliers attempt to show that it would be more cost effective for customers to buy from their standard range. This leads to an interesting spread of marketing approaches, with suppliers of made to order products competing against suppliers of standard made for stock products.

In many cases the seller is not selling a product but a capability to design, make or assemble something which does not now exist, be it a special purpose machine, an electronic control system or a mechanical subassembly. Very often the customer does not know exactly what he wants at the order placement stage and this will only become clear as the supplier's and the buyer's engineers work together on the project. Specification changes will occur and an important part of the sales task is to monitor these changes, explain how and why they have arisen and hence how they will affect price. There is a fine line between obtaining payment for all extra work incurred and not upsetting the customer and losing the prospect of repeat business.

(h) *The product often becomes part of the customer's product*

This important difference gives rise to the chain of derived demand (see below). The existence of supply chains creates problems not only because of the multiplier factor effect on demand changes but also because it is difficult to resolve the conflicting requirements of different parts of the chain. For example, should aero engine manufacturers concentrate on satisfying what the aircraft manufacturers say are their requirements, or what the airlines say are their requirements, or what the public say are theirs?

2.6 Chain of derived demand

Companies producing industrial products normally depend on derived demand. That is their customers are not the final consumers, and their demand is derived from the demand of other businesses along a chain, for example see Fig. 2.4. This means that companies in the chain have to look forward at the demand for the products at the end of the chain if they are to be able to forecast demand for their own products. This is particularly crucial in the case of products built for stock because of what is known as the multiplier effect.

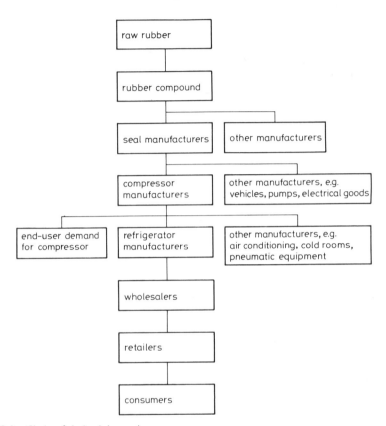

Fig. 2.4   *Chain of derived demand*

To examine the effect in more detail consideration need only be given to part of the chain. Suppose there is a reduction in demand for refrigerators of 10% and that both retailers and wholesalers reduce orders to keep their stocks at twice the usual periodic demand, then it may be seen from Table 2.1 that by the time the 10% reduction reaches the refrigerator maker it has become a 90% reduction. (For simplicity it has been assumed that for each refrigerator maker there are ten wholesalers and for each wholesaler, ten retailers.) If demand reduction continued to be multiplied in that way, businesses further up the chain would be faced with no orders at all. However, the refrigerator maker, because of employment and other reasons, may be tempted to only reduce his rate of manufacture by 10% per period. In that case his stock levels will rise rapidly. If demand were to stabilise at 70% of its previous

Table 2.1   The effect of destocking

	Period	Retailer × 10	Wholesaler × 10	Refrigerator manufacturer
Existing demand		10	100	1000
Usual order level	1	10	100	1000
Usual stock level		20	200	2000
Reduced demand		9	70	100
Reduced order level	2	7	10	900
New stock level		18	140	2800
Reduced demand		8	60	400
Reduced order level	3	6	40	800
New stock level		16	120	3200
Revised demand		7	50	300
Revised order level	4	5	30	700
New stock level		14	100	3600
Revised demand		7	70	700
Revised order level	5	7	70	700
New stock level		14	140	3600

In practice there will be a time lag between each stage; thus the figures shown against Period 1 and Period 2 will only apply directly to the retailer. The wholesaler would not be aware of any changes in demand until one period had elapsed, that is until the retailer had placed his revised order. Similarly the refrigerator manufacturer would receive his revised order one month later from the wholesaler and consequently would be operating two periods behind the retailer. Thus each column in reality would be displaced one period in time behind its predecessor.

level, the refrigerator manufacturer would be faced with the problem of either maintaining stocks of 3600 units instead of the 1400 he would prefer, or of reducing stocks by decreasing production below 700 units per period, (bearing in mind the problems of stepping production back up again should demand start to expand once more).

The problem would be repeated with the compressor maker and the seal maker. If the retailer, the wholesaler or the refrigerator maker did not respond immediately to the reduced demand, in the belief that it was temporary, then the effect down the chain would be more dramatic, possibly leaving the refrigerator maker with such large stocks that he would be forced to reduce production well below the 700 mark. Although managing the stocking policies of its distribution network can help the refrigerator manufacturer, this option is not open to manufacturers further down the chain. The only answer is to forecast demand.

Should demand begin to pick up, exactly the opposite effect would occur. By the time a 10% increase in user demand over three periods had worked its way along the chain, the refrigerator maker would be faced with a demand increase of over 100%. Clearly he could not cope, and even if he could respond in the short term by increasing output by about 10% per period, he eventually would run out of stock. Unfortunately, manufacturers have often not been able (or willing, a matter of confidence that the upturn has really arrived) to respond so readily to demand increases, and while initial increases may be covered by overtime and recruitment, plant and equipment which has lain idle or even been scrapped during a recession takes longer (and requires investment) to be made operational.

2.7 Ratchet effect

Delivery delays resulting from this multiplication of demand changes in a chain has been the cause of many businesses, and indeed industries, being permanently affected, particularly by imports. Thus, as each expansion follows each recession, companies who are not good at forecasting find that they are unable to meet the increased level of demand. They lose sales to competitors. A customer lost is often a customer permanently lost and so by the time the demand increase has begun to stabilise, and the company has been able to re-establish its manufacturing capacity, it finds that the level of demand left for its products reflects this loss of custom. The company is never able to expand during the boom back to the size it reached during the previous boom. Hence when the next recession comes the company shrinks a little smaller than last time. Companies who do not learn the lesson can easily shrink to half or less of their former size during the course of a few economic cycles. This affect has been termed the ratchet effect (see Fig. 2.5) and it vividly illustrates the worth of undertaking forecasts so that production can be adjusted ahead of changes in demand.

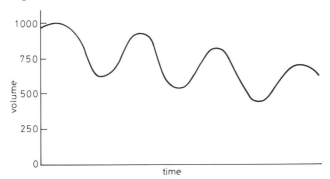

Fig. 2.5   *The ratchet effect*

2.8 Marketing response to a changing market environment

In the last chapter it was shown that the industrial market environment has changed. The current situation may be summarised as follows:

increased national and international competition;

rapid advances in technology;
increased costs of development and product launch.

Companies must respond to these changes in one of the following ways:

(a) Identification or creation of new customer needs and new competitive differences.
(b) Introduction of new technology either in the manufacturing process or in the product.
(c) Innovation of new products, services, methods of distribution and promotion.
(d) Improved organisational efficiency.

Suppose a company producing specialist gear box oil suddenly discovered that changes in gear box design would make specialist oil unnecessary in about two years from now. The first response may be to estimate the number of gear boxes in use and the rate at which they would be phased out. On the assumption that current market shares would be maintained it could be calculated how long it would be before production became uneconomic. Consideration would be given to whether some competitors would drop out quickly and to whether others would reduce prices substantially in an attempt to increase their market share. A second response might be to seek other uses for the oil. A third response could be to examine the new designs to see if a new specialist oil could offer sufficiently superior performance to justify its use over normal oil. A fourth response would be to plan a replacement product with a different end use. This is an example of a threatening change from the macro environment.

Consider car wheels. Declining UK vehicle production may mean that eventually, as has happened with other vehicle components, the unit costs of European rivals will reduce sufficiently below UK unit costs that the cross channel transportation cost barrier can be surmounted. UK producers will either have to prevent that happening, by obtaining export orders and maintaining volume, or by reducing their unit costs in some other way; otherwise they will have to find an alternative product.

Change produces opportunities as well as threats. UK Government sponsored changes to levels of redundancy pay and improvements in job security, combined with increased advertising and other recruitment costs, made it more expensive to employ and dismiss labour. As a result large companies found it more difficult to respond quickly to changes in demand, and this created an opportunity for specialist subcontracting companies who could provide the extra capacity when it was needed. Similarly, reduced spending power creates an opportunity for companies to introduce less expensive ranges; increased vandalism creates an opportunity to promote security alarms or security screens; increased petrol prices creates an oppportunity for more economical means of transport.

Occasionally, companies who are to the fore of their industry have the opportunity to create and fashion change. For example, the companies who first introduced fast foods were not only responding to a need but they helped to bring out and develop that need. Companies who introduced desk-top computers not only made it economic to satisfy a whole range of information processing needs, but by doing so, they made people aware of a whole range of user possibilities which had not been previously recognised. Companies which introduce quieter and easier to use machinery create not only a demand for their own products, but a demand for other makes and types of machinery to be equally quiet and easy to use.

The market environment is an environment of change. In order for a company to remain competitive it must be aware of all the changes taking place which will affect its business, and it must respond rapidly to those changes. The marketing discipline provides the means to sense, report and assess the impact of change. It helps ensure that companies respond to change and continue to produce, at a profit, products which will meet customer requirements.

Chapter 3

Organising for Marketing

3.1 Principles of organisation

An essential preliminary to effective marketing is a well thought out organisation. This chapter will consider some of the general principles of company organisation and then go on to examine some alternative ways of organising for marketing.

The aim of good organisation is to match the available resources as effectively as possible to the task in hand, and at the same time, make it relatively easy to monitor and control the total task by monitoring and controlling each part. The first step involves dividing the overall task facing a company into manageable parts or sections. Each section will tend to specialise in a particular activity which will be centred around functional skills, industry or market knowledge, product knowledge or geographic location. The scope of each manageable section needs to be chosen so that the responsibility for each section can be clearly allocated and the results easily monitored. Ideally, those in charge of sections should be given authority over all those areas which will influence their capability to achieve target results, but normally this is not possible and some compromise has to be reached. For example, the sales department's ability to achieve a sales target will depend on product availability, manufacturing quality, product design, brochure design, advertising campaigns, prices and many other factors over which they have no authority.

Similarly authority to take decisions should be limited to areas where the decision maker has personal responsibility. When a decision will affect other areas of the company, either recourse needs to be made to the next level up the hierarchy which does have responsibility for all the areas affected, or all the affected parties must become involved with and agree to the decisions. Special attention needs to be paid to grey areas where there is overlap of both reponsibility and authority, and this in a large measure is achieved by good communication.

On the whole specialisation brings with it efficiencies which arise from increased knowledge. However, increased efficiency arising from one type of specialisation (say product) has to be balanced against losses because of reductions in some other type of specialisation (say functional skills). For example, a company which produces several products may consider forming five separate divisions. Within each division there might be insufficient work to keep, say, a marketing research specialist, an advertising specialist or a market planner busy, and therefore these functions would have to be shared with other members of the division's staff, diluting the level of functional expertise. Division also creates inefficiency by way of duplication. Returning to the above example, the combined results of the five divisions would have to be sufficiently better than that currently being achieved to pay for five general managers, five production teams, five sales forces, five advertising campaigns and so on.

Another problem associated with the division of a company into sections is communication, and particular attention should be paid to this aspect of organisation. While communication between members of each section is normally good, because they have a common sense of identity and purpose, communication between sections tends to be poor. For example, heads of sections are prone to consider other sections as part of their external environment and hence something to be fought rather than co-operated with. This tendency is not helped because it is often necessary to ask each section of a company to work below its optimum efficiency in order for the overall task to be completed as efficiently as possible. Thus a particular production department may need to produce 500 units a week to operate most efficiently, whereas sales fluctuate between 250 and 800 units per week, and efficient stock control requires production to be varied between 350 and 700 units per week. Similarly a sales force might be most cost effective if it were allowed to handle ten products, whereas the rest of the company can only handle seven. This means that while heads of section are continually being asked to improve efficiency, they are at the same time told to operate in a manner which severely restricts that efficiency.

To overcome these sorts of problems it is essential to clearly communicate the overall company goals to each section of the company and to ensure that each section is aware of the difficulties facing all the other sections. It is to be hoped that such awareness

1   would encourage each section to plan its activities so that they fit in with rather than clash with those of other sections;
2   might reduce the amount of time managers have to spend 'selling' ideas which benefit their departments, to other departments,
3   would encourage the formation of informal interdepartmental communication links.

Linked closely to ideas of centralisation and decentralisation is the extent to which central services are to be provided. If a line manager was buying services from another company he would have direct control of the end result, but when he buys from an internal service department that control always seems to be more tenuous, simply because the service department has access to higher authority whenever it is considered that unreasonable pressure is being applied. That pressure is in any case limited as the line manager rarely has the authority to withdraw his custom from an internal department and so he may have to resort to the hierarchy to get things done to his satisfaction. In some cases, such dissatisfaction increases the rate at which line managers try to employ their own staff on such service tasks. In that event, higher level decisions about economies of centralisation versus decentralisation are needed.

Similarly, while staff planners normally rely on persuasion to get line management to adopt their ideas, if the direct approach fails, they too have to fall back on their boss, and the formal hierarchy. This type of problem is worse where the staff specialist is used to monitor the performance of line departments and to recommend how improvements can be achieved. The chances of a close staff—line liaison in such circumstances, without there being considerable management effort, are low. These centralisation/decentralisation and staff/line problems, are less obvious in small organisations because individual jobs often combine several specialist tasks. Nevertheless, they exist in concept and should be considered before an organisational structure is adopted.

Good organisation involves making the best trade off in given circumstances between different forms of specialisation, economies of scale, duplication, control and communication. In other words there is no universally 'best' method of organisation. The method of organisation must be appropriate to the circumstances and just as circumstances change so must the method of organisation. Particularly in the case of high technology companies the exact nature of the product and the market changes frequently, and it is vital not only to review organisational structure frequently, but also to build a flexible structure so that it can be changed as the demands on it change. In today's rapidly changing world, it is unlikely that the form of organisation which was appropriate eighteen months ago will be exactly appropriate today.

The most common methods of organising are by function, by common products or services, by projects, by common customers or by geographic area.

3.2 The functional organisation

The classic functional organisation tree is something like that shown in Fig. 3.1. The job functions are more or less self-explanatory but a brief summary is given in Table 3.1. The overall functions required of a marketing department remain more or less unchanged whatever the industry. Its responsibility is to determine and forecast market requirements, to set marketing objectives and performance specifications for new products, to investigate other growth opportunities such as acquisitions, and to manage the distribution, promotion, pricing and selling of the current product range.

Marketing departments should be kept as small as is compatible with properly undertaking each of the specified activities; they exist to increase profits not to drain them. As a result many industrial marketing departments are small, often consisting of less than half a dozen people. Thus, although for the purposes of illustration each function has been described as if it involves a separate person or group of people, in practice one person may undertake more than one of the functions described. Such people have been termed multi-specialists and their all-round ability is vital to the success of small and medium sized companies. For example, a marketing manager might undertake planning and pricing, supervise any marketing research, be involved in the preparation of brochures and advertisements, as well as going out selling to customers. However, just because roles are combined, that does not mean that any of the activities should be ignored and not carried out. It is better to chart all the roles separately, before they are combined under individual job titles.

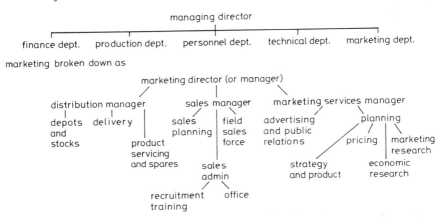

Fig. 3.1 *A typical functional organisation tree*

In some companies where more emphasis is given to selling, a sales director may report direct to the managing director and be responsible for distribution and marketing services as well as direct sales. In many such companies marketing services have a limited role. A compromise adopted in many UK companies is to employ a marketing manager with responsibility for marketing services, at the same level as the sales manager (see Fig. 3.2). In these circumstances the managing director

Fig. 3.2 *Typical organisation tree in a sales oriented company*

Table 3.1   *Summary of marketing tasks*

Marketing management   Develops marketing objectives, strategies and action programmes. Sets standards of performance and the company's marketing style. Organises, hires and trains section managers. Is responsible for maintaining overall progress towards objectives. Maintains top level contact with customers.

Sales management   Organises, hires and trains the sales force who are the final link in the marketing chain. Maintains senior contacts with customers.

Marketing research   Is one method of gathering data for companies' marketing information systems (see Chapter 4). The type of information sought includes the size, growth and location of markets, price patterns, market attitudes and needs, and levels of competitor activity.

Economic research   Provides data on the business outlook.

Advertising and public relations   Creates an awareness and an image of the company and its products.

Product planning   Helps ensure that the right products are available at the right time and at the right price.

Product servicing and spares   Ensures that the product is able to continue to perform in the manner promised. It encourages repeat business.

Distribution   Ensures that the product is available where customers wish to buy it or use it. Can include selection of outlets and management of stocks and delivery services, so as to minimise cost for agreed levels of customer service.

Administration   Records progress, sales, profits, stock levels versus budget. Can act as an internal sales force.

---

effectively assumes direct responsibility for the marketing management function described in Table 3.1.

The relative prominence given to each part of the marketing department will depend on the importance of that part to the success of the company – as perceived by the Board. Thus in some industries, e.g. small electrical components, well organised distribution is crucial to success, and in that case the distribution department may be set up as a completely separate functional department reporting direct to the Board. In other industries, e.g. electronic control panels, where distribution involves factory to factory delivery of made to order products, distribution may report to the works manager or in some cases even to the financial controller (who often seems to pick up general administrative responsibilities that no one else wants). Similarly a company producing and selling armaments may place less emphasis on marketing research or advertising and place more emphasis on direct selling and technical development, whereas the priorities of a company producing mechanical handling equipment might be completely the opposite.

A functionally organised marketing department is ideal for a company with relatively few product ranges where each functional head can understand and control his function across the whole width of products. Each functional department offers the possibility of extensive facilities, of in depth functional or specialist expertise and of economies of scale.

3.3 Product group organisation

In some cases, either because there are simply too many different products for a single department to deal with efficiently, or because major differences in marketing strategy are appropriate to different products or groups of products, a product based marketing department may be adopted. In this case the specialisation sought is different. It is specialisation by way of detail knowledge of the product, of prospective customers, of relevant new developments, of the competition and of how profit can be improved. The product team is close enough to the market to see areas of opportunity and potential problems, which would not be apparent to people operating in a functional department who have several other products to be concerned about.

The introduction of the role of product manager is normally credited to Proctor and Gamble, circa the late 1920s, and was followed by other consumer goods companies. The product manager (sometimes termed brand manager) was allocated responsibility for meeting sales volume targets for a single product or product group. He was expected to prepare a marketing plan for his product and to ensure that the agreed action programmes were implemented in terms of advertising, distribution, pricing, promotion, packaging and production. However, the product manager was not provided with any executive authority. His was a staff rather than a line position. It was necessary for him to attain his action programme by persuading the line managers in the various functional departments to actually undertake what needed to be done. The structure would have been on the lines of Fig. 3.3, the dotted lines showing the 'persuasion' organisational links.

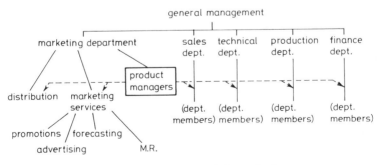

Fig. 3.3 *The position of product managers in a typical organisation*

The product manager's authority was to stem from his detail knowledge about everything to do with his product and how it should be marketed. Should the persuasion route fail, the product manager had recourse to the formal organisational structure via his boss, who would normally be the head of the marketing department.

The expected advantages were; first, that there would be efficiency by way of specialisation, second, that there would be clear accountability for product volume, and third that having several product managers competing for the use of company resources would help ensure that those resources would only be used in an efficient way. The main disadvantages were caused first by the classic problem of allocating responsibility without authority, and the stresses and tension which that imposes on job holders. Secondly, because the people appointed to the job tended to be young, inexperienced and on the way up, this meant that on first appointment the product managers tended to stumble around and needed a lot of support from functional departments. By the time they really had become experts they tended to be moved on to other jobs, either because they showed considerable promise or because the stresses were proving too much, leaving the people in the functional departments once again to be the experts until the learning cycle repeated itself. The short job tenure tended to lead to a short term outlook rather than a long term outlook and the long term view had to be superimposed from above. Thirdly, product managers only held responsibility for sales volume and not profit, and this naturally influenced the way they approached their job.

Although this staff role still exists — with improvements — in some large companies producing consumer goods, in engineering companies product managers tend to have been given line authority and this has made them more effective (but see Hise and Kelly [8]). The extra responsibility has been allocated gradually and for different reasons.

Often the first step has been to provide product managers with a budget for advertising, exhibitions, marketing research and the like, so that they are able to call on and to control marketing services rather than relying on persuasion. Similarly a budget has sometimes been allocated to product groups to 'buy' manufacturing and technical services. Secondly, product managers have often been allocated their own sales team because, in engineering companies, when a product group structure is appropriate, it is usually also sensible to divide the sales force by product rather than geographical area (see also Chapter 14); often using product managers to replace area sales managers. Thirdly, because much of the specialist knowledge about a product will be technically based, it has been natural for product managers to gradually begin to specify in increasing detail the technical as well as the performance specifications that products need to meet. However, where market demand is technology lead and where the technology is particularly complex, the extension of the product managers authority into the technical area is usually limited.

This broader span of authority, which now includes strategic and operational marketing, means that in many cases there is no need for a separate head of marketing and that leads to the type of organisational structure shown in Fig. 3.4.

As product groups grow in size, product managers begin to employ their own staff to undertake functions which were previously available to them only as a central service. In this way they are better able to control the direction, the quality and the spread of the work undertaken. The sales team are often the first to follow this route, followed by marketing services, product development and finally manufacture; the exact order being dependent on the degree of commonality of each function with other product groups. Thus if the manufacturing process for a product group can largely be undertaken on the same plant and equipment used for other product groups, responsibility for this function is likely to be transferred to the product manager later rather than sooner, if at all. Various parts of the accounting and personnel functions may also be transferred depending on the economies of scale involved.

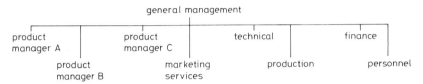

Fig. 3.4 *Product management in an engineering company*

If a product group continues to grow and it is forseen that it will remain a viable business entity, then the obvious development of this process is for the product group to be made into a division, with the product manager becoming the (general) manager. The organisation has come full circle, back to a functional structure; at least until the division itself grows to the point where it too begins to diversify its products.

3.4 The matrix organisation

It should be clear by now that the division of the overall business task revolves largely around a matrix of:

Marketing   Development

Sales   Manufacture

The choice of whether or not to sub-divide any part of these functions involves a trade-off between the factors which contribute towards efficiency, namely: economies of scale; duplication; specialisation; control and communication. The outcome need not be clear cut. For example, it is common for accountants to maintain a (professional) reporting relationship to the head of the finance department, although they have a direct line responsibility to a product manager. On the other hand, the direct line responsibility may be to the financial controller, and yet the accountant could spend all his time working with a particular product group. Similar split responsibilities often occur in the case of marketing research, advertising, development, distribution and manufacture. This form of organisation is called a martix organisation (see Fig. 3.5).

The dotted lines in Fig. 3.5 indicate indirect responsibility links. Obviously the linkages need not be as shown, and depending on the outcome of the above-mentioned trade-offs, production, marketing services or the technical group may have a direct link to their respective functional departments and only an indirect link to the product group. The strength of the various links will depend not only on the logical trade-offs referred to above but also on the strengths of the various personalities involved.

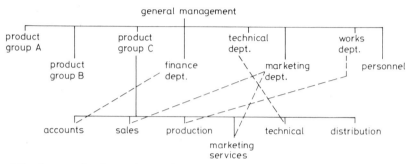

Fig. 3.5   *An example of a matrix organisation*

This form of organisation is particularly appropriate where it is forseen that the next generation of products will require a different way of dividing up the task, and therefore staff working for the product groups need to retain a strong hold on their general functional specialisms and not become too narrow in outlook, so that they can either return to their functional departments or be re-allocated to a new product group when the current product group breaks up. A matrix organisation enables staff to be moved in and out of product groups as the work load changes, and in this way enables companies to be very flexible.

3.5 Project based structures

A particular form of matrix organisation is the project based structure. The structure is common among contracting companies who bid for the privilege of designing and supervising the construction of large items of equipment, such as buildings, chemical plant, manufacturing systems, parcel handling systems or whatever. As projects have finite lives, project teams will continually need to be dissolved and reformed, and therefore a matrix structure is normally appropriate. The number of professions or functions which report to project managers will vary in accordance with the complexity of the project but normally would only include technical, production, accounts and possibly sales (see Fig. 3.6). In these circumstances, a major task of marketing departments will be to direct bidding efforts towards contracts which seem to offer the best long term prospects. They might, for example, forecast that there will be a growing demand for a particular type of plant and hence suggest that, in order to gain experience and thereby reduce future costs and create a relevant track record (a platform for future sales efforts), the company should make considerable efforts to obtain contracts for that type of plant even if small initial losses will be sustained.

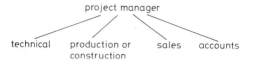

Fig. 3.6   *Project management responsibilities*

In order to be successful, it has been shown that it pays to concentrate on a relatively small number of contracts and that a multi-discipline team is needed to properly assemble and present a bid to the potential customer. Thus the sales effort will also be organised on a matrix basis with bid teams continually being formed and dissolved. A bid team might include one or more people from sales, accounts, estimating, design and production.

Once a project has been gained, sales staff will normally turn their attention to other projects. However, they should maintain a close link with existing projects and customers so that they can help present (the inevitable) changes to project costs and timings, and more easily discern follow up sales opportunities.

Many engineering companies produce made to order products which take between one month and perhaps nine months to manufacture and test. The size of individual orders is a relatively small proportion of the total turnover and hence members of each 'order' based project team will normally be working on several orders at the same time, moving from one to another as the workload changes. Obviously they have to co-operate if they are to achieve an efficient outcome, but formal responsibility for meeting cost and time targets usually remains with departmental managers, rather than being allocated to a project manager. This represents a rapidly changing matrix structure with a strong functional base.

3.6 Customer or industry based structure

Sometimes it becomes apparent that the needs of particular groups of customers, normally from different industries, are sufficiently different to warrant a distinctive marketing approach. However, the product, or at least the base product from which individual options may be offered, will be common and therefore it will not be sensible to divide the manufacturing and development functions. Only the marketing department need be divided. If this is not the case a product based structure is likely to be more appropriate.

Where customer groups are not very large or the differences between them are relatively slight, it may be decided that marketing services can be handled from a central unit and that only the sales and the service department need be divided by customer group (see Fig. 3.7).

Fig. 3.7   *An industry based structure*

[1] Sometimes there is a general sales manager reporting to a marketing manager.
[2] Sometimes the service manager will report to the sales manager.

On the other hand, where the customer groups are sufficiently large and different that staff have to specialise, then the marketing department may be divided in the way shown in Fig. 3.8. Advertising, public relations and economic research tend to be the skills most easily transferred across product or industry boundaries and hence are usually the last to be sub-divided.

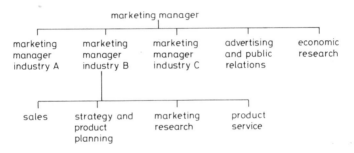

Fig. 3.8   *Alternative industry based structure*

The main advantages of a customer based structure arise because the marketing and sales teams become well known in the industry and are therefore well placed not only to sell, but also to find out about future industry requirements. This enables the company to adapt its product range to meet these requirements. Thus a customer based structure is particularly appropriate for companies who follow a differentiated marketing strategy (see Section 6.10).

3.7 Geographic based structure

In a small country like the United Kingdom it is unusual for industrial companies to divide themselves on a geographical basis. The general exceptions are sales forces, service departments and distribution depots, but even when there are regional sales, service and distribution offices, other departments are usually based at a head office.

Companies operating in more than one country have a wide range of organisational options to choose from and can readily adopt any one or a combination of the options already discussed. It is usual for companies who only export moderately to undertake most of the marketing planning from the UK. However, it is extremely difficult to plan effectively without detail knowledge of local conditions, and hence companies who operate in this way are very dependent on the quality of published data and the quality of the information fed back to them by their representatives. In some cases this information is supplemented by marketing research undertaken by a research agency located in the relevant export market. The selling can be undertaken by UK based export salesmen, or by agents appointed in each export market, or via local sales offices.

As the importance of a particular export market grows, then the number of independent functions undertaken by the local office will grow in a manner similar to that described for product groups, until in some cases a manufacturing facility may be established. While marketing planning authority may be vested in the local organisation, strategic planning is not usually delegated and a head office based marketing department with worldwide strategic responsibilities will inevitably remain in existence. The reasons for this, as opposed to the product group case where a central department may cease to exist, are probably based on the uncertainties introduced by distance and differences of culture.

Chapter 4

Information

4.1 Information provides a factual basis for decisions

Why is information needed? First of all to provide a firm basis upon which management can make decisions and exercise control. Information is the starting point for setting strategies and action programmes and this is why information search is the first element in the marketing loop (see Fig. 1.1.)

Without good information it is difficult to make sensible decisions. Unfortunately it appears that much apparently simple information is not known to many company managements. Many companies delude themselves into believing that they understand their market, but often they do not. Some do not know in detail how much of exactly which product they sell to each customer group, let alone at what profit. Many do not know the profit they earn from individual model variations within a product line; they make do with global figures. Many more companies fail to understand why some customers buy their products rather than those of their competitors, while others do not. It is not that the information is not available, it is simply that it is not recorded, analysed and presented in a usable way. Even where information is recorded and analysed, this is often only undertaken once or twice a year, perhaps when the annual operating plan is being prepared or revised. Worse still, many decisions are based on 2, 3, or even 4 year old marketing research reports.

To be useful, information must be up to date, and this implies continuous gathering and recording as a matter of routine. Gathering information continuously also enables trends and turning points to be identified, and this is important because they indicate when changed policies and action programmes will be needed. Gathering up to date intelligence is one of the first considerations of a military commander and so should it be in business.

4.2 Information provides early warning of change

Taking the military analogy a little further, if one was engaged in a conventional military campaign it would help to know that the enemy was going to attack in, say,

3 hours time. That would provide time to organise the defences and the outcome almost certainly would be better than if the first one knew of the attack was when the first shell landed. Decisions taken at relative leisure are more likely to be effective than panic reaction, and therefore obtaining early warning represents a second major reason for gathering information. Information buys time: time to think, to plan and to act.

4.3 Information time horizons

If information is to be used satisfactorily for planning and control it is necessary to obtain information about the future (see also Chapter 5) as well as about the present. In fact information can be divided into three time horizons as follows.

4.3.1 Long term

Information about the future, about economic social and technical change and about government policy is needed to provide early warning of the opportunities and threats which are on the horizon. Long term information provides the bases for strategic planning and for capital investment decisions and should be used by companies to determine their long term objectives and direction. It involves the identification of broad trends so as to help decide, for example, whether to invest in Germany or India, in heat pumps or gas boilers, in tractors or combine harvesters.

In order to detect trends, this type of information needs to be collected on a continuous basis and reviewed at regular intervals. For example, a few years ago it was recognised that the costs of sea fishing were increasing and the world fish population was decreasing at a rate which would cause fish prices to rise inevitably and steadily. At some point – placed anywhere between ten and thirty years according to the forecaster – as fish farming technology improved, the economic selling price of farm fish should drop below the price of caught fish. Based on these forecasts companies could decide whether they wished to enter the industry, and if so, when.

This raises an interesting issue of timing; whether it is better to become involved at an early stage of a new technology or market demand, and invest considerable sums in developing a saleable product, or whether it is better to wait until an economic saleable product is nearer reality and build on what others have already achieved. The extreme case is to wait until the market has been clearly established and then bring out a copy product. In order to take these sorts of decisions it is necessary to visualise what will develop from what now exists, with what probability and when, and to do that it is essential to have access to some form of long range information system.

4.3.2 Medium term

Medium term information (6 months–3 years) is required to identify more immediate needs and trends. It may be gathered in discrete lumps by statistical market research, competitor research and customer research, or continuously via publications

Table 4.1   *Examples of medium term information*

Market size	Market potential	Market trends
Market structure	Market share	Overseas markets
Marketing methods	New products	Competitive climate
Competitive prices	Competitive processes	Competitive products
User attitudes and behaviour	Governmental factors	Distribution methods
Company performance	Shipment and packaging	Profit
Costs and pricing	Own product	Services

Each category could itself be expanded, for example:

Market size   Size of total market, measured in units and money
Rate of change in size and identified causes of change
Percentage imported, and rate of change
Export markets
Factors limiting the size of market

Market structure Factors preventing/favouring emergence of new competitors
Factors reducing the number of existing competitors
Segmentation by geography, size of user, industry type/quality/
design/price of product, type of distributor
Number, size, profitability and market share of main competitors
Percentage of market served by importers

Market trends   Rate of change in total market and each segment
Causes of these trends – economic, social or technical change
Changes in user industries which will affect demand
Changes in non-user industries which could lead to new demand
Change in competitor market shares (including imports) and
preferably by segment
Causes of these trends, i.e. changes in product, promotion price
or distribution
Trends that are likely to attract new competition or reduce the
number of existing competitors

Profit   What is the operating profit, by segment, by product and what is
the trend (last year, 3 years ago)
How is the cost structure made up and how has it changed

New products   Given the changes in customer needs and tastes, competitive
offerings and technology, what new products should be developed
(therefore are those already in the pipeline likely to be winners or
losers)

or by direct contact with the market place. It is usually supplemented by taking account of short term trends in long term information.

Medium term information is most commonly used for setting the following years sales forecast. However it is also required for annual marketing, production and financial planning, to enable decisions to be taken about product replacements, product modifications, process modifications, new promotional strategies and so on. Examples of the type of data sought are given in Table 4.1.

4.3.3 Short Term

Short term or feedback information is required in order to be able to monitor the effectiveness of current plans and the manner in which they are being implemented. This type of data should be gathered continuously from reports which may cover all orders obtained, orders in hand, despatches, cancellations, quotations outstanding, stock levels, number of enquiries received, number of service calls and so on. It can be used to monitor functions such as quality control, service, promotion and advertising, methods of dealing with enquiries, exhibitions, packaging, delivery, distribution and sales (see for example Fig. 4.1). Most of this information is available in most companies and it only requires formalisation of its collection and presentation to provide a valuable source of data.

	This year	Last year	3 years ago
What percentage of turnover is spent on selling for:			
The total company	— —	— —	— — —
Each product group	— —	— —	— — —
Each sales territory	— —	— —	— — —
Each salesman	— —	— —	— — —
Each customer industry	— —	— —	— — —
Each major customer	— —	— —	— — —
What percentage of enquiries are converted into orders for:			
The total company	— —	— —	— — —
Each product group	— —	— —	— — —
Each sales territory	— —	— —	— — —
Each salesman	— —	— —	— — —
Each customer industry	— —	— —	— — —
Each major customer	— —	— —	— — —

Fig. 4.1 *Example of the type of information needed to monitor effectiveness of sales strategy*

4.4 What information should be sought

Within each time horizon information is needed about the environment, about the market, about the product and about company performance.

4.4.1 The environment

The nature of the marketing environment has been dealt with in Chapters 1 and 2. Information should be sought with respect to the economy, technology, social tastes and patterns of demand, government policy and competitive impingement from other markets. The latter category is one that has been overlooked in the past, but it is becoming more important as more and more different technologies and industries try to satisfy the same basic demands. For example, companies manufacturing metal cutting machine tools have to take account not only of other manufacturers of competitive machine tools and of improvements in metal forming, casting, fabrication, sintering and electrical machining, but they also have to take account of improvements in non-metallic materials which could cause the volume of metal used by industry to reduce.

4.4.2 The market

A wide variety of information is needed about the market (for examples see Table 4.1). When seeking information about market size, care must be taken to closely define the exact market that is being investigated. Is it, for example, the market for machine tools or for metal cutting machine tools or for lathes or for CNC lathes? It is also important to be aware of the differences between ultimate market potential, immediate market potential and market size. Ultimate market potential is the volume of sales which would be achieved if everyone who could conceivably have a use for the product, bought as much as they wanted. It assumes an infinite level of marketing effort. This is a higher sales volume than immediate market potential, which is equal to the sales volume if everyone who could afford the product at its current price bought as much as they could afford. Market size or market demand is the actual volume of sales which it is expected will be achieved, usually measured over one year, given the forecast product prices and the forecast level of marketing effort.

Immediate market potential can be increased by reducing price relative to inflation and this is usually brought about by improvements in technology (e.g. microcomputers). These same improvements may also extend the versatility of the product and thereby increase the ultimate potential. However, changes in technology in other areas may reduce the need for the product and therefore reduce the potential.

4.4.3 The product

The product range needs to be compared with what is available from direct competitors or is about to be launched by them. Information is sought with respect to relative performance, features, quality, reliability, ease of use, appearance, expected life and price.

4.4.4 Company performance

A vast range of feedback information is normally gathered about company performance (see Sections 4.3.3 and 4.5). However, it is also important to monitor company performance in the longer term, to establish trends and to discover whether there has been a gradual change in any aspect of the competitive position. Once a trend has been recognised its cause can be sought and remedial action initiated.

These different types of information can be linked together to help solve specific problems. An example of such a linkage is given in Fig. 4.2.

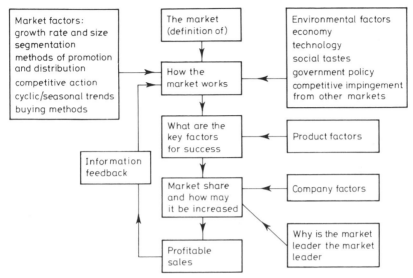

Fig. 4.2   *Information flow diagram to show use of information to help solve a typical problem, namely, how to increase market share*

4.5 Information sources: records of company performance

Having considered why information is required and what information should be sought it seems logical to go on to consider how information should be obtained. A prime source of relevant information are records of company performance such as monthly or weekly sales of each product to different customers. From such simple data it is possible to identify trends about the changing importance of different products, of different customers and of different categories of customer. It will be clear which customers are buying more, which are buying less, who are the new customers and who are about to become ex-customers. Analysis may indicate why what is offered is no longer appealing to some, while it is becoming more appealing to others, and that may reveal changing patterns or marketing emphases.

When combined with similarly recorded data on selling costs (sales force, advertising, exhibitions, brochures) or on the percentage of enquiries converted into orders, it is possible to cross-check conclusions being developed about when products should be replaced (see Chapter 7). Thus prior to a sales decline, products may begin to cost more to sell, and/or become increasingly reliant on new customers, and these sorts of symptons should be taken as a warning that a detail evaluation is needed. Consideration of the reasons given by the sales force as to why customers are being lost or prospects not converted should give a clear lead to how to improve what is being offered; of how it no longer quite meets changed market needs. An analysis of service records and guarantee claims may also help in this respect.

A veritable wealth of information is available to most companies as a result of their day to day activities, if only it were regularly recorded and presented in a usable format (see Section 4.18). For example, a record of all the companies who had ever enquired about a particular product would provide a valuable starting point when trying to assess the size and nature of the total market.

4.6 Information sources: company contacts with the market

Any member of a company who goes out and makes contact with suppliers, with customers, with competitors or anyone else in industry is a potential source of market data. They are continuously subject to all kinds of verbal and visual information. Staff are more likely to report back what they discover if it is clear to them what information is needed and how it will help the company towards greater sales, now and in the future. This is a matter of training and communication.

The most obvious and most prolific source is the sales force. Some people may say that the role of the sales force is to sell and that it should not be bothered with other distractions such as data gathering. In any case, data from salesmen is likely to be biased. Both these criticisms can be met by recording on standard report forms data that clearly helps salesmen to sell (see Fig. 14.4).

Another underutilised source of information is the technical applications engineer; the man who has to discover how to adapt the product so that it can meet the individual requirements of each customer. In the process the applications engineer is gathering absolutely vital information about customers' needs, which, when put together with information from other applications, can often lead to desirable product modifications literally becoming self-apparent.

An equally important source of information is the service engineer. The service engineer is in continuous contact with the people who actually use the product and who almost certainly will be very willing to express definite views about it, especially to someone who is clearly not trying to sell something. Admittedly the views of service engineers are often already gathered when consideration is being given to how the product can be made more reliable and easier to service, but with a little training service engineers could gather information about how products are actually used, how they could be made easier to use, why they were really bought, how they could be modified to extend their use, and in particular to provide early warning that the product is considered to be dated and no longer exactly what is required.

In all cases the first step to gathering the information is an easy to use report form to be filled in after every visit. The second step is a little instruction about what is needed and the questions which should be asked. The third step is to provide some evidence that the information will actually be put to good use.

4.7 Information sources: publications

There is a huge range of data published every day. Guides to reference books and information sources are published: there are even guides to the guides (e.g. see Wills [9]). A list of some of the more common sources is given in Fig. 4.3. In the case of press articles, research indices exist which list any published information relating to any number of selected subject areas. The indices can save much time providing of course that the subject under investigation falls squarely within one of the listed subject headings. The very breadth of the available information is itself a hurdle.

The reference sections of large city libraries or university libraries are a good starting point and the staff are invariably helpful. Examples of other useful locations are the Department of Industry Statistics and Market Intelligence library, the City Business Library, trade sections of embassies, NEDO and the Euopean Community Information Office. Very often many of the relevant publications can be obtained by simply walking round a relevant exhibition. The search is usually a step by step process, information from one source leading on to the next source.

All published information must be evaluated for consistency and bias. The method of compiling information into what appears directly comparable reports might be quite different. For example, some reports referring to lifting appliances might be referring to the whole system of hoist block, electric motor, chain and hook; others just to the block itself. Production figures have to be compared with sales figures, and different reports may quote different units, for example, production of copper pipe may be quoted in pounds sterling, mass of copper or length of pipe. In other cases there may be leads and lags in statistics, with apparently comparable data actually based on what happened during different time periods. Care must also be taken that the data is the latest available and has not been subsequently updated or modified. In certain areas reports by, say, the CBI, the TUC, the Friends of the Earth, or individual companies would not be without bias. In order to compare data, the assumptions, the data gathering, and the summarising methods of each data source must be assessed.

Normally it is not sensible to rely on the accuracy of data gathered from a single source − it is much better to cross-check. Sometimes it is not possible to make much progress without using several sources. For example, in spite of the mass of information available, it is amazing how often one will find that the specific data one is searching for (say UK production of gas burners) is not published in an immediately usable form, because the figures have been combined with others into some broader data category. In that case annual sales volume might be estimated by:

1 Estimating competitor sales from company and financial reports and discussions with agents, distributors and customers. Sometimes a direct request to a competitor will yield up a sales estimate, albeit an optimistic one.
2 Finding out sales of a common component from its suppliers.
3 Making an estimate of known production capacity and adjusting for stocking/ destocking.

Government, official, semi-official

Census of production
Census of distribution
Monthly digest of statistics
Business monitor
Treasury forecasts
Overseas trade accounts
NEDO reports

Customs and excise export/import figures
OECD reports and statistics
United Nations reports and statistics
Nationalised industry reports
CBI, TUC reports
Patent files
British Standards Institution reports
Monopolies Commission reports

Press (specialist and daily)

Articles   Surveys   Technical reports   Adverts

Directories

Kompass   Kelly's Yellow Pages   Year books   Who owns whom   Trade directories

Financial

Extel cards   Moodies cards   Stockbroker reports   Economic reports from the banks, The IMF and other forecasting centres

Financial records held in companies house   Inter company comparisons

Other

Trade association publications   Company brochures   Buyers guides   Published market research studies
Scientific and technical research associations   Universities

Fig. 4.3 Sources of published information

4 Conducting a field study among users.

5 Calculating the number of salesmen employed by all competitors and multiplying by an estimated average sales target for each salesman.

4.8. Information sources: formal marketing research

Formal marketing research is normally relatively expensive and therefore only used when the other sources cannot provide the necessary information. Marketing research can be used either to gather a limited range of information (because of costs) on a regular basis or to obtain on an occasional basis, broader information about, for example, possible new market areas, customer views on a prototype, confirmation of ideas about a change in the nature of market demand, or potential customers buying criteria. However there are significant drawbacks to information obtained only on an occasional basis. First, by the time the need for the information has been recognised and the results made available, many of the possible decision avenues may no longer be open. Second, discontinuous information cannot be used to reveal trends.

Most industrial companies cannot afford their own marketing research department, but many can afford a specialist who can undertake occasional studies, and in the case of larger studies help choose an agency, prepare the brief, guide the research and interpret the findings. However, project size is not the only reason for choosing an outside agency. Sometimes agencies can obtain more information than someone working directly for a company, simply because they do not have to mention the name of the company sponsoring the research. It is also true that in some cases, agencies are more expert at extracting the relevant from the mass of data available, interpreting it sensibly and presenting it in a useful form. On other occasions it may be decided to use an agency because it is felt that an outside report would carry more weight with the decision makers and would be more obviously free from bias.

4.9 The research brief[1]

In view of the fact that most research projects are specifically targeted, the first step must be to define the requirement and the best way of doing that is to prepare a research brief. The brief should list the following:

(a) the decision which will be taken on the basis of the information gathered;
(b) the information that will be required (Wilson [10] provides a comprehensive check list) and to what level of accuracy;
(c) from whom the information will be obtained and how it will be gathered (including recommendations on whether an outside agency will be required);

[1] Much of the information in sections 4.9, 4.13, 4.14, and 4.15 is based on Wilson [10].

(d) how the reliability of the data will be checked;
(e) the analyses of the data to be undertaken;
(f) any constraints such as finance, time and confidentiality.

The brief should be agreed with whoever has requested that the project be undertaken to ensure that the information researcher and the information seeker are in accord. This will help clarify the information seeker's objectives and avoid him being presented with a report which does not help him in his decision making process as directly or as fully as it otherwise might. If it appears from the brief that the desired level of accuracy cannot be achieved, or that the research cannot be completed within the time scale set, or that the quality of the decision will be insufficiently improved to generate enough profit to pay for the research, then it is best not undertaken.

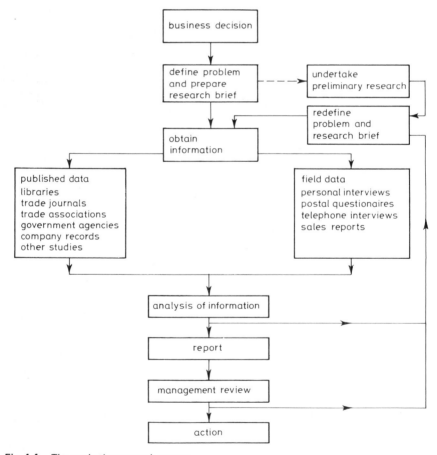

Fig. 4.4   *The marketing research process*

4.10 General research methodology

Once it is clear what the decisions are, and hence the exact nature of the information to be gathered, consideration can be given to methodology. In some cases it is necessary to undertake some preliminary work before an acceptable brief can be agreed, in particular with respect to the nature of the information to be obtained and the sources from which it is to be gathered. Information can then be collected via desk research and field research. Fig. 4.4 illustrates how this fits in to the overall marketing research process.

As soon as information is available it should begin to be processed. It is only by beginning the analysis that areas of misunderstanding, lack of data and bias can be identified. If analysis is left until the end of the field study and these types of problems left unidentified, it will inevitably become necessary to repeat some of the field work at extra cost, both in financial and in time terms, or to make do with an incomplete report. Basic decisions will have to be taken about what credence is to be placed on unsubstantial data, what information is invalid or should be ignored, how conflicting information is to be reconciled, how comparable different data sources truly are (units, methods of recording etc.), and particularly how data are to be summed. The next stage is to decide whether it is possible to form and test any hypotheses and hence draw conclusions. Once the analysis is complete a report will be drawn up and submitted to management for consideration and review. If the report is considered by the information seekers to be deficient in some way then clearly the cycle will have to be repeated (if sufficient time is available).

4.11 Choosing field data sources

Apart from company personnel there are eight sources of field data, namely customers, potential customers, competitors, suppliers, customer's customers, agents or wholesalers, and independent experts (journalists, consultants etc.).

In research studies it is usually impossible to make contact with all the potential sources of information. It is necessary to choose a small number or sample of people (or companies) to represent the whole. It would seem to be ideal to be able to define the whole (that is the total number of people who are sources of information) and to randomly select from them, without bias, a sample with whom to make contact. If, for example, one was undertaking research into consumer views on lawn mowers one might validly consider that all households who have gardens be considered as potential sources of information. It would then be necessary to assemble a list of all such households in the country, and using random numbers, randomly select the required number of households to contact — the sample size being chosen in accordance with the accuracy of the information required (reference should be made to the books on statistical sampling if more needs to be known on this subject). However, not only is this a very costly and time consuming task, but in the case of face to face interviewing, it would result in considerable travelling time in order to contact what would inevitably be a widely scattered group of people. In order to overcome this problem sampling is often undertaken in stages. The first stage might be to randomly select a number of centres of population and then pick a representative sample from within each of these centres. The size of each sample being proportional to the number of households with gardens in each centre. This is known as cluster or area sampling.

If there was reason to believe that views on lawn mowers would be different among city dwellers, town dwellers and the rural community, then each of these could be considered as a separate whole or universe, with the centres of population being chosen randomly from each community. The number of cities chosen and the sample size within each city would have to reflect the proportion of the households with gardens which are in cities. Similarly for towns and rural areas.

Subsequently within each centre, the households could either be selected at random, or if it was felt that predefined differences existed according to house-holders' incomes, size of garden or age, it would be possible to further subdivide each type of community before the random selection process was undertaken. In other words it can be beneficial to divide the whole universe into a series of smaller universes when it is known that each has different characteristics. This makes the actual survey more manageable and the results more useful. It is known as quota sampling. If subsequently two or more sub-universes exhibit similar characteristics that does no harm to the validity of the study.

4.12 Choosing sources in industrial markets

Because of the nature of industrial markets, very often no attempt is made to con-tact a statistically representative or significant sample of the whole market. In the first place all industrial customers are not equal. In any industrial market there will inevitably be some customers who buy more than other customers. Hence the first step may be to divide the market into broad categories such as very large users, large users, medium users and small users. The number of small users is likely to be much larger than the number of very large users but their total impact in terms of total sales may well be much less. Hence it is more sensible to select the number of customers to contact in each category in proportion to the buying power of that category, rather than in proportion to the number of companies in the category. This is illustrated below:

customer category	number of customers	% of all sales	number contacted
very large users	15	30%	15
large users	100	30%	15
medium users	300	20%	10
small users	1000	20%	10

The impact on company policy of the views of each large user will be much greater than the views of each small user and the sample represents this situation. However, care must be taken to count individual divisions and sites of large companies separately, whenever their buying is not centralised. A related problem is to ensure that the person contacted in each company holds an equivalent job; thus if one questioned the chief draughtsman in one customer category but the chief engineer in another customer category one would never be sure if any differences of opinion revealed were more related to the job role rather than to the customer category.

In some cases where, say, half a dozen customers represent 50% to 60% of a market, it is probably wise to visit each of them more than once, possibly visiting different departments. It would be foolish to waste time contacting, say, 50 small users unless one felt they might have special requirements which it was worth trying to satisfy. In that case the subject of the study would be different: it would be concentrated on the needs of the small users rather than on the market as a whole.

If little is known about potential users and their level of demand, not even the broad size categories outlined above can be used. One of the objectives in this situation is to try to define the market. In that case a possible solution is to visit the obvious or well known users of the product and build up information as one goes. Initial visits would not only involve asking about the product, but also what other companies or categories of company are known or thought to have a use for the product. Gradually, as more is learnt about different categories of user, a more systematic approach can be instituted; by continued face to face interviews, by using a postal questionnaire, or by desk research. Even then, especially where the budget is limited, one will not be sure that one has encompassed all of the market.

If it is necessary to obtain reaction to a proposed new product from an incompletely defined market the only sensible approach is to continue questioning until one is sure that no new views or data are being obtained, and that the percentage of respondents expressing a particular viewpoint has stabilised. In this way a picture is gradually built up, and as the study proceeds the views gathered will become more representative of the whole, although never completely so.

An alternative solution might be to post a questionnaire to every company in every industry category (obtained from directories) which one thought could contain potential users, either simply asking whether they had a potential use for product X, or listing the potential uses for product X and asking whether they had a need for any of those functions to be undertaken within their company. One might find that only 10% in one category would say yes, 30% in another category, 70% in another, 1% in another and so on. Even if one had the finances available to carry out such an exercise it would not completely solve the problem. First, one would not be sure, unless every questionnaire were returned, whether the 10% category really contained 20% potential users, and so on. Secondly, some of the largest users may not have replied and would be left out of any subsequent research. Thirdly, there might be some other categories which had not been contacted at all. Luckily the companies that do reply will usually represent a sufficiently wide cross-section of the market to enable the study to proceed, and these sorts of uncertainties can be reduced by building up information about other users during the course of the study as outlined above.

In many studies and particularly when dealing with highly technical subjects, one is not always sure at the start of the study what questions need to be asked. However, in a manner similar to that described above it is possible to build up knowledge from the earlier visits. Once it is considered that a full understanding of the relevant issues has been formed, it is a simple matter to re-establish contact with those companies visited in the early stages and ask them the missing questions. This is another case where one may wish to undertake a series of face to face interviews prior to sending out a postal questionnaire.

Thus a combination of techniques and sources is often needed to build up a reasonable picture of a market, of market needs and of the size of the market (usually cross-checked with desk research). The aim is to build up a sufficiently reliable picture such that if someone else repeated the survey, say, one month later, they would reach the same broad conclusions. It is rare in industrial marketing research to have sufficient numbers in each category of information source (e.g. material suppliers, large customers, small customers, customers' customers, agents, wholesalers, etc.) to make statistical techniques valid or worthwhile. In many cases, especially if one is seeking opinion, it makes more sense to seek out experts, that is the well informed, rather than trying to contact an unbiased section of opinion, although it is important not to fall into a journalistic type approach of regularly 'tapping' pre-identified sources. Some attempt must be made to obtain a representative section of opinion.

4.13 Postal questionnaires

Postal questionnaires are one of the main ways of obtaining field data. An example of a typical questionnaire is shown in Fig. 4.5. The generally accepted advantages of postal questionnaires are listed below:

1 In spite of their high redundancy rate (a 10–15 percent response is considered good), the cost per answer is low.
2 Busy people can reply at their convenience.
3 Questions requiring facts to be looked up or requiring a considered response can be properly answered.
4 Personal shyness on personal issues is avoided.
5 There is no interviewer bias in the manner in which questions are asked or answers recorded.

The generally accepted disadvantages are

1 The recipient's understanding of a question cannot be clarified before it is answered.
2 It is easy to put a questionnaire to one side and not to answer it at all or to pass the questionnaire down the company hierarchy so that it is eventually filled in

INSTRUCTIONS

The following questionnaire has been pretested on a small sample and it has been found that the average time to complete it is approximately 3 minutes. Simple user instructions have been placed in the left hand margin. Regardless of the number of questions you are able to answer, please return the questionnaire in the prepaid envelope enclosed.

PERSONAL INFORMATION

(1) What is your name? ....
(2) What is the name of your company? ....
(3) What is your position within the company? ....

GENERAL MARKET INFORMATION

(4) What is the approximate size of your company? ....
Number of employees ....

(5) Does your company presently use ballnose or diesinking cutters?

(PLEASE TICK)   YES ☐   NO ☐   (if No, do not continue the questionnaire but please still return it to us)

(6) What type of ballnose/diesinking cutters are you currently using?

(PLEASE TICK)
High speed steel ☐	Others ☐
Solid tungsten carbide ☐	Don't know ☐
Tungsten carbide tipped ☐	

(7) Which company manufactures your present ballnose/diesinking cutters?

(PLEASE TICK)
Carboy ☐	Osbourne ☐
Sandvik ☐	Others ☐
Clarkson ☐	Don't know ☐

(8) On average how many new ballnose/diesinking cutters do you buy in a month? .... per month

(9) When a ballnose/diesinking cutter becomes blunt do you usually

(PLEASE TICK)
Regrind on the premises	☐
Subcontract out the regrinding	☐
Throw it away	☐

(10) What is the most common material your company machines
Cast iron ☐	Other ☐
Tool steel ☐	Don't know ☐

PRODUCT OR INDUSTRY SPECIFICATIONS

(11) Please indicate the most common end user industry or industries for your moulds?

(TICK AS APPROPRIATE)
Plastic ☐	Metal ☐
Rubber ☐	Other ☐
Glass ☐	Don't know ☐

(12) Please indicate the most common depths of mould you currently produce?
0–1″ ☐	6″ + ☐
1–3″ ☐	Don't know ☐
3–6″ ☐	

(13) What are your ballnose/diesinking cutter diameter specifications?

(TICK AS APPROPRIATE)
Under 12 mm ☐	31–40 mm ☐
13–20 mm ☐	40 + ☐
21–30 mm ☐	All ☐
	Don't know ☐

(14) What are your ballnose/diesinking cutting length specifications?

(TICK AS APPROPRIATE)
Half times diameter ☐	Over two ☐
One times diameter ☐	All ☐
Two times diameter ☐	Don't know ☐

Thank you very much for taking part in this survey. Please return the questionnaire in the prepaid envelope enclosed.

Fig. 4.5 *Die and mould manufacturer's questionnaire*
This questionnaire about milling cutters was sent to all known UK die and mould manufacturers and achieved a 70% response

by someone who has not got access to the relevant data or whose views are not the same as those of the person to whom the questionnaire was originally addressed. This problem is compounded because the name which is placed on the questionnaire is often the name of the person to whom it was originally sent rather than the name of the person who actually answered it.

3 People give up early, often after only six or ten questions. Questions requiring effort of thought or facts to be looked up are simply missed out, or the first thing that comes into the respondents head is written down. Again there is no certain way for the researcher to differentiate between well thought out responses and casual responses.

4 Complicated questions cannot be asked.

5 Follow up questions are difficult. There is no progressive learning as outlined in Section 4.12.

6 Questionnaires can get passed on to competitors or deliberately filled in to be misleading (sometimes because the respondent wants to make his company out to be more healthy than it really is).

In order to maximise the effectiveness of postal questionnaires certain basic rules should be followed.

1 Find out the name and position of the person in each company from whom a response is sought. Aim at higher rather than lower levels.

2 Present the covering letter and the questionnaire well. Make it look important using good quality paper and a printed layout.

3 Prepare a covering letter setting out acceptable reasons for wanting the information and include some incentive to reply. Emphasise that even if all or nearly all the answers are negative, returning the questionnaire will still be extremely helpful.

4 Make it easy to answer the questions. A yes/no or multiple choice question is much more likely to be answered than an open ended question, but the option to say 'I don't know' should be included. Where a rating is required a five point scale should be used, e.g:

	Very		Not	
Vital	important	Important	important	Irrelevant

More divisions introduce unnecessary complexity and confusion; fewer divisions leave insufficient scope for choice.

5 Questions should be unambiguous and to ensure that they convey the same meaning to all readers they should be tested on a number of people prior to the circulation.

6 Answers sought should be factual rather then opinion based and personal or confidential information should be avoided if possible, or at least it should be made clear that it is understood that answers to such questions may not be forthcoming.

7 The question sequence should be logical, the most important questions come

first and as few questions as is compatible with obtaining the essential data asked. The form must include questions which will (a) identify the respondent, (b) check that he is qualified to answer the questionnaire (e.g. does your company buy wire strippers or are they ever likely to, and are you the person who chooses which make to buy), (c) provide the data sought, and (d) attempt to check the honesty of replies. This latter objective may be achieved by asking questions to which the answer is already known or by including alternatives in multiple choice questions that do not exist, such as a false name of a competitor or a false price range. If one of these false alternatives is ticked then clearly the respondent does not know much about the subject area, is careless or is deliberately trying to be misleading.

8 Include an incentive to reply. In industrial marketing research, this normally takes the form of promising to send a summary of the results. Little things like enclosing a stamped addressed envelope also help.

9 Do not use bought mailing lists. They are too general, usually out of date, assembled from the same directories that everyone has access to, and remain the property of the mailing house, making follow up difficult.

4.14 Personal interviews

Personal interviews are the second major way of obtaining field data. The major advantages of personal interviews are:

1 A large number of questions and complex questions can be asked; sample products can be shown or demonstrated.

2 New areas can be investigated and the depth and quality of the questions asked can be improved as the research proceeds.

3 One is certain of the status and qualifications of the respondents. The validity of replies can be checked via follow up questions, by physical signs such as facial expressions and tone of voice and sometimes by a tour of the premises.

4 The percentage of sources chosen who are actually met and from whom responses are obtained will be high. People who are genuinely interested in the subject area rarely refuse an interview, first because they know an interview is a two way process and they will be talking to someone who has just visited their competitors and/or suppliers and/or customers, and secondly if someone is prepared to take the time and trouble to come to visit, it seems positively rude not to see them.

The main disadvantages are:

1 The high cost of time and travel.

2 The length of time that is needed to complete a series of interviews.

3 The replies will be biased by how the questions are asked, how the interviewer—interviewee relate to each other and by how the interviewer records the replies.

4 Replies to questions will be instantaneous and may be different to the reply

which would have been obtained if there had been time to consider and to look up data.

There are three types of interview pattern: structured; semi-structured, and unstructured. In a structured interview the interviewer asks a list of prepared questions in a given order and records the replies. While this ensures that the whole questionnaire is completed and the interviewee clearly identified, the advantages for industrial marketing research do not usually outweigh the costs *vis-à-vis* postal questionnaires, especially as companies will inevitably be fairly widely scattered. In a semi-structured interview a list of questions is prepared and they are all asked during the interview, but in any order according to the drift of the conversation. Follow up questions can be introduced. In an unstructured interview the interviewer simply has a list of areas for discussion and while he will try to keep the conversation within these areas, a fairly broad approach is taken enabling the interviewee to talk about what interests him and is important to him. In this way valuable insights into the real nature of the market need can be obtained. Even with unstructured interviews it can be sensible to take a list of prepared questions on which specific data is sought, to act as a check list so that if these questions have not been answered by the end of the interview they can then be asked.

To be able to undertake marketing research interviews properly requires training, but there are a few basic rules worth mentioning:

1   At the start of the interview, its purpose should be explained. A check should be made as early on as possible to ensure that the person being interviewed is in fact qualified to answer the questions.
2   Notes should always be taken during the interview, otherwise vital points of information will be forgotten. Permission to take notes should always be asked for.
3   It is essential to recap at the end of the interview, to ensure that the notes properly reflect what was said and that there was no misunderstanding. Such a recap often brings new valuable thoughts into the interviewee's mind and offers him the opportunity to be more specific or even to change his mind.
4   The conversation should be allowed to develop naturally. It should not be forced as this makes the interviewee feel nervous. He senses that he is being examined in some way.
5   The interviewer, although not necessarily a specialist, must be able to talk knowledgeably about the subject.
6   Care must be taken not to ask questions in a way that indicates the response expected.
7   It is not advisable to undertake marketing research interviews by accompanying salesman on their visits. The presence of a salesman undoubtedly inhibits replies.
8   It is important to find out whether the views expressed represent official company policy or are personal ones. In the latter case it is necessary to form judgements about whether or not they are widespread within the company.

4.15 Telephone interviews

Telephone interviews are the third major way of obtaining field data and they fall midway between the other two with regard to cost, question complexity and questionnaire length. Their particular advantages are as follows:

1 In spite of the time wasted trying to identify and to get through to the right person, a telephone survey can be completed rapidly.
2 The respondent's identity is fairly clear.
3 Fairly complex questions can be asked and the interviewee has a chance to check that he properly understands the questions before answering.
4 A prepared questionnaire can be used and referred to while talking. Often a considerable number of questions can be asked.
5 The interviewee feels completely relaxed, he is in his own office and can simply put the telephone down any time he wants. He is in control and is not bothered by seeing his responses being noted down.
6 The telephone is particularly useful for asking supplementary questions following a face to face interview or a postal questionnaire. The person's identity is in that case already established and contact relatively easily made. Following a postal questionnaire much increased clarity and detail can be obtained via the telephone, or reasons elicited as to why a postal questionnaire was not returned. The telephone can be used to present the views of others who have been interviewed to see if those views are confirmed or denied and to see if the respondent's previous viewpoint will change when faced with contrary arguments.
7 Chosen respondents who cannot be reached or who refuse to co-operate can be rapidly replaced by second choice respondents as long as they are representative of the same market sector.
8 It is often possible to catch busy people who would not take the trouble to fill in a postal questionnaire or who would not be prepared to devote time to an interview.

The main disadvantages are

1 It is easy to be transferred to someone other than the identified contact and it is then difficult to establish quickly whether they are really qualified to answer the questions.
2 The validity of responses is difficult to check.
3 It is not possible to use visual material unless a letter is sent in advance.
4 Responses will be immediate as there will be no time to look up data.

4.16 Causes of incorrect information

However much trouble is taken some of the information recorded will not be correct. Much attention is paid in statistical techniques to minimising the effect of random mistakes in the information received. Over the course of a study, random mistakes should largely self-cancel and in any case they are often the least serious of the problems.

A more serious problem will be that much of the information gathered will be opinion and not fact. Many people give the first answer that comes into their head and that might not be the same as the answers they would have given if they had taken the trouble to think or to look up the relevant facts before replying. Many people genuinely do not know whether they would buy a particular product or not. It looks appealing to them, they are genuinely interested and they may say so, but that does not mean that they will buy. An even more vital use for the available funds may crop up between the research and the product purchasing decision point, or a better alternative product may become available, or the responsibility for making the decision may be shifted to someone with different priorities. In other cases the views expressed during an interview may turn out to be personal ones and not to be company policy, or the wrong person within the company may have been interviewed, someone who is not the decision maker. Sometimes the misrepresentation is deliberate. In industrial marketing research the number of information sources used will be much lower than in consumer research and hence inaccurate information from one large user can introduce more misleading conclusions than fifty poor responses among five hundred in a consumer survey.

A third source of inaccuracy is bias; bias of the researcher who is looking for a particular viewpoint to be expressed or who tends mainly to record views which conform with his own, and not so often record views contrary to his own. This is especially a problem from midway through a project when the researcher has already begun to draw conclusions and will be unconsciously leading the respondent towards confirming these conclusions. Attempts to save money by undertaking all interviews at an exhibition will also introduce bias, because only those people who are particularly interested in the subject will have attended the exhibition. Similarly, postal questionnaires introduce bias because only those really interested will reply. People who are really interested in a subject are rarely typical.

A fourth cause of incorrect information is distortion. Distortion is introduced when the report produced inaccurately reflects the information provided. This is one of the greatest sources of error in marketing studies and anything that can be done to improve the accuracy with which answers are transcribed and summarised may have a greater effect than the most careful of sampling techniques.

Perhaps most significant of all, much marketing research only provides a snapshot fixed in time, and the moment chosen may not happen to be typical. If the research were to be repeated in, say, three months, a completely different picture may emerge. This problem is made worse because many companies continue to use marketing research reports which are two or more years old. Unless marketing research is supplemented by continuously gathered and evaluated data of the type described earlier, the results cannot be placed in a proper frame of reference and this may lead to false conclusions.

4.17 Marketing research summary

The starting point for any study should be published data. Industrial markets are complex and statistical techniques are rarely applicable (which is not the same thing as saying that published statistics are not very useful — they are). Industrial marketing research is rather like a jigsaw, trying to fit together a lot of uncertain items

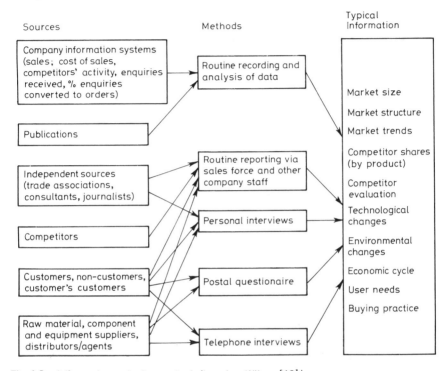

Fig. 4.6 *Information gathering methods (based on Wilson [10])*

of information so as to build up a picture. Some customers and suppliers are much more important than others and the effort should be concentrated accordingly. The research budget is often very low, often only sufficient to allow one part-time person to undertake the study and it is rarely possible to undertake more than twenty interviews. Hence it is important to use a combination of techniques, perhaps laying the ground work by a postal questionnaire or sandwiching a postal questionnaire between earlier and later face to face interviews. Much information of importance can be obtained via the telephone, by finding out why postal questionnaires have not been returned (which will often lead to a telephone interview), and by checking back with those questioned earlier and facing them with alternative viewpoints or asking supplementary questions. A low budget means that maximum use needs to be made of the other sources of information outlined in this chapter. The inter-relationship between different information sources, the methods of getting at them and the type of information they produce is summarised in Fig. 4.6.

Finally, it should be emphasised that marketing research is an information gathering function. In order to ensure the research is effective, it is necessary to become involved in defining the nature of the problem faced and the nature of the decisions to be made from the information gathered. However, marketing research should not become involved with building action programmes from the information, although it is often asked to do so. Admittedly it is part of the task to interpret the information gathered but that is not the same thing. The whole essence of marketing research is that it is undertaken before a decision is taken and not, as is unfortunately too common, used to justify decisions already taken (even to the extent of broad hints being dropped about what findings are expected), or to help furnish explanations of why things have gone wrong. At least in the latter case there is some hope that the information gathered will actually be used to improve the situation, despite the alienation which will be caused when the research findings are inevitably critical of what line management has already undertaken. Far better to undertake the research at the beginning before wrong decisions have been made.

4.18 Marketing information systems

In this chapter we have considered why information is important, what information is needed, what it is used for, and how it may be gathered. How can all this activity be incorporated into a logical system?

Companies need a system which will continuously obtain information from a multitude of sources and assemble it into a form which meets the requirements of different parts of the organisation. Data users do not want to be swamped by masses of reports, they only want information that is relevant to the decisions that they are trying to make at a given moment in time. Designing a good information system requires an understanding of what each part needs to know rather than starving it of vital material of flooding it with superfluous material. The following steps are involved:

Identification of relevant information from publications, questionnaires and personal contact.

Classification of the information into subject areas and in accordance with the established veracity of its source (i.e. sort fact from opinion). A suitable indexing system is essential.

Recording the information either verbatim or in summary form, with or without analysis. Information may be recorded on paper, on microfilm or on computer disc/tape.

Retrieval of the information via the indexing system to cover only the areas of interest and the level of detail needed.

Reporting the information, usually in summary form, but with reference to sources where more detail may be found.

The study of methods of classifying information is a subject in its own right. What is sought is a method of achieving a hierarchy of detail and cross-referencing so that it is possible to access only those parts of the mass of information available which are needed for the specified purpose, and without having to waste time on material which is not directly relevant. If more detail on a particular part of the data is required this should be readily available. For example it is possible to obtain data on price, sales volume, export sales volume and market share for a number of

Period: ....

Competitor	Machine	Home built or imported	Price	Sales volume	Export sales volume	Market share
Company A	X1	H	—	— — —	— —	— — —
	X2	H				
	X3	H	—	— — —	— —	— — —
	Y1	I				
	Y2	I	—	— — —	— —	— — —
Company B	X2	I	—	— — —	— —	— — —
	X3	H				
	X4	H				
	Y2	I	—	— — —	— —	— — —
	Z1	H				
	Z2	H				
Company C	X1	I	—	— — —	— —	— — —
	X4	I				
	Z1	H				
	Z2	H				
	Z3	H	—	— — —	— —	— — —

Fig. 4.7 *Example of competitor data file*
The file would include this information for several periods so that trends could be established

different types of product made by various competitors from the file illustrated in Fig. 4.7. If a decision maker wanted for some reason to know the market share held by company C in product category Z1 then it should be possible for him to access that data without being swamped by all the other data and having to waste time sorting out the relevant numbers for himself.

A further example of the possibilities is shown in Fig. 4.8. This type of data about existing customers could easily be obtained from sales visits reports, and subsequently analysed in many useful ways. The primary frame could easily be linked to a file of outstanding quotations so that when a customer made a progress telephone call the relevant data could quickly be brought up on a VDU. The customer list could be extended to include potential customers, providing not only a means of estimating sales potential (see also Section 5.16) but also a ready made schedule for mail shots and for salesmen's cold calls. A medium sized engineering group has actually implemented such a system. The list of potential customers was built up by eliminating from a very large externally supplied list of all those companies who could conceivably be potential customers, companies which did not exhibit identified characteristics of existing customers.

3000 customers or potential customers could be profiled.

Primary frame	Secondary frame by product*
Name, address, postcode	Criterion for selection of product
Telephone number	(1—5 rating for each)
Contact name	Price, durability, availability,
Geographic area	dimensions, finish produced,
Representative code	material being finished, etc.
Distributor code	Competitors' products bought
Size of customer	Name, model, value, quantity
Usage per annum	
Type of products to be sold	

Final frame by product*

Potential sales per annum	Value of business in last 12 months
Potential included in this year's sales forecast	Value of orders placed this year
	No. of salesmen's calls this year
Estimated profit contribution (value)	No. of mailshots this year
No. of years a customer	Date received catalogue

* That is data is recorded by product code as well as by customer code.

Fig. 4.8 *A customer information file*

Although low cost computing is making such a system an economic possibility for more and more companies, especially where all that is required is a reworking of data collected for other purposes, it is still very expensive, and indeed unnecessary/ impossible to try to cope with all the information that companies are exposed to. Therefore it is imperative that companies define what information they need for their key decisions; decisions which will determine their future success. Fig. 4.9 illustrates the information categories which have been selected by one British engineering company. Initially the available resources should be concentrated on key information. Only when the information system has proved its value should consideration be given to expanding it to deal with the merely important. Any gaps in the continuously gathered information can be filled periodically by specific information gathering efforts such as marketing research.

To make an information system work it normally will be necessary to appoint someone to be responsible for the system (possibly as part of his job) with the

Contents

Chapter 1 Internal data

1 Despatches
2 Sales
3 Orders
4 Net orders weekly
5 Quotations

Chapter 2 UK market data

1 Market size
2 Market share
3 Imports
4 Exports
5 Trade
6 Market study group
7 DOI statistics
8 MTTA survey

Chapter 3 Competition

1 Lost order analysis
2 Names
3 Distribution
4 Prices
5 Production and sales

Chapter 4 International

1 Distributors list
2 International market share
3 Market share
4 Country profiles

Chapter 5 Forecasts

1 2 week
2 This year
3 5 year
4 CBI survey
5 Henley
6 NMTBA
7 FT survey

Chapter 6 Financial

1 Competitor results
2 Pricing analysis
3 Price/quantity curves
4 Exchange rates
5 FT index

Fig. 4.9 *Example of a company marketing manual*

authority to insist that all information which has been agreed to be relevant is gathered by the various company departments and passed on to him to classify, record and later to retrieve. This person in effect becomes the focus for the information system, see Fig. 4.10.

If such a person is appointed it is very tempting for him to issue regular general reports. However, 'general', by definition, means that what is contained in such a report will not be exactly what the salesman wants nor what the planner wants nor what the development department wants. It is better to provide company staff with a directory of the information that is available and instructions about how it can be accessed when required. If access is easy and superfluous data not reported, the system is likely to prove popular. Once established, the ongoing running costs of a recording-retrieval system suitable for forecasting and decision making will probably be no more than is already spent on attempts to obtain information on an *ad hoc* basis.

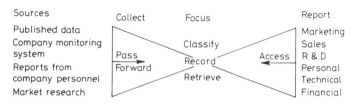

Fig. 4.10   *A focussed information system*

4.19 Using information

It has been emphasised that information is the cornerstone on which good decisions are built. Running a business without information is like negotiating an obstacle course with one's eyes shut. Opening one's eyes does not guarantee that one will not trip up occasionally but it certainly helps. Information reduces the risk of making a bad decision. It does not ensure a good decision. What companies should do is to decide what information is needed in order to reach a decision, compare that with what is available, and try to fill as much of the gap as can be done economically and within the decision timescale.

However, no matter how much time and effort is spent on gathering information it will never be possible to gather all the relevant information. It is important to be able to judge when a sufficiency of information has been made available, otherwise decisions can be put off indefinitely (of which there are many examples) or more money can be spent on information gathering than can be recouped from improved decision making. Even more important is to be able to recognise from the mass of information available what is relevant and what can safely be ignored. 'The critical information problem is not the lack of relevant information, it is an overabundance of irrelevant information.' (see Ackoff [11]).

Similarly to the way increased production automation has downgraded the manual skills of the shopfloor worker and increased the importance of the skills of the system designer and the 'tape' producer, computerised management information systems can shift the decision making influence towards the designers and operators of the system; people who are supposedly less competent to make the decisions than the authorised decision makers. This shift in power occurs because much of the skill of operating a management information system lies in extracting the relevant from the irrelevant and presenting that and only that to the decision maker. In a way this seems to take away some of the decision makers options and in many cases decision makers feel obliged to establish a second informal and unfiltered information channel as a check. Because they understand the informal channel, they are more likely to believe the information it provides and perhaps this explains why so many major decisions are made which appear contrary to the information which is formally made available. It is important to recognise what is happening and to try to ensure that the decision makers understand enough about their formal information systems to feel comfortable about using the information that they provide.

Chapter 5

Forecasting

5.1 Why and what to forecast

The time needed to implement many business decisions makes it difficult for companies to respond quickly to the unexpected. It is more efficient to plan ahead, but to do that it is necessary to forecast what lies in the future. Good forecasts open up opportunities for companies to be first into a new field, first with a new product, first to identify a new customer need. In industries where the scale of investment is such that it takes many years to amortise, forecasting is a prerequisite.

The areas of forecasting of interest to marketing departments generally correspond to the areas of information search dealt with in the last chapter, that is, the environment, the market and company performance. In an ideal world one might wish to produce a forecast for everything, but because forecasting is expensive, that is not possible. Instead, extensive use should be made of published forecasts (especially economic and social) prepared by specialists who have the expertise and resources to produce better forecasts than anything individual companies can achieve. These forecasts exist as indices/indicators, as investment intentions/business confidence surveys, as part of industry surveys, as well as full blown forecasts with full explanatory texts. As with information, the way to find out what is available is to consult major reference libraries, trade associations, professional bodies or government departments. However, it is essential to be aware of and to understand the assumptions on which these forecasts are based if incorrect inferences are to be avoided. Where published forecasts are insufficiently specific for company needs, they can be used as part of the input to a company's own forecasting effort.

Limited forecasting resources make it necessary for companies to concentrate on factors which will have a major impact on their future well being. These factors must be identified. For the most important, an appropriate forecasting technique should be chosen; with the remainder being monitored via business contacts and general reading. Particular attention should be paid to differentiating between those factors over which the company has some control and those over which it has no control (see Section 1.5). Forecasting tends to concentrate on the latter, whereas the former tends to be monitored (and to some extent forecast) as part of the control process. In either case, being aware of the critical factors and the probable manner of their impact gives an organisation a head start. It is able to monitor the key variables, and as soon as they start to change, action programmes can begin to be modified to take account of the forecast impacts.

5.2 Choice of forecasting method

The economic value of forecasts (and information) can be considered equivalent to the difference in the quality of the decisions which will be taken with the forecast (information) and without the forecast, measured in terms of profit or discounted cash flow. While this cannot normally be accurately assessed, the amount spent should nevertheless be broadly matched to the importance of the dependant decision. Fig. 5.1 illustrates an attempt to do just that, by linking some of the forecasting techniques described in this chapter to typical decisions which have to be taken during a product's life cycle (see Section 7.2). The choice of forecasting method will also be affected by practical matters of forecast preparation and implementation. The factors to take into account can be summarised as follows:

Time horizon	Subject of forecast	Method	Typical decision area
Long term; 2 years plus	The environment	Qualitative	New factory, major plant, new products
Medium term; next year	The market company sales		Minor plant and equipment, product modifications, exhibitions
Short term; this year	Company sales	Quantitative	Manning, stocks, sales thrust, promotion

There is no point in using sophisticated numerical techniques on poor quality data. In general short term forecasting tends to be heavily based on quantitative methods (see Table 5.1), and long term forecasting on qualitative methods (see Table 5.2). The output from the longer term qualitative techniques may of course be used as inputs to the quantitative techniques or used to review and perhaps modify their input. The situation may be summarised as follows:

1 Importance of the forecast to the future of the company.
2 Extent to which forecasts are incorporated into the company planning and decision making process.
3 Management sophistication; ability to communicate the problem to forecasters, ability to understand the basis of forecasting techniques and ability to translate forecasts into action plans.
4 Cost of preparation.
5 Availability of required forecasting expertise.

Stage of life cycle	Product development	Market testing and early introduction	Rapid growth	Steady state
Typical decisions	Amount of development effort Product design Business strategy	Facility size Marketing strategies including distribution and pricing	Facilities expansion Marketing strategies Product planning and control	Promotion, specials Pricing Production planning Inventory level Change of life cycle phase
Forecasting techniques	Scenario building Delphi studies Demand analysis Diffusion studies Impact analysis Theoretical limits test Technological mapping Strategic studies Opportunity identification Market surveys Input Output analysis Substitution forecasting	Market surveys Subjective forecasting Substitution forecasting Probability forecasting Model building	Statistical analysis of sales and trend extension Correlation Probability forecasting Market surveys Model building Life cycle analysis	Statistical analysis of sales and trend extension with special emphasis on market share Correlation Probability forecasting Market surveys for tracking and warning Life cycle analysis

Fig. 5.1 *Matching forecasting techniques to a product's life cycle (based on Chambers, Mullick and Smith [12])*

[Reprinted by permission of the *Harvard Business Review*. An exhibit from 'How to choose the right forecasting technique' by J. C. Chambers, S. K. Mullick and D. D. Smith. Copyright ©1971 by President and Fellows of Harvard College. All rights reserved]

6   Accuracy requirements of the data base.
7   Availability of required input data.
8   Sensitivity of forecast to environmental conditions.
9   Speed of preparation and time available for forecasting.

Qualitative techniques are particularly vital when trying to look at the future with imagination in order to identify major changes in technology, in social habits, or in the economic situation. The impact of such quantum leaps is normally considerable – possibly requiring divestment, diversification or considerable new investment – and hence much attention should be paid to identifying them.

5.3 Technological forecasting

It seems sensible in a book targeted at engineers to begin with technological fore-

Table 5.1   *Quantitative forecasting techniques (based on a table in Sasson [13])*

1   Product life cycle analysis
Assessing how long demand for a particular product will be maintained.

2   Extrapolation or trend extension
Extending historic data into the future. Methods of recording data for trend extension include moving averages, exponential smoothing and adaptive filtering.

3   Correlation
Relating the activity or event to be forecast to another data series which can be forecast with greater ease or accuracy.

4   Probability forecasting
Assigning numerical values to predicted events (e.g. how much will company A buy next year or what is the probability of obtaining a given order).

5   Model building
Building up a series of assumptions about how a number of factors will inter-relate to produce the forecast outcome (usually in the form of a series of simultaneous equations).

6   Substitution forecasting*
Assessing the rate at which an existing technology will be replaced by a new technology.

7   Test marketing
Releasing the product only to selected (typical) potential customers; usually geographically based in the case of consumer products. The sales results are extrapolated to encompass the total market, and sales growth and ultimate penetration of the market forecast. A very expensive method, even if the test is of limited spread and duration, because of the commitment to manufacturing facilities.

* These techniques are particularly associated with technological forecasting.

Table 5.2   *Qualitative forecasting techniques (based on a table in Sasson [13])*

1   Scenario building
    Asking many people from different specialisms (usually experts in their area) to describe the future as they see it. Extracting common elements and building a picture of the future.

2   Delphi studies*
    Asking a panel of experts to predict future events and to estimate the earliest, latest and most likely times when they will occur. Initial estimates are fed back to the panel until concensus is reached.

3   Diffusion studies*
    Assessing the potential application of known innovations in other fields.

4   Impact analysis*
    Forecasting the effect on the world of various highly likely events. The focus is often on technological advance and the impact that it will have on customers needs. Group discussions by experts often yield unexpected problems and areas for developments.

5   Theoretical limits test*
    Examining the impact of extending existing technical, scientific and social ideas to their limits.

6   Technological mapping*
    Assessing future competitiveness by analysing technological capabilities of direct and indirect competitors.

7   Strategic studies
    Forecasting the nature of competitive business activity.

8   Opportunity identification
    Identifying new customer needs and identifying new ways of satisfying current needs.

9   Market surveys
    Assessment of future buying patterns and competitor activity as a result of a directed investigation concentrating on making contact with customers. It can be used to forecast total market size as well as company sales volumes.

10 Input—output analysis
    Relates inputs such as socio/economic/technological data to outputs such as market and sales growth, usually via a model so that the effect of changing each input can be investigated. It may also be used in relation to the derived demand chain, to show how changes in one part of the chain when inputted to another part will affect the output of that part; or indeed how a competitor introducing a new product might affect the sales of all the other competitive products.

* These techniques are particularly associated with technological forecasting.

Table 5.2   *Continued*

11 Concensus of opinion

This is a much used and purely subjective technique where the opinion of company executives and outside experts is gathered (via day to day business contacts), reviewed in company meetings or simply within peoples minds, and formed into a view of the future. This is often the method adopted by top management (see Section 4.19) to test the validity of forecasts reached by more formal methods. It can be dangerously introspective because the views obtained will tend to reinforce each other (i.e. all from the same industry or the same job role) leading to over or under optimistic forecasts, e.g. steel output, car output and business confidence forecasts.

12 Normative relevance analysis

Working back to the present from an actual or assumed future requirement to see what needs to be done to make it attainable.

13 Morphological analysis

Using a matrix of all the conceivable approaches to a problem to help generate opportunities for a novel solution.

casting. Technological forecasting forecasts changes in technology; its influence on what products can be made available and its influence on people's expectations about what they will need; so that companies are better able to decide upon the level and direction of their research and development programmes. The most common methods have been marked with an asterisk in Tables 5.1 and 5.2.

It has already been emphasised that the rate of technological change is increasing and hence any lead companies can gain over competitors by obtaining an inkling of what is to come is especially valuable. Failure to keep up with technology has been a frequent cause of business failure. Some companies have clung to a technology which is no longer competitive, others have failed to fully exploit the latest technique, and others have fallen into the trap of overestimating the appeal of a new technology and hence have never been able to recoup the research and development involved in its introduction. Technological forecasting is a way of trying to reduce these types of error, but to be cost effective it has to be targeted as specifically as possible.

5.4 Scenario building

A scenario is a look into the future, consisting of a picture in which the various elements are combined in a plausible and mutually consistent manner, such that the logical sequence of events by which the pictured future state could be reached from the present state is clearly demonstrated (for example see part 2, Section A of Kotler and Cox [14]).

Scenarios are intended to be illuminating rather than predictive and as such do not reduce the risk of decisions. However, if two, three or four alternative scenarios are developed then the risk of a particular business decision can be evaluated, by examining how well the business would continue to succeed, given that decision in each of the possible scenarios. A decision which appeared to lead to success in all the scenarios would be low risk, and one which led to disaster in three out of four scenarios would be a high risk decision. In that way trade-offs between the risks and the benefits of alternative decisions can be made.

Scenarios can be very simple. A scenario for a particular industry could be produced by reading reports about the future economic, social, technological and political environment, and linking them to what is known about how changes to the environment will probably affect the industry. In most cases there will be published reports available speculating about the future of the industry, which will help the process. Most businessmen build up scenarios of the future in their minds, but unfortunately, very often they never get committed to paper, and as a result they are not compared with the ideas of colleagues, refined (perhaps using some of the steps outlined below), and used for forecasting purposes. It is suggested that production of written scenarios would be very cost effective for most companies, particularly if they took the trouble to identify the elements of the environment which were important to them, and collected reports, surveys and articles which referred to those elements. It almost certainly would be more important to identify the really major factors and pay very close attention to them, rather than try to cover all those of less importance. These reports could then be interpreted in a sensible manner to produce a written scenario of some kind.

At the other extreme, more comprehensive scenarios can be built up by asking panels of experts to put forward their views of the future, and combining them with all the published forecasts in a plausible manner. These broad scenarios would cover issues such as unemployment, union power, growth of the state sector, world trade, forms of political power, crime rates, environmental protection, use of energy, the division of the national purse, peoples values and lifestyle and so on. Usually at least an optimistic and pessimistic (and sometimes three or four alternative) scenarios would be prepared.

In order to relate these broad scenarios to a particular company it would be necessary to identify those areas which would most affect the fortunes of the company. Having identified each of the areas to be taken into account, the forecast state of as many of them as possible would be extracted from the broad scenarios, and their impact on the company assessed, so that appropriate strategies and action programmes could be evolved.

Large scale scenario building requires a vast amount of information to be processed and few companies find it cost effective to do it themselves. Instead, they prefer to buy the broad scenarios prepared by specialist forecasting organisations and combine them with relevant published material to form scenarios which are specific to their industries. A few very large companies find it worthwhile to commission forecasting organisations to prepare scenarios which specifically look at their business activities.

For most companies some middle ground between the very simple approach described above, and commissioning a comprehensive scenario, will be the most effective approach.

5.5 The Delphi technique

Delphi studies are started by making contact with a group of experts in the subject to be studied and forming them into a panel. Next the organiser poses a series of questions about how the future in that field might develop. For example, one question might be, 'what will become the most common automotive power unit during the next 25 years, and what is the earliest and the latest year when it can be expected to represent 50% of new power units'.* One answer might be:

Diesel reciprocating engines 1986–1993

and another:

Electric motors 2005–2015

Having obtained answers to all the questions posed, from all the panel, the organisers have to assemble the answers into a summarised list. In the case of some questions as many as ten alternative suggestions might be listed, each with a different time-scale. Each suggestion will be listed showing the % support, the extremes of the timescale suggested and the timescale supported by 50% of the experts who made that suggestion. To illustrate by continuing the above example, the replies to the first part of that question might be listed as follows:

	% support	Earliest date	Majority dates	Latest date
Reciprocating petrol engines	10	1985	1985	1985
Rotary petrol engines	10	1990	1991–1994	1997
Reciprocating diesel engines	30	1986	1988–1992	1998
Rotary diesel engines	5	1990	1992–1997	2004
Battery electric motors	20	1988	1990–1995	2003
Gas turbine engines	10	1990	1991–1994	1995
Gas reciprocating engines	10	1989	1993–1997	2000

These replies will be fed back to the panel and they will be asked to agree or disagree with each suggestion. Where they agree, they will be asked to suggest new time scales in the light of those provided. In cases where the experts disagree with a suggestion or with a majority timescale they are invited to include short reasons for their disagreement in their reply.

---

* Alternatively the question might begin 'For each alternative listed below indicate the probability that they will become the most common automotive power unit during the next 25 years . . .'. This form of question enables each expert to support more than one possibility – but space must be left for them to insert their own suggestions. The % support column in the above table would be replaced by a probability value.

Again the organiser will summarise the replies and send them out for a third round, asking panel members whether they wish to modify their previous views in the light of the new information. Theoretically the majority could move towards a well argued minority view and at the very least, awareness of other viewpoints will help them think more deeply about their own suggestions. By this stage the answers might be summarised as follows (the figures are purely fictitious):

	% support	Earliest date	Majority dates	Latest date
Majority views				
Reciprocating diesel	40%	1986	1987–1992	1995
Battery electric	25%	1988	1990–1994	2000
Gas reciprocating	15%	1989	1992–1996	2000
Minority views				
Reciprocating petrol	10%	1985	1985	1985
Rotary petrol	5%	1990	1991–1994	1998
Rotary diesel	2%	1990	1992–1996	2000
Gas turbine	2%	1992	1992–1994	1996

Reasons put forward to support minority views.
Reciprocating petrol . . . .
Rotary petrol   . . . .

In most studies by the end of the third, and certainly the fourth round, a clear consensus view (with one alternative receiving as much as 70% support) will begin to emerge. The value of this type of information to a company operating in the field of the study is obvious.

Delphi studies are conducted entirely by post and anonymously. First, to give panel members time to consider their reply, and secondly to avoid the views of the panel members being coloured by knowing who supports which proposal or by the force of someone's personality, as would occur if a roundtable discussion were held. In cases where panel members do not have equal levels of expertise over the range of subjects being studied, increased sophistication can be achieved by asking each panel member to self-rate his expertise on a 1–5 scale for each question answered, and weighting the replies accordingly.

The major problems involved with the method are obtaining agreement to participate from a sufficient number of experts (and at a reasonable fee), persuading them to reply promptly so that there is not a long gap between rounds which will result in loss of interest, maintaining interest over several rounds, not asking questions which generate so many alternative answers that subsequent rounds become unwieldly, and most important of all summarising the dissenting views in a succinct but sensible way.

Many companies in fact have enough experts among their own staff to carry out an internal Delphi study and the scope within a trade association is even greater.

polated. A sales forecast may be obtained by multiplying the percentage substitution at any point in time by the forecast market size at that same point in time. This technique has been 'proven' using historical data for many different technological substitutions such as detergents for soap, plastic for leather, or synthetic rubber for natural rubber in car tyres. The method works because once the take over of an old technology by a new one has progressed by a few percentage points, the takeover process normally continues to completion. When actually used for forecasting purposes account must be taken of outside factors such as an unexpected improvement in the existing technology, a diminished rate of improvement in the new technology because of a restriction of R & D funds or changed social factors, which may affect the rate of substitution by altering the comparative cost/benefit ratio of the two technologies.

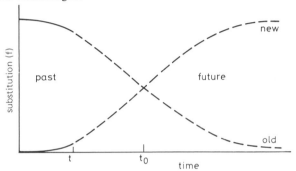

Fig. 5.2 *Rate of substitution for old technology by new technology*

A possible disadvantage to this technique is that in the cases of new technology which make a very rapid impact, by the time a substitution forecast has been made it may be already too late for a company to climb on to the band wagon. In these cases the information can be used either to confirm previous decisions or to modify them to a limited degree.

5.8 Forecasting market potential

Reference was made in Section 4.4.2 to ultimate and immediate market potential. Forecasting ultimate market potential at a given moment in time requires a list to be prepared showing every possible use of the product, the number of potential users for each use, and their maximum rate of use. For example, for radio telephones one might start as follows:

Use	Users	Number of users	Rate of use
Long range control	Armed forces Doctors Police Taxis		

Use	Users	Number of users	Rate of use
	Plumbers		
	Delivery drivers		
	Executives		
	Servicemen		
Short range control	Large factories		
	Building sites		
	Foremen		
	Police		

This is inevitably an extremely subjective procedure especially in the case of new technologies where one cannot possibly forsee all the uses and users. However, even allowing that the level of accuracy will be low, it at least provides a sense of to what degree further sales growth is possible. The next step is to compare the current sales volume with the potential and to forecast how long it will take to reach say 70% of the potential. Growth beyond 70%, given the inaccuracies, is likely to be uncertain. It is very dangerous for a company to be unaware that a market is about to 'top out', that is to reach saturation. Not only will forecast sales growth be unachieveable but the whole competitive situation will change in the same way that it does at the maturity phase of the product life cycle (see Section 7.3.3).

It is equally important to be aware of the immediate market potential. The difference between the two provides a good indication of the scope left for technical advances to make sales volume increases possible. Immediate potential has to be measured by systematic market research.

5.9 Trend extension

Virtually all companies try to forecast next year's sales, and inevitably part of the process will involve extending a graph of current and previous years sales. Most companies keep records of sales on a regular basis and ideally the sales figures will be kept separately for each product, each model and each customer category.

Two possible patterns are shown in Fig. 5.3. The first graph shows a reasonably steady state and in that case it would seem reasonable to assume that the steady state will continue for the next four quarters, and to predict next year's sales accordingly. It would be better to take account of known changes in the economic cycle and in product competitiveness (see Section 7.2) to modify the slope of the graph somewhat. Naturally the forecasts cannot be certain and hence an indication of the expected limits of accuracy should be made clear, based on statistical techniques as outlined below. In order to apply these techniques with confidence a basic level of statistical knowledge is essential and reference should be made to the appropriate texts.

Probabilistic techniques are used to set the limits of forecasting accuracy. That is the limits between which individual quarterly results can fall without causing concern that the fundamental nature of the prediction is incorrect. In what is termed a normal distribution, the standard deviation is a measure of the extent of the difference or deviation (σ) between the forecast or normal result and any individual result. In such a distribution 68% of the results will be within one standard deviation of the forecast result and 95% of the results within two

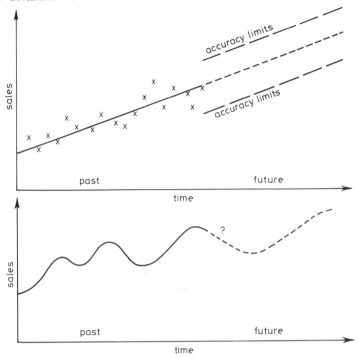

Fig. 5.3   *Sales patterns*

standard deviations of the forecast result. Therefore the normally adopted confidence limits are equal to two standard deviations on either side of the forecast value (say X), that is:

Sales forecast $= X \pm 2\sigma$

where

$$\sigma = \sqrt{[\Sigma d^2/(n-1)]}$$

and

$d =$ the difference between X and the actual sales (from Fig. 5.3) for each previous quarter

and

$n =$ the number of quarters for which figures are available

and

$\Sigma =$ the symbol meaning 'sum of'
(e.g. if $d_1 = 4, d_2 = 3$ and $d_3 = 2$ then $\Sigma d = 9$)

As long as the actual sales results fall within the confidence limits it may be safely assumed that the assumptions upon which the forecast was based are holding and that the forecast remains accurate. As soon as sales results start to fall outside the confidence limits, this can be taken as an early warning that the assumptions should be re-examined.

In practice it is common to find that the straight line or curve which best fits the plot of past sales against time cannot be drawn accurately by eye. In that case reference must be made to the various curve fitting techniques available. In some cases it may prove possible to derive an equation for the curve.

It is also common to find that the sales figures oscillate wildly (see second graph on Fig. 5.3). In other words there is either some kind of seasonal or economic cyclic effect superimposed on the trend, or there may be significant random variations. Genuine cyclic effects of both types will apply to all companies operating in the given market and hence their effect on the sales of an individual company can be eliminated by recording sales in terms of market share rather than gross sales. The market share trend can then be extended, and the variations resulting from the cycles reimposed to arrive at a sales forecast.

In the case of random variations the first step is to check that the variations are indeed random and not a result of a unique event such as a special offer by a competitor, a particularly effective advertising campaign or a temporary increase in demand (e.g. generators during an electricity strike). Such unique contributions should immediately be removed from the graph. In order to reveal the underlying pattern behind the variations which remain, techniques such as moving averages and exponential smoothing can be used. A moving average is the average of a past set of figures including the most recent figure, updated each time a new figure is available, as follows.

If M_t is the linear moving average of sales (s) calculated over six months then

$$M_t = \tfrac{1}{6}(S_t + S_{t-1} + S_{t-2} \ldots S_{t-5})$$

Next month the new moving average will be

$$M_{t+1} = \tfrac{1}{6}(S_{t+1} + S_t + S_{t-1} \ldots S_{t-4})$$

Thus each time a new result is added to the set, the oldest result is removed from the set. Since this method takes as much account of sales six months ago as in the most recent months it might be considered desirable to weight the figures such that

$$M_t = a_1 S_t + a_2 S_{t-1} + a_3 S_{t-2} \ldots a_6 S_{t-5}$$

where

$$a_1 > a_2 > a_3 \quad \text{and} \quad a_1 + a_2 + a_3 \ldots a_6 = 1$$

The trend of values of M_t over time can be used to predict next months sales. However, care must be taken because removing a bad month from the set increases the moving average just as surely as adding a good months sales. If the average is taken over too long a period important trends can be lost.

A special case of the last equation is the exponentially weighted moving average where:

new forecast = previous forecast

+ α(latest observation − previous forecast)

where α is a constant and lies between 0 and 1. Each new forecast is a weighted average of all previous observations and the weight attached to each observation will decrease by the fraction $(1 - \alpha)$ as past observations become more remote. If $\alpha = 0$ then the effect of the difference between the latest observation and the forecast made for that observation is being ignored. If $\alpha = 1$ the whole of the difference is being taken into account. Some experimenting is required to settle upon a value of α (usually between 0.1 and 0.3) which will give steadily accurate forecasts. The results of applying the formula successively with α equal to 0.5 is illustrated by the following.

Month	Forecast	Actual result	New forecast
January	£9000	£10 000	£9500 (for February)
February	£9500	£9000	£9250
March	£9250	£10 750	£10 000
April	£10 000	£9000	£9500

There are a number of other statistical techniques for dealing with random variations and interested readers should refer to the specialist texts.

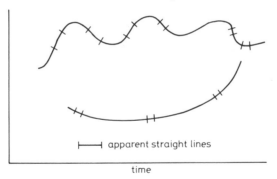

apparent straight lines

time

Fig. 5.4 *Short lived straight lines*

Trend extension relies on there being a straight line relationship between two variables. However, many straight line trends eventually begin to show signs of curvature. On any randomly drawn curvilinear line there will be straight portions and even on continuous curves if a short enough length is taken in isolation it could easily be mistaken for a straight line and lead to inaccurate forecasts, see Fig. 5.4. For this reason trend extension should be limited to short term forecasts, and a continuous check kept on how accurately the trend has predicted current results. As soon as there are signs of systematic deviation, the trend must be reassessed.

Trend extension techniques can be applied to variables other than company sales. One example is market size. Unfortunately published data is usually not broken down into sufficient detail to be useful for this purpose although reference should be made to publications such as *The Business Monitor* and to the statistics issued by Trade Associations in case something is available. Another example relevant to certain industries is to monitor how product servicing costs increase relative to production costs. In other words, at what stage will a durable become a non-durable. It is no longer economic to repair some items such as central heating water pumps, some radios and watches, small electric motors; it is cheaper to replace them. This trend is beginning to apply to certain production tools and it is important to identify the changeover point because production costs can be considerably reduced if the capability for the product to be serviced does not have to be designed in.

Trend extension can also be used to forecast levels of performance, such as noise levels of particular machines, machine tool accuracy, levels of house insulation or vehicle fuel economy and thereby provide a guide to future market requirements. In these cases consideration must be given to the influence of non-technical factors on the rate of advance. For example, the rate of increase of speed of commercial aircraft has been affected not only by technical constraints but by social pressures relating to noise, to not spending available resources in a way which seems to benefit so few people and the fact that on all but long hauls the total door to door journey time is more affected by airport and road congestion than by aircraft speed.

5.10 The experience curve

Learning curve theory states that the time needed to complete a given task is reduced as the person undertaking the task builds up experience of doing it; that is, the person learns to do it better. The Boston Consulting Group [18] applied this theory to industry and showed that for many products inflation adjusted unit costs reduce to between 70% and 90% of the existing unit cost, each time the cumulative production volume doubles, because of better product design and improved production and administrative (including marketing) processes. The relationship between costs and cumulative volume is called the experience curve, and the equation to the curve is:

$$C_n = C_m (n/m)^{-K}$$

where C_n is unit cost at a cumulative production volume of n and C_m is the unit cost at a cumulative production volume of m and K is a constant, dependent on the learning rate.

The value of K can be determined from historic data by plotting log (cost per unit) against log (cumulative production volume). (For more detail see also Abell and Hammond [19]. For example, in the mid-60s the inflation-adjusted price of a semiconductor reduced at a rate of 25% each time accumulated experience doubled.

It is possible to extend the curve in the light of sales forecasts, and forecast the expected production costs in twelve months or in three years time. Knowledge of these costs provides an efficiency target towards which the company must work if it is to remain competitive, because other companies in the field will also be moving along their own experience curve, and reducing their own costs. Cost reduction with experience does not happen automatically, it only happens because companies work hard to achieve it. Ideally it would be possible to plot average industry (competitor) costs against experience and compare it with the company's own results. Deviance above the industry norm would indicate that costs were above the industry average and deviance below the norm that costs were less than the industry average. Differences in slope of the plots would show whether the company was progressing sufficiently rapidly in order to maintain its competitive position.

The existence of the experience curve explains one of the advantages of dominating a market sector, namely that the dominant company accumulates experience faster than its competitors and is able to reduce unit costs more rapidly. It also explains one of the advantages of being first with a new product or into a new market sector; it offers the opportunity to keep costs below that of later arriving competitors and is especially useful in the early stages – increasing cumulative production volume from 10 to 1000 units increases cumulative experience by a factor of 10 whereas the volume increase from 1000 to 2000 units only doubles cumulative experience.

In practice there are problems. The closest one is likely to get to the zero experience position is the introduction of a new technology product into a new market. In all other cases companies will have some relevant experience (production, design, marketing, administration). In addition, cumulative experience applies not only to a company's direct experience but also to some extent to published and common knowledge experience in industry. Hence companies can never be sure exactly where on the curve they are. Experience can also be 'bought in', and therefore companies without direct experience need not start at the bottom of the curve. It is also true that costs tend to reduce in discrete lumps rather than continuously and that ingenuity and the introduction of new technology can often override cumulative experience, making forecasting more than 2 or 3 years ahead hazardous. However, with a bit of experimentation, a reasonable straight line cost reduction trend can be plotted using historic data.

Viewed from a different angle, being able to predict future production costs enables companies to deliberately price below their 'current unit cost + target profit margin' (see Section 11.6) in an attempt to make major gains in market share, in the knowledge that in a year or so costs will have reduced sufficiently to turn the loss into a profit. The initial lower price should increase market share, bringing with it economies of scale and a more rapid accumulation of experience, enabling costs to be more rapidly reduced than if the product had been priced higher. This seems to be the approach followed by many Japanese companies.

5.11 Forecasting unit costs

A similar approach can be used to predict future unit cost reductions as a result of the adoption of new technology. This is a different cause of cost reduction than cumulative experience although the two are inter-related. Projection of downward cost trends for existing technology and for known new technology may indicate a significant disparity, say in two or three years time. This is illustrated in Fig. 5.5.

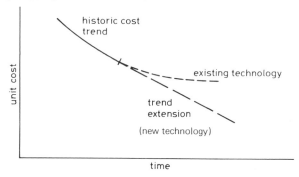

Fig. 5.5 *Unit cost trends*

Sometimes it is possible to temporarily keep on the lower trend without adopting the new technology because of government subsidies, reduced labour rates, import tariffs or the use of old and fully depreciated plant and equipment. Although unit cost reductions achieved by such measures can be continued over an extended time period, they are limited in extent and eventually it becomes impossible to keep on the trend. Unfortunately, by this time it is often too late to catch up the companies who introduced the new technology at an earlier stage. The loss of market share while the mistake is being rectified may be so great that insufficient revenue can be generated to pay for the catching up process.

5.12 Correlation

The idea behind correlation techniques is to relate company sales (or other variable to be forecast) to other readily available and accurately forecast data. Some of the best sources to use for this purpose are the official and semi-official statistical series referred to in Section 4.7, which are published by government departments, trade associations and by some specialist magazines. As with trend extension the further back the data can be traced and the relationship shown to hold true, the higher the level of confidence which can be placed on extending the relationship into the future.

The equation used to forecast UK demand for machine tools [20] is a typical example of correlation. Thus:

$$TO_t = -16.1739 + 5.8790 MP_t + 2.2878 P \& M_{t+1}$$

where

TO_t = % change in UK demand

MP_t = % change in manufacturing production

$P\&M_{t+1}$ = % change in plant and machinery investment

t = current year.

In this case there is considered to be a cause and effect relationship. UK demand (TO) is termed the dependent variable as its value is dependent on the values of MP, and $P\&M$, which are termed the independent variables. The values of the coefficients determine the extent of the influence of each independent variable, and can be determined by one of a number of curve fitting techniques, such as regression analysis. Where the relationship between the variables is clearly not linear it is sometimes possible to use regression techniques by changing the scale of one of the variables such that the relationship becomes linear, e.g. whereas S may not be proportional to X, S may be proportional to log X. Sometimes the dependent variable does not rise and fall in phase with the independent variables; for example demand for steel lags behind production changes in the metal working industry (the stocking problem). In yet other industries the time element between the dependent variable and each of the independent variables can itself vary and in that case establishing a working equation can become very complex indeed. Techniques are also available which will predict the error of the correlation between two or more variables, that is the degree of accuracy with which the value of the independent variables will predict the value of the dependent variable.

There are a lot of pitfalls in forecasting by correlation. First the chance of error is high because the independent variables are themselves subject to normal forecasting inaccuracies. Secondly, simply because it can be demonstrated that one variable (or set of data) varies in proportion to the values of another set of data, that does not mean that the changes to the second set of values cause the changes to the first set. Cause and effect is very hard to prove and the fact that the dependent and independent variables are proportionally related may simply be a result of chance circumstances. If those circumstances change, the proportionality may no longer hold. In marketing this situation is common, because circumstances inevitably do change. Luckily, as with trend extension, proving cause and effect is not essential as long as some proportionality, albeit temporary, can be demonstrated, and as long as the results are continually monitored for any signs of a change in the relationship.

5.13 Models

A model is a representation of reality that is adequate for the use we have in mind. Certain parts of reality are deliberately omitted because they are judged to be irrelevant. The resulting simplification of the real world problem or situation can be used to analyse, understand and to decide the most appropriate course of action. Some models are purely pictorial; they describe a situation in a way that helps us understand it, e.g. a technical drawing, an organisation chart, or various figures in this book (Fig. 1.1 and 2.1 etc.). Exploratory models are also descriptive, but they can be used to forecast or to show the consequences of changes, such as flow or system diagrams, or, for example, Fig. 5.8. Many exploratory models represent reality by a series of equations which try to relate changes in the dependent variable to changes in the independent variables. A correlation equation is in fact a very simple model. However each of the independent variables will themselves be affected by other variables and sometimes by each other (i.e. each variable will appear in more than one equation and will not truly be independent). Gradually a series of simultaneous equations can be built up.

Numerical models can very quickly become very complex and require the use of computers if the equations are to be solved. However, once models have been established as reasonably realistic representations of reality the effect of changing one or more of the variables can be investigated quickly and cheaply, and this is clearly of advantage when trying to decide at what levels to set the controllable marketing decision variables (see Section 1.5). In addition, the actual process of building a model adds considerably to the understanding of the reality being modelled, and as stated elsewhere draws attention to the major factors which should be closely monitored.

However, it should never be forgotten that a model is only a model and not reality. A model is a simplification of reality built up around a number of assumptions, some of which may not be correct. More important, some of the key variables might not have been identified and therefore left out of the model altogether. Only rarely are the equations used in models based on proven cause and effect and therefore they have to be continuously updated (see also Section 5.12). Hence the numerical results printed out by forecasting models should be treated with caution and interpreted in the light of other qualitative information available about the competitive environment and company strategies. The best models are often those which concentrate on the major variables, partly because the results of a simple model are more likely to be treated as guidelines rather than gospel, and partly because attempting to include too many minor variables can easily lead to a major one being overlooked.

Some of the established economic models are now available for company use and they offer the opportunity to test ones own assumptions about the relative importance of different factors, but without the need to painstakingly build up all the equations.

5.14 The PIMS model

Also available on a commercial basis is the PIMS (profit impact of marketing strategies) model. The PIMS model attempts to isolate and to determine the extent of the influence of factors which have a significant impact on the return of investment (ROI) and cash flow achieved by businesses. The model has been in operation since the early 1970s and is based on data gathered from about 2000 businesses — almost entirely divisions or subsidiaries of large corporations (and largely American) — about their competitive position and the market environment in which they operate. As a result 37 factors have been identified which together explain some 80% of the difference in ROIs achieved by these businesses. High confidence levels should be attached to the results for these types of businesses because of the large amount of data on which they are based, although the model has not yet been successfully extended to include smaller independent businesses.

The major factors which have been isolated are market share, product (or service) quality, and investment intensity (ratio of investment:sales). Other factors were, for example, company size, market growth, R & D expenditure, rate of new product introduction, marketing expenditure, capacity utilisation and the quality of company management (see Schoeffler *et al.* [21]).

However, the question of cause and effect, of whether, for example, superior product quality helps achieve a high market share or whether the economies of scale which can be achieved with a high market share enables businesses, if they choose, to invest in the design production and control capabilities needed to achieve superior quality, remains unanswered. In other words it is very difficult to accurately model how all the variables interrelate.

For this type of reason the model was strongly criticised in the 1970s. It was also criticised on the lines that, for example, knowing that a high market share would yield superior profits was not very helpful, if a company did not have the cash resources needed in order to improve its competitive position and hence its market share (see also Section 7.7.1). However, the fact that it is still supported by companies indicates that many companies find the results valuable.

Subscribers provide information for the data bank and in return can receive a multitude of reports. For example, it is possible to feed in marketing research data with respect to a new product, a new venture or a possible acquisition, and obtain a forecast of the ROI and cash flow that is likely to be achieved. By altering assumptions about sales, or market growth etc. it is possible to receive guidance about the security of the profit forecast and about the best strategy to adopt for the new business activity.

For existing businesses in a given set of circumstances (market growth, investment intensity etc.) a par value of ROI can be determined. Achievement of a ROI better than par is an indication that the business is being run efficiently — in the short term. The model can also indicate what longer term strategic changes (better product quality etc.) are necessary to move the business into a situation where the par ROI is higher (for more details see Abell and Hammond [19]).

More recent work (Buzzell and Wiersema [22]) on the project has indicated that for leading companies in well established markets, current market share and rank position in a market or market segment (i.e. is the company second, third or fourth . . . or tenth largest) is a major predictor of future market share, and unless the company is planning very major changes of strategy only small share changes can be expected. If that is the case then sales forecasting becomes very much a matter of forecasting market demand.

As an aid to decision making, forecasting models such as PIMS have a lot to offer but it is worth repeating that models are only a representation of reality, and the numerical results they produce must be interpreted with liberal doses of common sense. They are powerful decision making aids but they do not tell you what decisions to make.

5.15 Bayesian analysis

One of the simplest forms of subjective forecasting is to modify a sales forecast derived by simple trend extension or a model, in the light of available information about competitors, the economy or proposed company strategies. In many cases the effect of this information on sales cannot be derived from any rule and hence subjective judgement has to be applied. In an extreme case the application of subjective judgement may cause an upward sales trend to be modified to a downward trend. A mathematical model which helps the discipline and objectivity with which subjective judgement is applied is called Bayesian analysis. Its use in its simplest form may be illustrated as follows.

Assume that a sales forecast for a given product is prepared, but instead of just one forecast the marketing department is asked to provide an optimistic, a most likely and a pessimistic forecast. Suppose these forecasts are for 250, 150 and 100 units, respectively. The marketing department is also asked to state what they consider to be the probability of each of these sales forecasts being achieved. A probability of 0·9 means that nine times out of ten it is expected that the given event will occur and that one time out of ten it will not occur. Thus probabilities should always add up to one. This information can be represented as in Fig. 5.6.

Forecast	Probability
Optimistic : $E_1 = 250$	0.3
Most likely : $E_2 = 150$	0.4
Pessimistic : $E_3 = 100$	0.3

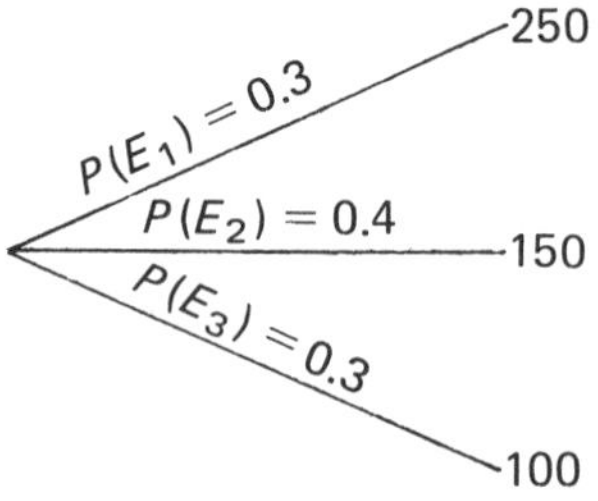

Decision tree diagram (right): branches labelled $P(E_1) = 0.3$ to 250, $P(E_2) = 0.4$ to 150, $P(E_3) = 0.3$ to 100.

Fig. 5.6   *A sales forecast indicating probabilities*

These initial forecasts and probabilities are referred to as the prior forecasts and the prior probabilities, and $P(E_1)$ is the probability of E_1, the optimistic sales forecast, occurring and $P(E_2)$ probability of E_2 occurring and so on. The diagram on the right hand side is the beginning of what is called a decision tree. From these three forecasts an average which takes account of probability, termed the expected (sales) value can be derived:

Expected value: $EV = (250 \times 0\cdot3) + (150 \times 0\cdot4) + (100 \times 0\cdot3)$

$= 165$ units

The expected value can be used for forecasting purposes.

Bayesian techniques can be extended to help evaluate whether or not a particular decision is worthwhile. For example, it might be decided to undertake a £20 000 advertising campaign and that might cause the forecasts to be revised as shown in Fig. 5.7. Hence the expected value

$EV = (300 \times 0\cdot3) + (210 \times 0\cdot5) + (150 \times 0\cdot2)$

$= 225$ units

If it happened that the gross contribution to profits for each unit sold was £500, the sale of the extra 60 units would yield £30 000 and the investment of £20 000 in the advertising campaign would have been worthwhile.

Posterior forecast	Posterior probability	
$E_1 = 300$	0.3	
$E_2 = 210$	0.5	
$E_3 = 150$	0.2	

Fig. 5.7 *Revised sales forecast indicating revised probabilities*

Used in this way the technique becomes known as a decision tree. For example, suppose a company was considering developing a new product with a research and development cost of £160 000 and a launch cost of £80 000 and it considered that the prior probabilities were as follows:

	R & D	Launch
Probability of success (S)	0.6	0.7
Probability of failure (F)	0.4	0.3

Success or failure of the research and development is measured in terms of a workable and saleable product being developed. It is assumed that in the event of failure the whole investment will be lost. Success or failure of the launch will be measured in terms of the degree of recovery of research and development and launch costs. In this case the success level of sales has been fixed at a level which will generate £450 000 profit (£170 000 net) and the failure level at the equivalent of $-£30 000$ net. If the launch goes ahead the expected profit will equal £170 000 × $0\cdot7 - £30 000 \times 0\cdot3 = £110 000$, and the expected profit for the project will be equal to £110 000 × $0\cdot6 - £160 000 \times 0\cdot4 = £2000$. This part of the decision process is represented on the upper section of Fig. 5.8.

The company next consider whether to undertake marketing research, with one

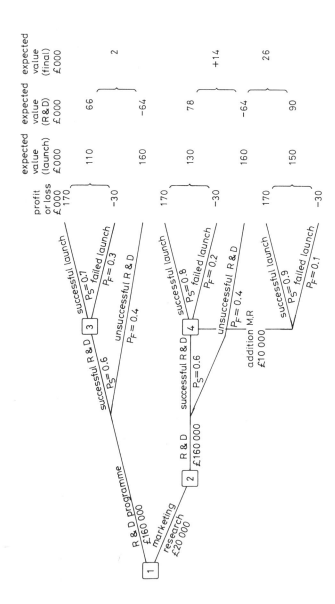

Fig. 5.8 *Decision tree*

□ decision points

1 to undertake MR or not

2 to cancel R & D programme

3 to launch or not

4 to launch, undertake further MR or not to launch

project costing £20 000 prior to the commencement of research and development and a second project costing £10 000 prior to launch. It is expected that the initial marketing research will provide information which will somewhat change the direction of the research and development such that the new product is more likely to be a sales success. Thus the revised probability of achieving the success level of sales is 0·8. Similarly the second marketing research project is assumed to improve the efficiency of the launch operation and to increase the probability of achieving the success level of sales to 0·9. For simplicity it has been assumed that the chances of the research and development itself being successful remain unchanged. The expected profit is calculated in exactly the same way as before, and it can be seen that both marketing research projects increase the expected value; the second relatively more than the first, but neither sufficiently greatly to offset the extra cost involved. Thus if both marketing research projects were undertaken the final expected profit would equal £26 000 − (£20 000 + £10 000) = −£4000, which is less than the £2000 expected without the research.

The decision tree could be expanded to look at the effect of the second marketing research project without undertaking the first, or to include more than two possible levels of sales following each decision point, or to allow the possibility that there was a prior probability that the marketing research would yield information which would lead to a decision to abandon the project completely. In that case the analysis becomes rather complex (see also Skinner [23]).

The advantage of the Bayesian approach is that it enables the effect on sales of a variety of factors such as advertising, attendance at exhibitions, stock levels and the like to be assessed in a subjective but disciplined manner, either one at a time or in combination, until it is possible to reach a reasonable and logical quantification of the subjective judgements. When the number of factors to be considered rises, the mathematics becomes complex, and it is usually more efficient to develop a model of the situation.

5.16 Sales forecasting using probabilities

A less mathematical, and perhaps to many a more useful, application of subjective probability is in building up sales forecasts from the reports of salesmen. The first step is for salesmen to consider each of their existing customers and to record on a suitable form (Fig. 5.9) the orders already obtained from them (category 1), and the level of orders expected (category 2), sub-divided into 'orders already being negotiated' and 'orders yet to be negotiated' if this is considered to be worthwhile. For category 2, salesmen will be asked to assess the probability of the predicted sales being achieved. Inclusion of these probability assessments enables the expected sales value (value × probability, as above) for each customer to be calculated. It is sensible to start with the largest customers first and to spend most time making those forecasts as accurate as possible. Clearly, small customers are not going to have such a great impact on total sales and hence they do not warrant as much

Category 1: Orders already obtained

	Quarter 1	Quarter 2	Quarter 3	Quarter 4	Annual total
Company A	100	30	10		130
Company B	150	40	10		200
—					
—					
Company X	60	20	10		90
Total					AAA

Category 2: Orders expected from existing customers

	Quarter 1			Quarter 2			Quarter 3			Quarter 4			Annual total		
	Value (V)	Probability (P)	Expected value (P × V)	V	P	EV	V	P	EV	V	P	EV	V	P	EV
Company A	300	0.8	240	300	0.75	225	350	0.7	245	400	0.6	240	1350	—	950
Company B	200	0.7	140	220	0.7	154	200	0.65	130	220	0.65	143	860	—	567
—															
—															
Company X	200	0.9	180	200	0.85	170	200	0.85	170	190	0.8	152	790	—	672
Total		—			—			—			—			—	BBB

Category 3: Orders from identified new customers

Company AA															
Company BB															
—															
—															
Company XX															
Total															CCC

Category 4: Orders from unidentified new customers

Customer group 1															
Customer group 2															
Customer group 3															
Total															DDD

Category 5: Unexpected loss or orders

															XXX

Fig. 5.9 *The salesman's sales forecast*

effort. Ranking customers by size will also help focus attention on where most of the selling effort should be made. Where salesmen are dealing with a relatively small number of customers, say less than 50, the above process can be undertaken customer by customer. Otherwise it will be necessary to divide the smaller customers into compatible groups and forecast a total order value and an average success rate for each group.

Having dealt with existing customers, salesmen should next consider new prospects. First (category 3A) companies which have already been visited but not yet converted into customers. Direct contact means that salesmen should be able to estimate their sales potential, and either individually or in like groups, be able to forecast the probability of gaining that business. The forecast probabilities should be compared with what has been achieved with similar customers over the past 2 or 3 years, to make sure that they are not wild over- or under-estimates. Category 3B covers customers who have not so far been visited. The value of their business and and probability of gaining it in the following year will have to be estimated entirely from records of what has been achieved in the past with customers in the same industry and of the same size, subject of course to changes in the business climate and in the company's competitive position.

Finally, each year a number of sales will be obtained from customers who have not been identified at the time the sales forecast is prepared. As nothing is known about this group of potential customers it is not possible to assign a probability, but at least a value of expected sales can be inserted (in category 4) based on past performance and on next years operational plans. Similarly, a single figure can be inserted for the whole year to represent the firm orders which will be lost quite unexpectedly. There are always some of these and it is unrealistic to ignore them.

This may appear to be an onerous job for salesmen (see also Section 14.3.1), and in a way it should be. Forecasting is an important part of their job because the preparation of a detail forecast will set them off on the right track. They will have had to think about where most of next years sales will come from. Therefore it is worth them raising the question of next year's sales with customers and potential customers and others in the industry over the five or six weeks prior to the forecasting deadline. Most existing customers will respond to the request for a forecast of their purchases for next year, especially if it is explained that that will help production planning and ensure a more reliable delivery. Certainly it is a technique which has been successfully applied with trained technical sales engineers. Forcing them to think in terms of probabilities seems to improve the quality of their subjective judgements. However, the wise sales manager will still vet each forecast in the light of his own market knowledge and the known optimism/pessimism of each salesman.

Naturally, when attempts are made to forecast sales more than one year ahead by this method, the level of certainty will fall dramatically and for that reason the time taken need not be as great. However, the temptation to quite arbitrarily add on an extra 5% or 10% or 1%, on the grounds that things are bound to be better next year, should be resisted.

In most companies the sum of the individual forecasts produced in this way (usually termed 'bottom up' forecasting) are compared with forecasts produced by trend extension and/or from models (usually termed 'top down' forecasting). These models should have been interpreted in the light of the expected competitive environment, and proposed company strategies. Thus if the turnover last year was £4 m, the economy looks 5% brighter, and the company's competitive position (because of its products, prices, distribution methods and promotion) has declined by 7%, next year's turnover would be estimated as £4 m x 1·05 x 0·93, that is £3·9 m. Any discrepancies between the 'top down' and 'bottom up' forecasts will be eliminated via a process of negotiation and subjective judgement, and the compromise figures used as the basis for other annual budgeting.

5.17 In conclusion

The aim of forecasting is to predict the direction in which events will move and to assess the impact of that movement on the organisation. The organisation then has to decide what to do about it. There is little point obtaining forecasts if they are not acted upon.

It seems to take two or three years before newcomers to forecasting properly understand the process and its value. Initially the best that can be expected is permission to continue forecasting, and only when it has been demonstrated − after the event − that taking account of these uncertain forecasts during the decision making process would have improved the outcome, will forecasting become accepted as a valuable process.

Some forecasting techniques operate by directly extending forward past trends. The advantage of these techniques is that they use facts about the product and about markets which are easily and quickly available, and directly relate to what is being forecast. Unfortunately the 'facts' are not always accurate and more importantly no account is taken of future changes in the influencing variables. As soon as an attempt is made to modify trends in the light of possible changes in these variables, the simplicity and directness is lost. That being the case, while mathematics provides a very valuable tool to help discipline the thought process, real world forecasts must inevitably be very largely based on subjective interpretation of how past trends will be modified by new conditions.

Subjective forecasting tries to predict what the future will be by jumping ahead, by making assumptions, by using the imagination. It ranges from completely intuitive judgements, through to carefully thought out but nevertheless subjective forecasts about the future.

The accuracy of forecasts which are neither very short term nor concerned with very slow changing parameters, tends to be low. For that reason forecasts should always be accompanied by some indication of the level of certainty or uncertainty attached to them, so that the extent of flexibility which must be built into plans based on them can be determined. Ideally, regular (at least quarterly) reviews should be undertaken of forecasts, and strategies and action programmes altered accordingly.

If they are to be accepted and acted upon, all forecasts should clearly state the assumptions on which they have been based and why it is considered that they are valid. To be used forecasts must be believable.

Chapter 6

Market Structure and Segmentation

6.1 Structural elements of a market

Reaching an understanding of market structure and of methods of market segmentation is an important preliminary to the planning process, because both exert a major influence on the manner in which companies are able to compete, and because understanding the nature of competition helps companies pinpoint where they should target their efforts if they are to maximise their competitive advantage.

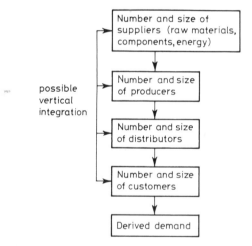

Fig. 6.1 *Structural elements of a market*

The major structural elements of a market (see Fig. 6.1) are the number and size of suppliers, producers, distributors and customers; the degree of integration between them; and, in the case of industrial markets, other companies and their customers further along the chain of derived demand (see Section 2.6). The influence on these elements of the technology used, potential economies of scale, barriers to market entry, the nature of the demand, and of the product itself, as illustrated in Fig. 6.2, will be considered in this chapter.

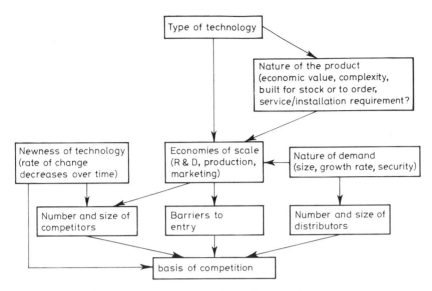

Fig. 6.2 *Influence of structural factors on the basis of competition*

6.2 Number and size of producers

The most significant element in a market is the size and number of producers, and this will be directly related to the amount of capital which can be attracted to the industry and to potential economies of scale. The volume of capital available to an industry will be proportional to the forecast of its future earnings. In other words capital will be made available if it is foreseen that a regular and reliable return on that capital is likely to be obtained over a number of years, and that will be dependent on current demand, the forecast growth of that demand and its security.

Security of demand is dependent on how vital the product is to the people who will be buying it. The more essential it is, the less it will be affected by the swings of the economic cycle and the foibles of fashion (and fashion does apply to demand for engineering products even if not to the extent of clothing). However, the chain of derived demand requires consideration to be given not just to immediate customers, but to the security of demand for the products of their customers, all the way down the chain. Security of demand will also be dependent on the current level of possible substitution from other products and technologies, and how the degree of that substitution is predicted to change with changes in technology (which will affect the nature of the demand as well as the nature of supply). In other words we are concerned not just with forecasting market potential and the overall rate of growth towards that potential, but in addition with short term fluctuations in the overall demand pattern, the reliability of the forecast and the possibility that the nature of the demand may shift sufficiently that it can be satisfied by other products.

6.3 Influence of economies of scale

The average size of producers will be dependent on the potential economies of R & D, buying, production, distribution, promotion and selling scale. Where there are economies of scale, companies grow steadily larger in order to take advantage of the cost benefits offered and improve their competitive position, although they tend thereby to reduce their ability to respond quickly to changes in demand and technology.

Economies of scale appear to take effect in three stages. First, economies of scale in production overcome distribution costs over an increasingly large geographical area. This stage is, of course, not only affected by improvement in the production process itself but also by improvements in transport and distribution efficiency. Naturally it is those companies who generate the greatest competitive advantage by way of superior production, design, organisation and marketing who gradually increase their market share and are able to take advantage of the existence of economies of scale.

At the second stage some companies become significantly larger than others. Their larger scale of operations enables them to continue to improve the efficiency of their production and marketing processes relative to smaller companies. Particularly in the case of frequently bought consumer products, high volume producers are able to use economies of marketing scale to erect significant barriers to entry; for example, while quite a few companies could afford to begin to produce washing powder, very few could afford the advertising necessary to make sufficient impact on the market to sell in sufficient volumes to run a cost effective manufacturing facility. Those that remain most profitable are also able to spend more on research and development and are most likely to be able to further improve their product and their process. Even if they are unable to generate many good ideas internally, they are able to buy in and develop the ideas of others.

At the third stage, diseconomies of organisational size (lack of motivation and bureaucracy) combined with the inevitable reduction in the rate of increase of economies of scale means that further increases in the geographical spread of distribution for a single production unit cannot be achieved (at least until the relative costs change further). However, the larger companies are still able to grow by setting up a number of factories in different geographic areas. This immediately reduces some of the diseconomies of motivation and distribution but without losing the economies of research and development and marketing scale, or the benefits of cumulative experience (see Section 5.10) and preferential access to funds.

However, where local selling and distribution effectiveness is more important than economies of production scale and international reputation, it is difficult for the larger companies to expand into overseas markets because the level of competitive advantage they can offer may be insufficient to enable them to gain a significant market share. Lack of share will prevent them establishing an effective local selling and distribution network and that will further diminish their competitive position. This is the classic chicken and egg situation, which can only be resolved by substantial investment, either in price cutting to improve market share or direct into a distribution network.

Until recently, economies of scale steadily grew across the whole of the manufacturing sector, and this forced more and more companies to seek survival by specialisation, or by moving out of manufacturing into the service sector. However, in many sectors; the latest generation of production equipment is more flexible and can be efficiently operated at lower volumes than its predecessors. This more flexible plant has been developed following recognition that the life of individual products and technologies is getting shorter (see Section 1.11).

Economies of scale appear to apply much less when the service element of what is offered is more important than the manufacturing element, if that exists at all. An extreme case is that of a window cleaner, where few economies of organisational scale apply. However, even here it is possible to grow beyond the one man business by good marketing; by persuading customers that one has more to offer, for example, reliably cleaner windows, regular service, the completion of, say, a large office block within a reasonable time scale or reduced price owing to better equipment. Perhaps a more sensible example is that of sub-contractors. Some sub-contractors have been able to afford machines which produce parts rapidly and to high quality standards, and which can be changed from one setting to another very quickly. As a result, these sub-contractors have offered better value for money, obtained more business and have continued to afford the latest machinery. However the economies are limited. Possibly one person can oversee three machines rather than just one, and maybe there are marginal economies in buying and selling, but these are unlikely to produce price advantages sufficient to make it worth while for customers to deal with a sub-contractor who is, say, two hundred miles distant rather than in the immediate locality, partly because of reduced delivery costs but particularly because of the lower costs of liaison.

Another example of limited economies of scale is where the competitive advantage offered is the capability to take a unique specification and turn it into a product. That capability is directly related to technical ability and it is only related to size insofar as the technical, production and financial resources required for larger jobs will be greater than for smaller jobs. However, once a sufficient size of company has been reached to enable the larger jobs to be undertaken, there are few further advantages of scale. A parallel case is the contract research and development companies where, although certain types of development cannot be undertaken without certain facilities and the ability to employ a multi-disciplinary team, the level to which these economies of scale can be extended is strictly limited.

6.4 Influence of technology

It is only where a standard product is being produced that large economies of scale will apply, and the degree of those economies will depend on the nature of the technology. The nature of the technology used within an industry determines the capital structure needed to operate the industry. Some industries are extremely capital intensive, such as the generation and supply of electricity or the extraction and distribution of oil. These industries require the investment of large amounts of capital before a company can even begin to compete. Economies of scale go hand in hand with capital intensity and almost inevitably the number of companies competing in such an industry will be small.

The barriers to entering such an industry are formidable. They are not simply the obvious financial ones of setting up process/production/extraction plant, distribution and administrative systems, and keeping in touch with improvements in technology, but also ones of establishing credibility with customers. Few companies, for example, would place total reliance on a chemical introduced by a company new to the chemical industry. Demand would initially be very low and it simply would not be possible to enter the market unless the process was viable at very low volumes (usually only possible when the technology involved is completely new and is not easily copied by the established competitors). Even then considerable financial backing would be required.

Companies entering these markets tend to aim at satisfying the specialist requirements of small market segments, not only because specialist products can demand a price premium but also because the volume of specialist demand is unlikely to be sufficient for the existing very large suppliers to respond to the new entry by rapidly copying the technology and using their larger resources to improve it. Should they do so, the established companies could use their reputation, superior distribution and price advantage (that is they could afford to temporarily operate at a loss in a small market segment) to eliminate the new competitor.

Technical barriers to entry can be increased by government regulations, usually in the form of minimum safety standards. Sometimes these are pitched at such a level that smaller companies are unable to attract sufficient capital to buy the plant and equipment needed to efficiently produce products to the required standard. More often the real problem is the time (often as much as two years) needed to obtain 'official' approval (e.g. see case histories[1] 2 and 10) for the new product. Delaying the commencement of sales can obviously make otherwise satisfactory projects uneconomic.

Barriers to entry are lower in newly established markets where there has not been time for economies of scale to exert their effect. Thus in the early days of biological engineering, companies were small, but they are now beginning to grow.

Economies of scale will also be mitigated by the rate of technical change. Normally the rate of technical change is most rapid when a technology is new. Where technology is changing rapidly it becomes less sensible to invest in very expensive dedicated plant and equipment which has to be operated at high volumes and which will only pay for itself over many years, partly because the nature and the level of demand is likely to change quickly and partly because the plant and equipment is likely to be quickly improved upon and will cease to be competitive. Where it has

[1] See page 382.

to be changed frequently, the payback period on plant and equipment needs to be shorter and this naturally leads to the purchase of less expensive or more versatile (and hence smaller) plant.

6.5 Influence of product differentiation

Arising quite naturally from consideration of the influence of technology on market structure is the question of product differentiation. In many product categories, customers find it hard to differentiate between what competing suppliers are offering. This is particularly true of commodities or of products supplied to a specified quality standard, for example, British Standard copper pipe, but it equally applies to commonly bought products, such as a packet of wood screws or a stapler. Small differences between products certainly favour the emergence of large production units, as it is unlikely that a small producer will be able to produce a standard product as economically and to as high a quality. The larger companies are often able to reinforce economies of production scale by increased weight of advertising, promotion and direct selling (often critically important in the case of undifferentiated products), and/or by superior distribution. Once established, distribution chains can handle other complementary products (often imported) and thereby increase their impact on the overall distribution of products to the market. Setting up a chain requires considerable capital commitment and its existence would not only represent a formidable barrier to smaller companies already in the market but also to companies seeking to enter the market. Quite naturally, given that it is hard to differentiate between competitors, most buyers will select the cheapest supplier. As a result, in these markets price tends to fall to quite a low equilibrium level.

Given that the main selection criteria is price, one might assume that the most efficient supplier could, by successive price reductions, gradually force its competitors out of business, until a monopoly was created, or at least a monopoly within a limited geographic area. However this does not tend to happen for a number of reasons. One reason is that most companies prefer to avoid the close public scrutiny which accompanies a monopoly. A second reason is that the basic price—profit—volume relationship does not encourage such a step. Consider a dominant company producing an undifferentiated product at a cost of 65p, selling 2000 units per annum at £1 and hence making a profit of £750. Suppose the company enjoys a 20% market share and the competition is as follows:

One major supplier	unit cost about 70p	10% share
Significant suppliers	unit cost 73–77p	40% share
Minor suppliers	unit cost 78–82p	30% share

If our company reduced price to 80p it would force a number of competitors out of business — optimistically, for example, all the minor suppliers and half the significant suppliers. If their market share were spread pro rata among the survivors our company would have obtained a 40% market share; reduced unit costs due to economies of scale of say 60p; and a profit of £(4000 × (0·8 − 0·6)) = £800. Encouraged, the company may repeat the medicine, reducing price to 70p. This time only the major competitor and two of the significant suppliers survive, such that our company now achieves a 60% market share, reduced unit costs of 58p (costs do not reduce in direct proportion to volume increases) and a profit of £(6000 × 0·12) = £720. So now, increased market penetration by price reduction has become subject to the law of diminishing returns and profit has started to reduce rather than increase. If the company subsequently were to allow its price to rise again, new suppliers would gradually be attracted back into the market and the company would be back where it started. The point then of this extreme example is that in markets where it is hard to differentiate one product from another, price will drop to a low equilibrium level. If price falls below that equilibrium level, the reduction of profits which that would bring about would tend to encourage prices to move back up to the equilibrium level. If prices rise above the equilibrium, there will always be some suppliers who will be tempted to increase their market share by reducing their prices, and competitors will be forced to follow − back towards the equilibrium level. A natural consequence of an equilibrium price is that the number of competitors in a market will be limited to those that can operate profitably at the equilibrium price.

Having a non-differentiated product is clearly not ideal for suppliers, and as a result they work quite hard to introduce differences in what they offer. That is, they seek to introduce reasons which will persuade customers to pay above the basic price. This is the heart of product differentiation; namely, introducing reasons to convince customers that the product is different and better, that is, worth paying more for. Usually the cost of introducing these differences is less than the price premium customers are prepared to pay to obtain them. In other words differentiation is the road to higher profits. Ideally each supplier would like to introduce differences that its competitors are unable to match; that is, to create a mini-monopoly so that the mini-monopoly can be exploited via a price premium. Now obviously a lot of the difference can be in the product, and the more complex the product the greater the opportunity to introduce differentiation, for example, houses, cars or machine tools. However, as technological knowledge becomes more widespread, these differences are not so much differences in fundamental performance as differences in detail. That is the manner in which the performance is achieved. They also tend to be short lived as competitors quickly introduce equivalents or copies. As a result, suppliers have been forced to look for longer lasting competitive advantages via distribution and promotion. In the case of straightforward products, such as solder or even filing cabinets, it is very difficult to introduce genuine product differences and their suppliers are forced to rely on non-product differences such as availability, appearance, after-sales service, guarantees, image, installation help, packaging, reputation, technical applications advice, user instructions and user training.

6.6 Number and size of distributors

The nature of the product will affect the distribution system used. Usually the higher the product's value; hence the greater its complexity and the fewer the number of customers; the more likely it is to be sold direct. In the case of relatively simple low value products sold to numerous customers, such as electrical components or small bearings, or products requiring regular servicing, producers tend to use existing distribution systems and they can do little about the size and number of companies within those systems.

The number and size of distributors relative to the number and size of producers will affect their comparative bargaining power and hence the percentage of total value added retained by each. The greater the bargaining power of the producer, the higher will be his selling price to distributors, as a proportion of the price that the final customer is prepared to pay. Thus if the producer's product forms a major part of a distributor's business, it will be vital to the ongoing health of that business, and hence the producer's bargaining power will be high. That power will be balanced if the number of distributors is small, because although the product would still be vital to them, withdrawal of their custom could have an equally vital effect on the producers business.

Similarly, the larger the number of suppliers to the market, the lower their prices are likely to be. If a producer has to buy steel, and has a limited choice of suppliers, his bargaining power is low. On the other hand if several suppliers are competing for his business, even if each of them is itself a much larger company, his bargaining power becomes higher because in effect the suppliers are bargaining against each other rather than against their smaller customer.

6.7 Horizontal and vertical integration

The nature of the product and the technology of its production will determine what has to be bought, and there is little that producers can do about the number and size of the various suppliers, although they can improve their relative bargaining power by growing larger, either by internal growth or by acquiring competitors; that is by horizontal integration.

Where particular supplies form a large part of producer's costs, or security of supply is essential, it may be cost effective for them to acquire one or more of their suppliers; that is to undertake backward vertical integration. One of the main reasons for integrating backwards has traditionally been to ensure security of supply when resources have been scarce. It has already been argued that the world's ability to produce has out-stripped demand, and hence security of supply is in general no longer the valid reason it used to be. A better reason for backward integration is that it can be foreseen that the life and earning potential of the supply industry is much greater than that of the producer industry and therefore it is sensible to use profits currently earned to secure the company's future. However, as one journeys further back along the supply chain one usually finds that the business becomes more capital intensive and requires different management skills. Unless there is a definite overlap of skills, whether in production, engineering, marketing or whatever, it is unlikely that the potential acquirer will be able to run the business any better than the existing management and attempts to do so may absorb so much time and capital that it can cause the original business to fail. Consequently this route needs to be evaluated very carefully indeed.

Not all companies become involved with backward integration as a result of a long term policy decision. Perhaps at some stage a supplier that they relied upon got into financial difficulties and required an injection of capital, or perhaps they were unable to find a supplier capable of designing and/or reliably producing a component to the desired level of performance/price. In that case producers are forced to take minority holdings in their suppliers or to undertake the design and production themselves. Although companies are increasingly examining the financial benefit of maintaining these sorts of business interests, they are still common, and have a major impact on the relationship between that supplier and those of its customers who are competitors of the company which has a financial stake in them.

Forward integration by acquiring distributors or customers, can be a less financially significant step as the capital involvement, at least initially, can be small. Some companies integrate forward on a very small scale simply to obtain first-rate market intelligence. Other companies become involved with the distribution system because they cannot achieve from the existing system the level of service and onward selling that they feel is necessary. If such involvement is to have a significant effect on their sales volume, the degree of involvement has to be significant and the capital commitment can then become very large. As with backward integration the efforts needed to be successful can be detrimental to the core business, but where it is successful, it can take over as the main competitive skill of the company.

6.8 Market segmentation

The market for a product or service may be considered as being that group of people who have some need or desire for the product and who are capable of being persuaded to purchase it. However all these people do not have exactly the same requirements, will not respond to the same stimuli in the same way and will not have the same resources. If these and other differences can be identified and grouped in a meaningful way, it may prove more profitable to offer variations of the product (or other part of the marketing mix) in order to cater for these differences. If that is so, these groups may be considered as separate market segments, that is, definable sub-sets of customers who can be sold to more effectively by offering them a non-standard marketing mix. In other words it is more profitable to offer a non-standard marketing mix than not to do so. The additional sales income will more than offset the increased costs of providing variety. However, care must be taken in one's enthusiasm not to generate unreal or unproductive segments. A segment is a segment only if it is more profitable to undertake a distinctive marketing management strategy.

Another way of looking at segmentation starts with the idea that people only buy products if they value what is offered at least as highly as the price. Some people within a market may only reach that state if what is offered generally is in some way changed. When there are enough of them, those people constitute a segment. Each member of the segment may have slightly different characteristics but they have sufficient in common to qualify for group membership.

Obviously some companies, when they analyse what they have to offer, will find that what they can offer falls more naturally into one market segment rather than another. In that case they can set about augmenting that natural appeal by appropriate product development, promotion, distribution and pricing. Deciding on the correct market segment to aim at, and the appeals which will promote the product in that segment most effectively, is often called product positioning. Thus if a product is incorrectly positioned its producers will be either trying to sell it to a market segment where it has little appeal, or even if the correct segment has been chosen, the product attributes most important to that segment will not be being emphasised (see also Markin [24]).

6.9 Methods of segmentation

There are a large number of ways in which a market can be segmented. The commonly quoted methods of segmentation are as follows:

(a) geographic — country, region, size of city or town, climate;
(b) demographic — age, sex, family size, income, occupation, religion, race, social class;
(c) purchase motive — practical need, luxury, prestige, excitement, copying instinct;
(d) volume of use or frequency of purchase;
(e) price — in some cases for price substitute quality; in other words some people will always buy expensive televisions and others always cheap ones and they require approaching in a different manner;
(f) purpose of use (or need fulfilled) — for example, beer can be drunk to quench thirst, induce stupor, to be social, for enjoyment of the taste, or simply to relax;
(g) type of user — for example, motor oil is bought by DIY enthusiasts, by other car users, by small garages, large garages, car manufacturers, fleet operators,
(h) product benefit sought — for example, long life, ease of service, noise levels, easily available, styling or whatever.

Market segments can be identified by statistical techniques which measure a number of different attributes or characteristics. It will be found that some attribute ratings are very similar for all the customers which make up a market (this is what defines them as members of the market). The ratings of other attributes will range more widely, but it may be found that groups of individuals have very similar ratings within the range. If groups of individuals have several ratings in common they represent the beginnings of a market segment.

In industrial markets ratings tend to be more subjective than in consumer markets and indeed some of the above categories do not strictly apply. Consideration focuses on:

(a) geography – country, region, climate;
(b) customer industry – different uses, priorities and method of contact;
(c) size of customer;
(d) price;
(e) type of use (e.g. a given tool might be used continuously, intermittently, at high load factors, at low load factors and so on),
(f) product features or product benefit sought.

As already mentioned in Section 4.12, variation in the size of customer is a particularly important feature of industrial markets. Larger customers warrant a greater concentration of effort than smaller customers, and a different sales strategy. In some cases the reason for buying a given product will be completely different. For example, a small company may buy a desk top computer and use it for accounting or customer records or some form of stock control, because that is all they can afford. A large company is more likely to buy a desk top computer for the convenience of a specialist user who does not want to bother to access a larger computer, or because the desk top is easier to use for the particular application, or because of lack of capacity on the larger unit.

It is often possible to consider more than one method of segmentation; in which case some combination of all of them might prove to be the most appropriate approach. For example, the market for pipe can be segmented *by type of user*:

(a) plumbers, DIY people, builders – that is, the installation of pipes into buildings either for water or for drainage;
(b) local authorities – that is, main property drains and sewers, road drains and sea outfalls;
(c) water authorities – water supply pipe across country and within urban areas;
(d) agriculture – for irrigation, for drainage and for sewers;
(e) the process industry – that is, easily cleaned pipe for food and drink manufacturers and corrosion resistant pipe for the petrochemical industry;
(f) oil supply industry – for overland and undersea use;
(g) gas supply industry – as above;
(h) electricity supply industry – to transport coal slurry or cooling water,
(i) sand, gravel, cement transportation.

By type of use:
above ground; below ground; under sea; on a structure (e.g. a bridge); in a house; as a drain; as a sewer; as conduit; to carry slurry or as part of a fire protection system.

By product features:
   pressure; rigidity; corrosion resistance; abrasion resistance; non-contamination; ease of joining; ease of handling; ease of attaching fittings; operating temperatures; fire resistance; and diameter.

By material:
   copper; cupro-nickel; aluminium; asbestos cement; clay; plastic; reinforced plastic; steel; lined steel; ductile iron; cast iron; composite (steel and plastic).

or by some matrix combination of all these.
   In other words one may legitimately choose to concentrate on high pressure steel pipe for use above and below ground for the oil and gas industry, or on lower pressure lined steel pipe for use above and below ground for the process industry, or on both, providing it was recognised that a different strategy may be needed in each segment.
   Our definition of a market segment gives us a guide to what is useful, namely that a segment is a definable subset of potential customers which can be more profitably reached by offering a distinctive marketing mix. We are seeking segmentation which will help the company offer better value for money and thereby increase its competitive advantage. The competitive advantage of a company might be its ability to distribute hardware, and the product may as well be valves or bolts as pipe. In that case the most appropriate method of market segmentation might be in terms of where the customer buys, making it possible to include other related products in each segment, providing that the same marketing approach can be taken for them.

6.10 Benefiting from segmentation

Segmenting a market involves identifying the peculiar needs of groups of potential customers so that those needs may be more exactly satisfied rather than included with the needs of other groups. Occasionally this process reveals a previously unrecognised specific requirement which no other producer has attempted to meet, and thereby opens up new profit opportunities.
   Some companies, once they have segmented a market, decide to offer several or all of the market segments which have been identified a different product and/or marketing programme. These companies are said to be following a 'differentiated' strategy (see Kotler [2]). Other companies, having made the attempt to segment, may decide that it is more cost effective to produce only one product, to offer it with as wide a range of appeal as practical, and to follow the same marketing approach across the whole market. In other words, product design, production, and marketing cost savings are forecast to outweigh the extra income from any increased turnover that could be achieved by a differentiated strategy. This approach to a market has been termed 'undifferentiated'. Alternatively, it may seem more profitable to follow a 'concentrated' strategy and concentrate on, and

hope to achieve a large share in, only some of the identified potential market segments. The target segments will be chosen to match the company's resources and capabilities; that is, where it has the greatest competitive advantage to offer. For example, a small company would find it difficult to pursue a differentiated policy in a large market, and in general is likely to follow a policy of concentration.

Inveitably there are shades between these three alternatives. It may be possible to offer the same product to different market segments but to change the sales message. For example, the same garden rotovator could be aimed at wealthy householders, at local authorities, at smallholders, or, in some territories, at small farmers. The product would be the same but the selling message would be different — the emphasis on timesaving and prestige at the one extreme and low cost, efficiency, adaptability and durability at the other. In other cases in order to maximise a favourable company name association across the whole market, the selling message for each segment might be the same, for example, value for money, but the manner in which that is achieved by the product might be different for different market segments.

Economies of scale may require that whatever is offered for sale is largely standard. In that case, it is important to try to create differentiation by offering options and alternatives to standard products rather than by generating completely unrelated offerings. Segmentation does not only involve isolating the differences, but also noting what is common, so that standard products with wide appeal can be designed, as a base upon which segment related options can be offered.

However, it is not always economic to try to sell to everyone. The cost of supplying some parts of the total market will be greater than the value placed on what is offered. For example, the large nationalised services such as electricity supply, letter delivery or rail transport, if they were not subsidised by other consumers, would not be able to offer many of their services in the remoter parts of the country at a price customers would be prepared to pay. Unsubsidised prices in these areas would raise prices to levels where users would switch to alternative services or simply forgo the benefits offered.

There is no point in identifying a customer group, creating a product and/or service to meet their needs, undertaking a special marketing programme, gaining a major share of their demand, if total profits are thereby reduced. Before deciding to concentrate on a customer group, the answers to the following questions should be sought:

1   How does the market sgement differ from the rest of the market and are those differences significant in marketing terms?
2   What special advantages can be offered and how is attention to be drawn to them?
3   What extra resources will be needed?
4   Will it be profitable?

It is very easy to create false and unproductive differences.

Chapter 7

Product Analysis

7.1 Introduction

Familiarity with three more important concepts is necessary before full consideration can be given to market and product planning. Product life cycles illustrate sales potential over time and help forecast when products will require replacing; portfolio analysis illuminates which products justify the greatest efforts; and gap analysis reveals the extent of the sales volume which needs to be generated by new products.

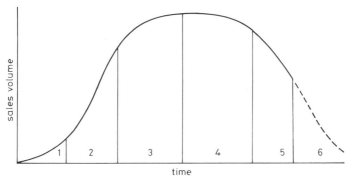

Fig. 7.1 *Product life cycle*
Life cycle phases
1 Introduction	4 Saturation
2 Growth	5 Decline
3 Maturity	6 Abandonment

7.2 Product life cycle

Manufactured products have a limited life. Product categories such as clothes, houses, and fasteners tend to have very long lives but individual product designs within each category will have much shorter lives. The length of a product's life can vary very considerably, from say 20 years for round bayed semi-detached houses, to

3 months or less for a fashion garment. Plotting the sales volumes of most products against time will produce the type of curve shown in Fig. 7.1. In practice, the graph will not be nice and smooth as depicted but will have many minor rises and falls along its path. The exact shape will vary from product to product, some rising steeply at first, and others more slowly; some having a long extended hump, others falling away very suddenly. However, the generalised product life cycle shape should always be discernible.

Product life cycles can be divided into six phases, as shown in Fig. 7.1. Different marketing strategies are appropriate for each phase (see Fig. 7.2 Sasson [13] and articles in *Journal of Marketing*, Fall 1981), and therefore it is important to be able to predict the turning points which mark changes from one phase to another. Obviously this is particularly difficult in the early stages of a product's life because there is little hard data to work on, apart from knowledge of the shape of the life cycle of previous similar products. However, it is particularly important to try to predict the turning point which marks the change from the introductory phase into the growth phase, if production is to be kept in step with demand and early growth is not to be dampened by supply shortages and late deliveries. To do that it is necessary to monitor:

(a) existing customers to see if larger orders are imminent;
(b) prospective customers to see how close they are to placing an order;
(c) the rate at which new enquiries are being received;
(d) the ratio of sales visits arranged/enquiries received;
(e) the ratio of quotations given/sales visits undertaken,
(f) the ratio of orders received/quotations given, to see if they are increasing.

If this data is interpreted in the light of the expected length of the selling cycle (that is the time between first contact with a customer and order placement) the onset of any order upsurge can usually be predicted.

Prediction of later turning points should be a little easier, and usually they can be forecast with sufficient accuracy for planning purposes. If that is not possible, simply tracking a product's life cycle is of value, because at least there will be an awareness of which phase the product is in, and marketing strategy can be amended accordingly. However, care must be taken not to mistake minor fluctuations for major turning points, and this can be achieved by interpreting turning points in the light of the maximum sales volume and product life originally forecast, and subsequent changes to the marketing environment which might cause that forecast to be no longer valid. For example, the major competitors may have introduced successful new products which will reduce the maximum sales volume achieveable and/or shorten the product's life. Alternatively, the market or the technology (see Sections 7.4 and 7.5) may have begun to decline. If a turning point occurs at what appears, in the light of all the available information, to be an unreasonably low sales volume, a temporary fluctuation should be suspected, and possible causes such as a sales drive by a competitor or temporary quality or distribution problems should be looked for. If the cause cannot be found or remedied then of course the temporary

Strategy / Elements of strategy	GROWTH	MATURITY/ SATURATION	DECLINE
Investment	Build market share for long-term profit	High short-term earnings medium cash flow	Maximise cash generation
	Maximise investment, subject only to ability to digest growth	Confine to selective/high return market segments, or to phase extension	Minimise investment, and consider disposal if the right opportunity presents itself
Risk	Accept reasonable levels	Limit	Avoid
Share	Build/diversify markets Seek new uses	Limited growth/protect position	Forego market share for profit
Pricing	Lead and exploit new product value/cost ratio (see Section 11.7)	Stabilise for minimum contribution	Above average, even at expense of volume
Products	Broaden product line	Differentiate product range — Specialisation — Applications — Performance	Prune product line
Costs	Utilise economies of scale rather than direct cost reduction	Aggressive reduction of variable costs economise on fixed costs	Aggressive reduction of fixed overheads
Marketing	Extend coverage: high level of effort	Maintain coverage	Cut expenditure

Fig. 7.2 *Marketing strategy over the product life cycle*

fluctuation could assume some permanence, and a major rethink of product planning and timing will need to be initiated.

A major life cycle turning point can usually be assumed when no such causes can be identified and this can often be confirmed by feedback from salesmen; they will know when the product is becoming easier or more difficult to sell, right across their spectrum of customers. Turning points can also be confirmed by cross referring to the ratio 'sales to new customers/sales to existing customers' and to the percentage of product which is being used in a novel way. For example, when more than two-thirds of the sales are to existing customers or for non-novel uses, this is a sign that the growth phase is ending.

7.3 Using product life cycles to shape marketing strategy

Since different marketing strategies are appropriate to different stages in the life cycle, each phase will be considered in depth.

7.3.1 Introductory phase

In the introductory phase the main objective is to persuade a sufficient number of customers to try the product so that a firm track record of successful in-use performance can be established which can be used to 'relaunch' the product into its growth phase. Potential customers for new technical products normally take several months to evaluate whether it is worth undertaking a trial purchase and several more months thereafter to reach a firm conclusion about the value for money offered. The more complex the product and the more novel the technology, the longer the introductory phase tends to be. As a result, the common marketing approach of undertaking a vigorous launch with much publicity, advertising, demonstrations, exhibitions and sales activity needs to be treated with caution. It may be more cost effective to reserve a major portion of the total launch budget until after that initial track record has been established. It can then be used to relaunch the product into the growth phase. It is likely to be more cost effective to limit the initial launch by targeting it directly at companies who are considered most likely to take the risk of trying a new product, namely: (1) companies who are trendsetters, that is those companies who are known to be favourably disposed to trying out the latest technology and the latest products (equivalent to 'early adopters' in consumer marketing); (2) existing customers with whom a close and trusting working relationship has been built up, in other words if the company introducing the new product says it will provide certain advantages, this class of customer will be less sceptical about the claims than most, and (3) companies who are dissatisfied with what else is available on the market, some of whom will almost be in the state of being willing to try anything.

If all goes well and the product performs as promised, then the word can be spread and the growth phase commenced, but if all does not go well the word also spreads; this time without any help. False starts usually take one of three forms. In the first form few people can be persauded to try the product because it seems to offer insufficient benefits to overcome the fear of trying a new product. This may be a result of (a) the product truly not having worthwhile virtues; (b) these virtues not being put across to potential customers in terms they can relate to, or (c) the risk element being unusually high (see Section 9.4). In the second form, customers are persuaded to try the new product but initial field use shows up real design deficiencies. Bad news spreads fast, and even if faults are quickly corrected, the cost of reassuring customers can be very great indeed. In the third form, teething problems prevent sales and profits taking off as planned. There may be unexpected production or distribution problems. The new product may get lost in salesmen's portfolios and not receive enough attention or it may be hit by a major competitive counter campaign.

Where a new product is a straight replacement many customers will be prepared to try the new product immediately, because of their successful experience with its predecessor. In these cases the introductory period can be very short indeed — as indeed can the growth period — and the initial launch and the relaunch into the growth phase can often be merged into one major operation. However the consequences of getting things wrong is much greater. There is much less time to put things right.

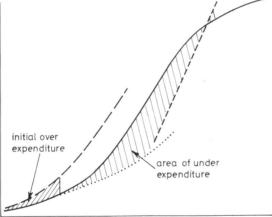

Fig. 7.3 *Mismatch of sales backing to sales growth*
——— actual sales
———— initial sales forecast
. . . . . revised pessimistic sales forecast
- - - - - revised optimistic sales forecast

In the introductory phase sales may well be below the break even point and hence when sales do not grow as rapidly as expected there is a strong temptation to abandon the new product. Alternatively, spending on promotion, selling and stock may be reduced, possibly just at the time when product sales would otherwise have started to increase. Having apparently been caught out once, companies are reluctant to step their expenditure back up until they have firm evidence of growth, and hence will tend to underspend during much of the growth phase (see Fig. 7.3).

Attempts to reduce the capital costs of the introductory phase by using only prototype plant and equipment very often do not work because of plant reliability and product quality reasons. This approach also introduces the risk of hitting teething problems on the full plant at a later stage when the sales volume and hence the consequences of setbacks in terms of lost profit and lost reputation are much greater.

7.3.2 Growth phase

The growth phase starts when the rate of increase of sales rises significantly. At this stage it pays more or less to relaunch, certainly to enter an era of very active selling and promotion. Admittedly, high spending will delay the onset of a positive cash flow but effectively managed it should improve the rate of growth, and providing the effort is sensibly sustained, the duration of the growth, and hence lead to greater overall profits. For technical products it is probably more sensible to leave the major product spending to this stage rather than undertake it at product launch, because the rate of response is likely to be greater.

Unfortunately there are inevitably common pitfalls. There are many examples of companies who have undertaken a costly and effective promotional effort only to see it negated because their dealers have run out of stock, or the product has exhibited poor quality as production volume increases, or the product has been subject to unexpected inservice problems. The time to sort out these types of problems is during the introductory phase.

Careful consideration must also be given to pricing policies (see Section 11.10). If the objective is to gain a dominant market share and long term profits then the price will be set lower than if the aim is to maximise profits at all stages. In this latter case the normal strategy is to price as high as possible and to reduce the price only as the rate of market penetration slows.

Very often the selling cycle is longer or shorter than anticipated (or the publicity and sales effort is more or less effective than anticipated), and as a result the move into growth is brought forward or delayed, creating the impression among the unwary that a product is going to be more or less successful than forecast. However these events are not likely to have affected the underlying demand, and the rate of growth will eventually settle at a level which will reflect that demand.

A related error is to mistake pent up demand for long term demand, and expand facilities far beyond what is appropriate in the longer term. For example, users may have been waiting for an easier to read 'X' meter for many years so that when one is launched, there will be a rush to buy — to the extent that existing meters are scrapped early, although they are perfectly serviceable. A sure sign of this is when customers who normally buy only two or three per year suddenly start talking about buying nine or ten per year. Once the pent up demand has been satisfied, sales will settle to reflect the underlying demand, that is the normal replacement rate for the meters, and in the meantime competitors will probably have introduced their own easier to read versions. However, perhaps this is a more desirable situation than finding that even though one has introduced a much more efficient version of a product, for example, a flow valve, customers will only buy as the old versions wear out, or as new systems are installed. In that case demand will build up very slowly.

7.3.3 Maturity phase

Sales growth will inevitably begin to level off; it always happens. Unfortunately many sales/marketing/general managers refuse to admit this possibility and after a period of steady growth continue to predict increasing sales. When sales begin to fall short of the forecast, rather than realising that this is the inevitable onset of maturity, they tend to redouble their spending on promotion and selling effort. Although some temporary improvement may result, the money spent is likely to be money wasted. By this stage some 85–90% of all those who are likely to buy the product are already doing so, or in the case of infrequently bought products they will be well aware of its existence and its potential benefits (or should be if the marketing effort has been properly undertaken). Many potential customers will be aware of other companies who are successfully using the product. Most of the potential customers who have not bought yet will not have done so because the exact need for the product has not arisen, and they will buy if and when it does. In these circumstances, other than when product variants and product improvements are being introduced (see below), it is sufficient to adopt a more moderate reminder level of sales and advertising effort; an effort which should retain current customers and prevent potential customers forgetting about the product and its potential benefits. The resources should be channelled into products which are in the earlier stages of their life.

Another common temptation and potential waste of company money in the maturity phase is to discount price in the hope that this will bolster sales volume. Although some sales increase may result, in the case of frequently bought technical products (e.g. components or consumables) there is a very real possibility that much of the increase will be caused by replacement stock orders being bought forward (and thereby increasing customer's stock levels) to take advantage of the discount. This is a 'once only' source of increase, and should the discount subsequently be removed, those stocks will be allowed to fall back to their former level, causing a temporary sales slump. The net effect will have been to sell the same volume but at a lower average price. At worst, introduction of discounting may be read by customers as a sign that the product is no longer selling as well as it should be or that is is about to be replaced, and this will encourage them to seek an alternative.

There are, however, two positive moves that can be made in the maturity phase. Sales volume can be increased by widening the sectors of the market that a product will appeal to. This is achieved by introducing model variants: if up to now sales have been achieved by a standard model, now is the time to introduce the product plus and the product minus. Development of these model variations should be started as soon as possible during the product's life so that they can be introduced either at the beginning of the maturity phase or as soon as the company resources are no longer fully tied up dealing with the growth of the original product.

The second positive move is to introduce product improvements or face lifts (as opposed to model variations) which will give the product a new lease of life and extend the maturity phase. Such planned product modifications can promote an image of a progressive company and generally take one of three forms:

(a) performance improvement − in terms that can easily be discerned by potential customers (e.g. longer life, reduced servicing, improved efficiency);
(b) style improvement,
(c) feature improvement − that is to increase the number of real or perceived user benefits such as convenience, safety, versatility.

For these moves to be successful the improvements must be perceived by customers as real. A high level of promotional and sales effort will be needed to draw attention to these improvements and as a result sales levels will frequently actually increase before falling back to the existing maturity levels.

However, it should not be forgotten that the competitors will not have been standing still and there will be a steadily increasing number of new products to compete against. By this stage marketing oriented organisations will have recognised that inevitably sales volume will begin to decline within a defined period, and that serious consideration must be given to the timing of the introduction of a replacement product. If the life cycle is short, development should already be well under way.

7.3.4 Saturation phase

In this phase the product has become dated and less competitive. Despite strenuous efforts sales volume will begin to fall. Even more than in the maturity phase there is a great danger of being tempted to overspend to try to avoid the decline. Remember, business success is measured in terms of profit and not sales volume. The only long term answer is a replacement product.

Nevertheless there is still opportunity for creativity by extending the length of this highly profitable phase. Sometimes this can be achieved by aiming the product at new and slightly different categories of customer. For example, the simple manual lathe has progressively been changed from being a major production machine to a toolroom machine to a jobbing machine and to a training machine. Its life has also been extended by entering new geographical markets where technology is less developed and where it again can assume its original role as a major production machine.

To ensure success in new market segments it is often necessary to change the product image. Unfortunately, changing the image of a technical product is not easily achieved, and if it is not well done it can leave customers confused between the old image and the new image with the result that the sales decline is hastened rather than delayed. Sales decline can also be staved off by appealing to customer loyalty and emphasising the low risk of using a tried and trusted product, even to the extent of making a virtue of old fashionedness. However, overdone this approach can harm the introduction of the replacement product, when it will become necessary to recreate an up-to-date image.

It is normally now too late to introduce product improvements. Unless the product is long lived or the costs are low, there will be insufficient product life left to recoup the investment. The only occasion when this can be justified is when a company has failed to properly plan its product succession and has to make the existing product last as long as possible.

7.3.5 Decline phase

The rate of sales decline has now begun to increase. If the replacement product is not ready then it will be necessary to try to minimise the rate of decline by carefully directed sales and promotion, and sometimes by minor repositioning. Major expenditure on new advertising themes or product revisions is likely to be wasted as there is unlikely to be sufficient time to reap the benefits. In any case it is doubtful whether drawing attention to an uncompetitive product is very helpful to the long term image of a company. The only customers still buying the product are those for whom, for some reason, the product represents special value. It provides exactly what they want in a way that more modern products cannot. This class of customer will go out of their way to continue to buy, will require a minimum of sales effort and often will pay a price premium.

If the replacement is well on the way, it will usually pay to continue to market the existing product even after the break-even point has been passed in the downward direction, in order to maintain a presence in the market, that is, customer contact and distribution channels. This presence has cost a lot of money to establish and would cost just as much to re-establish should it be lost. However care must be taken to ensure that pressure to complete development of the replacement is not lessened because the old product is still being sold.

7.3.6 Abandonment

This is not a life cycle stage; it is a decision point. The sales volume illustrated in Fig. 7.1 beyond this point represents what would happen if the abandonment decision was not taken.

The timing of abandonment, particularly of industrial products has to be thought out carefully. Frequently companies have to continue old products at a loss in order to maintain goodwill. For example, a chemical company which has customers who have processes dependent on one of their products has to give them time to adapt their process to the replacement product or find an alternative source of supply.

Buyers who have bought the existing product immediately prior to the introduction of its successor are another potential source of loss of goodwill. For example, if someone who had bought a £3000 microcomputer discovered a week later that it had been replaced with one at the same price which was capable of twice as many functions, he would not be very pleased. As a result it is now common practice to announce replacement models some weeks or even months prior to their launch and to heavily discount the old product in the meantime.

The exact timing of such an announcement is obviously critical, striking a balance between adequate warning and not selling at a discount for longer than necessary. The timing of the cessation of production will be affected by the volume of stocks being held in the distribution system. Most companies prefer to be left with some stocks of the old product rather than to run the risk of running out prior to the launch of the new. If that happens, the company is quite simply handing sales to its competitors, because most customers of most products (except capital equipment) cannot be persuaded to delay their purchase until the launch of a new product, which in their eyes may or may not be better than those currently available.

The enthusiasm displayed by the sales force for the new product also has to be handled carefully at this interim stage. Although it is beneficial to play up its virtues to try to prevent the loss of customers to a competitor by persuading them to hold back their buying decision, overemphasis will make the stock of the old product harder to clear. Finally there remains the question of stocks in the distribution network, and who pays for the off-loading once the new product has been launched. Advanced warning to distributors will minimise this problem, but the goodwill thereby gained has to be balanced against the inevitable loss of sales should distributors clear their stocks of the old model prior to the new one being launched.

If there is not a complete overlap of function the old product sometimes can be usefully continued even after the replacement has been introduced. An example was the continuation of the Leyland Mini after the Metro had been introduced. A further example are the lathes referred to in Section 7.3.4, where old models (although facelifted) have been successfully continued, albeit at a lower volume.

7.4 Using product life cycles to plan product succession

Apart from helping to determine appropriate marketing strategies, knowledge of product life cycles enables companies to plan for product succession. Ensuring a steady stream of profitable products is one of marketing's most important tasks. It is no good relaxing once a new product has been launched. The planning for life extension and eventual replacement should already be underway.

Many companies, when they become aware of the life cycle concept, find that too many of their products are in phases 3, 4 and 5. However, recognition is half the battle towards doing something about it. Companies who are not aware of the life cycle concept tend to wait for irrefutable signs of falling sales before worrying about a replacement, and that often is too late. With today's complexity of technology the time span from product idea, through development and testing, to launch can be longer than the life of the product itself. In such extreme cases it is necessary to be developing the successor's successor even before the successor is launched. In less extreme cases development of a successor has to be thought about in the growth or maturity phases of its predecessor, and only where the ratio of development time to product life is very low can development be left to the saturation phase.

The dangers of leaving development too late are several. Last minute development will inevitably be hurried and full pre-launch testing and debugging will tend to be skipped over. This will introduce the possibility that the new product will never fulfil its potential, not generate much positive cash flow and have a shorter life than anticipated. This in turn will lead to renewed attempts to develop yet another replacement in a hurry, but this time from a less secure position. Unless one is fortunate enough to obtain external financial backing (e.g. government subsidies) repetition of that cycle is one way to extinction.

Waiting until the existing product is selling very badly before introducing a successor will result in a loss of sales volume as illustrated by the shaded portion of Fig. 7.4*a*. It is better to introduce the successor while the existing customer base is still large and the reputation of the old product is still strong. There will be more existing customers to persuade to try the new product and therefore the introductory phase will be shorter and probably the growth rate steeper. Fig. 7.4*b* illustrates that the loss of sales is much less, especially when discounted sales of stocks of the old product (see Section 7.3.6) are added to the growing sales of the new one.

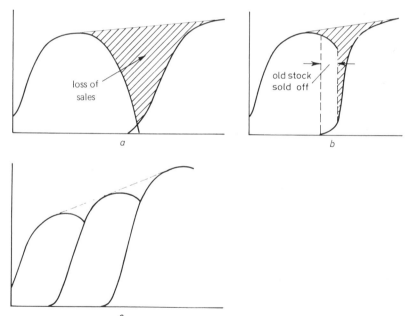

Fig. 7.4   *Product succession*
   a Existing product allowed to decline
   b Existing product reputation enhances new product growth
   c Successive products lead to steady growth

In practice there will be some dip in sales volume but in a multi-product company the effect of a small dip in one product should not be significant. The aim is to keep product sales volume more or less constant during the transition period such that the difference between introducing a new product and extending the life of an existing product becomes hard to detect. When product succession is carefully managed, continuing growth within the given product market can be achieved (see Fig. 7.4*c*), or at worst, loss of market share avoided.

Sometimes the progress of a product along its life cycle is hidden by increases in the size of the market. A product in a growth market might exhibit a steep growth phase followed by a period of steadily increasing sales, which could be interpreted as the maturity phase. However, if market share were plotted (see Fig. 7.5) in addition to sales volume, it would be seen that by the end of what seemed to be the growth phase, market share would already be well into the maturity phase, and that what appeared to be the maturity phase actually corresponded to the saturation and early decline phases.

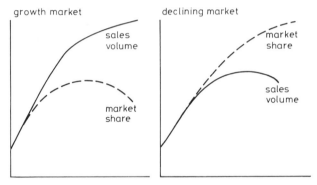

Fig. 7.5 *Market share life cycles*

By not appreciating this situation and not introducing a successor product the company involved would be paying a high price in terms of lost opportunity. A successor product capable of maintaining or continuing the growth of market share would have yielded sales far higher than the current product. Similarly, in a declining market the reverse situation can apply, and a product which is in fact still in its growth or maturity phases in terms of market share will appear to be in decline in terms of sales volume and may be unnecessarily replaced. This unnecessarily early warning means that the large number of companies which operate in declining markets can 'get away with' waiting for clear signs of sales decline before beginning to think of a replacement, and yet not suffer an erosion of their competitive position. They get it right by mistake.

Plotting market share as well as sales volume is the only sure way of eliminating the effects of the business cycle, and arriving at a true assessment of competitive position. In the case of international competition, domestic producers are frequently protected by import tariffs or other subsidies. Although it is fine to take advantage of such government help, it should not be allowed to hide the reality of the underlying competitive position and to delay product replacement. First, because of the opportunity cost referred to above, and secondly, should the subsidy be removed, market share is likely to drop very quickly. By the time a product replacement is designed and launched, market share could have fallen so dramatically that the future of the product line or indeed the company itself could be in jeopardy.

A similar position can arise when governments subsidise selected industries. Those industries are given a temporary cost advantage against substitute products from other industries and technologies, which can often lead to blinkered vision about their true competitive situation.

7.5 Technology life cycles

There has always been argument about what constitutes a new product as opposed to a product improvement. A simple way out of the problem is to define a product as new if more than 50% of the design has been changed. However it is not necessary for the technology to change because there are technology life cycles in addition to individual product life cycles. The individual product life cycles superimpose themselves on the technology life cycle as shown in Fig. 7.6. For example, each new design of steam locomotive represented a step along the steam locomotive technology life cycle and each new design of electromechanical switchboard represented a step along the electromechanical life cycle prior to the introduction of electronic switchboards (see also Ford and Ryan [25]).

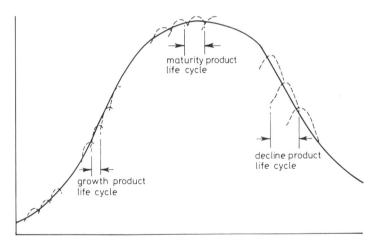

Fig. 7.6   *Technology life cycle*

In the growth phase of a new technology the rate of development tends to be much more rapid than in the latter phases and hence the life of individual product designs will tend to be shorter. As a result, companies operating in new technologies have to continually introduce new products simply to keep up, and often before they have been able to earn a reasonable return on the investment made in the existing product (see Section 7.6 and Scheuble [26]). As a result they require considerable cash injections (see also Section 7.7.1) and this in part explains why many growing companies in this situation end up being bought out by larger organisations.

Towards the end of the life of a technology, as with individual products, the incentive to invest in further development is low, partly because there is less time for the investment to be recouped before the technology is replaced and partly because most of the more obvious and less expensive improvements have already been made, and hence the chances are that those that remain to be discovered are not likely to be very cost effective. As a result, in the decline phase of a technology, products can retain their competitive advantage for relatively long periods and the return on the investment made in these products can be very high (see also Section 7.7.1). This tempts companies to stay in old technologies; which is fine providing the move into a newer technology is not delayed too long. For example, some companies who started in the electronics industry with discrete solid-state devices, did not recognise the importance of large scale integration and ease of programming sufficiently early to be able to establish sufficient experience and reputation in the new technology to compete with those companies that did, and with those new companies which sprung up around the new technology. Being unaware of technology life cycles, they underestimated the importance of the new technology and thought that they could continue to be competitive with the old one.

A classic example of getting it right was IBM, who recognised the change from mechanical accounting tabulators to electronics and changed their product range accordingly. At the other extreme was Facit, who clung on to making electro-mechanical calculators beyond the point of no return. Another well known example was Proctor and Gamble, who in the late 1940s recognised the importance of synthetic detergents, while Lever Brothers elected to continue with soap powders for a further three or four years. As a result Proctor and Gamble's US market share grew from 34% to 57% and Lever Brothers' market share dropped from 31% to 17% (Klaw [27]). Despite strenuous efforts by Lever Brothers since that time, they have never been able to regain their former parity and probably never will unless the situation is reversed when the next inevitable technology change comes along.

7.6 Life cycle expenditure and income

Life cycle expenditure and income is illustrated in Fig. 7.7. The life cycle curve, instead of representing sales volume or market share, has been drawn in terms of unit price, less unit production and other variable costs multiplied by sales volume (usually termed contribution). The curve has been offset below the zero cash flow axis by the amount of the fixed costs so that the area under the curve and above the zero axis represents the cumulative profit during a product's life. The break-even points in the upwards and downwards directions are marked 'A' and 'C' respectively.

Typical levels of investment needed to undertake successive steps in the product development and launch process quoted by the US Department of Commerce (see Chisnall [28]) have been shown in the rectangular boxes to the left of the graph. The area contained within the rectangles represents the cumulative investment in the product.

The expenditure mix will vary appreciably from product to product, but will of course add up to 100% for any given product. The time-scales shown on this section of the graph are illustrative; for example, the expenditure on plant and equipment often occurs within a very short time-scale but to represent that accurately, vertical extension of the rectangle would disappear well beyond the bottom of the page (to keep the area within the rectangle the same). In practice expenditure on categories will overlap and further marketing research/business appraisal will usually be undertaken at least once or twice during the period up to the product launch (see Section 10.10) but this has not been shown for the sake of clarity.

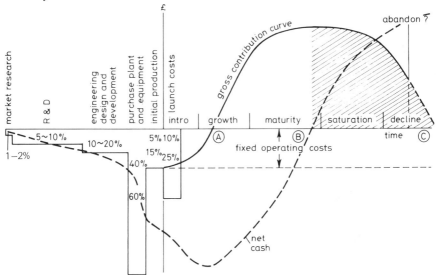

Fig. 7.7 *Product life cycle: expenditure and income*

The cumulative cash position has been illustrated (not to the same scale) by the dotted line and it can be seen that the cash outflow does not cease until the break-even point (A) has been passed. This is the point of maximum capital outlay, and from that point on the contribution from product sales begins to pay back the investment made. In the example shown the total investment is not recovered until the product is well into the maturity phase (point B). While some products achieve this position much earlier, especially those which are part of a planned succession strategy, the example illustrated is not uncommon. The shaded portion under the product contribution curve represents the net profit being earned by the product and it vividly illustrates why companies are tempted to extend product lives. It seems stupid to abandon a product when the net cash flow is still rising, and maybe when the return on the investment made or the product is still below target. However, the opportunity to maximise the return on investment on individual products sometimes has to be forgone in order to achieve the best long term return on investment for the company. Introducing the successor early should bring forward the point in its life when it begins to earn a net return on the investment made in it, such that the total profit earned by the two products will be greater than if the first one had been allowed to decline before the second was introduced.

Fig. 7.7 also illustrates the dangers of underestimating development costs and development times. Obviously the greater the costs, the larger will be the cash outflow, and the payback point will be reached later in the product's life. Perhaps less obvious are the problems of an extended development period. When the original marketing research was carried out not only should it have identified a clear competitive advantage for the proposed product, at that moment in time, but it should have tried to establish that that competitive advantage would still hold good, say, eighteen months later at the launch date, and a further eighteen months after that in the maturity phase. Eventually, progress by competitors will erode that competitive advantage and so a development programme which takes six months longer than forecast effectively lops six months off the product's life — and that will clearly have a very detrimental effect on the total positive cash flow earned by the product during its life. Underestimating on both counts seems to be universal, and attempts to get it right always seem to fail. The problem is overcome on the cash front by only going ahead with development projects which appear to offer a very high rate of return, so that after the development (and sometimes the launch) costs have inevitably over run, an adequate return can still be earned. The timing problem is generally overcome because everyone is as bad, or at least almost as bad, as everyone else and so the expected erosion of the competitive advantage does not happen as quickly as anticipated; except that occasionally it does, sometimes with disasterous results.

Finally, Fig. 7.7 illustrates that the best time to hit competitors hard is shortly after they have launched a new product. This is the period of maximum investment and maximum financing charges, and the longer sales growth is delayed, the lower the net product profit will be. From the point of view of companies introducing new products they need to enter the growth phase as quickly as possible, and as has already been stated several times this is most likely if a planned succession strategy is followed. Unfortunately, for companies introducing really innovative products the introductory phase can be extremely lengthy, and in that case adequate financing must be planned for and taken into account when assessing product viability.

7.7 Portfolio analysis

Some forms of investment, such as starting a new company, offer the opportunity to make a large gain or return on investment, but inevitably this opportunity goes hand in hand with the risk of making a loss, sometimes a considerable loss. Other investments (e.g. a building society account) only offer the opportunity to obtain a smaller return on investment but normally the chances of making a loss are commensurately less. Financial theories have been developed which show that an investor can maximise his expected gains at whatever level of risk he is prepared to accept by committing himself to a combination or portfolio of individual low risk and high risk investments.

A similar concept applies to companies (e.g. see Cordozo and Smith [29]). All but the smallest companies produce and market a portfolio of products, some of which offer the opportunity to earn high profits and some of which do not. The aim of good product planning is to attain a portfolio which offers the best long term prospects for the company, that is the best combination of return on investment and risk. A number of 'systems' have been developed to help companies try to assess where their products stand in relation to expected return and risk.

7.7.1 Boston matrix

One very well known system originally developed by the Boston Consulting Group [30] to help large companies examine the balance of their portfolios is illustrated in Fig. 7.8 (see also Abell and Hammond [19]). The potential rate of return on investment is represented by the market growth axis, because sales and profit growth is likely to be greater for products which are introduced into growth markets than for products introduced into declining markets.

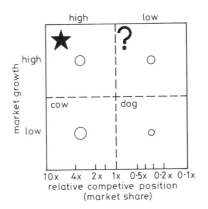

Fig. 7.8 *Boston growth/share matrix*
Circle size is proportional to product sales volume

The risk of failure to earn that return is measured by the company's competitive position, that is the relative strength of its design, production, marketing and financial capabilities. The company's strength in these areas will normally (see Buzzell [31]), but not necessarily (see Woo and Cooper [32]), be reflected by its existing market share, and when the Boston matrix was originally formulated relative market share was used as the sole indicator of competitive position. (If a company had a 10% share and the largest competitor 25%, then the relative competitive position was defined as 10/25, i.e. 0·4). While this might be considered oversimplistic (see Lorenz [33]), market share is a parameter which is relatively easily measured and in practice it provides a sufficiently accurate reflection of competitive position for the matrix to be used, providing that what is meant by 'the market' is carefully defined (see Goold [34]). For example, a company producing only low output portable compressors may have a small share of the total compressor market, a moderate share of the portable compressor market but a high share of the low output portable compressor market. It is this latter segment that they need to define as 'the market', providing it is a distinct segment with clearly separate characteristics, because the company will not be competing in any other of the segments encompassed within the broader definitions.

The share of 'the market' as defined above which corresponds to a 'high' relative competitive position will depend on the potential economies of scale relative to the size of the market. Thus in some markets a 10% share will correspond to maximum economies of scale whereas in others a 30% share would be required. In the former case a 10% share might be considered 'high', even though the largest competitor had a 20% share, whereas in the latter case a 10% share should be considered 'low'. Similarly, the definition of high and low growth will vary from time to time and from industry to industry. In a depression a 5% annual growth rate may be defined as high and the so-called low growth areas might actually be in decline, while during an economic upsurge a 10% growth might be described as low.

As can be seen from Fig. 7.8, the segments within the Boston matrix were christened cash cow, dog, question mark and star. Each of these segments will be considered in turn.

First, cash cows. Cash cows tend to be products which are in the maturity or saturation phase of their life. Sales will have grown as far as they are going to and in the process the product will have attained a high market share, and usually will be earning good profits (refer to Section 5.14). The technology will also normally be in the maturity or saturation phase and hence the market will be growing only slowly, if at all. The existing products should have a long life and it will not be necessary to invest heavily in new products. Nor will it be worth investing to try to increase that market share, because entrenched competitors made that difficult in low growth markets and because better opportunities to earn an adequate return on the incremental investment are more likely to occur in growth markets. Sufficient investment and product replacement to maintain the existing market share is all that will be required. High profits combined with low levels of investment quite clearly lead to a high positive cash flow. Hence the term cash cow. These products generate the cash to be 'milked' for other products in a company's portfolio. The positive cash flow could, of course, be further increased by not investing in the product at all, and letting market share decline — a favourite policy when a market is reaching the end of its life.

Next, the dogs. Dog products also tend to be in the maturity phase, but they will not have attained a high market share. They will also be in low growth, stagnant or declining markets. A low market share is linked to low profits and low growth is linked to low investment, leading to a small cash flow around the break-even point. When the matrix was first published it was suggested that existing dog products should not be replaced, there being no point in investing further, as there would be better returns to be made elsewhere. However, in an economic recession this is not necessarily so. If market demand is expected to continue for a number of years, it could be profitable to undertake considerable further investment in an attempt to improve market share. It is a case of balancing the forecast total increase in product profits over the remainder of the market's life against the investment needed, and if the investment funds available to the company are limited, comparing the forecast return on investment with other investment opportunities of equal risk. For example, the return on investment for a dog product might be 10%, whereas the return on a new product in a new technology might be 25%. This is where the risk assessment comes in. Investment in the dog product might be 65% certain to yield the forecast return whereas investment in the new product might be only 20% certain to yield the forecast return.

A good example of investing in dog products was Dunlop's decision in the late 1970s to continue to invest heavily in tyres. Tyres are in a declining market. On the other hand it is a market which seems likely to last at least another 50 years. It has been suggested that in another 15 or 20 years there may only be four or five major world suppliers of tyres left. The competitive pressures in a declining market will have forced everyone else out. Possibly each of the four or five could have cash cows on their hands. It was a case of investing in a long life dog in order to turn it into a cash cow, but which ran the danger that it would not be possible to sustain the investmant for long enough to reap the benefit. In other words, productivity and market share would not be increased fast enough to offset declining market demand and generate sufficient profit to sustain the investment.

Some dog products will be in the early phases of their life. In that case it is likely to be worth while to continue to invest in them until the maturity phase is reached. This is particularly true if the new product is a planned replacement for a predecessor which was in the cash cow category, as there is every chance that the product will eventually attain a major share of its market and move straight from the dog into the cash cow quadrant.

Even so, entirely new products are not normally introduced into low growth markets. It is much more common for new products to be launched into growth markets, that is, into the question mark sector. Because they are new, these products will not have achieved high sales volumes and hence will not be earning much profit. In growth markets, the technology will normally be in the growth phase and will be changing rapidly, and therefore products will tend to have short lives. A high level of spending will be needed to develop and introduce a stream of new products in order to keep up to date. In addition, heavy spending on marketing will be needed to expand the existing market share. The scale of the problem is illustrated below. An apparently modest target of increasing market share from 5% to 15% over 5 years, in a market growing at only 5% per annum requires an average annual growth rate in excess of 30%:

Year	Market size	Target share	Production	Growth rate
0	10 000	5%	500	
1	10 500	7%	735	47%
2	11 025	9%	992	35%
3	11 576	11%	1273	28%
4	12 155	13%	1580	24%
5	12 763	15%	1914	21%

If the money is not well spent, the products will remain in the question mark sector, eventually dropping into the dog sector as market growth slows and possibly never earning an adequate return on the investment made in them. Thus this category is a high risk category. If the hoped for sales volume growth does not occur, companies have to decide whether to continue to invest heavily, in the hope of gaining a high market share and hence high financial returns, or whether to withdraw. Hence the designation 'question mark'.

Star products are question mark products which made it. They tend to be in the late growth to early decline phases of their life and should be earning high profits. There will be further market growth potential and so most companies will not hesitate to invest further to protect their existing high market share. The high profits and high investment should lead to a break-even cash flow, preferably a slightly positive cash flow. Clearly, where funds for new product development are limited, preference will be given to replacements for star products because they represent the future profits of the company. Once the rate of market growth slows they should drop squarely into the cash cow sector.

Carefully managed, question marks which never made it into the star category might be succeeded by ones which cross over into the cash cow category rather than into the dog category, because as market growth slows and the rate of change decreases, some companies find that they are finally able to catch up and establish a firm competitive advantage. It should be remembered that a cash cow does not need to have a high market share *per se* but a sufficient share relative to that achieved by competitors in the industry to enable the company to generate and sustain a strongly positive cash flow.

The importance of having a balanced portfolio can now be seen. Companies need to market some question marks in order to develop a few stars, which in turn will become cash cows and generate the cash needed to finance the next generation of question marks. In a healthy company there should be more products in the question mark category than in the star category (up to two to one) to allow for failures, and a sufficient number in the cash cow category to finance the question marks. There should be relatively few dogs. A preponderence of products in the two lower quadrants of the matrix, assuming the markets have been correctly defined, is a sign of a company with a limited future unless strategies can be developed to correct the inbalance.

The matrix can be used for product planning by comparing the existing position of products with their expected position in one year and three years time. This will show up how the product balance will change unless appropriate action is taken. It is also revealing to place competitor's products on the matrix and thereby guess at what their product strategies are likely to be — but remember, because competitors have different skills and resources their market definitions are likely to be slightly different and that will affect how they view the situation.

The matrix must be used with common sense. The electronics market is a rapidly growing market, whereas the machine tool market is stagnant. That does not mean that all companies making machine tools who do not have a high market share should immediately move into electronics. Skills are not that simply transferred. What can be done is to classify different parts of the machine tool business into low and high growth sectors (although in absolute terms the high growth sectors may still be low growth in terms of other industries) and sort out the company's product lines accordingly. As stated above, what is meant by 'the market' needs to be defined with care and common sense. The definitions chosen must be mutually consistent so that all the product lines can be placed and examined, one relative to the other.

The Boston matrix is a useful tool. It can be used relatively easily, requiring at the simplest level only information about market growth and market share, and it graphically illustrates the product portfolio. However, too much should not be expected of it; it is only a tool. It is most useful when used alongside some of the other techniques described in this book (see also Wensley [35]).

7.7.2 GEC/McKinsey matrix

Many other more complex portfolio matrices have been developed. It has even been suggested that companies might find portfolio matrices more helpful if they generated measurement parameters (for each axis) specific to each product (see Wind and Mahajan [36]). However, increased complexity can make parameter measurement and rating more difficult, and lead to less reliable and less useable results. A more complex but still practical matrix developed by GEC/McKinsey (see Fig. 7.9) uses a nine segment matrix and relates industry attractiveness to company business strength (Karnani [37]). The definitions of business strength and industry attractiveness are deliberately broad so that a considerable number of factors can be considered. Business strength includes not just market share but other competitive factors such as company reputation, sales force coverage, the distribution system, customer service, production efficiency and financial strength (these factors could be weighted and scored as described in Section 10.8 to arrive at a rating). Industry attractiveness is assessed in terms of the market structure (see Chapter 6), that is, size and growth, barriers to entry, numbers of competitors and so on.

Each product is represented on the matrix by a small circle and the market share achieved by each product represented by the percentage of that circle which is shaded. One would normally expect high business strength to go hand in hand with high market share and vice versa, and hence products A and B appear to be anomalies requiring further investigation. If market share is less than it should be relative to business strength, this is a sign that it should be relatively easy to increase sales volume. Perhaps business strength has been increased recently and this is not yet reflected in terms of market share, or perhaps the restriction on sales growth is not lack of competitive strength but an inability to produce the product and to make it available to potential customers in sufficient quantities. This is a product with growth potential, and increased financial backing should be sought for a larger sales force, advertising budget, production facilities and so on. On the other hand, if the market share is high relative to the business strength, then that is a sign of vulnerability. One is in fact living off past efforts; on one's reputation. It will be relatively easy for competitors to erode the high market share. If the size and duration of the market seems to justify it, consideration should be given to investing in product design, process improvement and marketing improvement so as to improve the business strength and the company's competitive position. In both cases the decision whether to invest or not, or how much to invest, will be tempered by the industry attractiveness parameter.

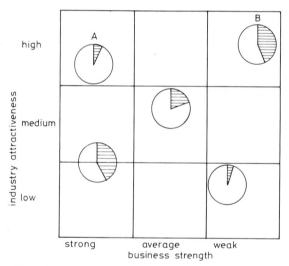

Fig. 7.9   *GEC/McKinsey business screen (from Karnani [37])*

7.8 Gap analysis

This is a straightforward technique (Kami [38]) which draws attention to any difference which may exist between sales forecasts and sales objectives. A graph of sales volume (usually expressed in financial terms rather than in physical units) against time is plotted for the past two or three years. Sometimes profit or return on capital employed is plotted rather than sales volume. The graph can be extended taking account of product life cycles, to show the forecast sales volume from existing products which will be obtained by following existing strategies, and this extension can be compared with the sales volume target. The difference between the two is the gap which has to be filled.

In order to obtain an accurate picture it is important to include in the projection the effect of actions which have already been taken but which so far have not impacted on sales volume or profits (e.g. a new product just launched, new staff recruited, a training programme started, improved production equipment just installed, introduction of computerised inventory control and so on) as well as the effect of forecast environmental factors which are beyond managements own control.

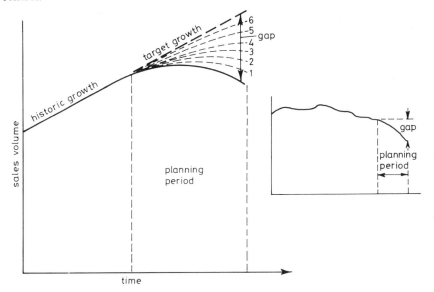

Fig. 7.10   *Gap analysis*

The usual form of the graph is illustrated in Fig. 7.10, but the inset shows what is realistically likely to be the picture in the current industrial climate. The gap can be progressively filled as follows:

1 Improve the effectiveness of existing sales and promotion activities.
2 Introduce product modifications and product extensions.
3 Introduce product replacements/improvements.
4 Sell the products into new market segments, that is, find new product users.
5 Broaden the product range.
6 Introduce a new related product range.
7 Introduce a new product into a related market.

These strategies are listed in order of increasing risk; that is, risk that the forecast sales volume will not be achieved. Implementation of one of the earlier alternatives is not a pre-requisite to the implementation of one of the later ones. If the volume objective is considered essential to the ongoing health of the company and cannot be achieved via the seven alternatives listed, then diversification possibilities can be examined. The experience of some companies has indicated that the chosen strategies have to be forecast to fill the gap three times over to ensure 100% achievement.

Gap analysis provides an excellent starting point for the planning process. It clearly shows what would happen if no new action were initiated.

Chapter 8

Planning

8.1 Why plan?

Usually companies' first priority is to survive. They try to do this by generating sufficient profit to satisfy shareholders and debtholders, and to reinvest in new capital equipment, new products, staff, and inflationary working capital. They try to generate sufficient profit in a competitive market by using their resources to meet customer requirements in areas where they can offer the maximum competitive advantage. In order to do that they have to forecast future customer requirements so that they can organise themselves to meet them as efficiently as possible. In effect they have to decide what needs to be undertaken during the coming 12 months in order to remain competitive for the following (typically) 3–5 years.

In order to organise themselves efficiently, most people find it helpful to write down what needs to be done in a logical sequence of steps, rather than simply starting at what seems the obvious place, and deciding what to do next once the first step has been completed. As tasks become more complex the potential for inefficiency grows and it becomes more important to consider in advance the pros and cons of alternative courses of action. It is too easy, when embroiled in sorting out short-term problems, to forget what the overall objectives are. For example, if one had been trying for three months to get a particular product feature 'right', it would not be easy to step back and examine whether the product could be marketed differently, either without that feature or with it operating in a slightly modified manner, unless the overall task objective — say to profitably meet an identified market requirement within a defined time-scale — had been written down.

Obviously planning involves some redundancy. All of what was anticipated will not happen: the unanticipated will happen. This uncertainty is often used to justify not planning at all. It is suggested that a flexible organisation can effectively respond to situations as they occur. Although this may be true to a limited extent, these responses are likely to be more effective if they are thought out in advance of the need to implement them (see Section 4.2), and formulated in the light of clear objectives.

In general the complexity of tasks increases as companies grow larger, and because of their higher momentum it takes longer for them to change direction. Therefore they have to look further ahead than small companies. The planning time horizon chosen will depend largely on the time needed to bring an idea to fruition (e.g. product idea to product launch). Although this is in part related to company size, it is also related to industry sector. In some industries it takes many years to design, build and commision new plant, let alone earn a reasonable return on it, while in other industries a payback within a year or less is possible. Where the rate of change is very rapid it is not sensible to plan more than a year or two ahead, although it is still important to scan the environment further ahead than that for signs of fundamental changes to come.

Plans also make it easier to delegate, to control, and to allocate resources. Delegation is achieved by allocating responsibility for defined action programmes to individual staff. Control is achieved by monitoring progress towards agreed objectives, and by initiating corrective action where necessary. Resources are allocated to those with plans which appear both promising and realistic, and who have performed well in the past. Others will probably have to trim their plans to the resources they are allowed to work with.

That leaves two significant spin-off benefits. First, information will be brought to the attention of higher management which otherwise would remain hidden, because managers are forced to yield up information in order to justify their targets and plans. Such information, when viewed from a broader perspective, can sometimes help to avoid major disasters. Gradually forcing out more information in this way is perhaps a justification for not immediately accepting the initial proposals of operating units (see Eliasson [39]). Second, the requirement to prepare and justify plans forces managers to look up from the short term and at the future; certainly 1 year and possibly further ahead.

The process of looking and of thinking about the impact of various types of change will make people more sensitive to what is going on around them, more aware, more flexible, more inclined to accept signals of change to come and to respond quickly to them. Many companies installing competerised accounts or stock control have reported that much of the benefit arose from the systematic thinking about what information is needed, how it is to be obtained, and how it is to be recorded. Similarly with business planning. The numbers themselves are not so important, it is how they are arrived at and how they are used which is important. To quote Eisenhower, 'the plan is nothing, planning is everything'. It is necessary for an organisation to be able to critically appraise its situation and its own activities so that it can decide how to progress that activity to greatest effect. After all, there is no point getting better and better at playing football in mud if the rest of the world plays on firm grass.

8.2 Planning alerts companies to gradual change

One of the major values of planning is the cultivation of an awareness of change and of gradual change in particular, so that steps can be taken now, to ensure that the organisation will be in the correct shape to survive in the future. Gradual changes in tastes or technology all too often still go unnoticed. For example, it seemed to take many companies a long time to appreciate that reduced transport costs and the economies of scale associated with many modern production plants require that many products are marketed on an international scale if costs are to be kept competitive. Much has been made of high wage rates to explain uncompetitive costs when a large part of the answer lies in increased volume. The British bicycle industry[1] did not understand for many years that people wanted a cheap bike for their small children rather than one which would last for fifteen years and for which a wide range of spares could be obtained. As a result, by the time they became aware, they had lost so much market share that they were no longer in a position to produce in sufficient volumes to reduce costs to the levels being achieved in other countries. Alfred Herbert did not see that more flexible and more automated lathes were wanted and that customers were less concerned with selection advice than with initial price. The UK motorbike industry did not understand that smoother, quieter and more comfortable machines were desired. It is not the large and totally unexpected changes, such as the 1970s oil crises, which are detrimental to companies competitive positions. These sudden unexpected changes affect all competitors alike and they all have to respond to the new situation as best they can. It is the large but gradual changes that cause the problems — if they go unrecognised.

8.3 Planning is systematic and hierarchical

'Planning is a systemised way of thinking ahead of time' (Eliasson [39]). It starts with the expectation of change. Change related to customers, competitors, technology, the economy, society or politics. Within each of these categories there will be some parameters which will affect companies more than others. These important parameters have to be identified, monitored and their impact assessed, for each market and market segment in which a company operates. Most of the information categories and the methods of analysing them have been dealt with in previous chapters, and the basic requirements are summarised in Fig. 8.1.

Less important parameters need to be identified but not monitored so closely. The very fact that they have been identified means that changes to them are more likely to be noticed and taken into account if they are relevant. Thus planning starts with a focused information gathering and forecasting effort. The results of this effort will be fed into the planning system and will form part of the basis for the initial setting of objectives (for more detail see Ansoff [40]).

Once information has been gathered, the planning process will evolve through three stages:

1 What are we trying to achieve — the objectives.
2 How are we to achieve the objectives — the strategy.
3 How are we to implement the strategy — the action programmes.

[1] Luckily they were rescued by the BMX craze, but have they learnt the planning lesson?

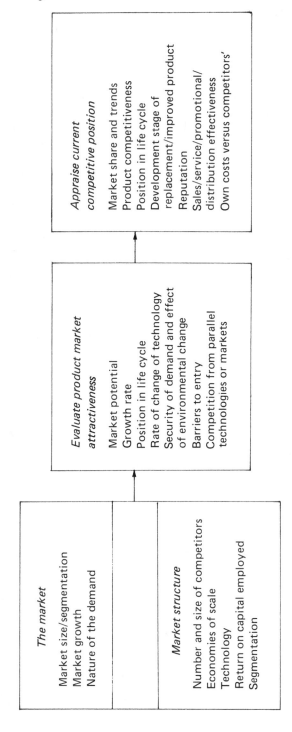

The market

Market size/segmentation
Market growth
Nature of the demand

Market structure

Number and size of competitors
Economies of scale
Technology
Return on capital employed
Segmentation

Evaluate product market attractiveness

Market potential
Growth rate
Position in life cycle
Rate of change of technology
Security of demand and effect of environmental change
Barriers to entry
Competition from parallel technologies or markets

Appraise current competitive position

Market share and trends
Product competitiveness
Position in life cycle
Development stage of replacement/improved product
Reputation
Sales/service/promotional/distribution effectiveness
Own costs versus competitors'

Fig. 8.1 *Appraisal of competitive position*

For example, a reasonable company objective might be to increase earnings per share in line with inflation. Given this objective the chosen strategies might be to (a) dominate the market and/or (b) cut costs by improved efficiency and/or (c) diversify into a chosen related area. From these strategies several different action programmes can be developed as illustrated in Fig. 8.2. Fig. 8.2 clearly shows planning as a hierarchical process — thus while at company level 'introduce superior products' is an action, to the department given the task it becomes an objective requiring its own substrategies and action programmes. The progressive nature of planning is also illustrated in Fig. 8.3, with each objective and strategy following on, and covering an increasingly narrow area of the company's operations (see also Lorange and Vancil [41]). The higher level strategies and action programmes tend to be longer term, and they set the decision limits (or objectives) for the parts of the organisation lower down the hierarchy. They should provide sufficient freedom to allow individual strategies and action programmes to be developed which meet those objectives, right down to the operating level where the action programmes will become very specific and short term, for example, 'visit customer A in week 5'. Thus a complete company plan consists of a whole series of plans; a broad company wide plan, divisional plans, product plans, functional department plans and even individual plans (see Fig. 8.4).

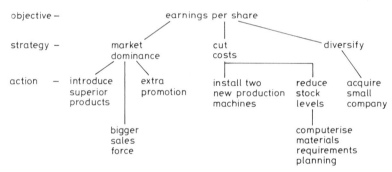

Fig. 8.2 *The planning hierarchy*

In the case of small businesses the planning process may be quite informal, involving the joining together of the views of the management team: views based on their feel for the nature of the market and how it is changing, which they will have gained by being in continual direct contact with that market. Even so some limited structuring of the thinking process will be helpful. In large organisations, faced with high levels of complexity and where the decision makers tend to be remote from the market served, more formality will be required to make the system workable. However, a good planning system is the simplest one which can achieve the desired results. If a dozen pages will tell everyone all they need to know, writing 100 pages is clearly counter productive. There is no virtue in a thick planning manual covering every conceivable issue for its own sake. The outcome of a thick manual will be an even thicker report. Planning systems should be fitted to the organisation, and just

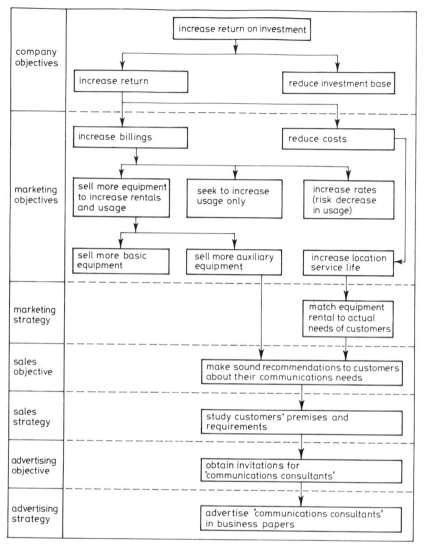

Fig. 8.3 *Hierarchy of planning objectives for a telephone company (from Winer [42])*

as the organisation itself should change in response to changed circumstances, so should the planning system be kept in step with changed needs as they evolve.

8.4 Planning is an iterative process

Planning is an iterative process, because corporate objectives cannot be realistically set in isolation. They must take account not only of information about the market, about the profits currently being generated, about the availability of outside finance, about the availability of personnel, but also of the practicality of the strategies needed to meet them. Detail planning in one area may reveal that what is proposed is not practical or efficient, or it may reveal that an alternative strategy would be more likely to be successful. For example, it may not be possible to meet target market shares at a price which would generate the target return on investment, unless the advertising strategy were changed. However, it would be unreasonable to change the advertising strategy without discussing the implications with other departments, because the proposed change may have an adverse effect on their operations. The aim must be to agree a strategy which is effective for the whole organisation and not just one part of it.

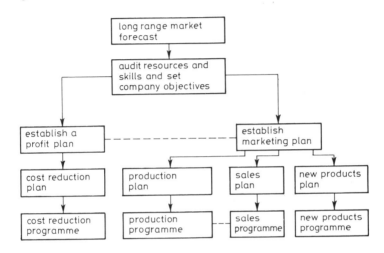

Fig. 8.4 *Progressive nature of company planning*

As a result, planning is a two way process. It starts with information being gathered at lower levels. That information is ordered and justified and progressed up the hierarchy. At the top it is combined with information from other sources — external to the company — and used to set broad objectives and strategies. These are taken back down the hierarchy and progressively exploded into more detail. Should the detail examination in any area reveal flaws, then these must be referred back up the hierarchy to be resolved in the light of the needs of other departments until an acceptable solution can be agreed. If agreements are to be reached reasonably quickly, this process should be kept informal during the early stages of the planning cycle, although it will become more formal as the cut off date for plan completion is approached. This process can be summarised as shown in Fig. 8.5.

Changes proposed at level 3 would normally be agreed and absorbed into a broader plan at level 2, and only in exceptional circumstances referred up to level 1 for review and decision. Changes at level 3 would of course affect level 4 and hence level 4 must be informed of any proposed changes to level 3, so that any parts of their planning process which will be affected can be placed in temporary obeyance, until confirmation of the changes at level 3 is received.

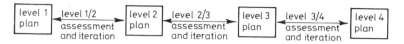

Fig. 8.5 *The iterative nature of planning*

8.5 Elements of a plan

8.5.1 Company purpose

Before planning is started, it is essential to be clear why a given company exists. It may exist as a means for the owner to pay less tax. It may exist as an outlet for its owner's interests and quite secondarily provide an income. It may exist to provide as secure an income as possible during the life of its owner(s) or it may exist as a means of creating wealth. Creating wealth is the purpose of most public companies (usually expressed in terms of share prices and earnings per share), but it is sometimes linked to a particular style of doing business or a particular industry — indeed many companies seem to prefer to go out of business rather than to move from one industry to another. These value judgements by top management probably exert more influence on company goals than the most detailed environmental scanning and planning, and this should always be borne in mind. The value judgements quite rightly shape how problems are approached, and the direction of the solutions chosen. The purpose of methodical planning is to draw attention to the problems, to possible solutions, and possible criteria for choosing between them. It does not seek to take away the right to choose.

8.5.2 Business definition

Once the overall purpose is recognised and agreed, the next step is to determine what business areas the company is to operate in if the purpose is to be achieved. Achievement is most likely if the company concentrates on areas where it can offer some competitive advantage. The starting point for determining where a competitive advantage could be offered is the company's existing resources and skills. A list of these can be prepared and compared with the resources and skills needed to make an impact in different markets. Having narrowed the field to markets where the company has at least half of the key resources needed, it is possible to group these various markets into different business areas (that is areas which require similar resources and skills). Normally the company will already be competing in some part of each of these areas, but not necessarily so.

It is not necessary or desirable for a company to compete in all of these business areas, although each should continue to be scanned for opportunities. For each area it is necessary to determine the incremental investment needed to compete effectively and the likely returns from that investment. Obviously the investment is likely to be least in those businesses where the company is most active and already has significant relevant resources.

It is logical to choose those areas which offer the best long term future for the company in terms of the rate of return on investment, the number of years for which that return should be achievable and the risks involved, subject of course to the company purpose as outlined above. These then are the business areas which the company should choose to compete in. As the resources available and resources required change, so too may the business areas chosen.

8.5.3 Objectives

An objective is a statement of what is to be achieved. In a business plan there will be a hierarchy of objectives corresponding to the different planning levels. At the top level the objectives will reflect the company purpose.

However, a good objective does not make a good plan. Sometimes better results will be attained from a more moderate objective and a good strategy, than from a good objective and a poor strategy. It can be better to reach where one expects to reach than to be left floundering in the middle of nowhere. Thus before objectives are finally adopted, the ability of the company to meet them must be assessed as the first iteration in the planning process.

Growth is sometimes quoted as a worthy objective but it is not without its dangers (see also Ramo [43]). Growth in sales volume can be accompanied by reduced margins, either because price has to be reduced to increase market share or because of increased costs (arising, for example, from a higher intensity of marketing effort, transportation over longer distances or an increased use of agents), which are greater than the economies of scale achieved. Even when margins are maintained, growth will require sustained investment and possibly a higher level of borrowing. Often a higher production capacity brings with it a much higher break-even and a greater susceptibility to small swings in demand. Thus before growth is planned for it is necessary to be very sure of the security of the sales forecast on which it has been based. It may be possible to operate at a lower volume and at a lower risk (but refer back to Section 5.14), so long as that will generate enough profit for the company to remain competitive in the long term.

Similarly, increasing the target return on assets above the existing level is not necessarily sensible. Higher returns are usually only achieved by taking risks. High risk means that the forecast profits from that business are less likely to be achieved, and unless the return on assets improves more than the risk increases, there will be insufficient extra profit generated to cover the inevitable failures, and hence the long term financial position of the company will have been worsened rather than improved.

Typical marketing objectives might be as shown in Table 8.1. Each of these objectives will need to be broken down into more detail by product, by sales area, by customer group etc., so that a series of lower level strategies can be developed.

Table 8.1

Market	Segment	Share target %	Volume target £k	Gross margin %	Time limit
A	1	10	100	20	1 year
	2	30	150	30	2 years
	3	40	300	35	6 months
B	1	25	50	30	9 months
	2	15	100	25	3 years
	3	10	100	20	1 year

8.5.4 Strategy

Strategy is a statement of how an objective is to be achieved, using available resources in what seems to be the most effective manner. A strategy is long term in nature and provides an overview within which shorter term action programmes can be formulated as circumstances dictate. Company strategies, if they are to achieve a major impact, should be as few in number as possible and be chosen so as to maximise the company's strengths and the opportunities available, and to exploit the competitors' weaknesses. A strategy can continue in force as long as the objectives, or the assumptions on which they were based, remain unchanged.

8.5.5 Action programmes

Action programmes are the detail part of a plan. They describe exactly how strategy is to be implemented in the short term. Actions that are timed for more than one year away need not be described in detail because they will form part of the following year's plan and will be determined in the light of the situation at that time. As that will inevitably be different to the current situation it is pointless wasting time describing in detail an action programme which is going to be changed before it is implemented.

Each action programme should consist of an unambiguous statement of what is to be undertaken, who is to be responsible and the date by which the action is to be completed. The detail included in action programmes will relate to the level of planning it refers to. It may refer to the introduction of two new product ranges or to the number of new customers to be sought in a given sales territory. It is only by preparing a series of action programmes, and by continually monitoring results achieved against those programmes, that companies stand any chance of achieving their objectives. Such monitoring is an integral part of the planning process and helps to provide early warning of change, and any need to reassess the appropriateness of the action programmes, the strategies and maybe even the objectives.

8.5.6 Budgets

The budget is a financial statement of the expected consequences of undertaking the agreed plan. There should be a financial statement for each level and for each part of the plan. Each statement provides a means of assessing the acceptability of the plan as well as numerical criteria against which its implementation can be judged.

8.6 Preparing a plan – the logical approach

The logical approach to planning outlined in many text books can be summarised as follows:

1 Evaluate and define the nature of the business a company operates in.
2 Analyse the company's present competitive position in its existing business and identify the key factors which will influence the probability of its continued success in that business.
3 Analyse the company's strengths and weaknesses: that is, evaluate company resources (financial, technical, human etc.).
4 Evaluate other business opportunities and threats.
5 Define objectives: such as continue/diversify/change the present business; or within the chosen business set financial, market share, resource acquisition and other targets.
6 Construct alternative strategies to achieve the objectives.
7 Select the preferred strategies and construct action programmes to achieve them.
8 Prepare detail sales targets and budgets which reflect the objectives and other action programmes.
9 Monitor progress against the planned action programmes and budgets, undertaking remedial action as necessary.

A more colloquial way of summarising the process is as follows:

1 Where are we now?
2 What are we capable of?
3 What do we expect to happen which is outside our control?
4 What do we want to do in the next 5 years?
5 How do we go about it and what resources do we need to do it?
6 Is it realistic and specifically what do we do next year?

The results of these efforts are normally expected to be written into a comprehensive plan format, perhaps of the type summarised in Fig. 8.6. In the case of a multi-division company, each division would normally prepare a separate plan and that would be consolidated into a single company wide plan.

8.7 Why the logical approach is rarely followed

Despite the logicality of the above approach few plans involve the selection of a preferred alternative from a series of possible strategies, with the other strategies

Summary of assumptions, results of environmental scanning and
market forecasts on which the plan is based:
  (a) Political, social, fiscal, economic and business
     environment for the next five or more years;
  (b) Competitive environment and market forecasts for
     the next five years;
      user needs
      products and services offered
      sales trends and market shares
      marketing capabilities and methods
      plant locations and capacities
      technological capabilities
      earnings records and returns on investment
      key factors in success (location, outlets, quality,
        service, price, cost, performance etc.)
      competitors' actions and reactions

Analysis:
  assessment of performance vs the industry
  assessment of performance vs major competitors
  priorities for resolution of problems identified
  priorities for exploitation of opportunities identified

Basic commercial policies to be followed:
  statement of fundamental purposes and beliefs
  corporate objectives: financial, physical and non-economic

Product/market strategy:
  objectives
  plans for growth products/markets
  plans for products/markets that are static
  plans for products/markets that are declining
  new products/markets envisaged
  new product/market gap

Marketing strategy:
  product development
  distribution methods
  pricing
  promotion
  profitability
  share of market

Detailed marketing plans:
  market research
  product planning
  market planning
  selling
  sales promotion
  sales service

Functional support programmes:
  research and development
  manufacturing
  physical distribution
  systems and accounting
  organisation and personnel

Financial summary:
  contributions by product, area, market segment, period
  functional programme costs
  profit plans
  cash flow
  source and use of funds
  analyses of alternative sources of capital
  analyses of discounted cash flows
  analyses of returns on investment

Fig. 8.6 *Format for corporate marketing plan (from Sasson [13])*

forming fallback positions (see Eliasson [39]). Why should this be? Possibly because the number of alternatives 5–10 years ahead is too great to handle; or possibly because by the time it becomes obvious that the 'most likely' plan is not appropriate, events will have occurred to make the fallback plans not quite right either. Hence it appears to be more efficient to develop one plan, to continually review it, and where relevant modify it to suit changed circumstances.

8.8 Preparing a plan – the normal approach

How is the practical manager tempted to plan? Remember he will be very busy keeping this year's results on par. If he is working for a large company he will probably receive a broad economic, social and technological forecast from a planning department, perhaps interpreted in terms of what that means for the company. If he works for a small company that stage may be missing completely. He will compare any forecast received with his own interpretation of what he has read, heard from his contemporaries, and seen on television, and will then consider whether any of this has any new implications for his own operating unit. He may well discuss his ideas with his colleagues. Very often, by this stage, managers already have action programmes in mind for the following year, based on a feel for the market which will have been built up as a result of operating in that market, and as a result of discussions with colleagues and with superiors. Providing the above mentioned forecasts do not alter this feel there will be a strong temptation to produce a plan which expresses the expected outcome of these action programmes as performance targets, that is revenue, operating costs and capital expenditure – incidently these targets are often misnamed forecasts but they are not, they are a desired outcome which is considered achievable by following the proposed programme of action. These targets are then generalised into business objectives and linked back to the action programmes via strategies, and presented with detail financial statements as a plan. In other words the hoped for results of the predetermined action programme are moulded into looking like acceptable objectives.

An outcome of this philosophy is that while financial statements *may* be an accurate reflection of what is proposed for the first few months, they will be little more than simple projections thereafter. Lack of real forward thinking means that as the time horizon extends and the percentage of sales volume represented by new products increases, often to include new products and markets which have not yet been investigated in detail, there is a tendency to arbitrarily decide that the company will do reasonably well in these unresearched areas and to set apparently easy to achieve market shares. How often do managers remark 'we must be able to achieve a 5% market share'. It all looks so easy when it is 2 or 3 years away. Sales forecasts which are not firmly based should only be included as speculative, and with wide tolerance bands.

Most managers hold to their predetermined action programmes quite dearly and take steps to help ensure that they are preserved. As a result, they will tend to interpret and present the information which is available to them in a way which is favourable to these predetermined programmes. This may mean exaggerating the benefits of proposed moves, exaggerating market growth forecasts, diminishing the impact of competitor strategies, and stretching to the limit of what is credible the resources needed to achieve the stated performance targets. The disguise is often helped because the comprehensive nature of the plans which are prepared at this stage make it very difficult for senior managers to see the wood from the trees.

There follows a negotiating process during which senior management try to tighten up on what has been put forward, because they will be aware that slack will have been built into the numbers, because the plan proposer – the manager – knows he will later be judged by them. This task is more difficult when senior management have no direct operating experience in the business that they are controlling, as it is difficult for them to challenge the assumptions and conclusions proposed. Usually some tightened targets are imposed and the manager comes away to revise his plan to meet those targets. This rarely involves a fundamental reworking of the whole plan – there simply would not be time. Instead, numbers tend to be juggled, and action plans reduced in scope and cost to arrive at the imposed target. In large companies this negotiation and alteration process can be repeated four or five times as the plan is progressed up the hierarchy and back down again.

If the manager prepares well, is a good negotiator and has a good record of meeting previous plans, the imposed targets should be achievable within the imposed costs limits – if not, he has problems; although in a fast moving world there is often sufficient change during the following 12 months to make it relatively easy to justify quite large deviations from plans. In either case the whole philosophy has been one of actions first, targets (or objectives) last, rather than the logical objectives first, actions last approach described in Section 8.6. The preparation of alternative plans rarely forms any part of the process. The net result is a compromise between what top management want to achieve and what lower levels of management say they can achieve. As with most negotiations all of the parties are left with the feeling that their views have not been properly taken into account. The chances of the agreed figures corresponding with what the operating unit would have set down had they been an independent business is a matter for conjecture.

This type of process can be summarised as follows:

1 Most operating managements have decided prior to drawing up a plan what they want to do, usually as a result to informal discussions among themselves; and the plan objectives and strategies are set out to justify those predetermined action programmes.

2 Recognising the negotiating process to follow and that they will be judged by how close they come to meeting them, operating units set targets which have slack built into them, so that after the negotiations have forced on them tighter targets, they will still be achievable. Unfortunately, of course, the very fact that

they are often subsequently achieved reinforces top management's view that they were right and the operating units wrong.

In other words very little genuine long range thinking occurs. In part, this may be because most successful managers are pragmatists, and hence as a breed are disinclined to conceptualise. Perhaps more important, many managers are rewarded in proportion to how well they meet the current year's targets rather than for their ability to plan ahead. As a result much of what planning has to offer – the value of the process itself – is lost. Managers plan reluctantly, concerned to complete the job as quickly as possible so that they can get on with what they feel is their real task: that of day to day operation. Real attempts to increase the long term net worth of a company can be subjugated to managers' desires for job security and promotion, and perhaps a feeling that they instinctively know best.

The same process, if not quite so contorted, also takes place in many smaller companies. Certainly the information base is usually more limited, the time horizons shorter, the number of pages filled in less, and the number of iterations fewer, but the plans still tend to be based on the actions first, objectives last philosophy. Although senior managers usually will have had direct operating experience in the business that they control, and will have direct informal information channels into its markets (and this makes the negotiating process much tougher for middle level managers), the real value of the planning process, looking ahead with imagination, will be lost. For example, 'pseudo' planning is unlikely to help companies to recognise gradual change, and alternative methods of responding to it.

8.9 How the planning process can be improved

It is suggested that the key step is to improve management attitudes towards planning, and that this can be achieved in four significant ways:

1 by improving the level of understanding about how planning can help a company survive;
2 by pointing out how planning can help managers in their day to day activities;
3 by simplifying the process as far as practicable,
4 by introducing incentives for managers to plan.

8.9.1 Understanding how planning helps companies survive
The reasons why companies need to plan have been dealt with in Sections 8.1 and 8.2. The essence of the message is that planning enables companies to determine what actions they should take now which will ensure that they will be competitive in the future; whether that be in three months, six months, two years or ten years. The message is probably best communicated by referring to past situations where panic measures have had to be taken to maintain a competitive position because of a failure to look ahead. Thus long range planning involves noting and forecasting

major changes – in technology, in methods of distribution, in the economic cycle, in spending patterns, in customers buying criteria – and organising to meet them. It is not a matter of extending annual budget numbers to three years or five years hence, numbers which in any case are unlikely to be sufficiently accurate to have much meaning. However, it does involve determining the amount of cash that has to be generated now, in order to finance the above actions, be they developing new products, moving into new markets, acquiring new skills, introducing new production techniques or whatever.

8.9.2 *Helping managers in their daily activities*
Some staff find it hard to work within agreed action programmes because of the nature of their work. These are the people such as production managers, foremen, service engineers, buyers; personnel who spend most of their working time responding to the unexpected. They say that there is no point in planning, that things change too quickly. This may be true if one were talking of trying to prepare action programmes to cover every detail of every day but it is not true of broad plans which set overall targets and allow flexibility of individual action. The message must be brought home that setting target service levels, production through-puts, unit costs, buying prices etc. should help rather than hinder performance, and that broad action programmes are intended to provide a framework which will help managers make the right response to the unexpected. If one is confronted with a hold up because of unexpected roadworks, it is not possible to select the best route to circumvent them unless you know your final destination and know which alternative routes are feasible. The plan may be seen as a map to which is attached target journey times and fuel consumption. Selecting the final route is management's task.

Similarly, the foreman often needs to know the output he has to achieve this week and next week and the week after when he is juggling men between machines and jobs, so that he can decide what can safely be put off until next week. Even a relatively detailed action statement such as 'introduce computerised stock control by March 1' leaves plenty of freedom for managers to organise the detail of implementation and to alter that detail as the situation demands. Only if some overriding major problem arises which cannot be circumvented should consideration be given to changing targets. For example, the service manager may be faced with much longer calls than planned for. Having a target immediately draws attention to the fact that there is a problem. Is it because the service staff are not working as effectively as planned or is it lack of co-operation with customers or is the cause a design problem or a production quality problem? The first reaction must be to find the cause and put it right rather than to set a new target.

Thus planning helps managers in their daily activities by providing them with a means of judging their own progress and by removing the need to constantly refer to their superiors before taking routine decisions. As long as a manager meets the targets agreed via the planning process, he can assume that he is performing adequately, and that his superiors do not need to know in great detail how the targets were achieved. Without a plan a manager has to operate in a vacuum with no framework to relate to.

Planning also helps managers run their own departments more effectively by avoiding panic reactions to change, by generating stretching targets for subordinates, by delegating detail and by providing a means of controlling subordinates performance — in other words by providing all the benefits set out in Sections 8.1 and 8.2.

8.9.3 Simplifying the planning process

The planning process can be simplified by accepting, for the reasons given in Section 8.7, that it is better to prepare a single valued plan, to monitor the environment closely, and to modify the plan as the situation demands. To quote the Textron Company 'planning is not pouring concrete': plans can and should be modified when necessary.

One way of simplifying the process would be for top management to begin it by asking each department/division/unit manager to set their own objectives, to explain why they believe those objectives are sensible, to explain how they could be met by following various strategies, and to list the broad financial implications. This fact-based statement could be discussed with top management and logical conclusions reached about its validity. Based on these conclusions and the needs of other parts of the company, unit objectives and strategies, and sales revenue profit and investment targets, which were broadly compatible with the company's overall profit and return on investment objectives could be agreed. Freedom from unnecessary detail should encourage these early discussions to be open and make it possible to discuss the implications of alternative strategies before settling on one.

These discussions should be extended to include all the interested parties at all management levels. In general, the more people who are involved in the planning process, the greater will be the awareness of the problems, opportunities and uncertainties facing the company and hence the more committed and flexible the organisation will become. Freedom from unnecessary detail should also reduce the risk of strategies being vigorously defended simply because of the amount of work which has been put into their formulation — once a lot of effort has been put into an idea, people tend to become committed to that idea.

It is then possible to begin to generate action programmes to meet the agreed sales revenue, profit and investment targets. To make this possible, agreed financial statements for each part of the programme would have to be developed so that trade offs could be made. Approval of this final detail plan should involve matters of detail, i.e. do top management really believe that action A can be completed by 30th March and will only cost £7000, rather than matters of principle. Following the maxim of only adding detail when it becomes essential, should make the planning process appear less formidable, less of a ritual and of greater practical value.

8.9.4 Introducing incentives to plan

Thinking ahead in the ways set out in Section 8.9.1 is more likely to be undertaken if regular performance review meetings concentrate as much on longer term strategy as on current year's results, thereby forcing managers to allocate time to obtain and interpret the information necessary to make such discussions sensible. These review meetings should also use the plan as a control and judgemental tool, by continually comparing actual performance against plan, and asking for explanations of the differences. For this to be effective the levels of uncertainty that were attached to the information on which the plan was based should be specifically stated. Otherwise they will be forgotten and the figures in the plan will come to be considered as achievable under all circumstances. Managers will find themselves pressurised to improve upon results which fall well within normal probability bands and this will not encourage the open flow of information which is needed to make planning work.

Another incentive is to make managers aware of how planning can be non-motivating, because being aware of problems usually helps people overcome them. Typical problems are:

1   In order to end up with one viable plan various parts of the company often have to modify what they originally proposed. The discussion involved usually generates a good deal of friction and can lead to major differences, frustration and future lack of co-operation. Part of this problem is that managers of divisions or departments tend to look on other parts of the company as part of their external environment and hence something to be fought. This problem can be reduced by focusing attention on broad external issues which all departments can agree to be important, and by rewarding managers (by promotion and salary) who think and act in the interests of the whole company rather than only in the interests of their own department.

2   Close study of competitors and understanding how good they are can be demoralising. Similarly, facing up to real weakness is something many people find hard, and is often followed by a period of seeing weakness everywhere and no strengths.

3   Finance to implement the proposed plan may not be available and hence a less than ideal plan has to be fallen back upon.

4   It is easy to over-react to a changing world, putting off doing things because their impact is forecast to be short lived. The real question is whether they are worth while.

8.10 Implementing plans

A plan is a framework for action to help that action to be more effective, and therefore its preparation is of little value if it cannot be implemented. Preparing a new plan only creates the potential for profit. It is the implementation which generates profit. Implementation requires staff co-operation and that is often not forthcoming if people feel that something is being forced on them. People like to feel that they have control over their own destiny, and they like to influence the manner in which proposed changes are implemented even if they appreciate that they cannot influence the nature of the change itself. At higher management levels some involvement with deciding the nature of change is expected and it is the price of co-operation (democracy versus dictatorship). If a new plan requires a major shift within the organisation this should be appreciated and implemented progressively in as small stages as time will permit. The better the planning the more time there will be. In other words organisational development should be undertaken in parallel with any other development work required by the plan. For example, if it is planned to set up a new product group on, say, 6th November, it would not be sensible to wait until 5th November to appoint a new product manager nor to wait until 7th November to decide how the new product group will link into the rest of the organisation. All the people involved, not only those who will be part of the new group, but also those that will be affected by its existence, need to be given prior notice so that they can adjust to the new state and maybe suggest better ways in which certain things can be undertaken. People do not like surprise. They need time to adjust and to be reassured that the new state will not be threatening to them. In other words successful implementation of plans requires people to understand in what ways following a plan can help them to achieve their own individual objectives, as well as wider company objectives. Obviously their understanding will be coloured by whether top management reward those who make serious attempts to follow the action programmes laid down for them.

8.11 Planning – a summary

The logical sequence of steps in planning is summarised in Fig. 8.7. However the planning process is not a one way trip through the steps. Planning is a circular, progressive and iterative procedure. Good planning begins by using detail information and forecasts about each part of a business's activities, to generate new ideas. These ideas are then consolidated, generalised, and processed upwards through the hierarchy. At the top level they will form part of the input into the setting of broad strategies. These strategies are then expanded into increasing detail and are gradually worked back down the hierarchy with a few iterations on the way. The difference between what went up and what comes down should reflect the overall company purpose and the need to balance the separate activities of each part of the organisation. It is the difference between planning for the future well being of the complete company, and planning the future of only one section of the company in isolation. If these differences are to be supported at lower levels they must be accompanied by acceptable reasons which stem logically from the broader picture. It is these logical explanations which are so often lacking and which leave the impression of top management manipulation of the company.

Too few company plans and forecasts (1) reflect potential acts and responses of competitors, trade unions, governments and public groups, (2) take enough account

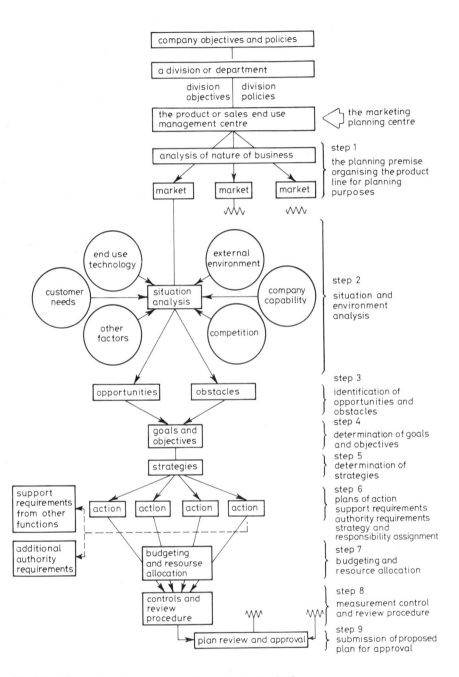

Fig. 8.7   *The market planning process (from Trowbridge [44])*

of sideways competition from other industries whose advances may make them future competitors, (3) concentrate sufficiently on what the company resources will allow to be achieved — realistically, (4) attempt to make good company weaknesses, and (5) delay the introduction of financial criteria until a broader look at the possibilities has been undertaken.

In general, companies plan to (1) stay in established markets and technologies, (2) maintain or improve past performance, (3) allow pockets of slack to build up in good times to be used as reserves in bad times, (4) concentrate on short term considerations in hard times even at the expense of sacrificing future growth (i.e. survival first). Standards of performance are always related to past performance. Plans are based on incomplete and incorrect information, to a large extent because information communicated upwards is deliberately biased because it is known that it will be used to control and assess individual performance. Major external changes are not planned for and instead early warning systems and systems to respond quickly to change are set up. However, where no structure is laid down for determining the response, companies become very dependent on the qualities and imagination of their top management. It is not true that in periods of great change formal planning does not work as well as in times of less change. In fact the reverse can be true because planning helps draw attention to that change, and it improves the early warning system. A plan is not a strait-jacket, it is a framework for action.

Chapter 9

Product Market Planning

9.1 What is a product market strategy?

It follows from Section 8.5.2 that companies should continually re-examine which markets to operate in and what products to offer for sale in those markets. Each product in each market is surrounded by a unique set of circumstances and problems, and as such represents a different activity and warrants separate consideration. Thus two products in a single market are considered to be in two separate product market areas (see Ansoff [45]). Each product market combination provides a strategic option which the company may choose to follow. Obviously not all of these options can be investigated in depth and limits must be set at an early stage in the planning process.

Within these limits, selection of preferred products and markets may be undertaken logically and the processes described in this book are summarised in Fig. 9.1. Using all the techniques described it is possible to:

(a) Determine which existing products need modification or replacement.
(b) Determine which market sectors are no longer worth servicing.
(c) Decide what scope there is to extend the existing product range.
(d) Decide whether existing products can be sold into new market sectors.
(e) Decide the nature of new products needed.
(f) Identify new market sectors that can be served.
(g) Forecast sales and profits for existing, modified, and new products and markets.
(h) Decide which products and markets should be given priority.
(i) Develop specifications for planned new products which can serve as design briefs and as a basis for business plans to exploit the planned competitive advantages in each product market area.

The strategy chosen will depend on the company's stance towards product development (see Section 10.5), its attitude towards risk, the availability of resources, and the rate of technological change in the industries in which it operates. Each product market is in effect ranked in terms of profit potential and risk, and those offering the best combination are selected as the ones in which the company should compete.

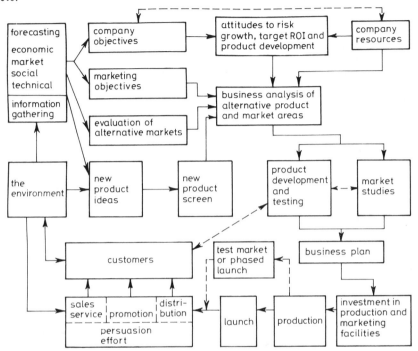

Fig. 9.1   *The product marketing process*

9.2 Evaluation of markets

The attractiveness of a market to a company is directly related to the structure of that market and to the competitive advantage which the company hopes to be able to sustain in that market.

In general, companies favour markets or market segments which exhibit the characteristics listed below:

1   The market is still in the growth phase. Demand is expected to continue for several years (relative to the forecast payback rate). Demand is not seasonal and does not fluctuate with the economic cycle. Demand currently cannot be, and is not forseen to be, capable of being met by substitute products.
2   There is under rather than over capacity in the industry and it is forecast that excess capacity will not arise in the forseeable future.
3   The barriers to entry are high and could be made higher as the market grows. The company has the resources to surmount the existing barriers. This state is usually associated with the existence of potential for economies of scale which so far have not been fully exploited.

4 Another form of barrier to entry is where the cost to customers of switching from their existing supplier is high or where the cost to customers of the product failing to perform as promised is high. In other words some parts of the market could be made into captive customers. Although this is the ideal state for an established company, new entrants must be very sure that they can offer sufficient competitive advantage to overcome this barrier.

5 The barriers to exit are not high. If it is decided to withdraw, close-down costs will not be high, or there will be a strong possibility of being able to sell out to another company. If the company is successful, low barriers to exit mean competitors are not so likely to fight to the last ditch.

6 The market should not be crucially important to existing competitors in the industry. If it is the only market in which they operate they are more likely to fight a new entry vigorously. On the other hand they may not have the resources, especially other sources of income, with which to fight off a determined campaign. On balance subsidiaries of large companies seem to give up more easily than totally committed companies.

7 The market is not dominated by two or three very large suppliers. The probability of being able to dislodge them will be low. On the other hand, a small market share might be attractive and the dominant suppliers may well welcome one or two smaller competitors.

8 The fixed to variable costs ratio is such that break-even can be achieved significantly below the expected sales volume.

9 The market is not dominated by a small number of customers who can exert considerable downward pressure on profit margins. Where the product forms only a small percentage of customers' purchasing budgets they are less likely to forcefully seek price reductions.

10 There is little history of production discontinuities in the industry arising from labour or material supply problems.

11 Supply prices are low; probably because the reverse of the characteristics outlined in 2, 4, 6, 8, and 9 apply to the supply industries.

12 It appears almost certain that the company is capable of establishing and sustaining a significant competitive advantage, whether that be in distribution, selling, promotion, production, design or a combination of all five.

However, these are not universally applicable criteria. For example, a company would normally find it attractive to enter a growing market because the market growth should enable the additional capacity which the company would bring to the market to be absorbed without causing any drop in prices, as well as providing opportunities for further increases in profits. However, entry to a static market may be logical and profitable if: (1) a company believed it had sufficient competitive advantage to enable it to operate economically at the lower price that its entry would produce, (and thereby force some of the existing competitors out of the business); (2) it was possible to forecast that the remaining life of the market in its saturation phase would be sufficient to yield a reasonable return on the investment made; or (3) it could be forseen that participation in the saturated market would provide an excellent lead into the market which was expected to supersede it.

Evaluation of the above characteristics should be undertaken by market research; in the proper sense of researching the market and how it works. In the case of markets where a company is already active it is possible to make use of continuously gathered information. For example, attention should be paid to:

1   the ultimate sales potential;
2   the immediate sales potential;
3   the sales penetration achieved by all competitors to date;
4   the total sales penetration achieved by the company's product;
5   annual sales achieved by all competitors;
6   the company's annual sales;
7   the percentage of sales which are replacement rather than new use sales,
8   the average product life.

Consider, for example, the following two 8 year old markets.

	Case A	Case B
Ultimate sales potential	£1000 m	£1000 m
Immediate sales potential	£600 m	£800 m
Total product in use	£400 m	£600 m
Total of company's own product in use	£180 m	£40 m
Total annual product sales	£60 m	£110 m
Company's own annual sales	£20 m	£20 m
Percentage of sales which are replacements	50%	20%

The ultimate sales potential and annual company sales are the same in both cases, but otherwise the situations are very different. In case A much of the immediate sales potential remains to be tapped. The percentage replacement sales is high and hence progress towards the immediate potential is slow at £30 m per annum. This should raise concern about whether the immediate potential is really as high as forecast, but if so, the reasons for the slow progress should be investigated. There is apparently considerable scope. However, the company is not maintaining its share of annual sales and these have dropped to 33%. This looks like a case for a revised product and a revised marketing strategy. In addition, providing the market need does not evaporate, there is considerable potential which it is not at present possible to tap but which may become a feasible proposition with new technology.

In case B, sales have risen rapidly and progress towards the immediate potential maintained. At the present rate the ceiling will be reached in a couple of years and hence the annual sales will drop dramatically as they become restricted to replacement demand. However 'our' company has been a late starter and is rapidly building up its share of annual sales and if this continues it may become strong enough to continue profitably in a stagnant market. This is a clear case for looking for new product uses and for planning for efficient low volume production so that other competitors can be priced out of the market as demand falls. It might be wise to plan a new product now, to be introduced ahead of the expected downturn, which will be both economic to produce at the expected lower volume, and will offer the maximum competitive advantage just at the time when demand begins to flatten and fall.

9.3 Evaluation of product and market related risk

Whenever a company introduces a new product there is a risk to that company that the product will not sell in sufficient volume to be profitable. The further removed the product from what the company currently produces, the greater the risk, because the existing proven capability or track record of the company is less relevant to the new activity. Not only does this increase the risk perceived by the buyer that the product will not perform as promised (see Section 9.4) with its associated downward effect on sales volume, but it also increases the chances of the company making other mistakes. The marketing department may for example misunderstand what the customer wants and lay down the wrong product specification (see Section 10.10); or the product development programme may not be able to meet the product specification; or the chosen promotion may not be appropriate; or the demand forecast may prove to be incorrect.

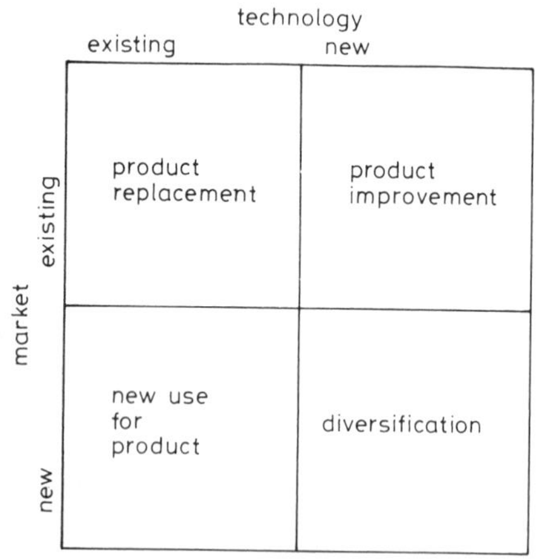

Fig. 9.2   *A simple market technology matrix*

Consider a single product company which finds itself unable to increase (or maintain) sales volume within its existing identified market area. The first reaction of such a company will probably be to check that its existing sales programme cannot be made more effective. If that proves to be the case, the company will be faced with four choices in order to try to increase sales.

These choices can be illustrated graphically by a simple matrix as shown in Fig. 9.2 (modified from Ansoff [40]).

In general companies succeed best by capitalising on their strengths and hence the first choice will be to keep within the existing market area and within existing technical know-how: that is, to replace the existing product with one which is fundamentally the same but offers greater utility to users; perhaps a more stylish model, or maybe one that is a bit quieter or easier to use. This is the least risk choice and customers can see that there should be little risk involved in buying the improved model. The second choice may be to find new markets for the existing product. Thus a computer previously used for payroll purposes could be sold for stock control or order processing. Sometimes slight modifications have to be made to the product to make it suitable for the identified new use. This choice is more risky than the first choice (see Section 9.4). The third choice might be to improve the existing product by introducing new technology in the hope of gaining a competitive advantage and thereby improving sales. The introduction of electric typewriters or, more recently, typewriters with limited memory capabilities represents such a step. In broad terms this third alternative is considered to represent an equal risk to the second alternative. They both involve taking one step away from the existing market and the existing technology. The fourth choice corresponds to the highest risk and involves changing both the technology and the market. This choice has been typified by the word 'diversification', that is, undertaking something completely different, such as a company producing castings moving into the production of electrical switches. However, interpreted literally as new market and new technology, the fourth choice could represent a less dramatic change.

What is considered to be a new market or a new technology will depend on the narrowness of the definitions used for existing markets and existing technologies. For example, if the existing product market were defined as low pressure PVC pipe for domestic use, then selling the same pipe for agricultural or industrial use would represent a new market, and producing and selling high pressure PVC pipe for industrial use would represent a new market and a new technology. On the other hand, if the product had been defined simply as 'PVC pipe', then all of the three alternatives would be included in existing market, existing technology. Product market definitions should be chosen in the same sort of manner as market segments (see Section 6.8), by setting boundaries around areas which require distinct competitive skills. If the number of alternatives attached to each element of the matrix becomes too confusing, companies should define a new matrix for each separable product market that they operate in. This means that if a company moves into a new element of the matrix, say via product improvement, then when the analysis is repeated at some future date, that improved product will become the existing technology—existing market element of a new matrix.

These four choices are illustrated in a slightly different manner in Fig. 9.3. The 'nuts and bolts' categories of product adaptation (existing technology—existing market), product modification (existing technology—new market) and product renovation (new technology—existing market) have already been dealt with. The other two categories would fit into the fourth element, new technology—new market, but would normally not be achieved directly as a result of company policy and

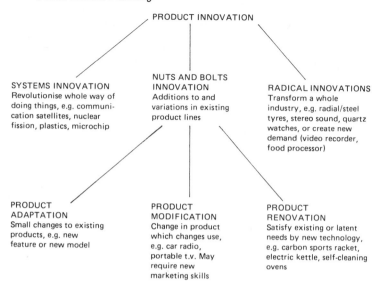

Fig. 9.3   *Product innovation (see Marquis [46])*
[Adapted by permission of the publisher from pp. 35—48 'The anatomy of successful innovations' in D. G. Marquis, 'Managing advancing technology. Vol. 1: Strategies and tactics of product innovation.' ©1972 American Management Association Inc. All rights reserved. This chapter originally appeared in *Innovation*, November 1969]

planning, because development projects are undertaken to meet a defined need, and not with the intent of transforming a whole industry or revolutionising a way of doing things. Such large scale possibilities only become apparent once the development programme is well advanced. At that stage, companies have to decide on the level of risk that they are prepared to accept in their attempts to exploit these large scale possibilities. At one extreme a company could try to use the development to attempt to dominate existing or even new markets. At the other extreme a company could ignore the larger possibilities and simply keep to the original objectives. In between lies a broad spectrum containing a mixture of own exploitation, joint ventures and licence agreements. It is a matter of balance between taking on a venture which is just too big for the company to handle, and extracting the maximum benefit from the new discovery. For all but the largest companies some form of licence agreement or joint venture with others already in the field is the most practical path.

The 2 × 2 market-technology matrix is a useful illustrative tool, but because each element is open to more than one interpretation it can become difficult to know where exactly to place a new activity. Adopting a 3 × 3 matrix (see Fig. 9.4) allows each element to be defined more closely and helps overcome this problem. The diagonal lines represent levels of increasing risk, as companies move further away from their existing activities. Sales might be increased by improved operational mar-

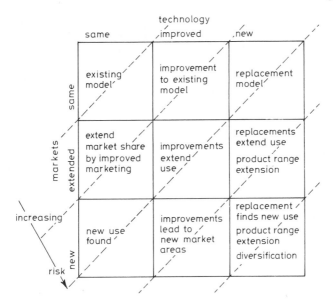

Fig. 9.4 *New activity choices and their risk*

keting; that is, by finding new users (customers) as a result of better selling methods, increased sales coverage, better and more advertising, more exhibiting and so on; or by entering entirely new market areas by finding new uses for the product. On the other hand sales could be increased by increasing the penetration of the market segments already served, by improving the existing product or by introducing an enitrely new replacement product. The value enhancement provided by either of these means may also lead to new market segments and/or entirely new markets being penetrated. An example of how the 3 × 3 matrix might be used in relation to computer aided draughting equipment is illustrated in Fig. 9.5. Other ways of using a 3 × 3 matrix are described, for example, by Severiens [47], who also links it to product life cycles, and by Johnson and Jones [48].

9.4 The buyer's risk premium

One of the reasons that risk increases as companies move away from what they currently undertake is that whenever anyone buys a product there is always a possibility that it will not perform as promised by the supplier. This possibility exists even when exactly the same product has previously been purchased from the same supplier, but the level of uncertainty will be much lower than if an entirely unknown product was being bought from a new supplier. The greater the uncertainty, the greater the risk in the buyer's eyes that he could pay more than the value to him of what he actually obtains. The difference between the value he hopes for and the value to him, should the product perform in what he perceives to be the worst possible way measures the extent of the risk premium that the buyer is paying. A buyer who has bought a particular product before and who knows that normally at least 95% of the expected value will be delivered, faces a low risk premium, whereas a new product from a new supplier could quite conceivably

| | | technology | |
	same	improved	new
same	computer aided draughting unit	easier to use, more versatile cheaper unit	more accurate line following improved definition 3-dimensional drawing
markets extended	education/ marketing persuades companies in more industries to buy	improvements persuade companies in more industries to buy	computer aided design/ manufacture
new	map drawing	illustration (for brochures or books)	process control

Fig. 9.5 *Application of a 3 × 3 risk square to computer aided draughting*

deliver only 50% value, or in some cases have no value at all, should it not perform as expected. The existence of this risk perception explains why, for example, a car main dealer can sell a secondhand car for several hundred pounds more than a small lesser known garage which in turn can sell it for more than a private individual.

Looking at this conundrum the other way around, it becomes clear that if the buyer is convinced that the product will perform as promised then he will be prepared to pay extra for that certainty.

Suppliers can reduce the risk premium perceived by potential customers in the following ways (in order of reducing effectiveness):

1 By demonstrating that other companies have bought the product and used it successfully in exactly the same way that the potential buyer intends to use it, e.g. a potential buyer of a new superfast glue wishing to bond rubber to rubber would like to see evidence of other companies using the glue to bond exactly the same types of rubber.

2 By demonstrating that other companies have bought the product and used it in a similar application, e.g. gluing different types of rubber or rubber to plastic etc.

3 If the product is relatively new, by demonstrating that the product replaces and utilises the know-how from a successful previous model — especially relevant to buyers of the previous model (e.g. fast glue) — or that a product of similar

design/use has been/still is produced, e.g. a glue which bonds plastic to wood or metal to wood.

4 By referring to a good overall reputation for delivering what has been promised.

5 By allowing a free trial (usually only possible with smaller items).

6 By guaranteeing a replacement within, say, 24 hours (but see below) or offering to reduce the invoice value, if the promised value is not forthcoming.

Although the newness to him of a product will be a major influence on the buyer's perception of risk, it will also be affected by the cost to him if the product does not perform as promised. Suppose a company is persuaded to purchase the latest 'super aero' compressor from an unknown company. One month after purchase it breaks down at 8.30 a.m. The supplier is contacted by telephone but he explains that his only service fitter is already out on call and will not be able to come along until 3 p.m. Even supposing that the fitter, when he arrives, is able to get the compressor working within an hour or two, rather than having to wait 2 or 3 days or even a week for a spare part, the buyer will have had a day's production disrupted. The cost to him of such disruption may already be greater than the purchase price saved by buying the less well known 'super aero' than an established brand. If that is the case

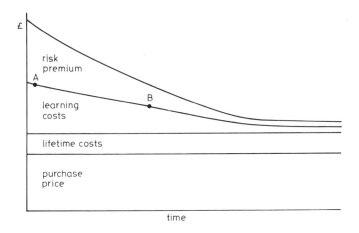

Fig. 9.6 *Perceived price of new products*
The scale of risk premium and learning costs has been exaggerated for illustrative purposes

it will be extremely difficult to introduce the 'super aero' to the market by means of a low price alone. In fact a low price may be counterproductive if it is read by buyers as a sign of uncertainty about product quality. The supplier may be more successful by trying to reduce the risk premium by guaranteeing reinstatement of air supply by some means within 2 or 3 hours. In the case of products where the risk premium is seen to be very high it may be necessary to provide the equivalent of a free standby compressor for a period of, say, 6 or 12 months until the new product has a proven track record of its own. Other examples of key equipment abound. Imagine the problems of trying to introduce a new material for sewerage pipe where, if it began to leak, considerable excavations would be necessary; or the problem of trying to break into the pressure vessel or defence markets. Reputation based on some previous success would be essential.

In addition to the risk premium, companies buying products which are new to them will be faced with the costs of learning how to use them in the most efficient manner. This means that the total cost faced by companies buying a product for the first time is much greater than just the purchase price (see Fig. 9.6). If the purchaser has direct experience of using a similar product, or if the product has been in use for some time and a general body of knowledge about it has arisen, then the learning period will be shorter than if the product is completely new, and the starting point on the learning cost curve might be at point B rather than at point A.

These considerations indicate why new products are often not bought as rapidly as their predecessors, and why the problems are worse for a company entering a new market area. They have little relevant track record to help them out. A somewhat better product is not enough; it has to be much better to overcome the buyers perception of risk. An alternative is to combine with a company who is already well established and well respected in the market.

The problem is compounded when really new technology is introduced. Not only is the perceived risk of it not working very high, but many potential customers will simply not know how to apply it to their circumstances. Considerable education and training will be needed before sales can be achieved and it is quite possible that customers will remain unconvinced for a very long time (e.g. vertical take-off aircraft or hovercraft or robots). The product is likely to remain in the introductory phase for a very long period and consequently the onset of a positive cashflow will be considerably delayed. The longer the time over which an investment remains unrecovered, the greater the chance of improved competitor products being announced which will make the attainment of a reasonable return on that investment impossible. In other words, with a very new technology, not only does the amount to be invested tend to be very considerable, but it is unlikely to be recovered on the first generation of products. This commitment to following the technology through should be clearly understood before the initial investment is made.

9.5 Towards a product market strategy

When drawing up a product market strategy attention is normally initially concentrated on existing products and markets, simply because they represent the lower risk options where a company has the most expertise and hence the opportunity to profit from that expertise. The objective is to operate in product market areas where a company can generate maximum competitive advantage.

Failing that, it is necessary for companies to move progressively outwards from their existing expertise into areas of increasing risk. Inasmuch that many studies of innovation have shown that it is the marketing problems which are the most common cause of failure and not the technical problems, it is probably better to give preference to known markets rather than to known technology unless the technology base is very strong. For example, a company making perhaps heat exchangers might consider that it could enter the air conditioning market relatively simply. All that seems to be needed is a compressor, an expander valve, some controls and a box, to add to the heat exchanger. However, in fact there would be a double competitive disadvantage. First, the company would be competing with a new product which did not have a proven track record and hence there might be some reluctance by customers to try it out. Secondly, the company would not have immediate access to a reasonable dealer network. Convincing the trade that the new product was worth supporting could be a greater hurdle than eventually persuading end users. Such an example also raises the interesting issue of whether it is wise to compete with one's own existing customers. Not only may the company not be successful with air conditioners but it may lose some of its heat exchanger business from existing air conditioner manufacturers.

Before any decisions are made it is most important to thoroughly evaluate the growth potential of new markets, and the ability of the company to generate and sustain sufficient competitive advantage to exploit that potential. The greater the competitive advantage the more likely it is that the choice will be successful. The actual choice will be circumscribed by company policy and will be largely dependent on where the company's major strength lies. If the strength lies in production rather than in selling, or in international financing rather than design, then the choice of product market should be made appropriately. Certainly the choice of which products the company will offer, and the choice of markets it will serve have to be made in parallel, with each product market representing a definably different area of choice.

Most companies do not produce and sell only one product. They try to ensure that the mix of products which they offer to their existing markets will maximise company objectives (usually profit), and they trade off increased sales volume against the costs of providing several products. Companies choose between the width of their product lines, that is the number and spread of product lines, and the depth of their product lines, that is the number of individual products in each line. The greater the product width the larger the number of market segments that can be served. The greater the product depth the greater the intended sales penetration within each segment. The range of choice faced at any time will vary with the size of the company and the size of the operation. Thus a large motor vehicle company may consider product width in terms of buses, lorries, vans, cars and motor bikes, and depth in terms of the number of models in each category, whereas a smaller company may consider product width in terms of different ranges of size of lorry.

Because on the whole it is more difficult to enter new markets than to introduce new products, companies tend first to increase depth and only to spread outwards when a significant gap starts to appear between growth targets and what can be achieved in the existing markets. Occasionally, of course, companies find themselves with such a significant technical advantage that they feel justified in moving into new markets in order to exploit that advantage, or because a great opportunity beckons.

Whichever product and markets are chosen, there will need to be continuous feedback to ensure that the circumstances on which the choice was based have not changed, and that the chosen strategy is still appropriate. It will be necessary to

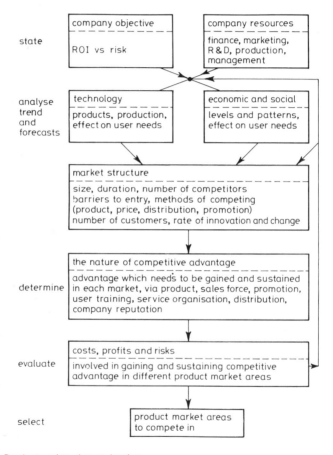

Fig. 9.7 *Product and market evaluation*

continuously compare market needs with what the company can best do and to draw attention to wherever there is a match. Ideally there should be more matches than a company has resources to develop, and only the best ones should be followed up; that is where there is a special technological lead, a special understanding or link with customers, or the marketing resources to enable a dominant market share to be obtained.

Diversification is the highest risk option and for that reason it has received considerable attention. It is the option where the procedures for evaluating the potential returns, and risks involved, are most widely applied. The procedures are exactly the same as for any other new or existing product market sector. The difference stems from the lack of relevant knowledge. Not only will the implementation of any plan be more difficult but the information base upon which the plan will be drawn up will be less sure. Reliance will have to be placed on formal marketing research and published data, because the valuable feedback element will be missing.

Diversification was a very popular method of growing in the 1960s and the early 1970s, but since then it has fallen from popularity because in many cases companies found that their lack of knowledge of new product market areas was such a great handicap, that they were never able to capture a significant share of the new markets. Although this may have been just acceptable in times of economic growth, in times of stagnation and depression many of the diversified operations have proved insufficiently efficient to withstand the increased levels of competition. Companies have found to their cost that on balance it is usually much more effective to take one step at a time.

The product and market evaluation process which has been described is summarised in Fig. 9.7. It really is a question of establishing exactly what the company capabilities are and of matching them with the key factors needed for success in different product market areas. Where a preliminary match is obtained it is necessary to examine in more detail the nature and level of competitive advantage which could be sustained and thence the costs, profits and risks of doing so. If the forecast results meet company objectives then it is worth considering the development of suitable products and marketing strategies.

9.6 The problem of product abandonment

Before leaving product market planning it is appropriate to renew consideration (see Section 7.3.6) of the problems involved in abandoning new products. More attention tends to be given to the problems of introducing new products than to the problems of abandoning existing products which are not to be replaced. Traditionally abandonment has been viewed almost entirely from a financial viewpoint, that is, is the product losing money and will it continue to do so, tempered by a consideration of opportunity costs, that is can the resources tied up in the product be used to achieve a greater profit elsewhere. Both are usually qualified by a sentimental attachment which grows up when a product has been handled for a number of years, and by the occasional need to carry a full line in order to maintain the sales of associated products. The argument is that some companies wish to buy all their bearings, switches or typewriters or whatever from one supplier, and will not buy from companies that cannot meet their full range of requirements. This argument is strongest for products which require servicing or require to be interchangeable. However, rather than relying on emotional subjective opinion, the potential loss of sales involved should be researched before a decision is reached.

In fact a structured approach should be taken to the whole question of abandonment by considering each of the following factors:

(a) Financial security — is the minimum return on investment required by top management being achieved? There is little apparent point in exercising great effort to achieve a return lower than that offered by the building societies. Clearly the further the return on investment is above the minimum, the less likely the product is to be abandoned.

(b) Financial opportunity — can the company's resources in terms of men, plant, money, distribution, and marketing tied up in the product, be used to achieve a higher return on investment elsewhere. For example, if production capacity were a limiting factor, the contribution per capacity hour freed could be compared with the loss of contribution from the product being considered for abandonment. However some resources simply are not transferrable and yield little monies if they are sold. In that case the opportunity cost may be nil and providing the marginal product is generating a positive cash flow there would be no financial reason for abandoning.

In addition, the risks involved in concentrating resources on a smaller number of products has to be assessed and compared with the risk related return being earned with the existing product. For example, a company may wish in the future to re-enter the particular product market being served by the product which is being considered for abandonment, and in that case the expenditure which will be needed to rebuild the customer base and the reputation to current levels, will have to be offset against the costs of continuing with a less profitable product. Obviously the decision will depend very much on how long it is before the product market is to be re-entered.

(c) Marketing strategy — if no alternative exists and some positive return is being obtained there would seem little point in abandoning unless the product is adversely affecting the company image. The need to carry a full line, market standing, market share, distributor agreements, stock levels, emotional involvement with the product, advertising, company image all need to be evaluated. Suppose, for example, that a product is to be deleted and not directly replaced because two other products in the line partially overlap with it. Salesmen may be disinclined to push what they consider to be less suitable products as hard as they push the product about to be deleted, and customers may feel that they are being fobbed off with second best. Customers who still have the product in use will want to be assured about continuity of servicing and spare parts. Deletion requires careful handling.

(d) Social responsibility — the main consideration under this heading is usually loss of jobs but sometimes it is the loss of important ongoing technical capability to the country as well as to company. In rare cases the loss of the product itself may be considered to be a social loss and any resultant publicity is unlikely to improve company image.

(e) Organised intervention — the abandonment of a product can sometimes promote official or unofficial union action or bring about government pressure. As with social responsibilities these arguments usually only apply where there is loss of jobs or the loss of what is considered to be an essential service.

It is important to logically think through all of the parameters and ramifications before a decision is taken. The decision need not be one of abandonment. Providing there is sufficient life left in the product market, it may be worth improving the poor product performance by a minor redesign (possibly via value analysis), by a facelift, by different product positioning, by different distribution or whatever. Sometimes a product can be sold to another company which has other competitive advantages which enable it to continue the product profitably.

The evaluation of mature products should not be left until they can clearly be seen to be in difficulties. Regular reviews of all established products are in order, so that the necessary decisions and actions can be initiated as early as possible. It is not good business simply to set the situation drift and to watch the product demand gradually dwindle. Letting the situation drift will almost certainly mean that resources are being tied up inefficiently (in terms of sales and promotional effort and in terms of stock and production capacity), and that when the end does come, customers will not be properly prepared and there will be loss of goodwill.

Chapter 10

Introducing New Products

10.1 The importance of new products

The introduction of new products is obviously a key part of a product market strategy. New products are introduced for a number of reasons, all of which are related to the need to establish and maintain a competitive advantage. The usual reasons are:

1 to replace an uncompetitive product or product range;
2 to extend the life of a product range;
3 to utilise unused capacity (production or selling);
4 to offset seasonal or cyclical factors;
5 to increase market penetration by broadening the product range;
6 to incorporate the latest technology (to reduce cost, to increase reliability, to improve performance, or to increase versatility);
7 to change product capability in line with changed customer requirements;
8 to take advantage of a new opportunity,
9 to take advantage of economies of development, production or marketing scale.

The importance of new products cannot be overemphasised; without them companies would quite quickly begin to run down (see also Sections 10.3 and 10.5), Particularly in the case of new technologies, where product life cycles are short, it is necessary to innovate and to replace uncompetitive products simply to stand still. In these circumstances all the new product capability of a company can quickly be absorbed by the need to replace or upgrade existing products. If a company is growing at the same time, the number of products it offers will have been increased. Before long the research and development facility will be unable to develop new products at the appropriate rate unless it too is growing in capacity. Unless this possibility is recognised and corrected, further growth will have to be achieved by introducing replacement products with a greater sales potential than their predecessors, or by expanding into new geographic areas, or by finding new users for the existing products, or by undertaking licence agreements, or by acquiring other companies.

10.2 Methods of innovation

Companies are not primarily concerned with invention, which normally relates to the conception of a new idea, but with innovation, which requires the successful commercial exploitation of a new or existing idea. Although much of the discussion about innovation is couched in terms of 'offensive' innovation aimed at increasing sales, much innovation is in practice 'defensive' and aimed at avoiding loss of sales.

To innovate it is not necessary to rely on a strong internal development department. It may be more cost effective to use the services of a commercial research and development organisation to undertake specific projects, rather than recruit extra R & D staff. A second advantage of dealing with an outside organisation derives from the fact that a formal contract to meet the defined product specification will normally be drawn up, and therefore any attempts to move away from that specification because of technical difficulties will be obvious, and therefore strongly resisted. Changes proposed by internal development departments tend to be resisted less forcefully, very often because no formal product specification has been drawn up to use as a control (see Section 10.10 and Skinner [23]). As a result, development which is contracted out often culminates with a product nearer to the original product specification than a product which is developed internally.

Another approach to innovation is to seek opportunities to obtain a licence to sell, or to produce and sell, the latest products of other progressive companies in the industry — although the choice is often restricted to overseas companies because of geographic competitive pressures. The licensor offers to provide the product and the technical know-how, and the licensee offers to provide knowledge, understanding and coverage of the local market place. Very often this is the quickest and best method of filling gaps between forecast sales and target sales (see Section 7.8).

Where companies wish to become involved in product production as well as selling then some kind of joint venture, with a new limited company being established under joint ownership, is often better than a straight license agreement. A joint venture combines the skills of the two companies and enables the financial burdens (and the benefits) of introducing a new product to a market to be shared.

On yet other occasions it will make sense to acquire a small innovative company which perhaps has considerable technical skills but not the financial or marketing resources to take advantage of them. Although acquisition appears to offer an immediate route to a new product or a new market, or a means of rapidly extending the coverage within an existing market, it is not without its problems. Most estimates place the failure rate, (in the sense of a below target return on investment), at well over one in three. Really successful companies do not wish to be taken over, and it is only those which have not been well run and either have generated insufficient revenue to finance the next stage of development or have encountered other operating difficulties, which will be readily available. If an

Table 10.1 Approaches to product and market development (based on Hill [49])

Internal development	Acquire specialists	Use external agencies	Acquire licences	Undertake joint ventures	Acquire companies
Advantages					
Maximum continuity and control of pace and direction	Extension of resources	Close control of direction, time-scale and costs	Select from part or completely developed products	Enables development to be undertaken which otherwise would be passed over	Immediate access to know-how and apparent time saving
	Control retained				
All know-how and profit retained	Development time reduced	Investment in facilities can be delayed until development known to be successful	Costs related to sales	Extends resources with ongoing gains in know-how via the the partner	Possibly the only way to obtain access to such know-how
	Profits and know-how retained	Profits retained	In case of proven products initial investment is low		Integration of resources may lead to other long term benefits
			Access to licensers know-how is gained		
Disadvantages					
Training can be costly	Search can be lengthy	Cost can be high but usually can be directly related to results	Lengthy search and negotiation process	Control and profits shared	Lengthy search and negotiation process
Progress inhibited by staff weaknesses and hence extended time-	Risk that past successes will not be repeated	Development know-how is not gained	Own further development restricted by		Really successful companies resist acquisition
					High initial costs and

scale and risk of development not being successful

Really original ideas may be lacking

Investment in facilities can be considerable

Risk of specialists leaving and of existing staff being upset

Effectively paying for the acquisition of facilities and know-how by others

licence and hence loss of control of product/market policy

Loss of profit via royalty

Own development capability may become neglected

high ongoing costs until the two organisations are successfully merged into one. Sometimes this is never achieved, with consequent loss of motivation and specialist staff

Problems of merging organisations leads to development delays and loss of profits for up to two or three years

Acquisition of unwanted staff and facilities

acquisition is forced through, the takeover price is likely to be greater than the normal valuation of the company, and this can tempt the acquirer to restrict follow on investment in an attempt to bring the total investment back in line with the original plan. Unfortunately, such restrictions may make the attainment of the planned sales volume impossible.

In addition, the takeover is likely to be resented, and this will delay the onset of efficient operations. The merging of two cultures is a difficult and time consuming business and the acquired company may not operate to its full potential for 2 or 3 years. Cash will need to be injected to compensate for the loss of revenue generation, as well as to finance the planned development programmes. The extent of the cash drain is often underestimated, although it can sometimes be partially offset by selling off those parts of the acquired company which do not fit with its future role. The extent of management attention needed to make an acquisition work is such that other areas of operation may suffer, and last, but certainly not least, customers may not see the acquisition as a good thing. A summary of the advantages and disadvantages of these approaches to innovation is given in Table 10.1.

10.3 Unnecessary innovation

Until recently it had been assumed that all companies require positive pressure to be exerted on them to encourage them to innovate. Such conservative companies only innovate when:

1 there are serious challenges, threats and instabilities in the environment;
2 these are brought to the attention of managers and consciously analysed, and/or
3 the control system reveals that the business is no longer as profitable as it used to be, and
4 organisational, technical and financial resources are available.

However, it has now been recognised (Miller and Friesen [50]) that, while many companies do fall into this conservative mould and if left to their own devices would innovate less, there are many other companies who have innovated successfully and who have built up a kind of innovation momentum, innovating more and more, sometimes past the point of diminishing returns. They innovate not to survive, but because the senior management enjoy the process and enjoy the challenge. These companies tend to be run by innovative chief executives who gather round them people of similar outlook and hence innovation becomes self-perpetuating. It is usually professionally trained engineers and scientists who are most likely to possess the knowledge and training to recognise the need for change and who possess the desire to innovate. These types of people are most likely to predominate in companies operating within the more rapidly changing and exciting technologies. These companies tend to possess good scanning systems and to be always on the outlook for change and new opportunity.

In these companies the emphasis of the marketing management task changes somewhat and should be aimed at bringing to light important inhibiting factors which will prevent every 'good' idea being followed up, and thereby automatically improve the innovation success rate and reduce the waste of resources. For this approach to be effective it will be necessary to encourage the company decision makers to take the trouble to analyse the information they receive, and to try to understand the underlying factors which will influence success and failure. Good control systems which bring to light the cost of past failures will be a great help in this respect. Very innovative companies tend to grow very rapidly, and as they grow the costs of failure tend to increase. Hence, unless the rate of failure can be restricted, these companies will run out of cash and will be absorbed into larger and more conservative organisations.

10.4 Organising for innovation

Successful innovation requires recognition of the fact that most companies tend to be organised to deal efficiently with short term problems, and while trying to maximise profits from existing products and services fits in well, innovation does not. The priorities and rewards of general managers and marketing managers are most likely to be related to current profits rather than to paving the way for the future. As a result it is often suggested that monies and management time spent on new product development might be better spent on improving sales of existing products. Certainly, problems with existing products should not be ignored because they are the means of generating the cash needed to keep the company in existence and to pay for the resources needed to develop tomorrow's breadwinners. The bread tomorrow argument is a common one and must be strongly countered. However, if a company is to survive it will need new products.

In general, innovative thinking flourishes where it is encouraged rather than criticised, where there is plenty of lateral rather than vertical communication, where there is plenty of interdepartmental transfer of personnel, where the company looks more at the future than the present, and where the company looks outward for opportunities rather than concentrating on internal problems. Innovation needs extra attention if it is to succeed, and that is precisely the reason why new product planning needs to be actively pursued at board level, and pressure brought to bear throughout the organisation to ensure that new products are properly developed and introduced into the operating units.

Many studies of the innovation process have been undertaken and in general (see Sasson [13] and Project SAPPHO [51]) they have shown that the characteristics of the more successful companies which the less successful companies do not have are as follows:

1 they make more use of market forecasting;
2 they are more familiar with target markets;
3 they understand user requirements better;
4 they concern themselves only with products whose launching costs are in balance with the size of the market and the scale of their production capacity;

5 they have better coupling with the outside scientific and technical community in the specialised areas concerned with innovation (e.g. they take licences, embark on joint ventures and generally tend to look outside);

6 they have better external communications;

7 they seek innovation more deliberately;

8 They encounter less opposition to innovation within the organisation on commercial grounds;

9 they employ larger teams at the peak of the development activity and achieve a shorter lead time from the start of a new project to the marketing of the product;

10 they benefit more from dependence on outside technology during production;

11 they give more publicity to their innovations;

12 they tend to drop products as the result of innovating others;

13 they devote more effort to educating users,

14 they employ greater sales effort.

Large companies tend to be more resistant to innovative ideas than small companies; partly because, as described above, the priorities of operating managements are short term, partly because professional managers, unlike entrepreneurs, are rarely adequately rewarded for risk taking (i.e. they are sacked if they fail but are rewarded little more if they are outstandingly successful rather than adequately successful), partly because innovation upsets the status quo, but mainly because in a large organisation so many people have to authorise an idea before it can be pursued that almost inevitably one of them will say no. The more innovative the idea the less its significance will be understood and the more likely it is to be rejected. History abounds with examples; aircraft companies rejecting folding undercarriages, Marconi rejecting Baird with his television and so on. Innovation seems to flourish best in small and unstructured organisations where there are not a lot of people whose job it is to say no. Many of the best new products launched by large companies have in fact been bought in from just such organisations.

Recognising that different types of people, with different values, cultures and priorities, are required for successful innovation, many large companies in the 1970s tried to splinter the innovative section of their organisation from the operational side (see Perel [52], and Radosevich [53]). The idea was that having identified the demand for a new product, the marketing and technical processes would be undertaken by a project team, under a new venture manager who would take the project through to launch, and who would have a direct link to top management — sometimes via a business development manager (or director), see Fig. 10.1.

In cases where innovation was directed at diversification, new ventures seemed to offer the opportunity to test the water in new product market areas before deciding to diversity into them on a large scale. Venture teams could be allowed to operate in chosen product markets for a year or so, prior to deciding whether or not to commit large scale investment. The direct operating experience in effect reduced the size of the risk involved. Should it have been decided not to diversify into the new area the venture could have been sold or closed down with relatively little financial loss.

However, most new ventures were not successful; large scale follow up investment was rare. Contributory factors seemed to have been:

1 Failure to appreciate how much time (5–15 years) and how much investment is needed to build a business from scratch.
2 Operational performance tended to be poor as a result of lack of experience and lack of scale. As a result the venture units lost out to mainstream business divisions in the competition for funds and this further reduced the rate of growth.
3 The recession in the late 1970s and early 1980s decided many companies to concentrate on their existing businesses, to conserve cash and to reduce risk. Hence small offshoots outside the main stream businesses were obvious targets for cuts.

However, the experience of running these types of new venture units did encourage many companies to establish multi-disciplinary project teams to control innovatory effort, and to that extent it has helped improve the success rate.

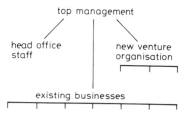

Fig. 10.1   *The hierarchical positioning of new venture management*

10.5 Scale of development effort needed

The rate at which new products are introduced will depend partly on the relative importance of the product in the marketing mix. For example, a company producing dog food probably does not have to worry much about updating the product as long as it is more or less edible; edible, that is, as far as dogs are concerned. The product will also have to look and smell reasonably attractive to dog owners. Companies producing dog food are much more likely to concentrate on distribution and promotion in order to attain a competitive advantage. On the other hand a company selling industrial boilers will have to concentrate on the product because potential customers will be careful to scrutinise the heat output per unit capital cost, and the running costs, and compare what is offered with competitive products.

The rate of new product introduction will also depend on the rate at which the technology is changing. Thus in the electronics industry the rate of introduction is very rapid, whereas it is quite slow in the case of metal cutting circular saw blades for example. Perhaps over-riding both these reasons will be the attitude of senior company management to new products (see also Section 10.3). The attitude towards product development will normally fall somewhere between the two extremes described below.*

1 The *pioneer approach.* Pioneer companies always aim to lead the field, to offer the latest technology and the latest production methods, and to introduce new products as soon as they are fully developed and tested, even if their predecessors are still selling well and have not recovered all their investment; on the basis that introducing a new product early will sufficiently enhance sales that the return on the total investment on the predecessor and successor products will be greater than if the introduction of the successor was delayed. Pioneer companies are also prepared to attempt to satisfy previously unforseen or latent customer needs (e.g. video recording). Sometimes they will use new technology to create a new way of satisfying an existing demand or even a different version of that demand (e.g. electronic games) or to fill needs that previously have been impractical or uneconomic to serve (e.g. computer aided manufacture).

2 The *follower approach.* Follower companies use well established technology and methods, very often copying existing product designs, and only aim at satisfying clearly established market requirements. The policy of such companies is to provide a reliable lower cost alternative to market leaders but with sufficient difference (and separate appeal) to take away market share from the market leader. The life of each product is often extended as far as possible — possibly with minor facelifts — in order to spread capital expenditure.

In general, pioneer products do pay off in terms of greater profit generation (see Davidson [55]). The market lead established before competitors introduce comparable products is not usually lost, enabling the extra revenue to more than offset the product market development costs. However, a pioneer policy requires an ability to absorb the cost of mistakes, both in terms of finance and image. A company which introduces too many new products that do not live up to expectations will soon gain a poor reputation and customers will not be prepared to try further new products that are introduced. A pioneer policy also requires ability to time new developments; not too early so that the product remains in the introductory stage for an unprofitably long period, but soon enough so as to be first. This tends to be very difficult to achieve in practice. Unfortunately, in high technology areas the penalties of failure are becoming high as the cost of innovative product development and launch rises, sometimes to a level which could jeopardise the financial status of the company itself. This trend towards high costs is leading more companies to consider joint ventures or to become followers.

The follower approach minimises risk and the level of capital expenditure required. Many profitable companies operate in this mode and their particular expertise will be in cost effective design, production, distribution or promotion

* Based on ideas from Ansoff and Stewart [54].

rather than innovation. These strengths are used to 'catch up' the pioneer companies. Following the leader requires a good task oriented development department which is able to quickly develop a competitive product at relatively low cost once it has been decided that a safe secure market demand exists. Timing is just as important as with the pioneer policy. If product launch is too early some of the pioneer risks will be run. If it is left too late too many competitors will have become firmly established to enable any significant market share to be quickly achieved (refer to Section 7.7.1). The first four reasons listed in Section 10.1 for new product introductions are the ones which are most likely to influence a follower company, whereas the second five will be most applicable to pioneer companies.

Finally, when assessing the development capacity which will be needed, allowance should be made for the fact that there will have to be quite a high degree of over provision of effort, simply because many projects will not succeed (see Section 10.6). Indeed, some projects will be dropped at quite a late stage, and some products which are launched will not be as successful as had been hoped. If more products than appears to be strictly essential are not being developed, companies get themselves into the position where they cannot afford any development or launch to fail, and this makes logical assessment of the product market position unlikely. At the extreme, many companies find all their hopes pinned on a single development programme.

10.6 Product development risk

The possibility of failure is something that too often seems to be forgotten as projects get under way, and members of the project team are blamed when a 50/50 project eventually does indeed fail. Worse still, the warning signs are ignored and the project continued long after it should have been abandoned. The losses are compounded. It is far better to accept that failure is possible and to plan accordingly.

If a higher risk project is to be undertaken, then, funds permitting, potentially less fruitful but lower risk projects should be pursued in parallel, to fill the gap in case the high risk project is not successful. If the products and markets being developed are crucial to the future of the company then wherever possible lower risk options should be chosen. High risk projects can only be undertaken with confidence if the resources required for them represent only a small proportion of the total resources available; otherwise the future of the whole company will be placed at risk — often a risk which is more chancy than the toss of a coin.

In an attempt to reduce the risk of failure, various systematic multi-stage approaches to product development have been proposed. One such is by Carson and Rickards [56], who propose a three stage process:

1 Search for opportunities.
2 New product development.
3 Commercialisation.

They suggest that the opportunity search should be preceeded by modelling corporate resources in three dimensions, in terms of raw materials, processes and markets. New opportunities can be identified by gaps in the periphery of the three-dimensional model formed by these parameters, or by extending the model along one or more of the axes. These opportunities can then be checked out in more detail, and a limited number of practical possibilities for product development identified.

These kinds of logical approach seem to be increasingly followed in the case of the development of new products. They are unfortunately not so often followed in the case of changes and improvements to existing product ranges, possibly because it is thought that the decision is less fundamental and that the case for going ahead is more obvious. However, funds committed to product improvement can be considerable, and it is essential to thoroughly evaluate the overall business effects of product changes and how they are to be introduced to the market place, if the changes are to be successful and properly accepted by customers.

The remainder of this chapter will discuss product innovation using the widely known headings established by Booz, Allen and Hamilton [57].

10.7 Idea generation

Many ideas for new products are generated following a study of market needs. Often the study is quite informal and sometimes almost unconscious. The 'study' may be a chance conversation with one or two customers, the reading of an article in a trade or technical magazine or an evaluation of competitor products at an exhibition. Many vital ideas are obtained from sales or service personnel who have used their contact with customers to find out what customers believe is wrong with current products and to find out what they believe will be required in the future. Where the same requirements are mentioned by several customers, they will be remembered and aired in corridors and in meetings until they either gain some support or are abandoned. Research has shown that up to 80% of successful new products are born in this way — as a result of intimate contact with customer needs and company resources. The suggestions will, again often unconsciously, take account of what the company is capable of, and will inevitably be largely directed at existing markets and technologies, or perhaps occasionally at market extension or technical improvements, that is the lower risk steps referred to in Section 9.3.

In a few companies the process is more formal. The formality is particularly valuable when consideration is being given to new product market areas, as it helps to make up for lack of direct experience. Formality usually takes the form of a committee who are made responsible for collecting relevant ideas (refer back to Section 4.18) from the sales force, development staff, other staff, exhibitions, the professional and technical press, market and technological forecasts, patent files, universities, other research organisations, overseas producers, competitors, consultants, government departments, marketing research studies and so on. Some companies successfully use suggestion schemes as inputs, but if these are to work the rewards to the idea originator must be substantial and demonstrably proportional to the value to the company of the idea.

If a market opportunity has been identified, but there is a shortage of ideas about how to take advantage of the opportunity, one of the more formally established methods of generating ideas might be undertaken. For example, 'attributes analysis' involves examining existing products and listing what is wrong with them from the customer's viewpoint. Attributes common to successful products are also listed. Consideration is then given to how best to correct the wrongs and to combine them with the rights. 'Brainstorming' involves forming a panel from a cross-section of interested personnel and arranging for them to meet at least two or three times in short succession. Two or three meetings are necessary before panel members are able to begin to think in the right way. At each meeting the panel chairman encourages a free atmosphere so that panel members are not shy about making even what appears to be idiotic suggestions. Those suggestions are not evaluated during these meetings. Evaluation is undertaken at follow-up meetings. 'Operational creativity' is a particular form of brainstorming where panel members are encouraged to talk around the subject area in the hope that ideas will emerge, rather than directly trying to think of those ideas. Unfortunately, the skills needed to successfully lead creative discussion are rare and group techniques can be expensive in terms of staff time.

Many ideas are not derived primarily from considering how to meet a market need, but direct from technical considerations. As a result of continued technical effort companies discover how to undertake production processes more efficiently or how to produce products with enhanced properties. The idea generating process is then working the other way round, and will focus on identifying how the technical breakthroughs can be exploited, that is, the new market needs and new market areas which will be opened up. This type of technology push occurs most naturally in industries where technology is developing rapidly and is in advance of market demand. New needs are satisfied before customers can recognise that the needs exist, let alone start to create a demand for them to be met. In some cases, by making technical advances it is possible to open up a whole new market by satisfying a latent need, that is, one which people were not actively aware of, simply because its satisfaction was not known to be possible.

As a technology matures and the rate of development slows, then customers begin to catch up technically and are able to think about and to formulate their requirements. Product development becomes market lead. In the transition period many companies keep thinking in the old way and introduce technically superior products which do not correspond with the requirements the market is now able to formulate for itself. Such products fail to sell well. It cannot be emphasised too strongly that a proper market study must be undertaken before product development is allowed to proceed beyond the early stages. Many companies have lost much money by ignoring this basic rule.

A particular form of user-based technology push occurs in the case of engineering companies who offer the capability to design and assemble one-off or small volume products. The new product ideas will come to the company from potential customers. These potential customers will approach the company because they are aware of its capabilities. The capabilities are in effect the 'product', and 'product' development is a matter of keeping the capability up to date and relevant to user needs. There is no point in being the best in the land at designing and assembling transfer machines if the trend of user demand is to move away from special purpose transfer machines towards more versatile equipment. Where the company also produces standard products, new standard products can often grow out of a special product designed to order. In that case the company has a head start in the form of a proven working design.

Depending on which research reports you read, apparently for every 70–100 new product ideas, only 10–15 will be worth pursuing beyond the initial screen and only two or three will be launched. Of those launched only about half will achieve an adequate return on investment. It is clear that whatever approach is taken to idea generation, many hundreds of ideas will be needed if companies are to ensure for themselves a succession of profitable products. Ideally ideas will be generated from parallel market and technical considerations but usually one or the other will predominate. It does not matter which, as long as both are properly taken into account during the screening process.

10.8 Screening

Having generated an idea, it needs to be examined to see if it is worth pursuing further. Examples of the criteria which might be used in the screening process are given in Table 10.2. However, more simply, the following three essential requirements should always be borne in mind, because unless at least one of them is satisfied a new product stands little chance of success. To succeed a new product must:

1 satisfy an existing need more cheaply;
2 satisfy an existing need more fully (i.e. better performance, reliability, versatility etc.);
3 satisfy a latent need at a price people will pay.

New product screening is best undertaken by a committee of between three and six people who can represent the major company departments and a cross-section of hierarchical levels, so as to minimise the risk of narrow thinking. Unfortunately, whatever the exhortations to the contrary, the views of the senior members will predominate and so they in particular need to be chosen for their openness of thinking. The accept/reject decision criteria at this stage come down to 'can our company develop a product which it can sell in sufficient volume and at a sufficient price which will provide an adequate return on the investment in that product's development, production and marketing', and 'can the company finance the development, the product launch and the initial production losses during the 1—5 year period which it is likely to take to move the idea from product development to profitable sales'. For example, if for some reason a company was having to reduce its level of debt, an otherwise good project which had high start up costs and an extended payback period might have to be passed over for a less worthwhile project with lower start up costs and a more rapid payback. It is also necessary to assess the risks of failure for the reasons mentioned in Section 10.6.

Probably over half the ideas will be rejected after a fairly cursory discussion. It will be obvious that the idea is not appropriate for the company. The remainder will require a somewhat longer appraisal and normally someone will be asked to generate some broad brush information about market appeal, market growth, forecast sales volume, forecast market share, technical feasibility, development costs, production costs, marketing and distribution costs, and competitive pressures. It is often easier to develop a new product than to develop a new market and so it may be more effective to look at the company's ability to market the product before looking at its technical ability to develop and produce it. However, if the product is an extension of an existing range, or clearly fits within an existing marketing network, then the technical assessment will assume priority. If the product is only par with what is available competitively then the company must have other compensating advantages to offer.

The evaluation should take account of the fact that the time and funds needed for development always seem to be underestimated, and multiplying estimates by a factor of two often seems to bring them nearer to the correct figure. The time value of money is normally also taken into account. Inflation aside, a cash inflow this year is worth more than exactly the same cash inflow next year, because cash received this year can be reinvested to obtain a higher cash flow next year. The time value of money is equivalent to the extra cash flow that can be earned as a result of that investment. Thus long term projects should eventually yield a higher return on investment during their profit making years than short term projects. This does not equate to excessive profits but simply to earning sufficient monies overall to make the investment economically worthwhile.

There will always be a strong tendency to lean towards new products which are needed to defend an existing market position, probably because of the investment which has been made in establishing that position. While the risks will be less than moving into less established areas, and the target return can be lowered accordingly, keeping the arguments logical may well encourage the company to begin to move into new and more profitable areas, rather than remain in their traditional markets until they have actively begun to decline.

A number of comprehensive checklists have been produced to help keep the idea screening process as logical as possible. They are based on the concept that each of the factors which will influence the success of a product should be listed, weighted in proportion to the degree of that influence and then rated (by the product development committee) in proportion to the competitive advantage which the company expects to achieve. Taking as an example from the simplified list

Table 10.2 *Specimen new product profile (adapted from Skinner [23])*

Factor	Necessary	Desirable	Contra-indications
Market characteristics	Not more than 60% saturated Growth rate at least 5% per annum	Less than 30% saturation Growth rate 10 +%	Over 60% saturated, coupled with growth rate of more than 15% per annum
Target sales volume (year 3)	£X000, to achieve target ROI	2 × £X000	Market share of more than 25% required to achieve target
Return on investment (year 3)	15%	20%	Capital costs uncertain
Production facilities	Capacity available. Supply lines clear	Technically compatible with existing lines	Unfamiliar technology
Competitive advantages	Comparable with existing competitive products on cost/benefit analysis	Points of superiority Lower cost	Competitors firmly established with major marketing strengths 'Single-line' competitors dominate market
Service facilities		Could be serviced by present staff with minimum extra training	Unfamiliar technology. Heavy expense in test equipment

Sales or distribution		Could be sold by existing sales force through present distribution channels	Necessitates a major change in sales and distribution methods
Sales promotion		Contributes positively to company range	Detracts from established image
Finance	Capital available. Puts no undue strain on company resources	Fits present pattern of company dealings (sale, rental, credit terms etc.)	Involves financial hazard outside existing expertise
Administration	Administrative costs must be capable of accurate assessment	Fits present methods of administration and accountancy	Involves completely new administrative procedures

Table 10.3

	Weight	Rating	Total
Market factors			
Product appearance	2	5	10
Product performance	5	3	15
Product durability	3	2	6
Product maintainability	1	5	5
Initial price	4	2	8
Life costs	2	4	8
Market growth	4	5	20
Cyclicity of demand	3	2	6
Total (marketing)	–	–	78
Financial factors			
Fit with existing operations	5	3	15
Development costs	4	3	12
Development time	3	2	6
Likelihood of development success	5	4	20
Patent protection	4	2	8
Investment in production facilities	5	2	10
Investment in marketing facilities	4	1	4
Launch costs	4	3	12
Expected profit margins	5	5	25
Total (financial)	–	–	112
Grand total	–	–	190

shown in Table 10.3, 'fit with existing operations', a new product which can be sold by the existing sales force would be rated higher than one which needed some extension of the sales force, which in turn would be rated higher than one which needed to be sold by an entirely new and separate sales force. Once all the factors have been rated, the ratings are multiplied by the weightings, and if the grand total falls below some predetermined cut-off value, the idea is rejected.

The length of the list of factors to be considered is a matter of choice and some lists extend to several pages, and some are so long that they involve inputting the ratings into a computer so as to make the arithmetic easier. Many different methods of numeric rating have been proposed and anyone interested in studying these further should look them up in texts on marketing, innovation and product development. For instance, one of the methods proposed by Toll [58], distinguishes eight main criteria:

1 performance factors;
2 stability factors;
3 growth factors;

4 assimulation factors;
5 marketing factors;
6 development factors;
7 production factors,
8 legal factors.

Each criteria is in fact the heading for a long list. Although a long list should ensure that no significant factor is overlooked, a major drawback is that at the early stage of a proposed development most of the questions cannot be answered; the criteria cannot be rated. There is unlikely to be any reliable marketing research at this stage, as customers are notoriously unable to offer sensible judgements about a product which is still an idea, about something they cannot see. In some cases it will be necessary to develop some form of prototype before any worthwhile views can be gathered. However, the main danger is that too much credence will be attached to the numbers. The weighting and the rating, and in particular the cut-off point, are all matters for subjective judgement. These judgements will be uncertain, especially in areas where the company has had little direct experience. Indeed, evaluations of the same idea by the same people spaced, say, 2 months apart, are unlikely to produce exactly the same numerical result. One might lie just above the cut-off point and the other just below. There is also a tendency to wish to change the predetermined cut-off value if an idea which is strongly supported by several influential members of a company, falls just below the existing cut-off value. The best way of using these methods is to keep them simple and to treat them as a decision aid rather than as a decision making tool. On balance they are probably of greater value at the later decision points in the decision making process than at this early stage.

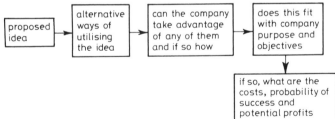

Fig. 10.2   *The new product idea screening process*

Ideas which pass the cut-off criteria will be taken on to the next stage. It may prove useful to re-evaluate discarded ideas from time to time as circumstances change. For example, although it may not be possible to meet an identified market demand at a saleable price with current technology, progress over the following 2 or 3 years may make an economic design feasible. The screening process can be summarised as shown in Fig. 10.2. It should be remembered that the purpose of screening new product ideas is to avoid wasting time and resources on those ideas which are least likely to prove successful. It is not intended that the winners should be identified at this stage.

10.9 Business analysis

Ideas which successfully pass through the initial screening should be subjected to a more formal appriasal before very much money is committed to their development. Should time be of the essence then development work could be allowed to continue while the business appraisal was being undertaken, but as soon as the analysis is complete a formal review should take place, preferably under the chairmanship of the chief executive.

The purpose of the business analysis is to forecast sales volume of the new product, the security of those sales forecasts, the profits which should be generated, and the costs which will have to be incurred along the way. Sales growth of innovative products is almost always overestimated. Sales forecasts must look secure for the planned product life and be based on market needs rather than on temporary factors, such as competitors who have fallen behind with their own product development or who are currently employing a poor marketing strategy but are in the process of updating. The entry of a new competitor is often the spur which provokes them to tighten up sufficiently to make the forecast growth impossible to achieve.

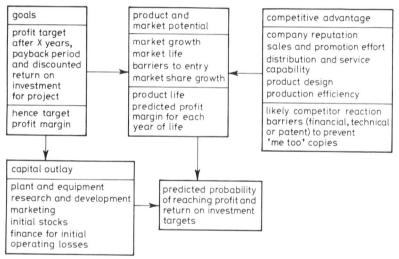

Fig. 10.3 *Business analysis*

Typical criteria used for business analysis are outlined in Fig. 10.3 (see also Fig. 9.7). The appraisal should also take account of the fact that studies into the failure of new consumer products (Angelus [59]) revealed that the major causes of failure were:*

(a) Little or no perceived product advantage from the customer's viewpoint — 56%.

---

* Reprinted with permission from the March 1969 issue of *Advertising Age*. Copyright 1969 by Crain Communications, Inc.

(b) Poor product positioning — 32%.
(c) Bad timing — 16%.
(d) Poor product performance — 12%.
(e) Wrong market for company — 8%.

In the case of industrial products 'little or no perceived product advantage from the customer's viewpoint' can usefully be restated as 'insufficient perceived advantages to offset the risk of using an untried product'. This is the largest cause of failure and arises because many companies fool themselves into believing that they are offering a better product. They fail to perceive the potential disadvantages. It is only by asking customers whether they would be prepared to pay a price premium for a new product that it is possible to discover whether it is seen as being better than what is currently available.

It can be helpful to present the results of business analyses on a standard appraisal form, because that enables the information to be presented in a standard way, which, once it is familiar, will be readily understood by the decision makers and will help them to assess what is being proposed, and to compare it with what has gone before. At a minimum the report should include:

1 a definition of the product and the market;
2 background on how the company became involved;
3 a market appreciation showing potential, penetration etc.;
4 detail product description and competitive advantages/disadvantages;
5 non-product competitive advantages and disadvantages;
6 a sales forecast, up to 5 years;
7 assessment of resources needed over the 5 years and leading up to the launch, and hence a financial assessment;
8 a clear statement of the risks involved (that is the sensitivity of the planned results to external influences);
9 an action programme covering development and launch.

Any financial forecasts should be subject to some form of sensitivity analysis to indicate how the values might change should business conditions change.

Product ideas which do not overcome this hurdle need not be abandoned. It may be possible to part develop them and to sell them to companies which are better placed to market them competitively, or the missing resources needed to attain a competitive advantage may be gained by combining with another company in a joint venture.

10.10 Development and testing

An outcome of the business appraisal should be a detailed product specification which interprets the market needs which have been identified (performance, price etc.) into a form which can be used as the target outcome of the design process.

The product specification should be prepared in consultation with the design department so that both parties are clear about what is to be achieved and why. The purpose of such liaison is to move the designer away from thinking purely in terms of function, although, of course, achievement of specified functions is an essential aim of design, towards thinking in terms of the qualities or attributes that the users are expecting from the new design. Thus the function of a keyboard may be to input signals into a computer, whereas the attributes associated with that keyboard are more concerned with the speed and ease with which it can be used.

Once the specification is agreed, it should be used to monitor the development process. Frequently requests are made to change the product specification for technical reasons, but before any change to that specification is agreed, the marketing effect of any such alterations must be researched, otherwise it would be too easy to end up with a product which would not sell, and the blame would rest squarely with the marketing department.

Prototypes should be thoroughly tested as part of the development process, both under controlled conditions and in conditions as close to the expected field conditions as can be achieved within the company. Further field testing of prototypes is a matter of choice, balancing the problem of secrecy and delayed product launches, against the risk of not discovering the inevitable flaws in the design which will only show up under field use. Real users will find snags that company personnel will not, simply because company personnel will automatically circumvent the snags and will be scarcely aware that they are doing so. Even users chosen to undertake field tests tend to treat prototypes more carefully than they would products which they have bought, and which are guaranteed in some way. This problem is easily solved where one is not evaluating a complete new product but only part of an existing product. It is probably legitimate in that case to incorporate the new part into a limited number of samples, and to carefully record to whom the relevant products are sold, and to monitor the results. If there are any problems then a particularly fast back up service or exchange scheme will have to be organised. In the case of very expensive plant and equipment the only way of undertaking any sort of field trial is to make it clear to initial customers that the product is very new and therefore it is being sold at a preferential rate, but with a first class back-up in case it fails to perform as expected. In the case of very major problems it may be necessary to offer another product in exchange. In all cases, successful field trials can be used to provide a preliminary track record which may be referred to when the product is officially launched.

A major problem with field trials of industrial products is that it is rarely possible to cover anything like the huge range of operating conditions which will be found in the market. If this were to be attempted the trial would become so large and costly as not to be worth doing. Hence typical uses, or the most strenuous known uses, have to be sought out. However, this is often not possible and field trials are often restricted to a company's longest standing customers, so as to minimise the problems of secrecy and the potential loss of confidence that will arise if the prototype proves unreliable or otherwise undesirable. For most technical products development cycles are sufficiently long, and the complexity of information which has to be gathered is sufficiently great, that 'tight' security is not essential, except perhaps to avoid the extreme of having a prototype fall into competitor's hands. In addition, time is rarely so crucial that a product launch cannot be delayed for a field trial. The most expensive stage to discover a mistake, in terms of cash and reputation, is after the product launch. Costs of checking and double checking are small in comparison.

Psychologically, the problem with field trials is that they come near the end of development projects, and if the results are negative they will cause projects to be delayed, and much of the development work to be repeated. However, the cost of delay and some redesign is low compared with the cost of launching a product which will not stand up in use. Think of the effect on company reputation. On the other hand it is often cheaper to leave trivial faults built in and to develop the sales strategy accordingly, rather than delay the launch and spend money trying to design out every single fault. It is a difficult decision to decide, especially in an era of broader and more expensive product liability, what can be acceptably — across the market — be left in as a known fault. All known faults can of course be put right at the first 'revision' stage.

Another common reason put forward for not undertaking trials is that many field trials are successful and logically therefore not worth undertaking. The better the new product appears to its proponents the greater will be the resistance to field trials. However, the reason for carrying out the field trial is to uncover the unexpected, and hence the surer one is that a field trial is not necessary the more certain it is that it really should be undertaken.

A field trial is not the same thing as a limited launch. A limited launch may be used in addition to a field trial to check that production equipment is working properly and to build up a track record prior to the main launch. In fact a limited launch usually forms a more realistic trial, with products being sold and used on a normal basis. Should there be any choice in the matter, initial sales should be restricted to customers for whom the effect of teething problems will be minimal and easily righted, and who may also provide future sales references. For many industrial products the need to undertake a deliberate limited launch is not very great because the rate of adoption by the market is likely to be relatively slow, providing time for product, production and marketing deficiencies to be put right during the introductory phase.

Whichever path is chosen it will be necessary at some stage to finalise upon the design. Practical difficulties will be encountered in the development stage such that the product which emerges will not be so universally good (i.e. have all the advantages) anticipated at the idea/business analysis stage. Hence further market studies are essential to check previous forecasts about demand and profits, although, providing it is planned for, less product advantage need not lead to product abandonment. Field trials may sometimes reveal that the product has been over-designed, that is it offers more than most customers are prepared to pay for, and in that case the design should be simplified.

The company now has to decide whether or not to launch the new product. The decision is normally taken by top management, not only because of the direct financial implications — in some cases the total investment up to this stage may represent as little as 30% of the total projected investment (see Fig. 7.7) — but also

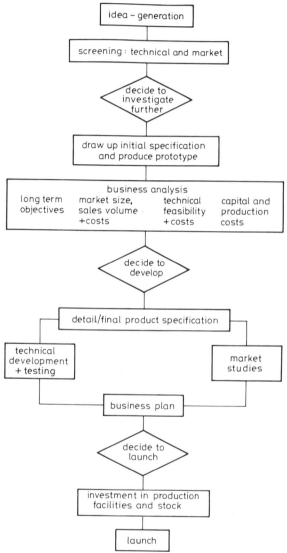

Fig. 10.4   *The innovation process*

because a failed product will have an adverse effect on a company's overall reputation and that could affect sales of its other products. This is the final major decision point in the product development process which has been described in this chapter. The process is summarised in Fig. 10.4.

10.11 Product launch

Product launches are usually associated with very active product promotion; promotion aimed at creating sufficient product awareness and interest to provide the sales force with enough enquiries to follow up, to make the initial sales targets realistic. In small industrial markets all that may be needed is a launch to the sales team, who will introduce the product to their existing customers. Direct contact is often able to generate more than enough enquiries for the introductory phase of the life cycle. This is often also true of product replacements where there should be a long list of existing customers to contact – unless of course the replacement has been left so long that the customer base has diminished significantly. However, in larger markets some back up – a press day, press releases, advertising – will be needed in order to create a sufficient volume of enquiries.

Whatever their scale, product launches should be undertaken as thoroughly and as professionally as possible, because if the launch is poorly done and the product fails, no one will be sure whether it was because of the poor launch or because the product fails to meet market requirements. It is better to launch well and then it will be obvious if the product is no good. A launch is more likely to be successful if:

1 The market sector which most needs the product (i.e. will value it most highly) is identified and the launch concentrates on that sector, and the reasons why the new product will be highly valued by that sector.
2 The product is only launched when it is fully developed and tested.
3 Considerable efforts are made to reduce the risk perceived by potential customers (see Section 9.4) and to induce maximum trial.
4 The costs and time-scale of the introductory phase are not underestimated.

The business plan should have included precise sales targets for each target market segment; e.g. customer category A: £X000 sales after 3 months: £(X + 10)000 after 6 months etc.

It is possible to set warning and pull out levels in a manner similar to that used by quality controllers. Should sales fall to the warning level a very careful investigation should be undertaken, and if no means can be found to improve the situation, withdrawal or complete replanning of the product will be necessary. Should sales fall to the pull-out level, unless it was obvious that the poor sales had been caused by a temporary problem which was already or very nearly solved, the product should be withdrawn before further losses are incurred. In practice, as the emotional commitment to the new product is by this time very high, few new products are killed off in one blow. Instead they tend to be gradually starved to death with less and less resources being made available for their production and marketing, until death is seen as inevitable and the final blow can be administered.

In many cases launch dates are fixed in the expectation that all the various aspects of the activity will come right on the day. Some of them inevitably will not; enough brochures will not be ready, salesmen will not be fully briefed, service arrangements will not be complete, demonstrations will not be available as hoped for and so on. Planning via critical path techniques is probably the best hope. Each department will be able to see how its efforts interrelate with those of other departments and particularly if there is an interdepartmental launch team, it is more likely that the various departments will communicate their problems to each other and possibly suggest ways of solving them. As with product development, the prime errors tend to be (1) unrealistically underestimating the time needed to complete the tasks in a normal workday atmosphere, and (2) setting unnecessarily tight launch dates — sometimes set to coincide with a major exhibition or simply because someone has committed themselves publicly. It is more important that the product is launched right, so as to shorten the introductory phase, than to be a slave to unnecessary deadlines.

Although it can help dilute competitors' publicity, launching at an exhibition does not necessarily obtain more publicity for a new product. In fact the effect can be less than launching at another time, as the impact may be lost among the counter publicity from competitors, and in any case most industrial buyers are unlikely to buy a brand new product at an exhibition, as they will have been unable to think about and evaluate it properly. Usually a launch creates a large number of leads, sufficient to keep salesmen busy, and therefore an even larger number of leads as the result of launching at an exhibition could be an embarrassment. It is probably better to exhibit the product sometime after it has been launched, using exhibitions to reinforce initial demand, rather than rushing the launch to meet an exhibition deadline.

An associated mistake is to launch a new product publicly before the sales force has been fully trained and has become knowledgeable enough to sell the new product effectively. This knowledge is best communicated individually or to small groups rather than to a mass audience. If the sales force is fairly large it is probably most efficient to thoroughly train area managers and to leave the responsibility for training individual salesmen to these area managers, possibly with one of the development team on hand to answer queries that the area manager is not yet able to cope with.

In some (large) companies the product development group will handle the initial launch and only pass the product to the established sales team once initial sales are established. This approach is followed to try to avoid the new baby being lost in the mass of established products and possibly die through lack of attention. Salesmen are unlikely to give as much time to a new, hard to sell product as they will to the established profit-making lines. At the other end of the spectrum, sales staff are sometimes pressurised into giving priority to a new product. However, the extent of any loss of sales of established products must be carefully assessed if this path is followed. Some middle way needs to be found.

In the case of industrial products there can be a long time-span between becoming aware of a new product and the decision to buy it, possibly because a formal trial is being undertaken, possibly because financial sanction is required, possibly because experience of other companies is being looked for, or simply because it is not clear how best the new product may be used. This is particularly true for capital goods where buyers are reluctant to try really new products and initial sales are likely to be very slow, and are best considered as a form of extended field trial. Thus once initial awareness has been created, further high rates of promotional expenditure are not likely to be cost effective and a less intense but sustained campaign should be followed until the growth phase is reached. The timing of the second front, that is in effect a relaunch at the start of the growth phase, is crucial. The selling message can now be reinforced by reference to user experience and for that reason is more likely to be believed. If the second front is started too early, much of the effort will be wasted, and if it is left too late, the onset of growth will be delayed and valuable income lost. Accurate timing is dependent on tracking sales volume and looking for signs of that first turning point (refer back to Section 7.2).

Chapter 11

Pricing

11.1 What is price?

When goods or services are transferred from one party to another it is necessary to set an exchange value. The seller seeks to influence that value by increasing the competitive advantage he offers as described in Section 1.11. The exchange value is usually measured in monetary terms as the price that the buyer will pay to gain ownership of the product.

The concept of price is somewhat complicated in industrial markets because the final price charged is rarely the published price. In many cases there will be no published price whatsoever and the two parties will agree on an exchange value by individual negotiation. Where a price list does exist, discounts will normally be allowed, proportional to the size of the order, or the cumulative order value, or the size of the customer (and hence his ordering potential) or the place of the customer in the supply chain (distributor discounts), or in return for ordering well in advance of the required delivery date, or very often to match the customer's perception of the value being offered to the price asked (i.e. to get the order). Discounts are supposed to reflect the economies of scale of the supplier but in practice tend to be chosen to match competitors' pricing structures. In some cases discounts are deliberately set at different levels to those offered by competitors so as to attract orders of a particular size.

Very often customers will not purchase a standard product but will order some combination of the available options and extras which will require a unique price to be calculated and agreed. Sometimes the agreed price will include an exchange element, such as a formal or informal agreement to place further orders of a certain size, or agreement that the seller will in turn make reciprocal purchases from the buyer, or provide some other goods or service which can be used directly by the seller or sold onwards to a third party. Barter of this kind is particularly common when selling to countries which are short of 'hard' currency, and local produce — often agricultural or mineral — rather than cash has to be accepted and sold onwards.

Price is thus the main, but not the sole, means of setting the exchange value of a good or service between two parties.

11.2 Pricing goals

Price is one of the four elements in the marketing mix (see Fig. 1.3). Of the four it is the only one which actually provides revenue to the seller rather than adding to his costs. Price is not an independent variable, and its setting is dependent on the setting of the other elements of the marketing mix and on the general economic and competitive climate. In general the other elements of the marketing mix are manoeuvred (for example, to increase product differentiation, see Section 6.5) in an attempt to maximise price, or at least the difference between price and unit costs. Thus the normally accepted pricing goal is to maximise profits, but to do that it is necessary to establish a relationship between price and volume, and as we shall see in Section 11.4 that is not easily achieved. As a result, other pricing goals are often adopted, namely:

1 Target rate of return on funds employed — measured after tax, this is usually 10–20%, (depending on the nature of the industry), in order to ensure ongoing competitiveness and liquidity. Companies tend to target pre-tax return on funds for different product lines at between 20% and 100%.

2 Target profit margin — this is a substitute for target rate of return, where experience has shown that a given range of profit margins produces a satisfactory return on funds in the industry in which the company operates.

3 Meeting the competition — this is frequently used as an easy way out, but if it is used blindly it can give up the use of price as a positive control element in the marketing mix. The prices to be met are not only those of the immediate competition but those of substitute products (see Section 4.4.1).

4 Generating cash — should the liquidity position of a company be in jeopardy cash inflow may be more important than profit margins. Sometimes the costs of holding stocks can be such that it will pay to sell off stocks at or below cost.

5 Discouraging competition — once a strong market position has been established it is a good idea to keep prices low enough to discourage new competitors from entering the market; that is, high enough to make an acceptable profit from an established business, but not high enough to encourage newcomers to risk the costs of starting up.

6 Target sales volume or market share — these targets are adopted if it is felt that a company's long term competitive position requires immediate profit to be foregone in order to increase sales volume. Price advantage can be combined with other available competitive advantages to attempt to gain the lions share of a particular market. This policy is often termed penetration pricing. Once the lion's share is achieved, price can sometimes thereafter be eased upwards. Reaction from established competitors must be planned for. An extreme form of this type of policy is elimination pricing where a company tries to price so low that it will force all or at least a large percentage of its competitors out of business.

7 Gaining prestige — many customers associate high price with quality. Classic examples are perfume, fashion clothes, and restaurants, but many engineering

companies use the same technique, pricing high to imply product quality, delivery reliability and so on. It is especially effective when it is difficult to objectively compare the performance of competing products, and price is used as a substitute yardstick. Obviously a prestige price has to be accompanied by a product which looks the part and which is promoted and sold accordingly. Sometimes companies deliberately price above the competition to keep volume low, in the knowledge that some people will be attracted by rarity value, but this is not common with engineering products.

8 Promoting products – in this case low prices are offered on a temporary basis in an attempt to persuade potential customers to place a first, second or third order, in the hope that they will be sufficiently impressed to place subsequent orders at the normal price. In the case of newly introduced infrequently bought goods, temporary low prices can be used to persuade a significant number of users to try the product and establish that crucial track record. An associated idea is to use 'loss leaders'; that is, a single product in a range is deliberately priced low in the hope that it will be bought and liked, and thereby stimulate sales of the other products in the range. However care must be taken that this does not create pressure from customers to reduce the price of the rest of the range.

9 Stimulating the sales of complementary products – products which are used together have to be priced together as sales volume will be interrelated. For example, cheap instant cameras can be used to stimulate sales of high margin film or cheap original equipment sales used to stimulate high margin spares sales. However, whole life costs are increasingly being taken into account both by customers prior to purchase and by equipment manufacturers before placing an order with component suppliers. Thus some manufacturers now insist that their components suppliers commit themselves to a reasonable spares pricing policy before they will sign a supply contract, as they are aware that high spares prices will have an unfavourable impact on their own reputation. Complementary promotional pricing also applies where the purchase of a particular brand (say of computer) makes the subsequent purchase of different brands difficult, because of system interchangeability and compatibility.

10 Keeping production capacity fully utilised – that is by 'off-peak' or 'marginal' pricing. Off-peak pricing is usually applied where there are high fixed (usually capital) costs and low variable costs, and where demand fluctuates in some regular manner, e.g. electricity supply, or transport. While demand is low, rather than leave facilities idle and receive no contribution towards the fixed costs of owning those facilities, it is better to try to stimulate demand by pricing the product at some level which is greater than the variable costs of making it available. For example, if the fixed costs of owning a ferry averaged £10 000 per day and the costs to actually run the ferry were £800 per day, then providing the service were priced to produce a sales revenue in excess of £800 it would pay to run the service. However, this means that at times of peak demand the price has to be set not only to recover the total daily cost of

£10 800, but also to make good the 'losses' incurred when demand was low. Similarly, companies with surplus manufacturing capacity can sometimes fill that capacity only at a marginal price, which does not recover all of their fixed costs. The dangers of filling capacity at marginal prices is that subsequent opportunities to fill the capacity at normal full cost price cannot be pursued.

11 Keeping colleagues happy — internal pressures often exert as much influence on the final price as external market pressures. Price setters in a company are subject to a multitude of group pressures (see Oxenfeldt [60]). The production department may press for a high price, the sales department for a low price and accounts for a logical cost plus price. The price setter will lean towards the views of whichever group he most wants to be associated with or to impress, or the group held in most favour by senior management — unless it is clear that his superiors value a fair minded independent approach which is seen to balance the various opinions.

11.3 Price tends not to be used aggressively

Despite being such a direct contributor to profits and having such a wide range of potential uses, advertised price tends not to be used aggressively by companies operating in industrial markets, and it is often set in a fairly perfunctory manner on a cost plus basis and within what is known to be the normal range for the product being marketed. Industrial companies often prefer to attain their competitive advantage from the other elements in the marketing mix. For example, very few advertisements for industrial products mention price, preferring instead to emphasise the other elements in an attempt to influence the exchange value. While many incentives cost less to provide than the value placed on them by customers (e.g. installation help which costs £100 to provide may be valued by customers as the equivalent to a discount of £120), care must be taken that the reverse situation does not occur, there being little point offering £15 worth of free service if the customer equates its value to a £10 discount.

List prices tend to be used to set the long term position of the company within the market (see Section 11.7) rather than as a short term response to fluctuations in market conditions and demand. Even where price reductions (or discounts) are offered during negotiations with individual customers, this is usually done not to attract the customer in the first place but to avoid the loss of a prospective order. In other words price tends to be used defensively rather than aggressively. This preference arises for a number of reasons, namely:

1 Customer reaction — price is closely linked with expectations and reputations (see Section 11.2 [7]). In many cases price is not the most important parameter used to assess the value of what is offered, with customers judging it more important to buy from the supplier offering the most reliable delivery, or the best quality or the greatest product range, and so on. In fact price is often used by customers as a measure of the likely dependability of a potential supplier. As

a result, publicly anyhow, prices are often set to place the product in the competitive price league (see Section 11.7) in a position which is consistent with the suppliers' overall promotional strategy. This leaves companies free to adjust to market conditions and to the bargaining power of individual customers by less visible means, such as discounting or the offer of free delivery, extra installation help, an extended guarantee or improved credit terms.

Another aspect of price and reputation is that customers tend to believe that products from reputable companies are more likely to meet the prepurchase description of the product than is the case with a less reputable company, and hence it is worth paying a price premium in order to deal with them. This process can be very clearly seen in operation when a new restaurant opens. Initially it has to charge prices which represent exceptional value for the standard of service provided, in order to attract customers, who hopefully will spread the word that this restaurant offers exceptional value and thereby start the process of building up a good reputation. As the reputation spreads and the clientele grows prices can be gradually raised, such that although some of the initial clientele will be lost, a sufficient volume of customers will be retained to keep the restaurant busy. There is no virtue in pricing so low that demand exceeds capacity. Conversely, there is a limit to the price premium which people will be prepared to pay, and once that limit is passed sales volume will decline if prices are raised further.

Even where companies have worked hard to differentiate what they produce from that of their competitors, customers do not always perceive these differences as strongly as hoped. This seems to be particularly true in markets where there are price bands (see Section 11.4.4). Unable to differentiate sufficiently closely between the value offered by different brands within each price band, customers tend to assume that the slightly more expensive brands are in some undiscernible way slightly superior to the cheaper versions. In that case they are likely to base their final choice almost on a whimsical basis; maybe there is something about one product which attracts them more than the others — which makes them feel good about buying it. This does apply to engineering products, where buyers, faced with largely comparable offers from suppliers, may, for example, place a contract with the company whose salesman they get on with best.

This means that if companies change their prices the volume response may be quite unpredictable, because by changing their established pricing patterns they would be transmitting signals to customers which would be contrary to their established image.

2 Competitor scrutiny — existing and potential competitors are always trying to estimate the cost and profit structure of one's product lines. Existing competitors will be anxious to match or better the value offered, and potential competitors may be encouraged to enter the market if the profit being earned seems high. Price is one of the most visible of all the competitive variables and hence price changes will be rapidly detected and responded to. Changes to the other elements of the marketing mix may take longer to detect and the responses longer to organise.

3 Time lags — in many industrial markets there will be long time lags between price changes and the resultant changes in sales volume, partly because of the existence of long term contracts, partly because changing supplier may require a procedural change (i.e. assembly or quality control) or even a design change, and partly because companies do not like to break established supplier–purchaser relationships (see Section 12.10.4). In the intervening period the selling company will have to finance its price reductions without the benefit of a commensurate sales increase.

4 Public opinion — even if a strong patent or market position enables a company to consider a higher price, it could also attract unfavourable publicity about so-called 'excessive profits', sometimes to the extent of persuading customers to place their custom elsewhere as soon as a suitable alternative becomes available, or adversely affecting the sales of sister products. Sometimes the publicity can attract government attention and interference, to the extent of trying to impose price levels from outside the industry.

5 Executive perception — attempts to maximise profits by whatever means go hand in hand with high risk. Boards of directors and shareholders tend to get more excited about the quality of management if profits start to fall below fore-cast levels rather than if they rise above them. As a result it tends to pay executives to minimise risk rather than to maximise profits, and that often means keeping prices within the normal accepted competitive range.

6 Price–volume relationship — it is extremely difficult, as will be explained in Section 11.4, to establish a firm relationship between changes in price and changes in product sales volume, with the result that the effect on profits of changing prices can be extremely uncertain.

11.4 Price–volume relationship

If it were possible to plot sales volume against price for a given product, pricing would be simple. For a range of prices it would be possible to read off the sales volume, calculate the sales revenue (price × volume), determine the operating costs and hence calculate the profit. Normally companies would choose the price which corresponded to the highest profit.

The slope of the volume–price graph is termed the price elasticity of demand (E) and is equal to $-\Delta V/\Delta P$, see Fig. 11.1. Thus if $E = 1$ a 10% reduction in price would increase volume by 10% and if $E = 0.5$ a 10% increase in price would cause only a 5% reduction in sales volume. The demand for a product is termed 'elastic' if a small price change produces a large change in volume ($E > 1$) and 'inelastic' if a large price change produces a relatively small change in sales volume ($E < 1$). In general the demand for products will be elastic if customers are unable to perceive significant differences between competing products (see Section 6.5), if the frequency of purchase is high (see Section 12.2), and if the unit cost is high. The demand for products will be inelastic if they tend to be unique, if purchasers believe them to be highly necessary, and if demand exceeds supply.

However, the concept of elasticity must be applied with care, because, as can be seen from Fig. 11.1 the value of E will vary as the price of a product changes. As normally used, it applies to the value of E within the accepted competitive price range. Outside these limits the effect of price changes would have to be reassessed. In addition, the value of E may well vary from country to country and therefore exporters would need to repeat their assessments accordingly. However the main reason why the concept of elasticity has to be used as a thinking aid rather than as a price rule is that for the reasons set out below, plotting an accurate price volume curve is very difficult.

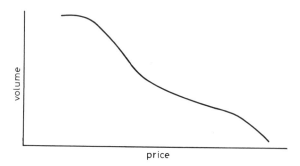

Fig. 11.1   *Illustration of price elasticity of demand*

11.4.1 Companies cannot systematically change prices

It is not practical for a company to charge one price this week, and another price next week, and another price the week after that in order to collect the necessary data to plot a price volume curve. In addition, time lags (see Section 11.3) make it extremely difficult to choose the right moment at which to measure the sales volume associated with each price. If measurement is left for several weeks in order to reach a steady state then the influence of other variables on sales volume is likely to become more significant. A less satisfactory way of arriving at a price volume curve would be to plot the price and volume of competitive products, and in some subjective way correct for differences in competitive advantage, but this is unlikely to be very accurate.

Perhaps the most practical alternative to monitoring actual price–volume changes, is to question customers about their likely reaction to product price changes. One such method (see Gabor and Granger [61]) involves presenting the product to a cross-section of customers and potential customers, and asking them whether they would buy the product if it were being sold at prices $P_1, P_2, P_3 \ldots P_n$, chosen to cover the normal price range for the product. The percentage of those questioned who would buy the product at each price is recorded on the buy–response curve, as shown in Fig. 11.2. At prices which are considerably below the normal product price range a large percentage of respondents may not wish to buy the product because they would instinctively feel that it was below the level at which such a product could be reliably produced – in other words either the product or the back up would not turn out to be what it purported to be, or the supplier would soon become bankrupt and the supply dry up. As the price asked is increased, a greater percentage of respondents will consider the price to be reasonable and would therefore affirm that they would buy. At higher prices still, an increasing percentage would believe that the price no longer represented good value for money and therefore they would not buy the product. Although the resulting curve does not represent a true price–volume relationship, it does at least give an idea of the price sensitivity of the product; very sensitive products having a very small hump with volume falling away sharply, and less sensitive products having a broader hump with volume falling away less sharply. Obviously this method is more appropriate for small easily displayed products than for large products or services, where reliance would have to be placed on description rather than on direct display.

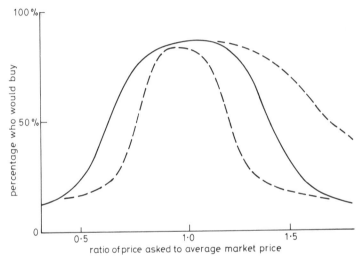

Fig. 11.2   *Buy response curve (see Gabor and Granger [61])*

When the method is used to price a new product, rather than display or refer to a prototype, it may be more appropriate to use the one or two competitive products which most closely match what is to be offered — partly for security reasons and partly because customers find it easier to answer questions about a product which is available and has been used, rather than about something whose performance has to be taken on trust, based on what those undertaking the survey say it will do.

11.4.2 A large number of interdependent variables affect price
Even if it were possible over the course of several weeks to change prices and to record the accompanying volume changes, one could never be sure that the volume change was caused only by the price change. During those weeks competitors may have launched a new product or changed their promotional campaign or their sales strategy or their discount structure; the economic climate may have altered, or even

the number of people away on holiday or away from work sick may have changed and influenced the sales volume. Although it is possible to correct for changes in these variables, the level of accuracy is not likely to be very high. Thus even if some price–volume relationship could be established at a given moment in time, perhaps via the buy–response curve, the influence on volume of these other variables will change over time and therefore that relationship will only hold true for a limited period.

11.4.3 Influence of industry wide prices

Companies operating within a specific market are more likely to be concerned with price relative to the price of competitors than with absolute price. The sales volume of a product may not be sensitive to industry wide price changes but may still be very sensitive to competitive price changes (e.g. petrol or steel). In these cases it is not possible in the short term for customers to stop using the product category, or even to use less of the product, in response to a price increase. However, if the industry wide price change remains in force and customers become confident that the price differential relative to substitute products will be sustained in most forseeable circumstances, then they may take steps to change to a substitute product. At an industry level, the volume response would considerably lag the price change which initiated it. For example, a general drop in the price of steel would have little immediate impact on the volume of steel consumed as customers would need time to redesign their products to incorporate steel rather than some other material. This makes the establishment of a relationship between price and volume even more complex.

11.4.4 Existence of price bands

In some industries there are clear examples of price bands — top of the range models may cost say between £5000 and £6000, mid-range models between £3500 and £4500 and bottom range models between £2750 and £3250. A product price of say £4750 would be seen by the market either as a low price top range model or as an expensive mid-range model. In the latter case there certainly would be little incentive to buy, and in the former case the cause of the low price might be interpreted as poor quality, poor back-up service, or lack of versatility, rather than efficient manufacture and marketing. Price bands become established because one supplier, seeking to be competitive with another probably very successful supplier, prices his comparable product very closely to that of his rival. So as not to be left out, a third and fourth supplier follow suit, until all the suppliers in the market are pricing within a relatively narrow range. Gradually that range becomes established as the band within which competitive suppliers will offer their products, and once formed, such preconceptions about what a product should cost are very hard to change, although it is possible via a sustained and hence costly promotional campaign. The efficient manufacturer who can genuinely offer his products below the accepted ranges may find his sales volume adversely rather than favourably affected. As a result of price banding, the price–volume curve may be discontinuous as illustrated below in Fig. 11.3.

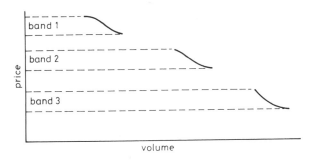

Fig. 11.3   *Price bands*

11.4.5 Link between price and reputation

As indicated in Section 11.3 [1], changes in price can often produce unpredictable sales volume changes. For example, where companies are well established, small price increases often do not result in a reduction in sales volume because existing customers are often reluctant to break an established buyer–seller relationship (see Section 12.10.4). It is difficult to predict the size of price rise which is needed to set off a reduction in sales volume, especially as it will be affected by the manner in which the increase is announced to customers, and the degree to which it can be linked to cost increases.

In addition, as indicated in Section 11.3 [3], any change which does occur is likely to occur gradually rather than immediately. This again makes it difficult to clearly link price changes with volume changes.

11.4.6 Influence of discounts

Very few industrial products are sold at list price, (see Table 11.3). The discount offered to different customers can vary widely (from 2% up to 50+%). Sometimes sales forces are issued with a series of guidlines which relate the size of discount that can be offered to a number of factors (see Section 11.1). Where these guidelines are made known to customers, it is theoretically possible to calculate an average price which could be used for price–volume predictions, but this is not possible where the guidelines are kept secret or where salesmen are free to negotiate individual discounts to whatever level is necessary in order to obtain an order. Thus the general existence of complex discount structures makes it more or less impossible to meaningfully associate a given price with a given sales volume.

11.5 Price–profit–volume relationship

For most established industrial products reducing an existing price is unlikely to increase profits because sales volume will not increase sufficiently to compensate for the loss of profit margins. Consider for example a product priced at £100 with a unit cost of £75, having a sales volume of 1000 units and hence earning a profit of

£25 000. If the price were reduced by 5% to £95, the sales volume would have to increase to 25 000/(95 − 75) = 1250 units, that is a 25% increase ($E = 5$) in order to maintain the £25 000 profit. The volume increase needed to maintain profits will vary in accordance with the initial profit margin as shown on Table 11.1. Of course the relationship is not quite that simple because unit costs normally decrease as volume increases and therefore profit margins will increase somewhat, but not normally sufficiently to maintain overall profits. Clearly, where the demand for a product around its normal price is very elastic (in this case > 5) then a price reduction within a limited range (until the value of E changes) can be profitable. However, in many markets price reductions are likely to be followed by competitors and therefore, because it is price relative to the competitors' prices rather than absolute price which has the greatest effect on sales volume, a price reduction will inevitably lead to lower profits.

Increasing the price of products for which demand is inelastic should substantially increase profits in the short term. Thus, if in the foregoing example $E = 0.5$, a 5% price increase to £105 would reduce sales volume by only $2\frac{1}{2}$% to 975 units, and profit would increase to £(105 − 75) × 975 = £29 250. All other things being equal, it can be shown that the price corresponding to maximum profit increases as the price elasticity of demand of a product decreases. However, unlike the response to industry wide price increases, the response to individual price increases tends, in most markets to be elastic. As a result it is difficult to increase profits by increasing price alone. Price increases have to be accompanied by increases in customers' perceptions of the value offered, and therefore increased profits will only accrue if that perception of value increases by an amount greater than the cost of achieving it.

11.6 Cost-plus pricing

Given that it is very difficult to relate sales volume and profit to price, it is not surprising that companies turn to simpler methods such as 'cost-plus pricing' and 'matching the competition'. Taking cost-plus pricing first, it would seem relatively straightforward to calculate unit costs and then to add a target profit margin to arrive at a selling price. However, as unit costs vary with volume, that begs the question of what sales volume should be chosen when calculating price. Suppose a company is faced with a first year's sales forecast of between 1000 and 1250 units. Cautious businessmen may favour calculating the price on the basis of 1000 units, but this may lead to a price which is too high to enable those 1000 units to be sold. In that case it may be better to take a risk and to calculate costs on the basis of 1250 units in the hope that the resulting lower price will help ensure that the higher volume will be sold. Extending this idea, second year sales volume may be forecast to be between 1250 and 1500 units, third year sales volume to be between 1400 and 1600 units and fourth year sales volume to be between 1500 and 1650 units. Why not then take a bigger risk and price on the basis of the third year's mid-volume, that is 1500 units.

Table 11.1 Relationship between price reductions, sales volume increases and profit (modified from Stapleton, [62])

Initial profit margin	90	80	70	60	50	40	30	20	10
Price reductions as a % of sales	Sales volume increase (%) required to maintain profit contribution								
1	1·1	1·3	1·5	2·0	2·1	2·6	3·5	5·3	11·1
2½	2·9	3·2	3·7	4·3	5·3	6·7	9·1	14·3	33·3
5	5·9	6·7	7·7	9·1	11·1	14·3	20·0	33·3	100·0
7½	9·1	10·3	12·0	14·3	17·7	23·1	33·3	60·0	300·0 loss line
10	12·5	14·3	16·7	20·0	25·0	33·3	50·0	100·0	
12½	16·1	18·5	21·7	26·3	33·3	45·4	71·4	166·7	
15	20·0	23·1	27·2	33·3	42·8	60·0	100·0	300·0	
17½	24·1	28·0	33·3	41·2	53·8	77·8	140·0	700·0	
20	28·6	33·3	40·0	50·0	66·7	100·0	200·0		
25	38·5	45·4	55·5	71·4	100·0	166·7	500·0		
30	50·0	60·0	75·0	100·0	150·0	300·0			
33⅓	58·7	71·2	90·8	125·0	200·0	500·0			
35	63·6	77·7	100·0	140·0	233·3	700·0			
40	80·0	100·0	133·3	200·0	400·0				
45	100·0	128·5	180·0	300·0	900·0				
50	125·0	166·7	250·0	500·0					

loss line

Admittedly, profit margins may be below target for the first two years, but thereafter they should rise above the target. In addition, the low price may help the company to rapidly gain market share and thereby reach the expected third year sales volume perhaps midway through the second year, and consequently increase the total profits earned during the product's life. These ideas can be pursued a stage further by taking into account the experience curve (see Section 5.10).

A frequently quoted case of a company taking calculated pricing risks of this nature is that of Texas Instruments, when they entered the hand-held calculator market in the early 1970s. As a result their prices were much lower than those of their competitors and they quickly gained a significant market share, passing the cumulative experience and sales volume on which the costs had been calculated much sooner than anticipated; a situation which led to some high profit margins. This type of approach to cost-plus pricing overcomes one of the major objections to the method, namely, that imposing from the start a minimum profit margin on every product or model causes prices to be set higher than the level which would maximise long term profit.

In spite of all the efforts, it may become apparent that the only way of reducing costs to achieve the target profit margin would be to manufacture at a higher volume than originally planned. How can this be achieved? By spending more on promotion and selling, by exporting or by upgrading the product in some way? It is now necessary to begin an iterative process of altering the various components of the marketing mix and projecting likely changes in the sales volume and total costs relative to such alterations, in an attempt to reach the target profit margins. It is not a simple matter to determine a valid relationship between the multitude of variables involved, and therefore the numbers which are arrived at are more likely to serve as useful guidelines than to provide definitive answers. Very often this iterative process produces a sales volume answer which is much higher than many companies are prepared to risk attempting to achieve, because of the large capital commitment which would be required. Instead they try to get by at lower volume, perhaps cutting production and marketing costs, and as a result never make an adequate return on the new product, and never earn sufficient profits to be able to keep up with technical improvements, until eventually they are forced to withdraw from that particular product line.

As a result of these sorts of experiences it is becoming more common in many countries to encourage companies to organise themselves to operate at what appears to be the most efficient production and marketing volume. Price is then set at a level which should enable that volume to be sold worldwide, even if that means initially operating at a loss, in the knowledge that operating at these higher volumes will bring economies of scale and gains in cumulative operating experience which are greater than those of most competitors, and that once a firm worldwide customer base has been established it may be possible to increase prices somewhat without loss of volume (see Section 11.4.5). Operating at these higher volumes not only enables companies to keep their costs at least as low as the best of their competitors but also enables them to generate sufficient revenue to be able to afford to introduce the latest technology. This desirable situation is unlikely to be reached if there is an insistence on achieving high margins from the start of operations, because volume will be limited by the resultant prices.

A fixation with cost-plus pricing can lead companies to the top of an unenviable spiral. They may find that their cost-plus price is not competitive, causing sales volume to drop below target. It will not be possible to reduce the fixed element of their costs in proportion to the reduced volume, and thus, if they wish to maintain their profit margins, they would have to raise their prices still further, with even more dire effects on sales volume. It will usually be better to accept lower margins for the time being and invest in building up sales volume, hopefully to the level where the traditional margins can be re-established.

On the other hand, where demand is inelastic, perhaps because of some product uniqueness, cost-plus pricing leads companies to underprice their products, and especially when demand exceeds supply it is usually more profitable to increase profit margins above the normal 'target' level. This begs the question of 'how much', and leads us back to the problem of relating price to volume. A possible solution to the problem is to examine what prices competitors are charging. Although there is no guarantee that they are not all underpricing, it is unlikely.

11.7 Matching the competition

This is the exact opposite of cost-plus pricing, and rather than simply allowing price to follow costs, price is matched to what the market appears to want to pay, sometimes thereby earning higher than 'normal' profit margins and sometimes earning lower than 'normal' margins. Ideally a company would examine the specification of its own product in comparison to the specification of what competitors were offering and place its own offering somewhere in a league table of desirability. Use of the buy—response curve is one method of achieving this objective. The position will, of course, not just depend on product attributes but on all the other factors, such as reputation, distribution and promotion, which contribute to a company's competitive position. The company could then set its price in relation to its league position (but see Section 11.3) and to competitor prices (see Fig. 11.4), to achieve some subjectively defined (based on previous experience) target value—price ratio.

Matching the competition seems a fairly safe policy, providing one has properly positioned one's product in the league table, and to do this one has to be aware of the buying criteria of different customers in different segments of home and overseas markets. However, it is often difficult to identify exactly what price competitors are charging because of the existence of discounts or price related incentives such as free delivery or free installation. Fairly careful research is needed. Matching the competition is a strategy which is particularly evident in oligopolies, that is markets with a small number of sellers. This idea is explored in more detail in the following section.

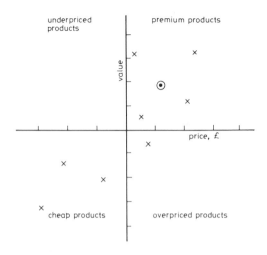

Fig. 11.4 *Value–price league table*
   × competitor products
   ⊙ own product?

11.8 Price and market structure

Market structure is a major determinent of pricing policies (see also Bain [63] and refer back to Sections 6.3–6.6 if you wish). It is important to bear in mind that suppliers rarely bargain directly against buyers. In such a situation the buyer would be pitching his need for what the supplier can provide, against the supplier's need to provide it, and an exchange value would be agreed. It is more normal for suppliers to be actually bargaining against their competitors. Buyers are able to exert pressure on one supplier by referring to what other suppliers are prepared to offer. It is for that reason that the number of sellers in a market affects price as much as the number of buyers.

In an oligopoly – that is where the top four suppliers have a combined market share of over 40% – the fortunes of each supplier will be very much influenced by the behaviour of the other suppliers, and to avoid the danger of a price war, a price leader is usually (unofficially) appointed – normally the supplier with the largest market share and/or lowest costs. Should one of the competitors actually reduce price below that of the price leader, presumably in the hope of some short term benefit, then very considerable pressure is likely to be brought to bear on him to conform, perhaps by some veiled threat about the others combining against him or by an appeal to common sense. Usually the other companies will try to combat the lower price by stepping up their marketing effort or by trying to tie up customers in long term contracts until the miscreant inevitably sees the error of his ways. In the long run all that the miscreant can achieve is to reduce his profits and the profits of his competitors, because ultimately if there are any signs of a significant shift in market share then the other companies in the oligopoly will be forced to reduce their own prices to protect their futures. Similarly, if companies other than the price leader choose to raise their prices, they face the danger that the others will not follow their lead. However, when the price leader raises his prices, because such a lead is normally followed by the other suppliers, it will not initiate any moves by customers to change supplier. If the other suppliers do not follow the lead, the price leader would be able to reduce his price back to previous levels, but this will not normally happen, because the price leader would only increase price if there was a clear informal understanding within the oligopoly that a price rise was appropriate.

From time to time there is public protest against price fixing practices and the protest is often followed by a governmental enquiry of some kind. These enquiries usually find that the price has been fixed at a level which enables companies to invest in research and development and in providing a service, and that the level of profits distributed to the shareholder is not excessive. Occasionally they find to the contrary and try to force the oligopoly to reduce its prices, but even where they have been successful in doing so the affects tend to be short term. An example in the UK (see Duncan Reekie [64]) of getting it wrong was where a government enquiry decided that Kodak was making excessive profits from selling colour film, and prices were forced down to what was considered to be a more reasonable level. All that happened was that Kodak's largest, but somewhat less efficient competitor, Ilford, was forced out of business and Kodak was left to pick up the benefits from the increased market share which was handed over to them. The extra economies of scale enabled them to achieve their former margins. Although it has to be admitted that prices were reduced, it remains a matter of opinion as to whether the overall public interest was served by the disappearance of Ilford.

Apart from public pressure, the existence of price leadership does not mean that price can be allowed to rise uncontrolled, because there is always the threat of new entrants to the market, either with a lower cost technology or with a substitute product. If the market leaders do not keep up with the latest technology and thereby allow a new entrant to use the latest low cost technology to surmount barriers to entry, that new entrant is very likely to obtain a significant market share before the market leaders are able to fill the technology gap that they have allowed to be created. In addition there is the increasing threat of international competition. The costs of entering a given market are lower for an overseas supplier than for a new domestic supplier. If an overseas supplier is able to use output from one of his existing factories, then the entry costs will only involve the costs of establishing a local marketing operation, a distribution facility, and, perhaps greatest of all, a sufficient reputation. Without the need to establish an efficient manufacturing capability it is possible for overseas companies to commence operations on a small scale, and to gradually increase their market share in parallel to improvements in their reputation and track record. Thus the skill of price leadership is to keep the market price high enough to make a sufficient return on investment to continue to attract investment to the industry, and yet low enough to discourage new entrants and to avoid excess capacity being created.

Mid-way between an oligopoly and a market containing many suppliers, many markets can be partially controlled by mutual agreement, for example via trade associations. Trade associations provide an ideal forum for discussions on industry costs. Although price need not be mentioned directly it is a fairly simple matter for members to reach an understanding about what constitutes an acceptable normal price. In many cases a well established company will become accepted as the price-value (see Section 11.7) barometer (see also Scherer [65]). Other companies in the industry cannot be forced to follow the barometer price but they are encouraged to use it as a starting point for their own price—value—volume calculations. Obviously each supplier's product will be different and in practice it is more likely that an acceptable price range will become established rather than a single price.

When the number of suppliers increases, it becomes more likely that one will choose to go his own way and price significantly above or below the barometer price. Certainly it is unlikely that a concerted industry reaction to such behaviour will be organised, if only because it would be very difficult with a large number of suppliers. However, more importantly where there are a large number of sellers, that means that there is some natural barrier which prevents companies expanding beyond a certain size, and in that case the fact that a small percentage of suppliers choose to reduce their prices is of little concern to the others, as the effect of any increased sales volume they achieve by the lower prices on each of the other suppliers, will be small.

There is little of relevance to say about the pricing behaviour of monopolies. International competition, and competition from substitute products, (e.g. for British Rail from road and air transport) means that there are few true monopolies. In the UK most near monopolies are nationalised industries, where price tends to be set by decree and by political considerations rather than by market forces. Possibly the nearest to a real monopoly is the energy industry where gas, electricity and coal are under national control, and oil is currently relatively expensive.

11.9 Price and the economic cycle

Inasmuch as supply normally exceeds demand in a recession, whereas in a boom there may be shortages, price tends to move in phase with the rise and fall of the economic cycle. However, it is not necessarily sound to initiate price reductions at the beginning of a recession. Faced with a shrinking market companies are obviously tempted to reduce price in the hope of increasing their market share and maintaining sales volume. Perhaps they believe that the volume effect of the increased market share will compensate for the reduced profit margins and that their competitors will not follow their price reduction; or perhaps more subtlely they initiate price reductions in the expectation that competitors will follow suit, in the hope that the general price reduction will help maintain market demand. However, because of the price—profit—volume relationship of Section 11.5 it is likely to make more sense to try to operate efficiently at a reduced volume, unless the forecast reduction is sufficiently high to take volume below break-even point. It is of course the recognition of this danger which has forced companies to turn towards more flexible production systems which can be profitably operated at low as well as high volumes.

A more sensible alternative to price reductions, especially for companies which have to operate a process which has a high break-even point, may be to offer especially low prices (say at full cost but with no profit margin), to one or two large customers to ensure that their business is secured. If most of the overhead costs are covered in this way, it immediately introduces much more flexibility into the pricing of the remaining output. A longer term strategic reason for initiating a price reduction could be an attempt to gain a larger market share during a recession, so as to be well placed to take advantage of the next upturn when it occurs. In the long term this may prove to be a more profitable approach than continuing to concentrate on making a profit at low volumes right up to the very end of a recession.

11.10 Pricing products

Ideally companies should fix the price of proposed new products in accordance with their findings about what the market will pay, and in accordance with their marketing strategy (in particular value/price objectives, see Section 11.7), and then design products to meet that price. In spite of the difficulties listed in Section 11.4, the price chosen will be derived from forecasts of sales volume at a range of possible prices; forecasts largely based on previous experience. In other words the value which it is intended to offer via the new product will be subjectively compared with what is currently offered both by the company itself and by its competitors. It is worth repeating that customers' perceptions of value will be affected not only by the various parameters of product performance and by the other elements of the marketing mix, but also by their perceptions of risk (see Section 9.4).

It is assumed that if the value/price ratio is kept the same as exists for current products then the new product should enable the company to maintain its current market share, whereas if the value/price ratio is improved market share should increase, but to an extent which will be uncertain. If the company believes that it can persuade customers to perceive greater value in what is to be offered, then it is possible to charge a higher price without altering the value/price ratio. Support for these subjective views can be obtained via market surveys or by plotting the buy—response curve, or sometimes by initially selling the product only to a limited but defined group of customers. However, as emphasised previously, the possession of information only reduces the risk of a poor decision, it does not guarantee success. Ultimately the decision will be subjective.

In the final analysis, it is necessary to choose what seems to be the best price in the light of the chosen marketing strategy and the available information, while at the same time being prepared to adjust it up or down as market reaction unfolds.

Some companies prefer to initially err on the side of a high price on the basis that:

1 A new product should have some genuine and unique advantage which some customers will pay more for.
2 Often initial high volume is not sought so that teething problems can be rectified.
3 High price, particularly where competing products are hard to compare, creates an impression of quality which will probably remain with the product even if price is subsequently reduced. This is particularly relevant if a higher price enables the promotional budget to be higher than at a lower price (see below). A high price can also have a favourable image effect on other products in the range.
4 Serious doubts about whether the price is too high can be tempered by opening offers. It is common for suppliers to openly state that they need to establish a track record for a new product and hence are prepared to offer it at below the normal price for a limited period. If subsequently the price does prove to be too high, the opening discounts can be continued until it is possible to effectively reduce price by not following normal inflationary price increases. Actual price reduction should be avoided because this will often be interpreted by customers to mean that the product is not performing as well as forecast and is not selling well, or that the quality has been reduced, or that the company is in trouble and needs a cash injection, or that the product is about to be withdrawn. In any of these cases the price reduction is more likely to reduce sales volume than to increase it. Unfortunately if the opening discounts are continued for too long, customers will expect them to apply throughout the product's life and may press for similar discounts to be applied to other products in the suppliers range.

Once demand from customers who will pay a price premium has stagnated, and sales volume begins to fall, some companies reduce price so that the product becomes attractive to a section of the market which does not value the unique benefits offered quite so highly. Once that sector has also stagnated the price may be further reduced and so on. In this way the price is set at the highest level commensurate with achieving the planned sales volume. This policy, which has been termed 'skimming the cream' (Dean [66]), can only be followed where one is sure that the uniqueness will not be copied before a substantial share of the total market has been gained, because otherwise one will be left with a high-price non-unique product, and with all the problems described in (4) above of trying to reduce price quickly. In that case it is better to take advantage of the temporary uniqueness, by trying to build up market share quickly through an extensive promotion campaign. Such a high-price—high-promotional expenditure strategy, designed to cash in on the uniqueness while it lasts, is sometimes called rapid skimming. It is rarely appropriate to industrial markets (see Section 11.3).

Other companies prefer to initially err on the side of a low price. A low price appears less risky as it minimises the chances of over-pricing and it should help products to move quickly into the growth phase of their lives. A rapid build up in sales volume is particularly important when unit costs are very volume dependent, and in those cases it is worth spending heavily on promotion to reinforce the low price. However, if product demand is not price sensitive and unit costs only reduce gradually as volume increases, then the benefits of a low price are less certain. A low price can bring with it the danger of an image of low quality, a fierce competitive reaction, and the possibility that demand will exceed the initial capacity to supply. Delivery delays or problems with quality as a result of trying to cope with unplanned for demand, can more than offset the beneficial effects of a low price or efficient promotion. In most cases customers prefer to take their business to their second or third choice of supplier rather than accept a long delivery delay from their first choice supplier. As a result it is no longer realistic to use a low price in order to try to ensure that demand always exceeds capacity, in an attempt to provide the security of an order backlog. Offering the product at an unnecessarily low price is in effect forfeiting profits which could be reinvested to ensure continued competitiveness, once that uniqueness has been copied or superseded.

For example, Jaguar Cars used to be so wedded to the value for money concept that they never tried increasing prices gradually to find the upper limit at which demand would approximately correspond to their production capacity. They preferred to have long waiting lists. Higher prices would have yielded higher profits which may have been used, for example, to keep the company independent. The extent of the under pricing can be seen by the relatively high price increases pursued more recently, which moved the Jaguar range from the medium to the high price range. The aim then is to set the value/price ratio at a level where demand more or less matches capacity to supply.

In spite of the logic of designing a new product to meet a defined market related price, there will inevitably be occasions where the unit cost at the forecast sales volumes of the new product, in its final developed form, will be too high to make the target price economically sensible. The common responses to this problem are to try to reduce costs by (1) examining production costs in terms of more efficient production methods, use of more economic materials, or a reduction in the number of product options offered, (2) considering a reduction in marketing costs (often with no commensurate planned reduction in sales volume), (3) re-evaluating the product design, perhaps undertaking value analysis, to see if a more economic design can be developed, and (4) accepting lower profit margins in the early stages of the product's life (see Section 11.6.)

An alternative response is to try to increase the value placed on the product by potential customers, for example, by introducing some extra uniqueness, or a somewhat different appearance, or by attaching some extra options or services to the product, or by presenting it differently. The choice between value enhancement and cost reduction depends very much on the type of product being offered, with obvious leanings towards cost reduction for non-differentiable products and components, and towards value enhancement for capital equipment. In markets where there are established price bands, the price/value combination may have to be shifted right up to the next band.

Although the discussion in this section has been directed towards new products, all the arguments can be applied when considering changing the price of existing products. However, customers usually expect to be able to relate any price increase on existing products to cost increases or to value increases, and because they have an existing value/price ratio to work from they can do this quite accurately. This linking of price increases to cost increases on existing products may explain why so many companies use cost-plus methods when setting the price of new products. As a result they often either set prices higher than is in the best long term interests of the company, or fail to take advantage of product uniqueness and price too low.

In the final analysis, customers' buying decisions are related to their perception of the ratio of the value to them of what is being offered to the price being asked. Providing the ratio is higher than one, there is an incentive to buy. One of the objectives of marketing is to get that ratio as high as possible for each prospective customer, and certainly higher than the ratio which is perceived to be offered by competitors. Where product prices are individually negotiated, this last step can be more accurate, with each customer being offered a price which reflects their unique value perceptions.

However, overriding that consideration, the price must be within the range that the target customer group is prepared to pay for the class of product under consideration. Thus if one wishes to buy a £10 000 car, one is not going to pay £6000 or £16 000, almost regardless of the value for money offered in those price ranges. The aim of good pricing is to set product prices at a level which falls within the range that the target customer group feels they are able to afford in relation to what is being offered, and which offers the supplier prospects of economically sensible long term profits.

11.11 Pricing product ranges

Companies which pursue cost-plus pricing often also believe that each model within a product range should pay its way. Because the cost structure of individual manufacturers may well be different to that of their competitors, applying a fixed profit margin to every product within a range can lead, as shown, to a set of prices which are not consistent within the existing competitive price range.

Competitive price range	£15/20	£25/30	£40/45	£60/70	£90/100
Base cost	£10	£20	£38	£50	£75
Cost plus 30%	£13	£26	£49	£65	£97
Market related price	£18	£28	£43	£66	£96
Percentage mark-up	80%	40%	13%	32%	28%

It is important for companies who market a range of products to present a consistent image for those products, and that includes consistent pricing. Sometimes this means accepting that the profit margin on some models within a range will be higher than on other models — possibly even to the extent of one model actually being priced such that the contribution it makes to overheads is not as great as the overhead costs allocated to it, although in that case the cost structure should be very carefully examined and perhaps some redesign considered. Should there be a 'loss making' model in the range, its continuation can be justified if its presence in the range sufficiently increases sales of the complete range to more than offset the losses. However this is difficult to definitely prove without actually withdrawing the model. As a result the decision will tend to be based on feedback from the sales force and perhaps on a market survey. The decision will also be significantly affected by the policy of major competitors. If all the competitors offer a complete range it will be necessary to have convincing reasons to go against the trend.

At the other end of the spectrum, should a company find that the unit cost of a new model being introduced into a product range yields a much higher than normal profit margin, it will probably be best to accept these higher margins rather than try to improve sales volume of the new model by a lower price. Such a lower price would create a pricing anomaly within the range, confuse customers and probably cause sales of other models to fall. Alternatively, the company may consider using the increased margins to slightly reduce the price of the whole range (but see Section 11.5). Of course it is quite possible, for reasons of appearance or performance or whatever, that the new model is not completely consistent with the existing range, and in that case it might prove more appropriate to introduce it as the first model in an entirely new range and to use a different generic name to avoid a conflicting image.

In general, companies selling a variety of product lines, with a range of products within each line, are not so free to maneouvre price as single product companies, because customers will compare one product line with another in terms of their place in the competitive league table and the value for money which appears to be offered. Inconsistencies seem to reduce customers confidence in suppliers. For example, the introduction of a low priced product range by a company which usually supplies high priced items might be taken as a sign that they are struggling and are desperate for sales, or that quality in general is to be reduced or that the prices of other product ranges will be progressively reduced. In contrast, a company which normally supplies low priced items may find that attempts to introduce a higher priced product, however good that product might be, are not successful because customers will assume that the quality is the same as the products in the other ranges, and that the new product has been mispriced.

11.12 Competitive bidding

Many industrial companies do not produce standard products, but unique products designed to meet a customer's specification. Such companies range from small subcontractors to companies building nuclear power stations, or turnkey factories or new harbours. They are not lucky enough to have published competitive prices available to help them set their own prices. Their starting point must be their own costs. Unfortunately, the level of these costs relative to those of the competitors will not simply be related to their operating efficiencies but also to their interpretation of exactly what it is that the customer wants, and how it is to be provided. Different engineers in different companies will interpret the customer's specifications of what he wants in different ways, and those differences can often far outweigh any differences in operating efficiency. For example, a company quoting to produce a particular electronic control panel arrived at a price per panel of £11 000, but because it was already busy and did not specially want the order, it decided to quote a price of £16 000. In due course the order was placed with them because the competitor suppliers had quoted in the range of £18 000–£25 000, itself a measure of the extent of differences of interpretation. On detailed post-order investigation it was discovered that the £11 000 interpretation was not exactly what the customer wanted, but was near enough to offer a better value/price ratio than that of competitors. Made to order products of this kind represent one of the few areas where individual engineering flair can outweigh the effect of scale of operation. The margin which companies can add to their costs will be related to their view of what their competitors are likely to ask to undertake the same tasks. This type of company finds itself in a competitive bidding situation each time it seeks an order, and it can legitimately decide to bid at a level which will be aimed at achieving one of the following objectives:*

1 Profit maximisation on this order.
2 Long run profit maximisation, or at least the achievement of an annual profit target.
3 Minimisation of competitor profit.
4 Minimisation of the risk of excessive losses on each contract.
5 Market share increase, i.e. to gain new customers or to maintain a steady work flow (equivalent in decision terms to trying to ensure that a given contract is not lost).

To illustrate the five possibilities let us consider a small order or contract where the cost estimate amounts to £7000. Profit associated with a range of possible bid prices is shown in Table 11.2. Let us suppose that our company is an efficient one

Table 11.2 *Contract pricing − OR approach (using an idea from Oxenfeldt et al.* [60])

Price	Profit	Contract probability	Expected profit
£10000	£3000	0·1	£300
£9000	£2000	0·3	£600
£8000	£1000	0·5	£500
£7000	£0000	0·8	£0
£6000	−£1000	0·95	−£950

* The following three paragraphs use ideas from Oxenfeldt *et al.* [60].

and it has kept a record of the prices competitors have bid historically, as a ratio of its own cost estimates, and has kept a record of which bids have been successful. This data can usefully be presented in the form of a histogram for each competitor, see Fig. 11.5.

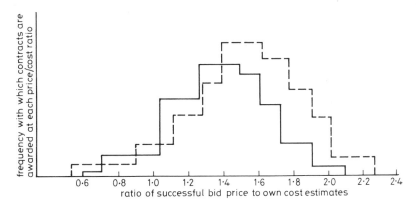

Fig. 11.5   *Competitor bid record histogram*

From such a record it would be possible to arrive at a broad picture whereby it is known that, because of their reputations, competitor A has to price at (own) cost plus *A*% to be successful, competitor B at cost plus *B*%, and so on. It will also be known that some competitors tend to bid at a lower price for certain types of contracts, and that other competitors tend to bid lower for other types of contracts. Based on this broad picture, and intelligence about how urgently each supplier needs the order, it is possible to arrive at an estimate of the probability that the company bid will be successful at each of a number of prices, e.g. as listed in Table 11.2. Using the concept of expected value (see Section 5.15), the expected profit at each price will be the product of the forecast profit and the forecast probability of obtaining the contract at that price. In other words, if the same rules were followed over a succession of different bids, then in the long run the number of successful bids would correspond with the probability estimates (i.e. 30 out of 100) and the expected profit would be earned.

If keeping records for individual competitors proves too onerous, the analysis could instead by based on records of the average bid levels of competitors. In general, as the number of competitors increases, the bid price which corresponds to the highest expected profit will decrease, because if there was a 0·8 probability that the average bid price of competitors was higher than the company's bid of say, £7000, and there were five competitors, then the cumulative probability that all five competitors would bid higher than £7000, would be $(0·8)^5$ or 0.33. Applying the data from Table 11.2 to the five objectives, the prices chosen would be:

1   £10 000
2   £9000

3 £8000, or even £7000, providing any contracts gained would not create capacity problems for more profitable contracts

4 £8000 — if for example company records indicated that its cost estimates were only accurate to within ± £1000

5 £7000 or £6000, depending on the investment to be made in building market share.

Companies with limited funds or with surplus capacity cannot afford to play the odds; they cannot afford to act other than to minimise the possibility of losing each contract and they exhibit different perceptions of risk and return to companies which have full order books.

Even supposing that it were possible to keep accurate and comprehensive records, and that it were possible to adjust the historic probabilities in the light of current conditions, it is unlikely that in individual cases the application of these types of operational research techniques would actually yield a 'best' result. In practice, rather like the football pools, the results, although they are influenced by form, are overridingly influenced by individual circumstances: one team plays better than usual and another worse than usual. Thus while on average competitors will bid to a pattern, on any given occasion one company may bid unexpectedly low; perhaps in the case of a subcontractor because they have relevant surplus capacity at the time, or have material left over from a previous job that can be used up, or in the case of a civil engineering company because it has achieved a superior design solution, or perhaps because a sudden move in exchange rates makes an overseas bid unexpectedly competitive. As with all models, the application of the above competitive bidding models will help improve a company's understanding of how the bidding situation works. However, the accuracy of the numbers which are produced is limited and as ever should be used as a guide rather than an answer.

Often a better approach to competitive bidding is to establish and maintain a close contact with the customer in an attempt to attain the status of 'preferred bidder'. This can in part be achieved by persuading the purchaser that the supplier is a reliable company to deal with, that is, it will actually perform in the way which is being promised. It can also be achieved by manoeuvering the final specification of what the purchaser wants, closer to what the supplier can best provide, and thereby away from what competitors can best supply (see Sections 15.5 and 15.7).

With luck, when the customer receives the competitive offers he may return to the preferred bidder to indicate that while he would like to place the contract with the preferred bidder, their price is a few thousand or a few hundred pounds too high to make that possible. In other words, selling non-price virtues means that one no longer has to make the lowest bid, but only to bid in the right range. (Clearly, if a company bids much too high even the most enthusiastic customer will not bother to give it a second bite at the cherry). Even at the second bite it is no longer necessary to match the lowest bid if the customer has been convinced that he is being offered a superior service. The above approach can even be seen to be of benefit with customers who are publicly committed to accepting the lowest bid which meets a publicly issued specification (e.g. government departments), because the contents of that specification will have been influenced, hopefully towards what the company can do best, that is most competitively. It also offers the opportunity to bid at a competitive price, because the company will know in detail exactly what the customer requires and that should open up cost saving opportunities.

Ensuring that one is in the right price range will still require knowledge of the likely level of competitive bids, and hence intelligence about competitive cost structures and current order levels. In addition, computer-based competitive bidding models can be used to help ensure that unnecessarily low bids are not made (rather than being used perhaps unrealistically to work out optimum bid prices).

Where the bid is for a design contract, companies often will bid at below their target margin because they are aware that during the design process, as buyers learn more about the intricacies and capabilities of the technology, the specification of what they want will change, and that should create the opportunity to introduce price increases – hopefully sufficient to allow the contract to achieve the normal target profit margins. It should not be forgotten that, just like the buyer, the supplier takes a risk when he contracts to supply something not yet designed, within an agreed time-scale and at an agreed price. Admittedly the contract can be subject to agreed waivers, such as delays caused by factors beyond the contractors control, changes to raw material and labour costs, and changes in the customers requirements, but rarely is any allowance made for unexpected development difficulties. Should they arise, they normally have to be treated as an investment, that is an investment in gaining knowhow which will help competitiveness in any subsequent contracts of a similar nature.

Operating in industries where orders are relatively large and are obtained infrequently can be a risky business. At any moment in time at least one competitor is likely to have excess capacity, as a result of failing to obtain previous contracts, and they will tend to bid at a level not far above their marginal cost to try to ensure that they obtain the next contract. This situation may be progressively repeated among all the suppliers (even though, overall, there is no excess capacity) and as a result contracts awarded at prices which are only just above the break-even point. Such consistently low profit margins would not allow for proper investment in improved methods or technology.

The situation is made worse in some international markets because companies often have to compete with overseas suppliers who have their home market secure, possibly via subsidies or tarriff barriers, and therefore are able to consistently bid at little over marginal cost. The only answers to this situation are lower costs through increased efficiency or design skills, or a much superior reputation.

A further interesting concept in the competitive bidding situation is that it can very often pay to bid well below the company's normal target profit margins. At the beginning of each financial year an estimate is likely to be made of the expected sales volume, and hence the average profit margin necessary to achieve the profit target. As the year progresses it may become apparent that a number of particularly profitable orders have made the achievement of that profit margin unnecessary on other orders. This provides freedom to bid at a lower price — possibly to reduce competitor profits or to keep volume near to full capacity. In many cases companies that have been operating in a particular business for several years are able to estimate the number of exceptionally profitable orders that they may expect to obtain during a year, and on that basis bid more competitively on other contracts.

11.13 Pricing capital goods

The problems of pricing capital goods which are made to customer order, are similar to those dealt with in the previous section. Although competitive bidding may still be necessary, supplying made for stock capital items introduces additional problems. For example, different customers will value different items of hardware and service differently. Some companies buying a complex machining centre may value a consultancy type of technical applications service (see Section 14.14) which helps them understand the capability of machining centres, and hence helps them to select and use one in an efficient manner. Other companies may believe they have a sufficiently competent staff of production engineers not to need such a service and they will not place any value on its provision. Similarly while one company may highly value the provision of an extensive service facility which will enable service calls to be answered promptly, another company may prefer to hold its own stock of spares and to undertake its own repairs and servicing. Inasmuch as suppliers' pricing structures will reflect their decision to provide the service(s), the latter type of customer may be encouraged to patronise other suppliers who, because they do not provide a service, offer a lower price. The only way the former supplier can combat such competition is by offering a discount to customers who do not want to make use of the services, but that would increase their price to those customers that do, and possibly make them more expensive than suppliers who continue to evenly distribute the cost of their technical applications services.

Another example of varying valuations might be where a particular machining centre was capable of performing an operational sequence which its competitors were not able to match. This capability will be highly valued by those customers who are able to utilise it, but not valued at all by those customers who have no practical use for that operating sequence. Again how does the supplier price* his product? At a level which will attract only the former customers, or at a level which will attract both categories? The decision will need to be taken in the light of the sales potential of each user category, unit costs, and the manufacturing capacity of the supplier. Even if the supplier decides to concentrate on the former group, how does he decide upon a price which reflects their valuation of the unique operating capability? Could he perhaps undertake a complex costing exercise for a cross-section of customers? Certainly it is possible to calculate the cost saving potential for one or two typical users, either based on the suppliers own estimate of typical user costs, or in collaboration with one or two well established customers, and to

* In the sense of setting an average price around which a discount structure can be built.

price accordingly. However, ultimately the supplier will be forced to rely on trial and error, further increasing the price if the sales response is much greater than planned, and reducing price if it is less than planned.

The problem is even more difficult to solve if the new product incorporates new technology. There will be little basis on which to set a price in relation to what competitors offer. In addition customers, and indeed the supplier, may not be aware of all the potential cost saving advantages of the new product, and hence the cost advantages of ownership. These advantages will obviously be affected by the costs of scrapping existing equipment; that is the undepreciated element of the price of existing equipment, less its current secondhand price, plus the disruption costs of removal and re-installation (e.g. lost production). As a result, suppliers of new technology products tend to price on the low side in order to move their products out of the introductory phase of their life cycles as quickly as possible.

In practice many of these problems can be overcome by adopting a flexible pricing policy (see Section 11.1), either negotiating individual prices with each customer, or offering discounts. Another way of simplifying the conundrum, especially where technology is changing rapidly, is to lease rather than to sell. This encourages customers to change more quickly to the latest models, because they simply have to compare the new model's operating cost savings with any difference in leasing charges, less some allowance for disruption, and they can leave disposal of the old model to the supplier. Leasing can be a useful strategy for the supplier of an untried product because it immediately reduces the risk perceived by buyers from the level of capital cost, to the level of the cancellation charges on the lease. However, in many cases the costs of poor quality or disrupted production are so much higher than the capital costs that leasing has only a marginal effect. Usually suppliers operate leasing schemes through finance companies, and they have to evaluate whether leasing can increase sales volume sufficiently to offset any financing charges incurred. Occasionally companies set up their own leasing organisation, in which case they have to evaluate whether the return on the capital tied up in the leased plant is sufficient to justify such an approach, particularly if that reduces the company's ability to borrow to expand its manufacturing or marketing or development capabilities.

11.14 Summary

Pricing is a complex subject and many alternative approaches are equally legitimate, (as a matter of interest the results of a survey into how British industry sets prices has been summarised in Table 11.3). For homogeneous commodity type products, where there is little possibility of product differentiation, price is arguably the single most important factor in the marketing mix. However, marketing departments continually seek to introduce some element of uniqueness to what they sell and in practice some degree of differentiation can be assumed.

As product complexity increases there is increasing scope for using non-price

Table 11.3   *How British industry prices (adapted from a survey by Atkin and Skinner [67])*

1   Responsibility for approving pricing policy usually lies with the managing director (35–38% of companies) often based on the recommendations of the marketing/sales director. Often price responsibility lies solely with the marketing/sales director (approximately 30% of companies). Individual pricing decisions are delegated much further down the hierarchy.

2   51% of companies use cost plus pricing (but most subsequently modify price because of non-cost considerations). The most popular non-cost methods of pricing are:
    refer to competitor prices: 81%
    market survey: 31%
    consult sales force: 14%
    follow market leader: 11%

3   Most companies use more than one pricing system, namely:
    published price list: 55%
    (for companies which use wholesalers: 94%)
    individual negotiation: 53%
    (particularly favoured by companies which sell materials and components for use in further manufacture)
    internal price lists (but not released to customers): 47%
    formal tenders: 43%

4   Discounts are nearly always offered, that is 70% of companies, rising to 85% where a price list is published.

5   Discounts tend to be related to customer category as well as purchase volume, especially for capital goods. Discounting by volume is more common with raw materials and components in which case:
    in about 50% of cases discounts are published, and
    in about 50% of cases discounts are entirely discretionary.

6 Knowledge of competitor prices seem poor:
  80% of companies claiming above average prices
  only 7% claiming below average prices

7 Companies change their price in the following situations:
  80% when costs increase
  47% when market prices rise generally
  39% when greater profit is required
  15% when market prices fall
  15% when costs are cut
  12% when a greater market share is sought

8 Changes to product specifications in order to reduce price are rare.

9 The effect of price increases is monitored by:
  comparing with sales in previous period: 73%
  recording changes in market share: 32%
  formal market investigation: 14%

10 Computer models are rarely used to help set prices:
   in the case of list prices: 13%
   in the case of tender prices: 4%

methods of competition and there are positive advantages in doing so, not least that of higher prices and higher profits. As a result, in industrial markets, companies rarely use price aggressively, perferring to concentrate on non-price factors.

Like everything else in marketing, it is impossible to choose an ideal price, that is one which will maximise profits. Companies simply do not have sufficient information available to them to reach such a judgement. Even if it were possible, the market situation changes so frequently that to maintain an optimum level, the price would continually have to be altered, and as explained at the outset that is not desirable. The best that can be done is to take account of as many factors as possible and to move the price into the right area for the target market or market segment. Having moved price into the right area, it can then be tuned to provide a value/price ratio which will be perceived by customers to at least match, and preferably somewhat exceed, that offered by competitors. However that only gets the initial price right; it has to be kept right. It is essential to monitor the situation and to respond to changed circumstances; in the short term by discounts or by value enhancing special offers, and in the long term by changing the basic value/price ratio offered.

Chapter 12

Industrial Buying

12.1 Why study buyer behaviour?

The answer is simple. Suppliers who understand why people choose one product rather than another and one supplier rather than another, can direct their product development, pricing, promotion, distribution and sales strategy more effectively. To do this they need to understand what motivates people to buy at all; how they go about searching for alternative products; and on what basis they differentiate between them.

Studies seeking the answer to these sorts of issues can be divided into two main types: those that concentrate on the processes and procedures involved, and those that consider the psychological aspects. Although some of the findings of the latter studies can be applied in a general way to industrial buying, the impact of the former is more obvious and for that reason this chapter will concentrate on them. However, no single model, or even combination of models, can fully explain buying behaviour in all circumstances; there are simply too many variables to cope with. Buying behaviour is dynamic, it varies from industry to industry, company to company, person to person, and from time to time, as well as with the nature of the purchase being made. At best, studying buying behaviour will make marketeers more aware of the broad issues, and hence perhaps more sensitive to the nature of problems that are likely to arise in a particular situation. This should guide them towards more effective marketing.

12.2 Consumers buy different types of goods differently

It is appropriate to begin by briefly considering consumer buying behaviour, partly because it has been very widely researched, and studies of industrial buying have used that platform of knowledge, and partly because industrial buyers are individuals and respond to stimuli in much the same way that other consumers do. Products, divided into durable, non-durable (including food and services), may be considered in terms of their frequency of purchase as follows* (see also Chapter 6, Markin [68]):

1 *Convenience goods* — frequently bought with the minimum of effort (i.e. soap, papers, food). These goods are normally sold in high volumes at relatively low margins and a relatively low price. There is little inherent product loyalty in most cases and when consumers visit their normal shop, if Brand X is not on the shelf, or Brand Y is on special offer, or Brand Z has a new eye catching pack, or there has been a good advertisement for Brand Q, then most consumers will forgo their normal brand for one of the others. Unless one of these alternative brands seems to be significantly superior in some way to the usual brand purchased, consumers tend to return to their normal brand — largely out of habit. Consumers do not differentiate between brands very highly on an ongoing basis, that is without advertising reminders. It has been cynically suggested that the job of promotion is to build insignificant brand differences into major perceived differences in the mind of consumers. Small changes in price will have a large effect on volume and it is vital to achieve as wide a distribution as possible and to maintain a highly effective level of promotion.

2 *Shopping goods* — infrequently bought items where quite a lot of care is taken about selection (e.g. televisions, refrigerators, clothes, holidays). Consumers shop around for what they prefer in terms of value for money. Unit price can vary widely and does not greatly affect the care taken. For example, nearly as much care will be taken over a £50 camera as over a £200 hi-fi system. However, as with convenience goods, if a given brand is not on the shelf of the first few retailers visited by the prospective purchaser, even if an advertisement has been seen and the brand asked for, many people will allow retailers to talk them around to another brand. Hence much marketing effort must be aimed at the retailer. Most consumers are not able to differentiate performance between products in similar price bands (e.g. televisions, gas boilers, tennis racquets, washing machines) and they rely very much on appearance, reputation (largely influenced by advertising) and on the retailer's advice.

3 *Speciality goods* — products which are unique in some way, for example, appearance, reputation, performance, and which will be specifically sought out (e.g. cars, caravans, expensive cameras, specialist magazines). In this case it is not quite so important for the product to be stocked by a wide range of outlets. The marketing strategy will concentrate on emphasising the unique qualities and their importance in providing favourable in-use experience. Consumers will be very largely influenced by advertising, magazine articles and the experience of acquaintances. Prices will vary but the mark-up will tend to be high.

These are just the main categories around which most products can be fitted. For example, short-lived fashion goods tend to be bought very much like shopping goods, and unless wide distribution is quickly achieved sales volume will be low. Products which need regular service tend to be treated as speciality goods, with

* This and the following section use ideas previously set out in Kotler [2].

service reliability often overriding product differences; even in purchases as major as a motor car some consumers will not change to a different make of vehicle if that means they have to risk dealing with a garage other than the one to which they are accustomed.

To summarise, consumer buying behaviour largely depends on the frequency of purchase (and hence the rapidity of consumption), the time and effort spent on purchasing, the significance of the purchase to the consumer, the rate of technical and/or fashion change, technical complexity, the inherent level of product differentiation and the consumer's need for service. The importance of each factor will vary from product to product and from consumer to consumer. Marketing strategy has to be adapted accordingly. All these ideas have obvious implications for the marketing of industrial goods.

12.3 Basic consumer buying behaviour models

Many studies have been undertaken into buyer behaviour and various worthwhile models and theories have been developed (e.g. see Howard and Sheth [69]). However, the number of variables in a buying situation is large, and therefore many of the models are complex and difficult to understand. The way in which they can be applied to practical marketing problems is not always obvious. Probably some elements of all the models apply when people actually undertake a purchase, making it necessary for companies to try to evaluate how each of them will apply to a given product and a given market, as a first-step towards developing an appropriate marketing strategy. For simplicity, only the more basic ideas (also described in Kotler [2]) have been described here.

12.3.1 Buying stages model

This model follows the sequence of thoughts and feelings which go through buyers' minds as they move from being first aware that they may want to buy a product, through buying, to first use. There are five clear stages:

$$\text{felt need} \rightarrow \begin{matrix} \text{prepurchase} \\ \text{activity} \end{matrix} \rightarrow \begin{matrix} \text{purchase} \\ \text{decision} \end{matrix} \rightarrow \begin{matrix} \text{use} \\ \text{behaviour} \end{matrix} \rightarrow \begin{matrix} \text{post-purchase} \\ \text{feelings} \end{matrix}$$

At each stage buyers may change their brand preference, hence they need to be influenced in an appropriate way. The arousal of a felt need for a product may be a result of product (-class) promotion, or as a result of observing the use of the product by others (a kind of envy). The degree of prepurchase activity will vary as described in Section 12.2, according to the nature of the purchase and the manner of the purchase decision. Equally important is the customer's reaction when he first uses the product. If the product does not immediately perform as expected, this will induce uncertainties about whether a wise buying decision has been made; whether perhaps an inferior article has been bought. The provision of very clear and simple instructions (where appropriate) helps new purchasers quickly to get the best out of products and they are less likely to pass on negative messages to acquaintances. Even so, much advertising is aimed at reassuring recent purchasers that they have in fact made a good buying decision (see Section 12.10.7).

An alternative way of looking at the same idea is as follows:

Prospect stage — actively considering a new purchase.

Buying stage — has decided will buy and is evaluating.

User stage — latest purchase in use. Experience of performance in use (reliability, level of service) will affect next purchase decision. Not actively considering next purchase.

Each of these stages needs to be understood if they are to be effectively influenced.

12.3.2 Choice parameters model

This model considers how the underlying buying motive differs from the obvious product use and the apparent buying motive, for example:

Product	Use	Primary parameter	Secondary parameter
Cereal	Nutrition	Taste, bulk economy	Ease of preparation, slimming, health image, special offers of games on packet
Aspirin	Pain control	Effectiveness	Taste, ease of swallowing, no upset stomach, reassurance of popular brand

or to use an industrial example:

Cutting tools	Metal removal	Removal rate, surface finish, life, price	Productivity

Much effective advertising homes in on the secondary parameters to create brand differentiation, on the basis that all competing brands meet the primary parameters in some way.

12.3.3 Learning model

We respond by habit to certain stimuli. We all have certain drives (hunger, thirst, cold, sex, pain, fear). If a cue reminds us of an unsatisfied drive, then we will respond to it. Consider, for example, a repeated advertisement showing sizzling sausages; each time we see it we feel hungry; next time we shop for food we may think of sausages — hopefully even the right brand. We will probably not remember the brand name but the stimulus of looking along the shelf displaying different brands may subconsciously cause us to remember the advertised brand. Fortunately, or unfortunately, depending on how one views the world, this sort of stimulus does not last very long and hence the importance of repeated advertising over an extended period.

Habit forms a very large part of any purchasing behaviour; we normally prefer what we are used to. In order to break a habit the stimulus must be relatively strong and the product really must deliver what is being offered. For example, a new razor blade must offer a really much closer shave, because if on trial it is no better or worse than the usual brand, many people will return to the brand with which they are familiar and comfortable, unless, of course, there are other compensating benefits, such as being easier to dispense, easier to load into the razor, or being significantly cheaper. Breaking habits is a major problem in industrial markets (see Section 12.10.4).

12.3.4 The psychoanalytic model
People have many levels of motivation and if advertising goes against the hidden motives it will be unsuccessful. For example, it was found that the original advertisements for instant cake mixes aroused guilt feelings in housewives that they would not be good wives if they took short cuts with the cooking, and so the advertisements were changed to emphasize improved results rather than just time saving. However attitudes have now changed and current advertisers emphasize that these aids free time for other more "worthwhile" activities. Another example is the serious business magazines and newspapers while they appear to be sold because they are authoritative, many people buy them because it makes them feel important. (Similarly, say with personal dictating machines: efficiency or importance?) Successful marketing requires that the influence of these underlying motives is recognised.

12.3.5 Social psychological model
People are affected by their social contacts and their cultural norms. It is noticeable how ownership of items such as double glazing, video recorders, greenhouses, freezers, spreads within social groups. Once one or two become owners, others feel left out if they do not follow. People see others with a particular style of shirt, sweater or whatever and may feel impelled to follow. The pattern of uptake for a new product can be illustrated as shown in Fig. 12.1. The innovators will adopt anything new, just to be first. Product launches should be aimed at them, and at early adopters, in order to get a new product off the ground. Early adopters are on the look-out for new ideas and will undertake rapid but quite thorough evaluation. If the new product appears to offer a geniune advantage to them (an advantage may be measured in many different forms), they will try it out. Their motivation is to be opinion leaders. Thereafter personal influence will play an increasingly important role in the ongoing adoption of the product.

12.3.6 Buying role model
A number of different buying roles have been identified, namely, initiator, influencer, decider, purchaser, and user (see Webster and Wind [70]). In many cases

several of these roles will be combined. The list below shows who might occupy each of the roles for two different buying decisions:

Buying roles	Purchase of a drawing board	Purchase of a football player
Initiator	Draughtsmen or chief draughtsman	The player, or the coach/manager/chairman of the buying or selling club
Influencer	Everyone in the drawing office, the chief engineer, the buyer, the accountant, possibly the work study department	The fans, the media, other players, the Board and staff at both clubs. Other clubs who may bid for the player
Decider	Works manager or chief engineer	Chairman or manager of buying club
Purchaser	Usually the buyer	Usually the manager
User	The draughtsman	The club, the fans

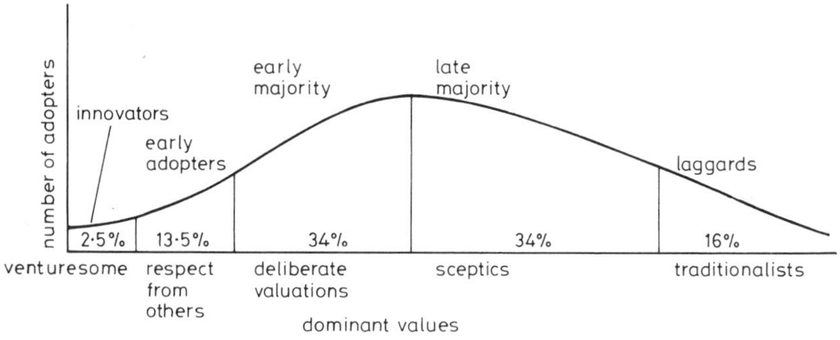

Fig. 12.1   *Uptake of new products*

Often the occupant of different roles will depend on the personalities involved. So for example, in some companies the chief engineer may simply indicate which drawing boards he is prepared to accept and leave the final choice to the chief draughtsman, whereas in others he will be the final decider. A recent *ad hoc* study into the purchase of computers suggests that in the case of technically complex capital goods the influencer role can be subdivided into recommender and influencer. The recommender is usually someone who has some technical understanding of the product to be bought and who is therefore given the job of investigating what is commercially available, and reporting back. As a result, this person attains a much higher level of technical understanding about the product to be bought and consequently it becomes very difficult for anyone else in the company to argue against his recommendations. Thus the recommender is able to exert much greater influence on the final decision than other less informed influencers, such as potential users or senior managers. Marketing management must appreciate the importance of all these roles.

12.3.7 Logical model

In some cases buyers undertake a logical analysis of their requirements, see Fig. 12.2. If it is assumed that rational buyers would buy whichever brands offered the greatest utility to them, a straight presentation of product features and performance capability would be the best approach. However, in practice few consumers remain uninfluenced by some of the factors referred to in the previous models. Given logical behaviour the important decision factors could be researched and utilised in subsequent promotions.

Fig. 12.2   *A logical buying sequence*

12.4 Industrial buyers

Following the above outline of some of the basic explanations of consumer buying behaviour, it is now appropriate to consider how industrial buyers behave. Clearly there are important differences as well as similarities. Industrial buyers have been portrayed as follows:

1 *Rational*: industrial buyers usually do not buy for themselves but on behalf of others, and therefore they need not become emotionally involved in the purchase. As a result they are expected to follow a logical sequence of buying steps in accordance with the logical model, namely, to buy only when there is a clear value-analysed need, to undertake a thorough search for alternative products and suppliers, and to compare them systematically on the basis of agreed buying criteria (for examples of criteria see Chapter 5, Hill and Hillier [71]). These criteria are expected to be agreed by the company departments which will be affected by the buying decision, and are expected to be as stated rather than hiding secondary parameters or psychological concerns. This logical approach should mean that industrial buyers, when presented with a superior product, will switch to that product and not continue with an old product out of habit or because they prefer dealing with a particular supplier. Industrial buyers are expected to search continuously for best buys.

2 *A team member*: most industrial purchases are not undertaken in isolation by only one individual. Usually several members of the organisation will be affected by the decision and therefore will wish to influence it. Sometimes this fact is

recognised by formally establishing a buying team or committee, but very often the team establishes itself informally as a result of individuals expressing an interest in the purchase and becoming involved in informal consultations. The buyer or 'decider' (from Section 12.3.6) normally acts as the focus of the activities. Being a team process is supposed to increase the logicality of the decision with non-logical individualistic views being smoothed away during group discussions, that is, when exposed to logical counter-arguments. The size of the team will vary greatly according to the nature of the purchase and each member of the team will occupy one or more of the buying roles described in Section 12.3.6. Alternatively, it has been suggested (Hill and Hillier [71]) that the buying team can be divided into an information gathering unit, a control unit (which determines the buying criteria) and a decision making unit (which decides between competitors on the basis of the chosen criteria). Although this concept is possibly easier for suppliers to relate to when deciding to whom they should direct their efforts, it can be seen that it has a direct link to the buying roles.

3 *Well informed*: it is expected that at least one member of a buying team will be technically competent to evaluate alternative products in some depth, rather than having to rely on the information salesmen and brochures provide. As a result it is generally held that it is necessary for suppliers to explain in detail how their products produce the performance which is being promised, rather than forcing buyers to take the performance on trust, via company reputation, as is done with most consumer products. It is also expected that buyers will be well informed about alternative sources of supply. A consumer setting out to buy, say, a portable radio recorder, would not be expected to take the trouble to find out all the alternative models available and all the different prices at which each model is being sold by all the local retailers. It is much more likely that the consumer will visit two or three, or perhaps if he is keen five or six, local suppliers and choose from those models in stock the one which seems the best value. On the other hand the industrial buyer, buying, say, an integrated circuit block, might be expected to know of each alternative make, and the price, delivery and reliability of each supplier. If this were the case, then logically every buyer would welcome every salesman with open arms, as they would be bringing new information to help with the all embracing search and evaluation process.

It should be clear from this picture of industrial buying that the person who holds the job title 'buyer' is not the only person involved. In engineering companies technical staff exert a major influence on buying decisions, often to the extent of specifying a particular make; for example, a design draughtsman may specify on his drawings the make of component he wants to incorporate in his designs. Often the buyer only enters the picture after the choice of supplier has been made on technical grounds; as a formality. Buyers are rarely allowed to choose for themselves what is bought.

Instead, the buyer's role is:

1 to negotiate prices and other terms of sale with vendors;
2 to keep company staff aware of alternative sources of supply and in particular of their pricing structures and their delivery/quality performance, thereby ensuring competitive purchasing;
3 to maintain good relationships with suppliers;
4 to manage the mechanics of order placement, chasing delivery, returning defects and authorising payments,
5 to influence colleagues to plan purchases ahead, and to order in economic batch quantities (materials requirements planning is a logical extension of this last role and in fact extends the role of the buying department).

Buyers only become decision makers when several technically acceptable suppliers have been identified or when the purchase is not considered important enough to involve several people. As a result, in engineering companies the buyer is often held to have a lower status than the specifying engineers, but usually neither has authority over the other and hence complex communications and motivation flows are set up. The buyer will often seek to gain power by modifying the decision variables so that his department has a larger say in the buying decisions than otherwise would have been the case. Clearly the buyer loses status if the decision is cut and dried in other departments. He then becomes merely an order clerk.

This means that suppliers have to actively sell to other personnel in addition to the buyer. To avoid terminology confusion from now on the term 'buyer' will be reserved for the person with that job title, and the term 'purchaser' will be used to indicate anyone else involved in the buying decision.

12.5 Industrial purchasing is not necessarily logical or thorough

For a long time industrial marketing tended to play down the fact that industrial purchasers are human beings and subject to all the same emotions, motivations, pressures, values and beliefs as consumers. After all, during their lunch hour or at weekends industrial purchasers become ordinary consumers. In other words they can be persuaded to buy other than with purely logical arguments. While industrial purchasers do not buy for themselves, they are still likely to become emotionally involved, because if a chosen supplier falls down on the job, that will reflect badly on them.

Rather than undertaking an all embracing search and evaluation process, individuals tend to simplify their problems by sub-dividing them, looking for acceptable rather than optimal solutions, dealing with problems on a one at a time basis rather than in parallel, trying to avoid uncertainty by establishing reliable relationships, looking for familiar solutions to problems, and looking for solutions consistent with previous experience and expectations. They change their behaviour to reflect past successes and failures. These generalised behaviour patterns, first postulated by Cyert and Marsh [72], can be applied to the industrial buying situation.

12.5.1 Decisions are affected by previous experience

The objectivity of buying decisions will be influenced by people's existing opinions of potential suppliers, formed from their own direct and indirect experience. Previous experience directly biases our perception of reality. To take a simple example, if one walks into a room at $20°C$ on a winter day when the outside temperature is $10°C$, that room will feel warm, whereas the same room at the same temperature on a hot day will seem cool. People also tend to generalise on the particular. For example, if someone has had poor direct experience of one division of a company he will often transfer that poor experience to all other divisions of the company; or if someone has experienced problems, say, with a particular belt drive, he is likely to be set against all belt drives. Rather than taking the trouble to re-evaluate suppliers who have not proved satisfactory in the past, attention will only be paid to suppliers who have proved satisfactory, and failing that, to suppliers who have not previously been dealt with. People use past experience to save time, and therefore searches for suppliers will tend to focus on areas where solutions have been found in the past.

Indirect experience is often as powerful an influence as direct experience. Indirect experience is gained by reading technical articles, adverts, and brochures, by attending exhibitions, by listening to what salesmen say, and by talking with colleagues. The problem with selling to people who have preconceptions, even if based on hearsay, is that they will see what they expect to see and will hear what they expect to hear. Thus if a purchaser has decided that a particular product is unreliable he will tend to extract from all that the salesman says, items which will confirm that view, and will tend not to remember items which are contrary to that view. Unless the salesman is aware of these prejudgements he probably will not contradict them sufficiently strongly to dislodge them from the purchaser's mind. If these prejudgements have been publicly stated then it is extremely unlikely that they can be changed, because of the loss of face involved. Where the views have not been publicly stated the chances of changing them are much improved.

12.5.2 Team decisions are often not logical

Anyone who has served on a committee will appreciate the truth of this statement. First, the views expressed by each group member will inevitably be influenced by the sales and promotional skills of alternative suppliers. Secondly, within any group there will be some who are worse at stating their case than others, who, although they may actually be correct in their views, allow themselves to be out-argued. Thus the views of the better talkers will carry more weight than the views of the poorer talkers. Thirdly, within any group some people will have more power and authority than others, and as a result their views will carry greater weight. This is a particularly important effect within companies, as those lower down the hierarchy will be trying to impress those higher up, and hence will tend to mould (often subconsciously) what they say, around what they believe those higher up will want to hear. In that case the chances of a cool logical well balanced decision are remote. Judgement will also be clouded by the extent to which individual team members want to be seen to conform with the group values, (which in turn will be affected by the extent that those values conflict with the values of other groups of which they are members). Senior executives are more likely to become involved in the more major decisions, and on the above basis, their presence may well hinder the process of reaching a best buy rather than helping it.

Fourthly, in order to counter personal power, groups often sub-divide into factions. When there are two or more equally powerful sub-groups then some compromise view is sought, and this can often degenerate to the lowest common denominator, that is the least bad solution that no faction will vociferously object to. Unfortunately that also often means that no one on the team actually believes that the agreed decision is a particularly good one, but at least an agreement has been reached and progress can be made. In many ways the larger the number of people involved in the decision, the greater the potential for arriving at an emotive or political decision rather than a logical decision. Alternative ways of resolving interfactional or interdepartmental conflicts are to favour the views of one group in one decision and those of another group in the next, or to allow different groups to exert dominance over different aspects of a single buying decision. These ways can make selling very difficult.

12.5.3 Industrial purchasers are not necessarily well informed
In industrial markets, products and their application tend to be technically complex and considerable knowledge and expertise is needed to understand what is offered. This is where perhaps some misunderstanding arises. The fact that a person needs to have a considerable technical background to reach the same level of understanding about, say, a flow soldering machine, that the average person will reach with respect to, say, the qualities of a pint of beer, does not mean that the technical expert is actually better informed than his consumer counterpart. In the case of really complex technical items, the engineers in the buying company are unlikely to have sufficient specialist knowledge to truly appreciate the various counter claims of the competing suppliers. For example, many companies cannot afford specialists capable of designing complex systems, and although, as would-be purchasers they may lay down initial performance parameters, they often have to rely on suppliers' advice about what they really need. In that case they have no absolute way of judging the capabilities of competing proposals other than by impression and reputation.

12.5.4 Industrial purchasers seek to reduce risk
Purchasers always try to avoid the risk of making a poor purchase. The cost to a company if a small component is not delivered on time, or has to be returned after goods inwards inspection, or even worse fails in final test or in service, will normally far outweigh the difference in price between a low price supplier and a medium price supplier. Failure in service requires the company to face not only the cost of replacing and retesting the faulty items, but perhaps more significant, loss of reputation and customer goodwill; the extent of which it is difficult to

measure either in terms of lost sales or increased promotional expenditure to re-establish an untarnished image. Hence the prime purchasing criteria must be that the product performance promised by the supplier is sufficient for the task, that the performance promised will always actually be achieved in use, and that delivery promises will be met. Price differences only become important when choosing between suppliers who meet all the above criteria. Obviously the more crucial purchases, evaluated in terms of cost to the company if the purchased product fails to live up to expectations, will be approached with more care than less important purchases will.

Purchasers try to reduce the risk of making a poor decision in three major ways:

1 *By using existing or past suppliers.* That is buying from companies who have satisfactorily supplied the same, or similar product in the past, on the basis that if suppliers have proved themselves reliable, there is no reason to believe that they will not continue in that vein. Very often this is taken to the extent of continuing to buy from a supplier who certainly no longer appears to offer the best value, rather than risk changing to another supplier who seems better, but may turn out to be worse. It is this continual preference to deal with the known that makes it so difficult for companies new to a market, and with a new product, to establish themselves.

2 *By using reputable suppliers.* Companies establish a good reputation by satisfactorily supplying a wide range of companies. Obviously satisfactory experience of others is not as reliable as first-hand experience, but unless there are specific contra-indications, reputable suppliers should prove to be satisfactory. Sometimes purchasers seek the advice of acquaintances in other companies whose views and values they trust, to try to confirm the validity of general reputations. This approach is particularly popular with senior executives, as they do not have the time needed to evaluate the various counter claims in depth.

3 *By seeking information.* Should there be no potential suppliers in the above categories, it is necessary to undertake a more extensive search for suppliers. Purchasers have to find out as much about each supplier as possible; by reading their advertisments and their brochures, by listening to their salesmen, by talking to other customers, by reading articles in the technical press, by attending exhibitions and demonstrations, and by undertaking evaluation and trials. This thirst for information is not an attempt to find a best buy but an attempt to avoid a bad buy.

On a more personal level, buyers and purchasers will be anxious to avoid the risk of a bad purchase because that would reflect badly on them and would affect their ego, their standing with the company, their chances of promotion, and in extreme cases their job security. The more important the purchase, the more dire will be the consequences of a bad decision (for example, one senior data processing manager was moved on because he chose a new computer system which proved not to be properly capable of meeting his company's information needs). Purchasers' levels of anxiety will also be related to their confidence that they can properly discriminate between alternative offerings, and to their sense of the security of their position within the company. Where the level of anxiety is high, purchasers are most likely to opt for safety and to choose a supplier with a good general reputation, rather than a supplier who seems to offer the best solution to the particular problem, because the good reputation can be used as some sort of defence if the purchase does not work out. Only if the anxiety level is low is there much chance of an objective appraisal. Thus companies selling to purchasers who are not technically competent and/or not secure in their job, need to emphasise reputation and make sure that purchasers are able to inspect other successful installations (this again provides a form of defence for purchasers if the product proves unsatisfactory; they can refer to the successful experience of companies A, B etc.).

Although middle managers tend to be risk avoiders and more concerned with survival than excelling, they do like from time to time to be seen to make a good decision. The more important the purchase, the greater the potential kudos involved in making a good decision, and the greater the apparent incentive to undertake a really thorough appraisal. However, risk avoidance tends to dominate, with many apparently extensive appraisals being undertaken to add to the defences should things go wrong, by 'proving' that the supplier with the best reputation is the best choice. It is part of the selling art to take advantage of these appraisals by persuading purchasers that in this particular case there actually will be virtually no risk to them in taking a decision not to choose the supplier with the best reputation, and therefore the prestige attached to taking an apparently bold step will far exceed any minimal risks involved. Apart from the methods outlined above, purchasers often try to avoid sole responsibility for a complex decision by deliberately spreading the risk and involving other staff in the decision.

12.5.5 Industrial purchasers seek satisfactory purchases rather than best buys

In other words purchasers undertake only a limited search for alternative products and alternative suppliers, just as consumers do. As soon as four or five, or less, technically acceptable suppliers have been found, the search process will be curtailed, and whichever of the four or five seems to represent the best value will be chosen. Further time and money (and remember time is money), will not be wasted in searching for more alternatives to evaluate, on the off chance that one of them may provide sufficiently better value to offset the increased search and evaluation costs which would have been incurred. It is more likely that the time could be spent more effectively on another task, perhaps clarifying requirements with the chosen suppliers in an attempt to improve the value of what they offer. The only exceptions to this rule are very large companies where purchases are large enough to justify a continuous search. In contrast, in smaller companies with a lower order value the search process tends to be quickly curtailed. This satisfying process does not mean that if a supplier actively draws attention to the fact that his product offers better value, that the information will be ignored, it just means that it will not be actively sought.

12.6 Processes used to search for alternative suppliers

These sorts of ideas led to suggestions (e.g. by Robinson, Faris and Wind [73])
that most purchasers follow a sequence of steps similar to that outlined below,
when searching for a supplier, only continuing to the next step if the previous
one has not yielded a satisfactory solution:

1 They affirm that there is a need to make a purchase.
2 If there is a current supplier, they evaluate whether their performance is still
   satisfactory. If so a repeat order is placed.
3 They search in their memory for a previous supplier of that product.
4 They search in company records for a previous supplier of that product.
5 They search in their memory or in company records for a current or previous
   supplier of a similar product.
6 They ask suppliers of similar products for their recommendations.
7 They search among brochures and catalogues on file within the company,
   that is among suppliers who have not been used before but whose products
   have been considered sufficiently interesting for some sort of contact to have
   been made.
8 They ask colleagues both inside and outside the company if they know of a
   reliable supplier.
9 They consult the advertisments in the relevant trade magazines.
10 They consult product directories, that is directories which list the name of
   every company which supplies the type of product being sought.

This search process is summarised in Fig. 12.3.

Obviously this sequence is not always followed exactly and sometimes one or
more steps are undertaken in parallel, but in general there is a tendency to start
with the known, the least risky and to move progressively towards the unknown,
the most risky. Small companies, because of their lack of resources are more
likely to stop earlier, rather than later, in the process. Sometimes to save time,
rather than move on to the next stage, the decision criteria are deliberately modified so that previously rejected suppliers can now be considered as acceptable.

The speed with which the process is undertaken will be dependent on the
urgency of purchase. In the case of an urgent purchase it is more likely that several
of the steps will be undertaken in parallel, that the sales organisations of possible
suppliers will be contacted by telephone and asked to present themselves the next
day, and that the purchase decision criteria will be less rigorously applied so that
a satisfactory supplier can be found quickly. In this urgent situation it is particularly
important for the selling company to be within the net of the earlier stages of the
search process, as the latter stages will invariably not be reached. If the purchase
is to be repeated, a more thorough search and evaluation may be undertaken in
time for the first rebuy (see Section 12.9), although the supplier chosen the first
time around obviously has an advantage.

Finally, depending on the importance of the purchase and the degree of uncer-

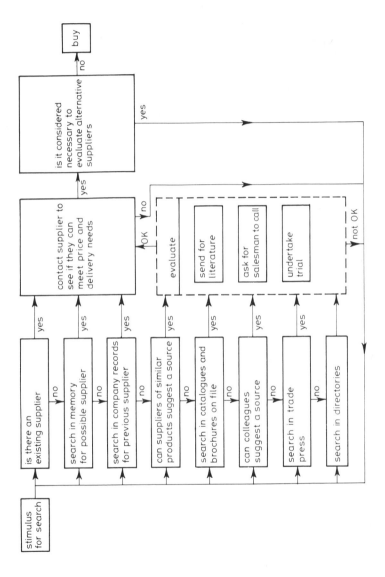

Fig. 12.3   Search process (from ideas in Robinson, Faris and Wind [73])

tainty about the reliability of the performance promises made by the short-listed suppliers, some sort of demonstration or trial may be undertaken. Whereas a standard well defined item, such as a particular type of diode, may be chosen straight from a catalogue, a non-standard less well defined item, such as an automatic soldering machine, may be subject to a trial.

12.7 Factors which inhibit a thorough search for and evaluation of suppliers

As indicated above, the search for and evaluation of alternative suppliers will not necessarily be thorough or logical. Various inhibitors are at work which make it sensible to undertake only a limited search and evaluation process. First the time available; the more urgently the problem needs solving the less thorough will be the search for alternative suppliers and the less thorough the evaluation of what they offer.

In the case of urgently required items a balance has to be struck between the cost of delay and the cost of buying an adequate rather than a good product. Usually the costs of delay are the overriding factor, or the purchase should not have been classified as urgent. Time constraints often force buyers to only spend time on items which are complex, or where there are problems, and in order to create sufficient time for these purposes, as many other purchases as possible are reduced to a routine habitual process. Suppliers who are difficult to find are not likely to be considered, especially where half a dozen names come readily to mind, unless all the initial batch of potential suppliers prove unsatisfactory in some way.

A second inhibitor is cost. If the product is such that proper evaluation would be expensive and time consuming, there is every chance that the evaluation will not be properly undertaken, and reliance placed on impression and reputation. Unfortunately it is precisely in these cases, where evaluation is complex, that it should be most thorough.

The effect of these two inhibitors is clearly illustrated by the way companies try to fill job vacancies. They advertise the vacancy and choose the best of those who reply, providing they meet the basic performance specifications for the vacancy. It is only at the highest level that attempts are sometimes made to evaluate all the people who can potentially undertake the job. The search and evaluation process is likely to be more extensive in the case of items of high value to a company because the difference between a good buy and an adequate buy will be sufficient to offset the costs of a more thorough approach.

A third inhibitior is that sometimes, even where a systematic evaluation against agreed decision criteria makes economic sense, it is not possible because of the nature of the purchase. For example, although it is relatively easy to judge between forklift trucks in terms of reach, lift, height, width, power consumption, noise, manoeuvreability and driver comfort, it is much more difficult to choose between alternative bids to install a ducting system. All that can be done, other than rely on impression and reputation, is to check some other previous installations. Even that is no guarantee that the proposed installation will be as good as the previous ones; maybe the foreman or the installation team will have changed in the interim. In yet other cases, the evaluation of alternative suppliers may not bring to light one which is clearly superior to the others. None of them is ideal, each having different disadvantages and advantages. Yet again purchasers are forced to rely on their subjective impressions and in this case the influence of the salesman often becomes the deciding factor.

A fourth inhibitor to the most cost effective choice is that there are insufficient funds to pay for it, and therefore a less satisfactory but cheaper alternative has to be chosen. The fifth major inhibitor is that purchasers continually seek to reduce the risk of making a bad buy (see Section 12.5.4).

12.8 How purchasing decisions are arrived at

Industrial purchasing can be considered as a problem-solving process which extends from the early recognition of a problem, through stages of fluctuating activity towards the eventual placing of an order. The process will be affected by the order value, the importance of the order to the customer's business, technical complexity, the number of potential suppliers, and the experience and knowledge of the purchaser. The process has been summarised in Fig. 12.4. The first step is the recognition of a need to make a purchase, which usually in industrial companies means that there is a problem which needs to be solved; for example, to maintain production, to improve product finish, to improve fatigue strength, to increase throughput on a particular process or to reduce stocks.

The next stage is to consider ways of solving the problem, quite often in consultation with potential suppliers, and to set the buying decision criteria. The decision criteria eventually arrived at are then compared with the packages (of problem solving benefits) offered by competing suppliers, and one of them chosen to be given the order. Technical superiority alone does not guarantee success, with orders often being placed with suppliers who give the impression of best understanding customer's problems, and of putting themselves out to help solve them.

The final choice may be by an individual, or more usually by a group or team. The choice will be strongly influenced by previous experience, by time, cost, and risk related constraints, and by social pressures exerted on and between the buying team.

Once a decision has been reached, the chosen product will either be subjected to a trial or bought. Occasionally a purchase can be deferred, either because during the evaluation process a more urgent use for the funds has arisen, or because the evaluated benefits of the proposed purchase do not warrant the expenditure at the present time. Once the product is bought, in-use experience, either good or bad, will become part of the purchasers' experience and will have a major effect on their subsequent choice of the same or similar products.

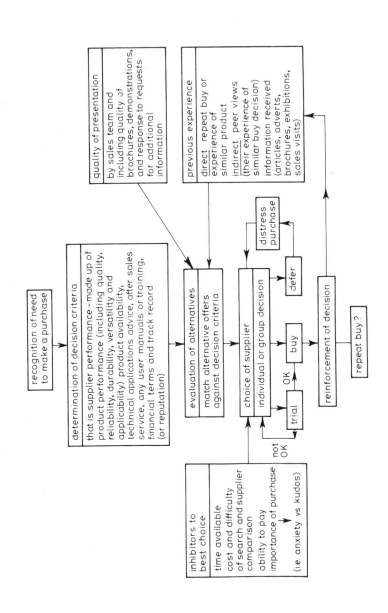

Fig. 12.4 Industrial buying process

12.9 Different types of product are bought differently

Companies undertake different types of purchases, and the nature of the purchase will affect how they go about deciding where to place their custom. For example, Lehmann and O'Shaughnessy [74] suggested that different sorts of purchasing problems would arise with the four product types listed in Table 12.1. If this were true, purchasers should use different criteria when choosing each type of product. A survey among 45 major companies confirmed that the most important criteria did differ as shown in Table 12.1. The high rating of delivery reliability for product type 3 was put down to the high overall importance of this factor, and the need

Table 12.1   *The most important buying criteria for different product types*

Product type	Description	Most important buying criteria
1 Routine order products	Frequently ordered and used, there is confidence in their ability to do the job and no problems in learning how to use them	Delivery reliability Price
2 Procedural problem products	There is confidence that they will do the job but personnel have to be taught how to use them	Technical services offered Ease of operation or use Training offered
3 Performance problem products	There is doubt as to whether the products will perform satisfactorily in the application being considered	Delivery reliability Technical service offered Flexibility of supplier in adjusting to customer needs Product reliability
4 Political problem products	There is likely to be difficulty in reaching agreement among those affected if the product is adopted; particularly if several departments are involved	Price Reputation of supplier Data on product reliability Delivery reliability Flexibility of supplier in adjusting to customer needs

to avoid such an obvious source of potential criticism from users, which would aggravate other potential problems. In the case of type 4 products, it was suggested that the priorities listed indicated a need for buyers to reduce personal risk, by being able to clearly justify the choice made. In practice, of course, a single purchase can give rise to more than one problem type.

Another method of classifying purchases was suggested by Robinson and Faris [73] as follows:

1 A new buy, that is the first occasion that an article of the specified type has been bought.
2 A rebuy, that is a straight repeat purchase of an article which has been bought previously (e.g. drills, stationery or raw material).
3 A modified rebuy, that is where the specification of the article required has been modified for some reason since the last purchase.

Companies are obviously most likely to place an order with an existing supplier in the case of a rebuy and most likely to undertake a fairly extended search in the case of a new buy. Unless they have an outstanding product advantage to offer it is very difficult for salesmen to break into a rebuy situation, and they have to wait for it to change to a modified rebuy. Likely triggers are irritation caused by a change in commercial procedures by the usual supplier, an unexpected price increase, a drop in product quality or delivery reliability, or a change in customer needs which will lead to a modification of the specification. In the case of modified rebuys, evaluation is likely to be limited to a small number of known suppliers, and only if these three or four are considered unacceptable will a wider search be initiated. In the rebuy situation commercial considerations are more likely to lead to a re-evaluation than technical considerations. In the case of a new buy, technical personnel will take the key decisions in the early stages, and technical considerations will probably limit the commercial choice to only two or three suppliers.

The articles being bought can also be classified as follows:

1 *Capital goods*
   Capital goods can be defined as goods for which the purchase cost is not written off against profits in the year of the purchase. Instead the cost is written off over what is considered to be a safe estimate of the useful life of the goods, i.e. a £20 000 computer with a life of four years may be written off at £5000 per year. Capital goods tend to be the purchases which can most easily be delayed (albeit unwisely, especially if the future of a company is dependent on having an up-to-date production or process plant), it being possible to continue operations using old equipment. The propensity to buy is much affected by the general level of business confidence, as this will dictate whether the equipment can be sufficiently utilised to repay its purchase price within a reasonable time-scale. Capital goods are normally treated as important purchases and most companies have formal approval procedures which have to be followed before the purchase is sanctioned. In other words the purchase decision will be considered in depth and a number of people will be involved.

2 *Goods bought for production*
   (a) Raw materials, that is materials, including components, sub-assemblies, nuts and bolts etc. which end up as parts of the final product. Purchases of raw materials cannot be put off if the company is to continue its operations. The initial specification and choice of supplier (i.e. new buy) usually involves a team of people and will almost certainly involve a formal product trial. However, once the initial choice has been made, rebuys will normally be left to the buyer and it is only if some dissatisfaction arises with the first choice supplier that any further evaluation is undertaken. Sometimes the buyer will be given the names of two or three technically acceptable suppliers and the final choice will be left to him on the basis of delivery and price. The tendency to continue to deal with those two or three companies who are selected initially will probably increase as computer controlled buying becomes more common and reordering becomes a matter of automated routine, organised to fit in with the production schedule. In these cases extended contracts with agreed call-off schedules may become even more common.
   (b) Consumables, that is items which are literally consumed during the production process but which do not form part of the final product, e.g. energy, cutting oil, solder, drills, mills and labour. The definition may fairly be extended from production to business consumables to include items such as stationery, factory rent, telephones, advertising, sales expenditure and so on. Buying the time of an advertising agency is just as much an industrial purchase as buying steel plate. As with raw materials most of these purchases are essential, and the buy decision is often taken by the department which will actually use the consumable item. In the case of 'standard' (and often low value) items the final choice between acceptable suppliers is often left to the buyer. This type of low value purchase is akin to the frequently bought consumer purchase, where it is relatively cheap to switch brands, just to check that alternative brands are no better than the one habitually purchased.

3 *Items bought for resale*
   Items are bought for resale whenever companies consider that they can efficiently market the product in question, but do not have the technical and production resources to manufacture it themselves. In this case the buying decision is likely to be made by marketing management or general management, subject to the advice of the technical and buying departments. The evaluation and negotiation process is likely to be lengthy.

A summary of the situation with respect to each type of article is shown in Fig. 12.5 (for an alternative classification see Chapter 2, Hill and Hillier [71]). The major sales influence in each case indicates where potential suppliers should concentrate their selling effort in order to maximise their influence on the purchaser's buying decision. Capital equipment salesmen should initially concentrate on influencing the decision criteria eventually to be set by the purchaser, (see also Section 12.10.2). By helping the purchaser understand what is important and how different models perform, the selling company strongly influences the final decision

	Capital goods	Production purchases		Items for resale
		High value	Low value and consumables	
Purchase importance	May be put off	Essential	Essential	Easily put off
Decision period or complexity	Extended and proportional to value. Often a made to order product	Initial selection extended. Periodic review else straight rebuy	Initially (may be) straight from catalogue else straight rebuy	Extremely variable Depends on extent of prior knowledge and on opportunities which crop up
Purchase frequency	Can be very infrequent (once in 5–10 years) or for low value items every six months	Fairly frequent	Very frequent	New buys rare; rebuys fairly frequent
Decision criteria	Applications advice (help with need assessment and understanding of how product works) Value added (to the business), versus cost of use (ownership) over planned life Installation help User instruction Versatility Service costs Reliability Energy costs	Reliability Results of trial Price	Ability to meet design criteria Reliability Availability Price (crucial as often treated as commodity type product; i.e. little differentiation between brands)	Availability Competitive advantage provided to buyer (i.e. profit potential)
Major sales influence	Setting of decision criteria	Ability to meet design criteria	Trial + catalogue quality	Proof there is a profitable market
Price	Competitive bids (for high value) List less discount	Individual negotiation or List plus discount	List less discount Occasionally individual negotiation	Negotiation
Distribution	Factory to factory	Factory to factory Some via stockists	Via stockists Some factory to factory	Factory to factory

Fig. 12.5   *Classification of industrial purchases*

criteria which will be laid down. While this also tends to be true of high value production purchases, buying companies often feel more confident of specifying what they want, and in that case the selling priority changes. It becomes necessary to demonstrate that a given product is the best fit with the specified criteria (technical and commercial). On the other hand, low value production purchases are often bought direct from a catalogue and the buyer is likely to choose from whichever catalogue he finds easiest to use. Providing the chosen brand performs adequately the chances are that no further evaluation will be undertaken.

12.10 Implications for marketing

Many of the implications for marketing management of the buying process have been mentioned in earlier sections of this chapter. Other implications will become apparent as you read other chapters of this book. However some of them are worth highlighting.

12.10.1 Buying team

This is perhaps the most important phenomenon of industrial buying. The more technically complex the product, the more important it is to the buying company, and the larger the company, the more likely it is that the buying process will be lengthy and involve a large number of people. It is crucial for suppliers to identify who is involved in the buying team, what their role is, and what their buying criteria are. Unfortunately, very often people try to keep their decision criteria hidden and therefore salesmen have to probe until they find them. Otherwise they may unconsciously say exactly the wrong thing or even sell their competitor's products. Very often the hidden criteria may be based on psychological factors, in particular in relation to job security and kudos. Where a buying team exists, it will usually pay to form an equivalent sales team. Very often the right person to speak to the prospect's design engineers or production manager, or buyer, or service manager is not the salesman, and the appropriate member of the selling team must be introduced so that a proper rapport can be established. In many cases the salesman assumes the role of an intelligence agent, finding out where the remaining problem areas are, relaying back the nature of those problems, so that the appropriate expert can make contact and help overcome the problem, whether it be in design, installation, training, servicing, delivery, packaging or whatever.

Ideally every member of the buying team should be sold in some way, but inevitably most of the effort will have to be concentrated on the decision maker, the recommender (if he exists) and the chief influencers. The sales team must identify who has the authority to commit company funds to the purchase and try to influence them directly. Failing that, the sales team must at least directly influence, or even better coach, whoever it is (often the recommender) who is to put forward the information upon which the spending authorisation decision will be based. In the case of important purchases a senior management committee or the board will usually expect to approve the proposal of the decision maker, that is to ensure that he has used the decision criteria which the board believes to be appropriate. If they do not agree with the criteria they will ask for the proposed purchase to be re-evaluated. In rarer cases the board may ask for two or three alternative proposals to be submitted from which they can make the final decision themselves. In that case it is vital to be aware of the board's decision criteria as well as those of the person who prepares the proposals. Very often the criteria are different. Many a sales attempt has failed because the most influential member of the buying team has been overlooked.

Within any group there will be opinion leaders and if they can be located and sold, they will often sell the product more effectively to other group members than could the product salesman, simply because people are more easily influenced by insiders (people they know and respect) than by outsiders. Very often the most important influencers may not be directly employed by the buying company: they may be consultants, architects or even one of the buying company's customers. For example, in the case of an electronic control panel, a customer may prefer a particular type or style of switch or instrument, in which case the panel manufacturer will have little freedom of choice, and salesmen would be wasting their time if they tried to persuade the manufacturer that an alternative type would be a better choice. They have to influence the end customer direct.

Each member of the buying team will have different motivations and priorities, and the salesmen must demonstrate their products in ways which reflect those motivations and priorities. For example, if one were selecting a container into which, say, a control unit was to be placed, the marketing department might be most concerned with the appearance and durability and size of the container, the production department with how easily components could be assembled into the container and with the reliability of delivery, the technical department with how well the container dissipates heat and allows control buttons and lamps to be ergonomically laid out, the service department with how easily the container allows key parts to be accessed, the transportation department with the degree of protection provided by the container, and the buying office with price, terms and ease of commercial dealings. Ideally each must be convinced in terms of their own priorities, but inevitably, the needs of one of the departments will override the needs of the others, and that department must be identified and concentrated on.

12.10.2 Different types of purchase
Obviously it is not possible to sell to everyone all the time and therefore it is necessary to try to determine whom to concentrate on at different stages of the sales effort (see also Brand [75]). Unfortunately, a survey into the construction industry (Bellizzi and McVey [76]) indicated that the Robinson/Faris buy classes are not necessarily by themselves a good predictor of who to influence. However, it is suggested that the idea of different buying roles and the Robinson/Faris buy classes can be combined with their ideas about the steps involved in the buying

process to identify whom to concentrate on at each stage (see also Johnston and Bonoma [77], and Hakannson [78]), for different types of purchase, as illustrated in Fig. 12. 6. The names of the departments who are less directly involved at each stage are shown in brackets (on Fig. 12. 6). For example, the analysis of alternative suppliers for a production component will be the prime responsibility of the design and production department, but the buying office, the service department and the marketing department may have important views because the choice will have an effect on their own activities. In the case of crucial components general management may also wish to be involved.

In the case of a new buy, technical staff tend to be given a clear run in the early stages, and where the problem is technically complex, they often appreciate help and advice on how to design a particular part of their product or how to solve a particular (say production) problem, or how to best select a particular component. In order to provide access to the specialist know-how of alternative suppliers when deciding how best to solve the problem, technical staff often initiate a search for suppliers (see Fig. 12.6) immediately following problem definition. Very often the company which offers the best solution at this stage is immediately chosen without inviting other companies to meet the proposed specification. The time to sell products whose application is technically complex is while the proposed solution is being worked out and not after formal enquiries are made. Even if a purchasing specification is put out to tender, the company which had most influence at the specification setting stage should have established itself as the preferred potential supplier in the eyes of the technical staff.

Properly undertaken, technical applications advice should be such that the selling company's product naturally emerges as the obvious choice to solve the problem. That is, the decision criteria will be influenced so that they become a reflection of what that supplier and that product can do particularly well, which their competitors cannot do quite so well (see also Section 15.5). In addition, technical staff usually regard suppliers who provide a technical advice service as more reliable and more likely to provide further help and service if subsequent operating problems occur. As a result, technical staff are often prepared to accept a higher price as a trade-off for the service provided. This trade-off is not always accepted by the buying office, but technical staff are often prepared to set the technical specification such that the freedom of the buying office to place the order with less co-operative but cheaper suppliers is limited. The only hope for competitors who only enter the picture much later in the decision making process (presumably owing to lack of market intelligence) is to enlist the help of buying departments, who will be anxious to press for a broader specification so that they can exercise some choice, and negotiate with respect to terms and delivery, rather than being tied down to only one supplier.

Providing a technical specification can be met by several competitors, the final buying decision is usually taken purely on commercial grounds, and in that case, step 6 becomes a two-stage process; a technical first stage followed by a commercial second stage.

Company department involved in process

Buying steps‡	Class of purchase	Buying role	Capital goods	Components	Consumables	Resale items
1. Problem realisation	new buy	Initiator	General management production† (or other user department)	Technical, Production (general management and marketing)	Production + (other user department)	General management Marketing
2 Problem definition		Initiator Influencers	General management Production (or other user department)	Technical Production	User department (technical)	Marketing (general management)
3 Proposed solution	modified rebuy	Influencers	User department and suppliers	Technical (production)	User department supplier (technical)	Marketing (general management)
4 Description of item needed		Influencers	User department and suppliers	Technical	User department	Marketing
5 Search for suppliers		Influencers	Buying (user department and general management)	Buying (technical and production)	Buying (user department)	General management Marketing
6 Analysis of alternative offerings		Influencers Decider* User	User department (Buying and general management)	Technical and Production (marketing general management, buying and service department)	User department (buying)	General management Marketing
7 Order placement	rebuy	Buyer*	Buying office	Buying office	Buying office	Marketing
8 Performance		User* Influencers	General management and user departments	All company departments	User department (buying)	General management

* In the sense used, the buyer, the decider and the user can be one of the influencers at the earlier stages.
† Production is the most likely user department but office equipment or test rigs will obviously be used by other departments.
‡ Based on Robinson and Faris [73].

Fig. 12.6 *Who to influence during each stage of the buying process*

At the other end of the spectrum, straight rebuys only involve steps 7 and 8, and are mainly controlled by buying departments. Where buyers have successfully pressed for a list of technically acceptable alternative suppliers, any dissatisfaction from them on commercial grounds, or from user departments on quality or delivery matters, can lead to a rapid reappraisal within the approved list (step 6). That being the case, suppliers must be careful not to upset their existing customers — for any reason. Of course the requirements of user departments will occasionally change, and that will necessitate a return to step 3.

Companies selling capital goods and other products made to order will appear to deal almost entirely with new buy situations. However, they are in fact normally dealing with a very long rebuy cycle, sometimes so long that the technology has advanced sufficiently to make the current product very different to the one bought previously, but if the personnel are still the same they will be influenced by their previous experience. Other companies selling raw materials or standard components will have to mainly deal with rebuys or modified rebuys. It will help them to sell more effectively if they establish in each case which situation they are in. In the case of the rebuy situation in particular, buyers become very discerning about small differences, and providing they have been given a list of technically acceptable suppliers they can sometimes be persuaded to place an order with other than their normal supplier by the offer of an improved commercial service.

As well as knowing who to concentrate on, it is also necessary to identify the buying criteria being used by the buying team. While Fig. 12.5 and the work of Lehmann and O'Shaughnessy [74] gives a general lead (Table 12.1), unfortunately any given product may be subject to different criteria depending on the application, the type of customer and the nature of the individuals involved. As a result, suppliers must try to see the situation from the customer's viewpoint and try to deduce what their key decision criteria will be.

12.10.3 Risk

Another significant idea to arise is that one of the prime aims of most purchasers is to avoid risk; the risk of the product not performing as promised by the advertising, brochures and the salesman — and in the case of industrial products the risk of not being delivered on time — as well as the risk of being blamed later should the product fail to meet expectations.

This means that there will be a strong tendency to buy from companies that have proved satisfactory in the past; for example, a buyer in a large motor company stated that they almost never bought from a supplier they had not dealt with previously, even though it was appreciated that something akin to a closed shop was being created. In the rare cases where no satisfactory previous supplier could be found, they looked first of all at suppliers who supplied competitors, or who had a good reputation as a supplier in a similar industry. In order to obtain that first order, the risk perceived by potential customers has to be reduced (see Section 9.4). Companies with a good reputation usually win the battle.

In the case of new products being introduced to the market, the social psychological model (Section 12.3.5) certainly applies, with some companies being in the vanguard and anxious to try whatever is the latest product, and others being conservative and not prepared to buy anything that has not been proved in service over a number of years. These characteristics are probably more a reflection of the personalities of the relevant job holders at a given time, than of ongoing company policy, and therefore attempts must be made to assess and to record the personalities of key prospects.

12.10.4 Established purchaser–supplier relationships

These relationships are common because it usually makes sense to prefer to deal with an existing supplier; a good long term purchaser–supplier relationship can be as beneficial to the purchaser as to the seller. It can be used to bargain for better credit terms, for preference on delivery, or for improved quality. A long standing supplier is more likely to help out in an emergency situation where parts are needed unexpectedly urgently. In addition, suppliers will come to know customers well and will be better placed to understand their exact needs, and possibly will modify their standard offerings (making it more difficult for competitors to break the link) to meet those needs as nearly as possible. In other words, purchasers are always seeking to establish for themselves 'preferred customer' status, and obviously sellers should try very hard to reinforce this desire as it works beneficially for both sides and repays the effort involved. It is common practice in industry.

It follows that breaking an established buyer–seller relationship is not easily accomplished. For example, a survey (Buckner [79]) among industrial buyers indicated that approximately half would not change suppliers for a price differential of less than 5% and that approximately one-fifth would not change suppliers for a price differential of less than 10%. Occasionally it is possible to offer such a significant competitive advantage that potential customers are willing to face the risk and disruption costs involved in changing supplier. However, it is normally necessary to wait until a modified rebuy opportunity arises, and even then it will be necessary to offer something better than can be offered by existing suppliers. In many cases buyers initially use the results of such a re-evaluation to pressurise their existing supplier to improve his service, and only actually change suppliers if that pressure does not yield a positive result. This type of 'false' interest has caused many a frustrating hour for salesmen.

Sometimes it is possible to edge towards breaking a close customer–supplier relationship by responding very effectively if called on to help out in an emergency situation, whether it be an urgent delivery or a request for a non-standard item. An effective response, even if it is not profitable in itself, is likely to be rewarded by a further order, which if it is again filled satisfactorily, can be the beginning of a series of orders. Certainly, if a company does not respond to a call for help it may as well forget any prospects of orders in the immediate future. Similarly it behoves established suppliers to respond to requests of this nature to avoid customers looking elsewhere.

Another way of breaking in is to take advantage of those occasions when companies decide to buy a given product from more than one supplier, so as to improve delivery and quality security. However, such opportunities do not occur very frequently, as most companies who are inclined towards 'second sourcing' are already doing just that. The problem then is that one of the best predictors of future purchase behaviour is the pattern of past purchases. People learn habits and it takes major stimuli to unlearn them.

On the other hand, once suppliers have gained new customers they should concentrate on making habit work for them. They should concentrate on avoiding actions which might stimulate existing customers to look elsewhere, and on establishing close social links so that if a commercial or technical problem does arise, it will be treated with tolerance, as long as the supplier is clearly making attempts at rectification.

12.10.5 Limited search

The best answer to this phenomenon, other than, of course, being an existing supplier, is to have a good overall reputation; to be the industrial equivalent of a household name, so that when purchasers are trying to decide who to approach about a new buy or modified rebuy the company name is among the first three or four that come into their minds. While this familiarity can be attained by advertising or through publications in the technical press, if there are a relatively small number of potential customers it can be more cost effective to achieve it by regular sales calls or by mail shots or by regular exhibiting, or by some combination of all of these.

Crucial to this process is the impression made by salesmen during their visits, and the efficiency with which customers and potential customers are provided with up-to-date copies of company brochures and catalogues, and are kept aware of the capabilities of the latest versions of the company's products.

12.10.6 Inability to properly compare competing products

Many standard products are almost indistinguishable in purchasers' eyes, especially where there is strong competitive pressure to manufacture to a given level of performance (e.g. to international or national standards say for nuts and bolts, electrical resistors or hose fittings). Given an adequate performance for these products, they tend to be treated like convenience goods with buyers leaning towards delivery reliability and lower prices rather than improved performance. If price differentials are low, buyers will tend to opt for the supplier who appears to be the easiest to deal with, and that often means the one they are used to dealing with, or the one whose salesman they get on with best. Thus the less exciting the product the more important it is to have a good salesman (see also Wilson and Fowler [80]) because lacking any other meaningful decision criteria the buyer will use the salesman as a substitute criteria.

Even where standard products are somewhat more expensive and perhaps less frequently bought, it may not be considered necessary to undertake a thorough evaluation of alternatives, and therefore this type of product is often bought via a local distributor and his advice is sought and acted upon. They are akin to shopping goods. Habit plays a large part in these situations, and competitors have to try to cause buyers to begin to wonder whether or not they are making their companies uncompetitive by using a supplier who is no longer the best, in the hope that the uncertainty will cause them to re-evaluate the situation.

The buyer of basic products is likely to be fairly low down the hierarchy and on the whole will not wish to become involved in making a decision to move beyond the list of preferred suppliers. A company wishing to break the closed shop needs to introduce some novelty into his offer so that it can be legitimately brought to the attention of more senior management. This novelty will have to be via non-product benefits (because as stated above improved product performance is not sought), such as the method and timing of delivery being arranged to suit customers, making ordering/reordering and invoicing arrangements particularly easy for customers, provision of extra technical applications advice, offering very long guarantees as a sign of faith in the product, or offering to buy back surplus stock.

In general there will be little personal anxiety or prestige factors involved in such relatively unexciting purchases and hence the route to success is to concentrate on keeping prices relatively low rather than on product improvement, and to offer a first class commercial service, especially reliable delivery.

12.10.7 Post-purchase dissonance

On occasions when a buying team has found it difficult to decide between alternative products, the team will start to see more clearly the disadvantages associated with their choice once it is brought into use, and this will cause them to start to remember the strong points of the competitive products. This will be stressful to them and has been termed post purchase dissonance (see Festinger [81]). In order to make life more comfortable again, the buying team will actively seek information to reassure themselves that their decision was in fact wise. If such information is not forthcoming they may well become disenchanted and not buy from that supplier again. The supplier must ensure that the appropriate information is available, both direct from salesmen and indirectly via advertisements (see Section 13.3.6), technical papers and technical articles.

The possibility of post-purchase dissonance makes it essential to follow up orders once they have been delivered to ensure that all is well. If all is well, the follow up will serve to reassure the buyer that he has made a wise choice, and will improve the favourable impression of the company and its products. Admittedly, if things have gone badly wrong purchasers undertake their own follow up, but if the product has not performed quite as well as had been expected, this may not have sparked off an immediate reaction, and following up will enable the problems to be put right quickly before a bad impression builds up. An impression which would not only adversely affect subsequent buying decisions but could also affect the experience based messages passed on to colleagues and peers in other companies.

12.11 Buying in the future

The advent of increasingly universal and low cost information systems makes it
possible to conceive of a time when much of the search process described in this
chapter will not be necessary. It seems suitable to suggest that in the not too
distant future buyers will to able to 'punch' product codes into their individual
data terminals to 'call up' lists of competing suppliers, and on request, displays of
the equivalent of brochures and price lists. More ambitiously, sales videos
describing competing products and how they can and have been used could be
'called up', along with background information about each supplier and a list of
satisfied customers that are willing to be contacted by potential purchasers. However, while this eases the initial search process, all the other implications of buying
behaviour (i.e. Section 12.10) will still apply. For all but the most straightforward
products, potential purchasers will still want to ask questions of suppliers and to
examine products 'in the flesh', and the final stages of the buying process are
unlikely to be substantially different.

Chapter 13

Promotion

13.1 Why Promotion is needed

Obviously companies need to draw the attention of potential customers to their existence, to their products, and to the other qualities that they have to offer. One way of doing it is by direct contact, salesman to customer, but where the number of potential customers is large, this is an extremely expensive approach, and is unlikely to be economic unless the value of each individual purchase is large enough to offset the cost of a salesman's time. However, because human memory is not perfect, creating awareness once is insufficient by itself. The awareness has to be maintained by constant reminders. This means that regular sales visits would be needed, considerably adding to the above costs. Instead, a method of making repeat contact with a wide audience, rapidly and relatively cheaply is required. The methods used come under the broad heading of promotion.*

Marketing promotion is an attempt to persuade prospective customers to undertake some action, to find out more or to buy, by appeal to reason and to emotion, and it involves the following activities:

(a) Advertising
(b) Exhibitions
(c) Direct mail
(d) Brochures
(e) Public relations
(f) Technical articles and conferences
(g) Sponsorship
(h) Free trial

The emphasis given to each of these activities will vary from company to company, product to product, and market to market in an attempt to create maximum impact

---

* This uses the term promotion in a broad sense rather than the sense of temporarily increasing the value of a product so as to persuade more people to try it, by offering, for example, 2p off the next purchase, or a competition, or an extra 30% in the packet, or a free gift. Much more detail on promotion in general is given in Hart [82].

from a limited budget. The way promotion works should become clearer as we go on, but the importance of using promotion to make product names well known can be appreciated from some research (see Leavitt [83]) which indicated that it is easier for salemen from well known companies to arrange a sales visit than for salesmen from less well known companies. It was also shown that people attach greater truth to what is said by salesmen from companies with a good reputation than they do to what is said by salesmen from other companies. In other words the risk premium that the buyer perceives, that is the risk that the product will not perform as promised, can be reduced by promotion. Promotion can build a favourable image; a favourable image reduces the perceived risk; reduced risk can lead to increased sales.

13.2 Popular Image of Advertising

When many people refer to promotion, or indeed marketing, they are actually thinking in terms of advertising, probably because advertising is crucial to consumer marketing and everyone is liberally exposed to it in everyday life. As a result advertising has received a lot of attention in terms of research and theories, and inevitably this chapter will to some extent reflect this situation. Most people have a view about advertising; some good, some bad. As an introduction to the subject some of the better known views have been summarised without comment (see Duncan Reekie [64] and Leavitt [84] for definite views and research). Readers will be better placed to form their own view having read the rest of the chapter.

(a) *The cost of advertising increases prices.* This view is partly made up of the belief that the price of an advertised product must include an element to cover the cost of advertising which would not be present if there had been no advertising, and partly of the belief that advertising can create a false image which leads people to believe the product has more to offer than it has, and thereby encourages them to pay 'over the odds'.

(b) *Advertising reduces price.* This view is partly based on the belief that advertising can reduce total selling costs, by saving salesmen's time. Advertising saves time by generating enquiries for salesmen to follow up and hence reducing the amount of cold calling needed, and by pre-selling customers and thereby reducing the time which has to be spent on each initial sales visit. This view is also partly based on the belief that advertising helps companies to sell more, either by improving their market share or in combination with competitive advertising, by increasing total industry sales. Increased volume reduces unit costs. It may also reduce the margin charged by distributors. This incidently raises the interesting question of whether advertising, by encouraging people to buy more than they would have otherwise, is a good or bad thing. Certainly our improved material standard of living during this century has partly been based on higher sales volumes.

(c) *Advertising creates preconceptions which cause customers to be less critical.* Advertising seeks to build up a favourable impression of the sponsoring company and its products. It is known that people practise selective perception, that is they only tend to see, hear and remember information which reinforces their previous views, and tend to reject information which is contrary to those views. Hence if advertising is successful at creating a favourable impression, during subsequent contact with the company, customers will be expecting and will tend to find information which reinforces that impression. A parallel view is that advertising can cause buyers to adopt non-logical decision criteria, possibly preventing them from making a best choice. For example, for many years the promotion for movable office partitioning emphasised ease of erecion and ease of taking down and re-erection. Indeed, a survey among buyers showed that mobility easily topped their list of decision criteria. However, another survey discovered that only 10% of partitions are ever moved (and probably not many times). One might logically assume that factors such as appearance or sound proofing would be more important than mobility, unless the advertising had brainwashed buyers. An alternative answer may lie in the fact that an important 'influence' in the choice between alternative suppliers will be the works service department − the people who actually have to put the partitions up. They are treated as the experts and they clearly will be influenced by ease of erection and less by appearance and sound proofing. The views of the people who actually have to sit between the partitions generally carries much less weight.

(d) *If the product does not match up to the expectations created by advertising then it will not be bought.* Most industrial buyers undertake some sort of systemised trial or at least attend a product demonstration where product performance can be evaluated. Many low value items or frequently bought items are bought in small trial quantities so that they can be tested under actual operating conditions. Obviously, if the products do not match up to expectations, there will be no follow-up orders. This has led to a general belief that only 'good' products should be heavily advertised, that is where use will reinforce the expectations, and so on in an upward spiral.

(e) *Advertising increases barriers to entry to a market.* Higher barriers to entry reduce the number of competitors in a market and by implication that encourages higher prices to be charged. They are therefore undesirable. The height of a barrier can be increased if considerable advertising expenditure has to be incurred by new entrants in order to overcome existing product loyalties. Certainly it requires a higher level of advertising to create an impact in areas where advertising is generally at a high level than in areas where advertising is generally at a low level. It has been stated that it is risky for companies to diversify into new product/market areas where they have no track record, and presumably that risk will be increased if existing competitors in the market operate with high advertising levels. In other words, the new entrant will have to spend more on advertising to create a significant track record in people's minds. On the other hand, where the general level of advertising is high, some segments of the market may be vulnerable to a specialist low priced, low advertising approach.

(f) *Advertising reduces barriers to entry to a market.* Advertising enables newcomers to draw attention quickly to themselves and their products. This leads to more rapid trial (the introductory phase) and offers the opportunity for companies quickly to build their sales past the break-even point. However, in industrial markets, design, development and production set-up costs are often more significant barriers to entry than advertising costs. It would appear that, where these other barriers are significant, companies actually spend less on advertising than where these barriers are low, which tends to suggest that companies do believe that advertising can create a substitute barrier. It is also true that where these other barriers are significant, margins tend to be high, but that does not mean that low advertising expenditures cause high margins, nor that high advertising expenditures cause low margins. There will be a number of other factors at work.

13.3 Role of Advertising

In industrial marketing, advertising is often less important than other types of promotion or than direct selling. Take for an example an established seller of major capital plant. Decisions to buy capital plant are not normally taken quickly and purchasers usually make special efforts to find out what major suppliers have to offer, before investigating a limited number of options in more detail. In addition, the number of potential customers in a given year in a given geographic territory is likely to be relatively small and this makes it economic for salesmen to contact them individually. Similarly, advertising need not be vital for small subcontractors who target their marketing at a relatively small number of potential customers. Although mailshots and local exhibitions can create some impact, most of their new customers are likely to be gained as a result of personal recommendation from existing customers. In general, as products become more complex, and as the number of potential customers decreases, advertising becomes less important to sales success.

On the other hand for newcomers to a market, or for suppliers of products which are bought by a wide cross-section of industry (such as electric cable or drill bits), advertising is likely to be the most cost effective way of generating and maintaining awareness of their company and its products.

Advertisements undoubtedly represent an attempt to communicate persuasively with potential customers. In other words advertising is not concerned with presenting facts in an unbiased manner, but with presenting them in a way which will present advertisers and their products in a favourable light, and which will thereby persuade readers that it is worth finding out more about the advertised products. In the case of cheap, simple, and frequently bought products, finding out more may take the form of undertaking a trial purchase, but normally potential purchasers will want to find out more about products before they buy. However, advertising is only one-way communication, advertiser to reader, and therefore it cannot provide that additional information. This means that potential customers are forced to contact the supplier or his sales agent, and that advertising by itself cannot sell industrial products. Its role in industrial markets is:

1 to create and maintain awareness of companies and their products;
2 to generate interest, differentiation, and image;
3 to establish supplier credibility, that is a favourable impression of companies and their products;
4 to persuade distributors and agents that the advertised products will sell well;
5 to generate enquiries, that is to pave the way for a sales visit;
6 to reinforce the purchase decision.

13.3.1 Awareness
As indicated in Section 12.6, industrial purchasers only tend to consider suppliers whose names spring readily to mind. Advertising can be an extremely cost effective method of keeping the company name and the product name in front of purchasers, providing that the advertisements are eye catching and are printed where they will be noticed. Continual repetition of the name should eventually lead to it being remembered. In the case of new products this role is especially vital, as it rapidly makes customers aware that something new (and better) is available, that (by implication) should be investigated further.

In the case of new technology, awareness of the company name has to be supplemented by awareness of the new technology and how it can be of benefit. Obviously advertisements by themselves cannot provide the necessary education, but they can generate sufficient interest to entice readers to attend relevant seminars (see Section 13.5.6) and conferences.

13.3.2 Interest and Image
A well conceived advertisement will not only draw attention to itself so that it will be read, but it will also generate interest in the product by referring to a number of benefits which product use will confer on the purchaser and on the user. Ideally these benefits will be ones which competitors find hard to match. If not, it may be that the benefits can be combined in a novel way to provide a unique package. Alternatively, emphasis may be given to benefits where the advertised product has some marginal advantage, or which have existed for so long that people have taken them for granted. In other words, an attempt is made to emphasise that the advertised product is in some way sufficiently different and better than its competitors, that buying it will generate greater in-use satisfaction. Advertisements try to create an image of what it is like to own and to use the advertised products; a sufficiently favourable image to make people want to find out more, and possibly to persuade them to pay a higher price (see Section 6.5), or at least to tip the scales in favour of the advertised product. This effort is only likely to be effective if it is reinforced

by user experience and if it is consistent with company image and other company advertising, and with the way the product is presented (including its appearance), distributed and sold.

Perhaps the only occasion when a supplier who is aiming at a national audience, need not depend on advertising to generate a strong image is where the competitive advantage he can offer, perhaps by a unique selling point, such as a low price or product features that competitors cannot match, is so great that the product sells itself and generates its own favourable image. Such products are rare, and even then initial sales are likely to be higher if some advertising is undertaken.

13.3.3 Credibility

Sustained advertising without a doubt creates familiarity with a product and the product's name. With familiarity comes the assumption that many people must have bought and successfully used the product (even if the reader has not), and hence the product must at least be adequate for its purpose. In other words, sustained advertising builds up an image over time to the point where customers forget that much of the image has been created by advertising rather than by product performance. It creates the equivalent of a track record in buyers' minds and hence is particularly important for companies entering new product markets. This means that the effect of advertising on credibility is cumulative (the longer the advertising continues the greater the credibility), and that money spent on advertising now, continues to have a positive effect on the market for many months. Credibility is also concerned with the image of the supplying company as well as with product image. Advertisements can help generate supplier credibility by explaining why a particular company has the resources and expertise to reliably produce/deliver/install/guarantee/service an outstanding product, and to go on doing so for a number of years.

Once supplier credibility is established it becomes easier for salesmen to sell (see Section 13.1), quite often to the extent where the better known company, provided it employs equally competent salesmen, is able to sell an inferior product against competition from less known companies. As a result advertising campaigns have a considerable morale boosting effect on salesmen.

Occasionally companies are forced by circumstances to change their method of operation, and if the change is to be successful, it usually has to be accompanied by a change of image. People do not change their views easily and in general will make small changes more readily than large changes. The implications for the advertising effort is that the image being projected should be changed in stages from the old to the new, even if this will take a year or two. Attempts to change image quickly and in one large step are likely to create confusion about the company in customers' minds. Where there is confusion there is uncertainty and lack of credibility, and where there is lack of credibility there is loss of sales.

13.3.4 Distributor Enthusiasm

Credibility is especially important for companies selling via distributors. The last thing intermediaries want is for their sales efforts to be wasted on hard-to-sell products when they could earn more by concentrating on easier to sell products. As a result they try harder with products which they think will sell easily, and on the whole they tend to believe that well advertised products fall into that category. This belief must be in part experience based, but also stems from the fact that a sustained advertising campaign (a) should generate enquiries for their salesmen to follow up, (b) should make potential customers more inclined to see and to listen to their salesmen, and (c) is a sign of a substantial capital commitment to the product by the manufacturer, which should mean they believe that it will sell well.

Where products are well established, manufacturers should be able to establish their credibility by pointing to their past sales record and to their current sales volume, but even then more weight is likely to be attached to that record if there is a steady advertising campaign — for all the abovementioned reasons. Some advertising is aimed directly at intermediaries (via trade publications) but they can also be influenced by advertising aimed at end users.

A more direct way of using advertising to engender distributor enthusiasm is to undertake a joint supplier—distributor advertising campaign in local or specialist media. Usually the advertisements spotlight both supplier and distributor names (and addresses), and the quality and reliability of the distribution service offered. The aim, of course, is to generate enquiries for distributors to follow up themselves.

13.3.5 Enquiries

One of the major purposes of advertising industrial products — especially new ones — is to generate enquiries. It is hoped that advertisements will draw attention to themselves, and that they will create sufficient interest to persuade readers to send for more details (i.e. literature) or to request a sales visit. In both cases the customer initiated contact provides a lead for salesmen to follow up, and the opportunity to multiply the interest and credibility. However, it is surprising, in view of the importance of enquiry generation, how many advertisements still do not clearly display the company address and telephone number, or do not build in a reply coupon.

As a product becomes more familiar, the number of enquiries generated by each successive advertisement will decrease, but very often at a surprisingly low rate. While some people respond to advertisements in order to build up a library of catalogues, or because the contents seem so interesting that they want to find out more for general interest, most only respond when they are actually considering buying the type of product being advertised (representing what is known as a hard enquiry), and therefore advertising must be repeated if it is to be effective.

The enquiry generating role is more important for products which are aimed at a diverse market and where the name of individual suppliers does not spring readily to purchasers' minds. Few people would be able to list immediately the names of the manufacturers of say, industrial warm air space heaters, let alone the manufacturers of other competitive types of space heating equipment. Should it become necessary to purchase this type of equipment, prospective customers may well consult one of the relevant magazines and send for details from say the half dozen suppliers whose advertisments motivated them to do so. Similarly, for someone deciding to enclose say some electrical circuitry in a metal or plastic container. Who makes those? This situation is more common where the number of suppliers is large and where the number of potential customers is also very large. If the names of individual suppliers are well known, then advertising tends to revert more to an awareness and credibility maintenance role.

13.3.6 Reinforcement

It has been established that buyers, particularly those who have bought a particular product for the first time or for the first time for several months suffer from post-purchase dissonance (see Section 12.10.7). It is not part of human nature to live easily with such uncertainties and so people seek reassurance that they have in fact made a wise decision. They become some of the most avid readers of product advertisements and look for statements about the product that they have just bought which will reassure them that they have not been taken for a ride and have made a sound buying decision. They also practice selective perception, and try to interpret information in competitor advertisements in a way which will be detrimental to those products. In other words they try to read into advertisements exactly what they are looking for, rather than comprehending what is actually said. So far there seems to have been little attempt to actively make that difficult.

13.4 The Advertising Process

Having considered the role of advertising it is now appropriate to consider the practical problems of organising a cost effective advertising campaign. Even though the depth of analysis at each stage may be limited in a small marketing department, it is recommended that the following steps are always followed:

1 Identify potential customers.
2 Determine their decision criteria.
3 Based on these criteria, decide which competitive advantages to emphasise.
4 Decide on the advertising messages to be transmitted.
5 Decide on the media which will most cost effectively transmit the messages to the target audience.
6 Decide how best to present the messages, given the target audience and the media chosen.
7 Decide how much to spend.
8 Decide matters of timing, frequency and coverage.

The last six steps are interrelated and decisions will have to be taken in parallel. However, for clarity each step will be discussed sequentially. Discussion of how much to spend has been left until the last section of this chapter.

13.4.1 Audience Identification

The first step towards cost effective advertising is to clearly identify one's customers, that is not only which companies but which people or job roles in those companies, especially the initiators, the influencers and the decision makers. This is, of course, fundamental to all marketing. Having identified whom the target audience is, it is possible to find out what media they read, watch or listen to most widely, and to establish what their buying criteria are; in particular what they believe to be important, and indeed what they believe to be not important, about the type of product to be advertised.

13.4.2 The Message

The choice of advertising message will depend very much on the nature of the target audience, their buying criteria, and the choice of media. It is common in the case of consumer products to survey existing customer attitudes towards the product to be advertised, so that they can be compared with the attitudes that advertisers wish customers to have, e.g. tasty, luxurious, reliable or whatever. It is then a question of deciding in terms of message, media and presentation, how to effect the desired attitude change. In industrial markets it is considered that attitudes are very directly affected by how well a product meets defined buying criteria and therefore advertising messages emphasise product benefits in terms of those criteria.

Ground rules for advertising messages (quoted from Chorafas [85]) are that they should be:

(a) believable
(b) brief, even if this means leaving out relevant points
(c) stated in a positive manner rather than a negative manner (e.g. using super toothpaste makes your teeth whiter rather than makes them less yellow)
(d) not copies of other successful adverts (thereby causing confusion)
(e) stated simply and not confused by overly clever writing
(f) the most important message should be incorporated in the headline as this is the only part of the advertisement that many will read.

Sometimes the message emphasises a particular and unique competitive advantage in an attempt to build up the importance of that advantage as a significant decision criteria in the purchasers' eyes. In general the message is that we are different and better because . . . . The message is repeated as frequently as possible in a number of different ways, first because repetition builds memory and image (the illusive track record), secondly to avoid boredom, and thirdly because different people react to and see stimuli in different ways, and so repeating the message in different ways will ensure that it is comprehended by a wide cross-section of readers.

Not only will people react differently because of their role in the buying process and because of the demands of the industry in which they work, but because of their individual natures. For example, within any buying team, those who have been conditioned to obey instructions will respond best to advertisements which more or less tell them why they should choose the advertised brand. Others, usually higher up the hierarchy, react against such obvious attempts at persuasion and respond best to advertisements which demonstrate a professional approach and which merely suggest that it is worth taking time to investigate the product more thoroughly. Yet others are suspicious of all advertisements and respond best to amusing advertisments, or ones which seem to simply present the facts rather than persuasive arguments. No single advertisement can appeal to all three categories.

This problem is further complicated if the same product is to be sold to more than one market segment. The decision criteria of different segments will differ in some definable ways, and hence, logically, the advertising message to each of these segments should be different. However, quite often customers in different segments will read the same magazines and the same journals and it would be fatal to insert three or four successive advertisements, each with a completely different message. Although it means foregoing one of the major advantages of segmentation, it may be necessary to adopt a main message with universal appeal, and rely on sub-messages to appeal to individual market segments.

The only way to retain a totally differentiated approach to segments would be to introduce slight modifications to the product such that each could be given a different brand name and advertised separately. This would enable a unique set of qualities for each product or brand to be promoted. However, such an approach would introduce various diseconomies of scale, and in particular in the present context, decrease the repetitive effect of a given level of advertising expenditure. It is possible to minimise this diminution if the company name is retained along side the individual product name, but this would restrict to some degree the variety of selling messages which could be used.

13.4.3 The Medium

Once the message has been chosen it is necessary to select media which will deliver that message effectively and economically. The usual medium for advertisements for industrial products is the technical, professional or trade press, but sometimes the range of prospective customers is so wide that no single magazine, or even small number of magazines, seems to provide adequate coverage. In that case it may prove more cost effective to advertise on television or in the national press, as has been done for products like crop seeds, fertilisers, forklift trucks or parcel transport services.

Advertisers are faced with a very wide choice of magazines and papers and it is necessary to try to match the readership of each with the different categories of customer which have been identified. Certainly habit plays a major part in reading preferences, with engineers, buyers and others looking wherever they are used to looking for a given type of information. Thus if new air filters, for example, are usually advertised in a particular magazine, it is not likely to be sensible to advertise heavily in some other media. Considerable reliance is inevitably placed on circulation and readership figures provided by publishers. It is not the total figures which are important, but the breakdowns which enable the number of relevant readers (that is readers who fall into one of the chosen customer categories) to be assessed. On this basis it is possible to estimate the cost per 1000 potential customers who are likely to be exposed to the advertisements.

Once a first-order match has been obtained, consideration should be given to the images presented by the magazines and to whether they reinforce the existing image of the advertiser and of the advertised products. Some magazines have a higher standing than others. For example, it is held that: (1) the editorial content of professional journals has a higher credibility than the content of other journals and that this credibility tends to rub off onto the advertisements; (2) magazines which are paid for rather than received free are more likely to be closely read and to be taken home, and (3) magazines which are read at home are read in a more relaxed manner with readers usually prepared to spend more time on the content, and hence advertisements in these magazines are more likely to be noticed and remembered. This is one of the arguments for placing advertisements in the Sunday colour supplements or on late night television slots.

Some magazines have a long shelf life and tend to be widely circulated within companies rather than remaining with the initial recipient. A long shelf life is important because if a purchaser has reached the stage when he has decided to consult magazines for advertisements about potential suppliers, he will tend to glance not only at current issues but at any other reasonably recent issues which are readily available to him.

To summarise, media selection must be preceded by a clear definition of the target audience. Subsequent choice will tend to centre upon the cost per 1000 potential customers reached (i.e. who will actually read the advertisement) but with the following provisos:

1   Some publications help reinforce a particular image.
2   Some publications are more read than others by decision makers rather than by influencers, and therefore are likely to generate more hard enquiries, even if less enquiries in total.
3   Segment division of the market may show that use of particular restricted readership publications can be more effective than the higher circulation general magazines.
4   Experience may indicate that some magazines are more closely read than others or that they have a longer shelf life; in particular, magazines tend to be read more leisurely than newspapers.
5   The dynamics of television advertising may be considered essential to get the message over properly. It is generally considered that a television advertisement gains more attention than a printed advertisement as a result of the combined impact of the spoken voice and the moving picture. In addition the recipient is relaxing with time to spare. Some industrial products are advertised on television because, in spite of the high redundancy, these advertisements still reach a high percentage of the target audience. Radio advertisements are more easily ignored.

6 Justification of the extra cost of colour advertisements in terms of image and attracting attention is something that can never be proved, but must be considered.

7 Space is available at shorter notice, or changes can be made nearer the publication date in certain publications.

8 Publications which offer reply paid cards to readers generate a high proportion of time wasting replies.

Although it may be heresy to suggest it, the most practical approach to media selection may ultimately be one of trial and error. Suppose that some half dozen generally relevant publications have been identified. It might be wise to advertise initially in all these publications. The impact and enquiry rates could be monitored, and after a predetermined period, the least successful publications dropped and the expenditure concentrated on the remainder. This process could be repeated until the total number of enquiries received for the same total expenditure began to decrease.

13.4.4 Presentation

Once the message and the media have been chosen, consideration can be given to how the message is to be presented. Somehow the advertisement must be designed so that it draws attention to itself and subsequently appeals to the different values and perceptions of the range of people who are potential customers. This is where the creative flair of advertising agencies comes into its own.[*]

The advertiser's responsibility is to communicate to the agency all he knows about the market, how it works, the buying decision criteria, the standards and values which apply, as well as all he knows about the product and the benefits it can provide to users. In addition, advertisers must communicate to agencies the personality of their companies. Companies develop a personality because of the way they go about their business. This personality will be moulded by the standards and values of the chief executive and will be reinforced by the type of people who are recruited. This personality should come across in advertisements, because if a different personality is communicated, then when potential customers contact the company, their first impression will be contrary to their expectations, and this immediately will create uncertainty in their minds about whether the advertised claims about the company and its product are really true. Subsequent attempts at reassurance and selling will have been made unnecessarily difficult. Consistency at all times is a cornerstone of good promotion and good selling.

Once the agency has prepared some alternative outlines, there is a tendency for a final choice to be made on the basis of a subjective judgement by a small group within the sponsoring company. Although it is accepted that the final decision is likely to be subjective, unless the subjectivity is disciplined in some way, the systematic approach outlined in the rest of this chapter will be devalued. It is far better to try out the alternative outlines on one or two long established customers,

---

[*] For interesting surveys into client–agency relationships, see Hart [82].

and maybe on one or two prospective customers, to find out which one conveys the main message most clearly and most memorably.

Much industrial advertising appears to be very straightforward, drawing attention to the product and emphasising its virtues, but with little consideration of purchaser motivation and of personality and image. Although there is a need to put messages across in a readily understood and positive way, that does not mean that advertisements have to be unimaginative. The visual impact should reinforce the message, be it one of quality, prestige, reliability, innovation, value for money or whatever. It is said that pictures are worth a thousand words, and certainly in the case of advertisements which are often only glanced at, pictures can much more quickly convey an impression than can words. In many cases all the reader will see is the headline, the picture, and, if the advertisement is well conceived, the company or product name. Pictures are absorbed more unconsciously than words and hence strike deeper and leave a more lasting impression. As a result, advertisement pictures are often designed to appeal to our hidden motivations rather than to logic. Reading requires conscious thought and hence the appeal of texts has to be more rational. However, there is little point in using a great visual idea if it does not reinforce the basic message.

It is no good emphasising the high quality of the product if the advertisment gives the appearance of being cheap. The use of naked ladies may attract attention to an advertisement but very often the product message is subsequently not read, or is dismissed because people instinctively do not believe that solid reliable suppliers of industrial products would resort to such an obvious trick. Similarly, the use of other gimmicks can backfire, as gimmicks tend to be associated with gimmicky companies, possibly with ones who have money to burn, and that is not consistent with the image of a supplier of a reliable good value for money product. Some attempts have been made to show engineering products being produced on the latest equipment, or being used in especially arduous conditions, or being developed in well equipped laboratories, but in general industrial advertisements do not seem to make full use of the visual possibilities.

The well known mnemonic AIDA was conceived by Strong [86] in 1925 to summarise and to help people remember what constitutes a well conceived advertisement. Such an advertisement:

attracts *Attention* to itself, if it is to be read at all
creates *Interest* in the mind of the reader sufficient to
lead to *Desire* to find out more which in turn will
lead to *Action* of some kind — usually making contact with the supplier

It is still relevant today.

13.4.5 Advertisement Positioning, Timing, Size, Coverage and Frequency
Advertising budgets for industrial products tend to be low in comparison with consumer products and hence special attention has to be given to obtaining maximum impact from a small number of insertions. Many people believe that the

effectiveness of advertisements can be related to their position in magazines. Obviously advertisements on the outside cover, or even on the inside covers, are more likely to be noticed. However, within a magazine some advertisers prefer to be near the front because they believe that many people only look at the first few pages in a magazine; others believe it is good to have an advertisement at the back of a magazine because some people flick through from the back, and others still believe that advertisements should be in the middle of a magazine, among the text, that is, the parts which will be actually read. Possibly different magazines are in general read in different ways, but there are enough different people around and their moods change sufficiently frequently to make such generalisations dangerous.

Some advertisers concentrate on a particular time in the year. However, advertising which is timed to reinforce peak demand is too often counter productive because there are insufficient stocks in the distribution system to satisfy the demand thereby generated. This problem does not apply so directly to industrial products where there is a relatively long lapse of time between initial interest and order placement, but it is nevertheless a potential hazard which should not be ignored. In the case of companies which make products to order, it is not low stock levels which will be the hazard, but lack of design capacity or lack of assembly capacity.

Some companies do not advertise during the holiday months of July, August and December, in the belief that magazines during those months are less thoroughly read and that major purchase decisions are less likely to be taken. Others believe that it pays to concentrate advertising around a relevant trade exhibition, partly to counter the expected increase in intensity of advertising by competitors, partly to encourage customers to visit their exhibition stands, and partly because bumper show issues tend to have a longer shelf life than ordinary issues. However, this effort may well be wasted if many readers are put off by the sheer volume of advertisements in bumper show issues, and hence pay little heed to any of them. In addition people's itinerary at exhibitions might be more likely to be influenced by the classified lists in exhibition catalogues or by well thought out advertisements in catalogues, or by posters outside the venue, or by opinions formed well before the exhibition.

Next, it is necessary to consider the trade-off between coverage, size and frequency. At any moment in time some potential customers will be actively considering making a purchase, and an advertisement may stimulate them to enquire about the advertised products. There will be other potential customers who are not actively considering making a purchase and an advertisement will not create such an impact with them, but if it is repeated it should help create product awareness, so that when these potential customers do become active they are more likely to notice subsequent product advertisements — providing that there are such subsequent advertisements. Suppose one can afford the equivalent of 20 full-page advertisements during one year. It would be possible to insert a full-page advertisement in ten different publications in January and to repeat the process in February. While this would ensure customer coverage and a significant impact in those months, by April or May the effects will have worn off and the product may gradually be forgotten. Quite often it takes three or four or more successive insertions before some readers notice an advertisement, and so a large number of potential customers simply will not have become aware of the advertisements at all. If the magazines chosen are published weekly rather than monthly then shelf life will be shorter and the impact of a couple of insertions could be minimal.

A second possibility would be to insert the full-page advertisement ten times in two magazines. This might be particularly appropriate if it has been decided to concentrate on a single market segment rather than the whole market. Monthly insertions would enable awareness and credibility to be quickly built up with readers of those magazines (and incidently maximum advertising discounts to be obtained), although if the publications are weekly rather than monthly the impact will be proportionally reduced. Nevertheless, coverage is being sacrificed to gain repetition.

A third possibility would be to adopt half page or quarter page advertisements and so increase the frequency and coverage. A lot of research has been undertaken into the impact of different sizes of advertisements, but there is no cut and dried data available which would inform the would-be advertiser whether in any given case it is more cost effective to pay for, say, seven half-page advertisements rather than for about eleven quarter-page advertisements or four full page advertisements. Some people believe that a half-page advertisement creates almost as much impact as a full page advertisement because it is large enough to be noticed and to be associated with a quality product. They choose accordingly. Others believe that it is possible to follow a full-page advertisement with one or two quarter-page advertisements, because the quarter-page advertisements are likely to be noticed by those who have already seen the full-page advertisement. This is selective perception again, with people noticing things that they are already familiar with. Unfortunately it is not always possible to design a single advertisement which will be equally effective on a full page as on a quarter page, and certainly not on a half page, and as a result some of the economies of using more than one size will be offset by additional design and make-up costs.

Yet others believe that quarter-page or even smaller advertisements create sufficient impact for their purposes. Some prefer to insert a relatively small advertisement in weekly publications believing that regular appearance in widely read publications, preferably in the same position on the same page each time, will be more effective than fewer larger advertisements. Certainly it may be more effective at getting the name widely known, but little product information can be communicated. The message that can be put across in small advertisements has to be different to that which is possible in large advertisements, but that does not make one more valid than the other except, of course that the smaller one is less likely to be noticed.

A fourth possibility would be to space the advertisements, say, every other month, or to adopt a series of bursts, say over three successive months, followed by a gap of three months and another three month burst. Using bursts enables the advertisements to be spread throughout the year without entirely losing the impact that repetition brings. If there is a gap of three months it is unlikely that those who noticed the previous insertions will have entirely forgotten them and their memory will be sparked off again and further reinforced by a second three month burst. Some advertisers favour the view that it pays to have longish gaps between bursts because that will enable each burst to be longer and the effect of repetition will build up quicker. Others favour insertions every other month in the belief that this provides the best of both worlds because the gap is short enough for there to be an easy memory carry-over from one insertion to the next.

Taking as variables the number of magazines to be used, the size of advertisement and the insertion rate, the advertiser has a matrix of possibilities to choose from, for example:

Number of magazines	Number of insertions in each	Size of advertisement	Frequency
2	12	Full page	Monthly
4	6	Full page	Alternate months or 2 month bursts or 3 month bursts
4	10	Half page	4 month bursts with 1 month gaps or every month except 2
6	6–7	Half page	Every other month or 2/3 month bursts
6	11–12	Quarter page	Monthly

The number of possibilities is almost endless. The advertisement size, coverage, frequency conflict may be summarised (Broadbent [87]) as shown in Fig. 13.1.

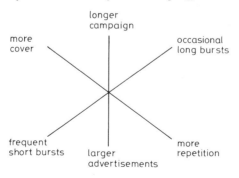

Fig. 13.1 *Advertising conflicts*

One way of making it easier to make final choices between these alternatives is to prepare a media schedule (see Fig. 13.2). A media schedule illustrates very

Media	Daily Weekly Monthly	Advert size (length) and insertion cost	Advert preparation cost	Total budget	Insertions (week nos) 1	2	3	4	5	6	......	49	50	51	52
National press															
Specialist press Trade															
User															
Television															

Fig. 13.2 An outline media schedule

clearly the level of cover and repetition which will be obtained for a given budget and choice of advertisement size, type and position. If the cover and repetition seems insufficient, additional schedules, based on different budget and advertisement size/type/position assumptions, can be prepared and compared, in an attempt to arrive at a logical decision.

Unfortunately, there is no one best solution. Although attempts can be made to monitor the effectiveness of different advertisement sizes, positions, frequencies and coverages, few combinations will be possible within a realistic time period. Once outside that time period, other circumstances will have changed so significantly that previous results will no longer be directly relevant — even though they relate to previous advertising of the same type of product to the same type of customer. As a result, advertising decisions often tend to be a matter of personal preference. However, that preference may be more effective if it is based on an analysis of the spread of customers to be reached, the readership overlap of different publications, the credibility and image of different publications, the length of the buying decision cycle and publication shelf life, seasonality of demand, and the type of image to be created.

13.5 Exhibitions

13.5.1 Why Exhibit?
Exhibitions are an important part of the promotion of industrial engineering products. They provide the opportunity to undertake initial sales interviews with reasonably interested prospects — if they were not interested they would not have come to the exhibition or entered your stand — without the costs of identifying individual potential customers, or making individual sales visits. Exhibitions should be used to create an interest in the exhibiting company and its products, and to generate leads for salesmen to follow up, rather than to gain immediate orders. Exhibitions also provide the opportunity to demonstrate products or at least models of products.

The quality (and size) of the stand itself, the way products are displayed, the professionalism of stand staff and not least the number of other customers on the stand, serve to reinforce the image of the company being promoted by advertising and by salesmen. In some cases a stand can actually create the first favourable impression which will be subsequently reinforced by noticing company advertisements. These opportunities will be lost by an untrained and unprofessional approach to prospects by stand sales staff (selling from a stand is different to the normal industrial selling situation and therefore special training is needed), by an undermanned stand, and by leaving literature lying aound. For example, a partially interested prospective customer may decide that obtaining literature for future reference is all that his degree of interest justifies, but if he can do this without making contact with stand staff so that the interest (and hence memory) can be multiplied, and his name and address obtained, the cost invested in order to get him on to the stand will for the most part have been wasted.

Just like advertising, it is difficult to judge the cost effectiveness of attending an exhibition. Obviously it is possible to ascertain the number of visitors to an exhibition, the number of visitors to a stand, the number of enquiries received, the number of follow-up sales visits arranged and the value of orders which are eventually obtained. However, it will not be clear how many of these orders would have been obtained had there been no exhibition stand, nor how many more or less would have been obtained if more or less had been spent on the exhibition, or if the money had been spent on a different exhibition, on advertising, direct mail or on extra salesmen.

13.5.2 Types of Exhibition

Exhibitions range from major international events involving many hundreds of exhibitors and thousands of attendees, through small local exhibitions which may have as few as 30 exhibitors and perhaps a couple of hundred attendees, to individual exhibitions where, say, 30 or 40 already identified prospects are invited to a venue to see and discuss the product of an individual manufacturer. A summary of the alternatives is as follows:

Type	Cost	Relevance
International	High	Important if selling overseas, especially in host country. Prestige.
National – general	Fairly high depending	Opportunity to make contact with a broad cross section of potential customers.
or		
specialist trade	on size	Opportunity to make contact with particular market segment.
Local – general or specialist	Low	Contact with users in a given locality.
Single company	Low	Contact with pre-selected potential customers.

13.5.3 International Exhibitions

The major costs involved in exhibiting are staff time, travel and accommodation, space rental, stand building, transport of equipment, piles of literature and associated advertising. All but the latter will definitely be higher at international exhibitions, although sometimes they can be reduced by sharing a stand with other exhibitors.

Most of the people attending a major international exhibition will inevitably be from the country in which the exhibition is staged and therefore, unless a company is actively marketing its product in that country, it is difficult to justify the relatively high costs involved. Admittedly there is an element of prestige, and it is nice to be able to refer to the model which was exhibited at the Tokyo World Fair or whatever, but if one is not actively selling in Japan, the cost can only be justified if sufficient potential customers from countries in which the company is actively selling will be attending, or if the exhibition will be given prominence in the specialist press of those countries.

13.5.4 National Exhibitions

Major national exhibitions fall into two categories; general and specialist (that is single industry), and it is often very difficult to decide which to attend. For example, a company producing electronic control equipment could legitimately exhibit at exhibitions dealing with mechanical handling, machine tools, process engineering or packaging. For a control equipment supplier such exhibitions could be considered as general, with many of the attendees looking for control equipment only incidently, possibly as an ancilliary to other plant and equipment. However, they provide the opportunity to influence end users and to contact a range of equipment manufacturers, who presumably will be exhibiting, in an attempt to start to persuade them to fit the said control equipment as standard to their products. On the other hand, the electronic control equipment supplier could choose to exhibit at specialist electronics exhibitions. There are unlikely to be many end users at such exhibitions, with many of the attendees coming from direct or indirectly competitive producers, or from companies seeking components to incorporate in their own equipment, or as a package to supplement their own equipment.

The initial choice will have to be based on a comparison of who has attended in the past – job titles and company names – with known customer categories. If the major part of company sales are to original equipment manufacturers then in general it is more likely that the design and specifying engineers in those companies will attend a specialist electronics exhibition, or even better a control exhibition, rather than a general exhibition. On the other hand, if considerable sales are made direct to end users, then the general exhibition will provide the more cost effective approach.

The cost of exhibiting at national exhibitions is usually to a large extent proportional to the size of the exhibition (which is usually a reflection of previous year's attendances). On the same basis as advertising expenditure, if the stands of one's competitors are large, it is necessary to have an equally large and expensive stand in order to be noticed and to create the desired image. However, companies who have a smaller market share can 'get away' with a smaller stand than market leaders without loss of face, and a large stand for them would create a proportionally greater impact than for a market leader; that is, the number of people attracted to the stand will be larger in comparison with the current customer base. However, enthusiasm by smaller companies towards large stands should be tempered, because if a large stand is followed by a smaller one the following year, comparisons will be made and speculation about falling sales may be started. Similarly, companies who have regularly exhibited at a particular national exhibition become afraid to withdraw in case this starts off rumours about financial difficulties (presumably arising from falling sales) and hence doubts about product quality, continued availability and so on. Whether running counter to customer's expectations does have such dramatic effects has not been conclusively proven, but fear of the possibility certainly influences this and much other marketing thinking.

13.5.5 Local Exhibitions

Attendance at local exhibitions does not raise such problems. Local exhibitions are targetted at industry in a particular geographic area and their content can be fairly wide ranging as well as specific to a particular product category or categories. These exhibitions tend to last only one or two days and stand rental and erection costs are low. If it is intended to exhibit at many small exhibitions it is usually cost effective to pay for a purpose built portable display which can be readily assembled at exhibition sites within a couple of hours; often by the personnel who will man the stand (and usually only two are needed). Choice of which exhibitions to attend will be influenced by any regional concentration of prospective customers, and to some extent by the degree to which these prospects are likely to be encouraged to attend the exhibition by organisers. The wise exhibitor should supplement the organisers' efforts with his own direct promotional activity – usually by mail – although this may not be necessary if the exhibition subject is very specific. It is a moot point whether being present at local exhibitions brings the company into contact with more potential customers per £ spent than large exhibitions, or indeed whether prospective companies who attend the one do not also attend the other. Busy people may be more likely to spare the time to visit a local exhibition and therefore people who had to miss a major exhibition may make a point of filling the gap by attending a local exhibition. It is fair to say that, in general, the level of staff who attend local exhibitions tends to be lower than that at major exhibitions, and therefore local exhibitions enable the exhibitor to make contact with a broader section of the buying team, although in some cases their only selling use is to provide leads into more influential members of that team.

13.5.6 Single Company Exhibitions

On occasion it will pay a company to organise its own series of local exhibitions or presentations, usually in a hotel or similar venue, and to invite a fairly large number of potential customers, both in terms of the number of companies and of the number of individuals, to visit the exhibition at any time during the day – say from 10 a.m. to 9 p.m. These exhibitions provide a cost effective way of either undertaking an initial sales meeting, or supplementing a previous meeting, by being able to refer to the exhibits and by introducing other personnel in attendance.

An alternative approach is to hold a series of formal presentations during the day to explain what the product range can do, how and why; followed by informal discussions and demonstrations. This enables the technically expert to make a professional presentation to prospective customers, often thereby creating a higher level of interest than could be achieved by salesmen alone, and sometimes reducing the number of visits needed to complete a sale. It is particularly advantageous for technically advanced products where customers can be inhibited by a lack of understanding of how the product works and what it will do. These occasions are often promoted as technical seminars rather than as exhibitions so as to set the right mood and to avoid an over emphasis on selling, although all the audience will be aware that some selling activity will be inevitable.

Many seminars are used as an adjunct to a mail shot. The invitation to attend a semi-educational event often greatly improves the response rate. Even if all the respondents do not eventually turn up, the sales force has been provided with potentially valuable leads. If the pitch is made right, it is often possible to attract higher echelons of management than the sales force would normally be able to reach. The audience will all arrive at the same time and so the time available to speak to individuals will be more limited than with the all day approach. Seminars primarily serve as an introduction to a company and its products (providing leads for salesmen to follow up) rather than providing an opportunity to gain immediate orders. In spite of providing incentives such as free food and drink, the geographical area which can be covered by a single venue will usually be limited to a radius of, say, 30 miles, although it does no harm to invite prospects from further afield. As there will be many localities with an insufficient number of prospects to make a local exhibition cost effective, the geographic coverage achieved is likely to be patchy and will need to be supplemented by other promotional means.

One such alternative is to take the demonstration to the customer, usually in a specially fitted demonstration van. Demonstration vans are normally associated with large vehicles which are expensive to buy and to fit out, and this perhaps explains why they are not very widely used. However, they not only take the product to the customer but also encourage the customer out of his office into the salesman's own territory. In the case of small products which could adequately be displayed and demonstrated in 30 cwt or 2 ton vans, maybe more consideration should be given to providing some salesmen with mobile offices and display centres rather than company cars. The merits would depend on the travelling distances involved and the importance of demonstrations and ready reference to prepared display material to the selling process.

13.6 Direct Mail

Rather than wait for potential customers to identify themselves by responding to an advertisement or by turning up at an exhibition, all companies take active steps to identify potential customers for themselves by talking to existing and past customers, by examining exhibition attendance lists and directories, and by undertaking marketing research. However, knowing that a particular company is a potential customer is of little use unless individuals within that company can be identified and contacted. Although this is part of the salesman's task, it is often cost effective to supplement their effort by mailing information. If the presentation of the information is sufficiently attractive and the subject of the information is of interest, the recipient will respond by requesting further details. Just like advertising and exhibiting, direct mail provides a source of leads, but it probably has less effect on company image because the content of 'mail shots' seems to be readily forgotten and is not usually sent repeatedly to the same prospects.

Unless a mailer provokes fairly instant action it is not likely to be successful. To achieve this effect the contents of the envelope actually have to be read. A very high percentage of direct mail receives only a 10 second glance on its way to the waste paper basket. The first need then is an eye catching statement which will ensure that the recipient will at least read the next statement. This is most likely to be achieved by referring to what the product has achieved for others. Within a minute or so the reader will have decided whether this is a subject of interest to him or to any of his colleagues (getting a mailer into the out tray with someone else's name on the top is in itself a major achievement, as the second recipient is more likely to give it a longer read out of respect for his colleague). If the reader carries on beyond that minute the mailer has succeeded to some extent in drawing attention to the company and its product, even if there is no subsequent response. The reader may unconsciously remember the name and notice company advertisements, such that when a need does arise, the company may be among those which are remembered and contacted.

There is normally some argument about whether it is better to send a specially designed mailer or to send a letter, either by itself or with single or double sheet literature. The barrier to action in the former case appears to be less; that is, filling in the mandatory reply card to send for the company brochure, rather than asking a salesman to call. Some people believe that a specially designed card or folder is more likely to be read, while others firmly believe that the first few lines of a letter are more likely to be read, if only because initially it can be mistaken for normal correspondence: a few lines in which to gain the interest of the reader. If leaflets are sent as well, then the purpose is obvious, but the letter may be glanced at anyway. As with advertisements it is best to undertake some form of trial; perhaps sending the proposed mailer to 20 prospects and then following up three or four days later to find out what action, if any, has been generated.

Finally, a word about costs. The unit cost of specially designed mailers will be more than a letter by itself, but normally less than a letter plus leaflets, even allowing for the cost involved in subsequently sending out leaflets to those people that do reply to the mailer. Providing the addresses are carefully chosen, direct mail can be a cost effective way of generating enquiries, in spite of the normal very low response rate. A 10% response would be considered a very good result, a 5% response as normal, and in some industries it is considered that a 2% response is sufficient to justify the effort.

13.7 Other Promotion

13.7.1 Brochures/Catalogues
Sometimes it would seem that manufacturers forget that brochures are an important promotional tool. Literature is an important part of the image building

process and any expectations of a reliable efficient supplier built up by advertising and/or a good salesman can be negated by cheap looking and poorly presented literature. By the time he reads a brochure, the potential customer has had his interest aroused by colleagues, by an advertisement, at an exhibtion, or by a mailer. The brochure is an opportunity to reinforce that interest; it is a form of extended advertisement.

Brochures also serve as reference documents, both where initial interest does not lead to an immediate order and indeed where it does, for future occasions when the need to buy that class of product or service (re-)arises. A point often overlooked is that most literature will be filed in a buying office or technical department library. Catalogues which last well, are kept updated, and stand out on the shelf, are the ones which tend to be referred to most frequently. A common and sensible approach is to obtain sturdy binders with the company name prominently displayed on the face and on the spine and to supply these to established customers, and to companies who have been identified as major prospects. The binders can be filled with general sales and technical data sheets, applications manuals and user instructions. Individual publications can be updated and circulated more frequently and more cheaply than a comprehensive manual, and the receipt of frequent updates keeps the company name to the forefront as well as promoting an image of an efficient and go ahead organisation. Less certain prospective customers can be supplied with individual publications as appropriate, at a significantly lower cost.

The quality of literature is especially important for those relatively simple products which tend to be chosen and bought direct from a catalogue rather than as a result of a salesman's efforts. These tend to be well known, well understood and relatively low value items such as resistors, solder, drawing office materials, fasteners, switches and so on, where most competitive products will meet customer's performance requirements. For these items, choice of supply is frequently left to the buying office, and other things being near enough equal, the buying office will tend to patronise the supplier whose catalogue is the easiest to use.

13.7.2 Public Relations
The objective of most public relations (PR) activities is to persuade the media to publish or to broadcast items about the company and its activities which will help keep the name known and help create a favourable image. Although even small companies can undertake this function for themselves it is often subcontracted to a specialist agency. Large companies and consumer products companies have gradually increased the percentage of their promotional budget allocated to PR, as it has come to be recognised as an increasingly effective way of influencing opinion, be it employees, financiers, customers or government. Engineering companies, other than the very large ones, have not moved so far down the track, and apart from efforts targetted at employees, PR is aimed at customers via the trade and technical press.

The basic vehicle is the press release, where a few paragraphs of information are written about the company, preferably accompanied by a photograph or two, in a form which can be inserted in relevant publications with the minimum of editorial effort. It has been established that readers assign a higher level of credibility to information which is read as part of the editorial text of a publication, than to information contained in advertisements. This high credibility, together with the fact that no payment has to be made to the journal for space, makes PR an important promotional tool. A single press release will often generate more enquiries than an advertisement and is generally much cheaper, but of course it is not possible to ensure that press releases are published month after month.

To help ensure insertion, press releases have to be newsworthy; for example, announcing a major advance which will lead to improvements in industrial efficiency, explaining how a customer has saved money and/or increased sales by using the said product, or outlining how a large order (preferably export) has been achieved. For magazines where insertion is considered especially important, the mailing will be preceded by a 'sales' telephone call so that the press release is noticed and given some thought when it arrives, rather than being despatched straight to the waste paper basket.

Less common and more difficult to achieve is the publication of a longer article about the company written by a member of the company's staff. It really has to be newsworthy. Equally difficult to achieve is a 2–3 page feature article, written by magazine editorial staff – usually following a visit to the company. However, such articles represent very cheap publicity.

Stylish logos, smart letter heads, smart and visually outstanding company vehicles, all serve to draw attention to the company name and add to the image. Even the way operators answer the telephone, and the neatness of typed letters have their effect, and as such are part of the PR effort.

13.7.3 Conferences and Technical Articles

Some companies encourage their professional staff to give papers at conferences and to submit papers and articles to professional journals. Part of the reason is good personnel management, because such participation in one's profession improves motivation and job satisfaction, but the other part of the reason is marketing based. A few customers will attend the conference and a few more will read the relevant journal. However, a wider impact can be achieved by obtaining reprints of papers and articles and circulating them to customers and prospective customers. Reading a technical assessment of a product which has been published in a leading professional journal, albeit written by a member of the suppliers staff, carries a much higher credibility than articles in lower status journals and particularly articles which are obviously of the PR variety. Publication of articles in professional journals creates an image of a company which is at the forefront of its technical field. This approach need not be limited to the technical capabilities of the company, and a similarly positive image can be created by articles about other areas of company activity, such as manufacturing management, accounting, training, personnel or distribution. To some degree this type of thinking can culminate in companies encouraging their senior executives to take part in public affairs and to become widely known, because there is prestige attached to employing well known personalities — in whatever field.

13.7.4 Posters

Posters play a very minor role in the promotion of industrial products. They are mostly seen at the approaches to exhibitions, to remind those entering that 'Brown's Boilers' are good and can be seen on stand 123. They can also be occasionally seen around football grounds or at other major sporting events, or in railway stations and air terminals. The reason that they are not more widely used is simply that there are few places where there is likely to be a sufficient concentration of potential customers passing by to make a poster worthwhile. They are not likely to be cost effective for specialist products and their use at sports fixtures and travel termini tends to be restricted to products which are very widely used throughout industry.

13.7.5 Sponsorship

General sponsorship of sporting and other events is another method of promotion which is little used by industrial marketeers because for them it is not a cost effective way of keeping the company name in front of customers. It is also possible that sponsoring the Horse and Hounds Cup or whatever would not convey quite the solid reliable image most industrial suppliers are trying to build up. Sponsoring more 'worthwhile' events, such as the longest flight by a man-powered aircraft or the greatest distance travelled on one gallon of petrol, or offering prizes for technical achievement or for successful small business ventures seems to fit better with the desired image. Sponsoring events or competitions where the sponsor's product is actually used can be seen to be more relevant, whether it be tractor pulling, apprentice of the year, or trips round the world or up the Amazon. Such sponsorship provides material for advertisements, press releases, articles and for salesmen to talk about. In general, companies that do use sponsorship tend to be the larger industrial companies who are interested in reaching broad sectors of industry.

13.7.6 Free Trials

Free trials of industrial products are very common. Customers are encouraged to take sample products for evaluation, sometimes to test to destruction. Very often suppliers will actively participate in and shoulder some of the costs of these trials, partly because the results, if successful, can often be used in subsequent publicity, partly because the tests will add to product application know-how, and partly because that may be the only way to achieve a sale.

If normal in-use experience is required rather than a specially conceived trial, customers may be encouraged to buy on a sale or return basis, such that if they are not satisfied after the agreed period of use they may return the product and obtain a refund. Free trials, while they can be costly, are a very powerful promotional tool, aimed at obtaining immediate sales rather than building a long term image. However, companies who gain a reputation of being willing to participate in trials do little harm to that image.

13.7.7 Packaging

Packaging of industrial products does not have the major display attraction and image building role that it has for consumer products. It is primarily concerned with effective protection for the product during storage and transportation, and facilitating easy and safe handling, at a minimum cost and commensurate with any minimum safety standards which exist. However, a well packed product can still promote an image of smartness, efficiency and quality, as well as save money by reducing transit damage.

13.8 Promotional Budgets

The mix of expenditure on promotion within UK industry revealed by Gentry and Rodger [88] is shown in Table 13.1. It would appear that some 50% of UK industrial companies spend less than 1% of their turnover on promotion and some 75% spend less than 2%, and that because of the economies of scale involved, the percentage spent by large companies is less than that spent by small companies. However, there is likely to be quite a large variation between companies in the same industry because no logically sound and reliable method of determining how much to spend on promotion has been formulated (but see Faris and Buzzell [89] and Lilien [90]), let alone for deciding how to divide the budget between advertising, exhibitions, public relations, direct mail and other promotional activities.

The lack of a single established method stems from an inability to directly relate changes in levels of spending to changes in sales volume. One reason for this lack of success is that there are too many other interrelated factors influencing sales volume, such as business confidence, competitor activity, product attributes, sales force efficiency, distribution efficiency and so on. A second reason is that the effect of many forms of promotion, particularly advertising, builds up gradually. Thus efforts made now to improve company image and reputation may still be contributing to increased sales in 6 months or in 2 years time.

Instead less direct methods of evaluating effectiveness have to be adopted, (see Chapter 12, Wilson [10] and Kinnard [91]) such as the number of enquiries generated, or the level of advertisement/company name/product name/message recall among customers and potential customers. If any attempt is to be made to measure the effectiveness of a particular campaign, then campaign goals must be set in terms of these measurable factors and not in terms of overall marketing objectives, such as increased market share or profit enhancement. In consumer markets, it is usual to make some attempt at measurement; first by asking members of the target audience whether they recall any advertisement, poster, exhibit or special offer for a specified type of product; secondly by asking whether they recall the promoted product name(s); and thirdly by asking what else they remember about the promotion. They may also be asked to state what they think about the product (attitude testing), to check if it corresponds with the messages being presented to them.

Table 13.1 *Type of promotional expenditure as percentage of total promotional budget by type of product sold*

Type of promotion	All companies	Industrial products				Products sold mainly to the final consumer
		Raw materials	Component parts	Capital goods	Other end products	
Professional/trade journal advertising	27.9	37.2	36.6	25.3	26.5	17.1
Technical/product literature	23.2	21.6	28.7	28.3	21.9	18.8
Trade shows/exhibitions	15.1	12.5	18.1	21.4	14.8	12.9
Newspapers	10.4	11.7	3.0	6.1	10.4	17.7
Public relations	7.3	7.7	4.4	8.8	8.1	6.7
Direct mail	5.3	2.9	3.4	4.8	8.6	6.7
Television	2.4	1.4	–	–	–	7.2
Film	1.6	1.6	0.8	1.2	2.0	1.1
Other (special offers and promotions)	6.9	3.5	5.2	4.7	7.9	11.7
(Base)	(197)	(48)	(34)	(48)	(36)	(54)

However, care has to be taken in measurement, as exemplified by the case where a survey after a particular advertising campaign revealed a very high product name recall rate. It was only when a follow-up survey was undertaken and people were asked to recall the selling message, that it was realised that it was not the current campaign that was remembered, nor its immediate predecessor, but the campaign before that! On the other hand, without the follow-up campaigns, memory of the earlier one may not have been so clear. This vividly illustrates the way in which the effect of promotion, and advertising in particular, builds up gradually over time. The rate of build up and the time lag involved can rarely be discerned and this further complicates the task of measuring effectiveness.

Few sellers of industrial products can afford to undertake measurement as a separate exercise, and have to rely on reports from salesmen about customer attitudes and about where they first heard of the product (see Fig. 14.4). However, just because less is spent on monitoring, that does not mean that monitoring is less important, and vigorous efforts should always be made to record the effects of promotional campaigns.

Because there is no one best way of setting the promotional budget, different companies use different approaches. Methods adopted by UK industry (from Gentry and Rodger [88]) are shown in Table 13.2. Popular alternatives are outlined below. None of them really takes account of the cumulative effect of promotion and treats it as a capital item; as an investment in future sales. Instead, they all, in some way, try to relate the expenditure to sales volume in the year in which the expenditure is to be incurred.

13.8.1 *Matching Historic Levels of Expenditure*
Nearly all companies keep records of how much they spend on promoting different products in different years and it is relatively easy to cross-refer to the product sales volume achieved in those years. The figures can be subjectively adjusted for changes in the economic cycle, in competitive position and in competitor spending, and hence the level of spending required to achieve the current sales target for each product can be estimated. This is not a very exact method but it is straightforward and hence popular. Usually most emphasis is placed on what happened in the immediately preceding year and little account is taken of the cumulative effect of advertising. Even where elements of the other methods are adopted, almost inevitably they will include some reference to past experience.

13.8.2 *Budgeting to spend a fixed percentage of Forecast Sales*
This method allows more money to be spent if forecast sales are high, and therefore it would appear to relate the level of expenditure to what is needed to achieve the sales forecast. However, when sales are at their peak, the track record of a product will be bringing repeat orders (see Section 7.3.3), and therefore lower levels of promotion are often adequate. The time to spend heavily on promotion is when products are new and sales volume low. Perhaps a better approach would be to set different percentage levels for each stage in the life cycle, but once an attempt is

Table 13.2   Setting the overall promotional budget: main method used by type of product sold (percent)

Means of setting budget	All companies	Industrial products				Products sold mainly to the final consumer
		Raw materials	Component parts	Capital goods	Other end products	
Intuition, experience	39	50	39	38	54	32
Specific task method	39	43	34	41	44	32
Fixed percentage of projected sales	16	3	16	14	7	29
Fixed percentage of previous year's sales	7	5	11	7	7	6
Matching or relating to market shares	4	2	–	2	–	10
Matching or relating to competitor's expenditure	1	–	–	–	–	3
Historical trend	*	2	–	–	–	–
Amount of cash available	*	–	–	2	–	–
No information	5	5	3	2	5	6
(Base)	(228)	(60)	(38)	(56)	(41)	(63)

* = less than 1 percent.

made to fix different percentages for each product at each stage of its life cycle, we take ourselves right back to the unanswerable question of how much. The percentage actually chosen is usually historically based, with perhaps some adjustment for current trading conditions. A further disadvantage of the fixed percentage approach is that it tends to amplify the effects of the economic cycle, because less will be spent in a recession when sales are low and more spent when sales are high.

13.8.3 Matching the Competition

This seems a sound approach because the impact made by promotion is proportional to the degree to which the promotion stands out from that of competitors. It has been shown that those who advertise considerably less than competitors face higher direct selling costs. But which competitors should one match?

If one has a 5% market share, should the expenditure be matched to others with a 5% share, or with the average level of spending by all competitors, or pro rated to the spending of the market leader to give the same percentage of sales figure. Inasmuch that it is the absolute level which determines impact, the percentage of sales is probably not relevant, unless it could be shown that all the more profitable companies in the market were spending at a different percentage level to the less profitable companies and that the absolute levels differed widely. There is no guarantee that any of the competitors are themselves spending wisely and following them may represent lemming-type behaviour. Perhaps the answer lies in studying any changes in the level of spending of competitors, followed by changes in their market share (suitably corrected for variations in other influencing factors). Unfortunately it is very difficult to obtain this type of information, and even when it can be obtained there remains the overriding problem that the quality of promotion can have as much effect on impact as the level of spending, and one company spending less, but effectively, may be generating more business than another spending more, but less effectively. Of course, if the objective is to gain market share, then perhaps matching the competition is not a wise course to follow.

13.8.4 Residual Money Approach

If the net profit after all expenses (including reinvestment) except promotion were to be calculated for some target sales volume, this 'residual money' could be considered to correspond to the maximum amount available to be spent on promotion. More usually residual money is set in terms of "price less target profit margin less other unit costs" × "forecast sales volume". Since a company's best products are likely to be the most profitable, some justification for the residual money approach can be found in the belief that promotional expenditure is most effective for 'good' products, where performance in use reinforces the image being promoted.

However, there is no logical reason to single out the promotional budget for this type of treatment − why not the research and development budget or the sales budget? The method suffers from the drawbacks of the fixed percentage of sales method, that is spending at the wrong times. Promotion is most needed when profits (and hence residual money) are lowest, to help increase sales volume and reduce unit costs, and is least needed in the saturation/maturity phases of a product's life when profits are greatest. Some companies overcome this drawback by forecasting the total residual money which should be available during the expected life of a product and then allocating that amount to different stages of the life cycle in whatever way they believe to be effective. For example:

Market share	Residual money	Advertising spent
1%	− £5 000	£60 000
4%	£10 000	£70 000
7%	£35 000	£70 000
10%	£60 000	£60 000
13%	£100 000	£50 000
13%	£100 000	£40 000
10%	£70 000	£40 000
7%	£40 000	£20 000
Total	£410 000	£410 000

However, this takes us back yet again to the subjective judgement of deciding how much to allocate to each stage of the product's life.

13.8.5 Task Related Method

This appears to be an 'ideal' approach where somehow one is supposed to estimate the amount of expenditure required to achieve a specific objective or task. As explained earlier, this objective cannot be defined in terms of a target sales volume and some substitute has to be chosen. In industrial markets, a possible measure of the impact made by promotion is the number of enquiries which can be related back, via customer recall, to a single advertisement or a series of advertisements, or to a particular exhibition or direct mail campaign. It is not a foolproof measure because some of the enquiries may have been received in any case, without the promotion, and it takes no account of the cumulative effect of advertising on the rate of conversion of enquiries into orders (i.e. easing the salesman's task), but at least it is a readily recorded measure of effectiveness of previous campaigns.

In principle these records could be used to calculate a promotional budget. For example, suppose a company earns a net margin of 10% on sales; then to pay for a £10 000 promotion it would have to sell an extra £100 000 of product. If the average order size were, say £5000, then 20 extra orders would be needed. If the historic rate of conversion of enquiries into orders was 20:1, then 400 enquiries would have to be generated, but that is only a break-even situation, and a more likely target would be 450 or 480, in order to earn a reasonable return on the £10 000. It is now a matter of consulting company records to see whether any of the available forms of promotion would generate 450 enquiries from £10 000 worth of expenditure. If the answer is yes then it is likely that money should be spent.

However, just because spending £10 000 in the past has generated 450 enquiries, that does not mean it will do so again. In any case most companies do not keep sufficiently comprehensive records to make a task related approach possible, and many would argue that it would not be cost effective to do so. Instead they use past experience as their yardstick, suitably modified by subjective judgement of changes in competitive position, and by market buoyancy.

13.8.6 Budget Setting Recommendation

The impact made by promotion depends not just on the level of spending, but on its effectiveness and on the other elements of the marketing mix. Hence, just as with pricing, no single definitive method of setting the level and mix of promotional expenditure can be recommended. However, useful guidance can be obtained by constructing a simple model, using historic data, which relates promotional expenditure in the current and previous years (say five), market size, market growth rate, the other elements of competitive position (e.g. product, price, distribution, existing reputation) and the level of competitor promotional spending, to the market share actually achieved. Some form of subjective rating system for the elements of competitive position, and simple estimates of competitor spending should be sufficient. The purpose of the model would be to feed in various levels of promotional expenditure until the predicted market share equalled the target set. In no way would such a model indicate an optimum spend, but at least it would take into account the major influencing variables in a subjective but ordered manner, and therefore should at least ensure the amount spent is of the right order.

13.9 Looking ahead

As suggested in Section 12.11 it is possible to foresee the time when the equivalent of advertisements, brochures, price lists and mailers, as well as sales videos will be transmitted to customers along data links. This method of presenting information to the market will obviously alter the economics of promotion and the promotional mix. For example, the possibility of transmitting videos to customers at relatively low cost may make it less necessary to hold exhibitions, and in many cases will eliminate the preliminary visit in the direct selling process. If, as suggested in Section 12.11, a comprehensive product-supplier information system were to be set up, subscribing to such a system may significantly reduce the need to advertise in other media; certainly it would eliminate the enquiry generating role, although the familiarity/image creation role may well be unaffected. However, eventually magazines and journals may no longer be printed. In that event consideration would have to be given to whether it would be sensible for adverts to share a screen page with editorial text. The concept of separate advertising pages preceding and following the editorial content would no longer be relevant, as most 'readers' would not call them up, and instead would probably refer to any product-supplier information system which was available.

Obviously it is not sensible to think about the possibilities in detail until the relevant technology is available. Nevertheless, an awareness of what media may be provided in the future should encourage marketeers to actively look out for new possibilities, and to take advantage of them as soon as they become economically feasible.

Chapter 14

Sales Force Decisions

14.1 Introduction

This chapter will examine how sales targets can be translated into individual sales quotas and how sales forces can be organised and managed to try to minimise the cost of achieving those targets. Although for the purposes of this chapter topics have had to be dealt with separately and in a particular order, this does not mean the decision making process should follow a similar order, or that any topic should be considered in isolation. Variables in one subject area will not only affect other variables in that area, but will also affect variables in many other areas. For example, before a realistic sales budget can be drawn up, the role of the sales force, the sales force size, the sales force structure, and the sales target must be determined, but the size of the sales force will itself be dependent on the sales volume target set in the annual plan. In other words it is necessary to move back and forth between the relevant decision variables until an acceptable overall state is reached.

14.2 Role of the sales force

Before considering sales force size and structure in detail it is necessary to determine the role to be played by the sales force within the marketing mix. In some cases, such as life insurance, the salesman is the dominant factor, whereas in other cases, such as petrol retailing, there is no face to face selling to the end customer. Broadly, the more complex the product and the more it has to be fitted to individual customer requirements, the more important it is to communicate through a salesman rather than via the written word, because this enables the seller to help the potential customer to accurately understand the exact nature of his needs. Once those needs are properly understood, the seller is more likely to be able to offer a package of benefits which potential customers will buy and which will prove satisfactory in service. There is nothing worse than finding that a particular material or component or item of equipment is not performing to the customer's satisfaction through no fault of its own, but simply because the real requirement was not understood at the specification stage. It is part of the sales task to help the customer to properly understand his requirements, and therefore to order correctly, because it is the reputation of the vendor and not the reputation of the customer which is at stake, if for whatever reason satisfactory performance is not achieved.

As products become more technically complex, more time has on average to be spent with each customer. Selling a particular rubber compound to a potential user is likely to take several times the time needed to sell a duplicating machine. Some customers require a detail technical appraisal of a potential application, amounting in some cases to a design consultancy. The level of effort required, particularly for materials or components to be incorporated in a new design, often extends to becoming involved in the manufacture of a prototype, the organisation of trials, and the interpretation of results. In the case of products using the more recent technologies, part of the selling role is educational; explaining to prospective purchasers how the product works, why it is an improvement on what has gone before and what benefit this can confer on the user. In addition, more complex products require more intensive post-sale follow-up, to ensure that they are being used correctly and to customers' satisfaction. Luckily, the value of individual orders tends to increase with technical complexity, and therefore fewer customers have to be visited to attain a given sales target.

In general then, as products become more complex, or the average order size becomes larger, or the number of customers becomes fewer (see Section 13.3), it makes sense to spend a higher proportion of the marketing budget on the sales force. Although some promotion is still necessary to help generate awareness and a reputation in the market as a whole, it will normally be more important to make personal contact with the companies which are most likely to place orders during the following year.

14.3 Sales force size

Since it can be legitimate to try to increase sales by spending relatively more on promotion than on the sales force, or vice versa, there is no general rule whereby one can stipulate that a company of a given turnover in a given industry requires a sales force of a given size.

A method of approximating the size of sales force needed to undertake the workload associated with achieving a given sales forecast is now described. The method assumes that sales force efficiency is not improved above the level achieved historically, but methods of checking that efficiency are suggested.

14.3.1 Sales forecast

Sales are normally forecast using some combination of the methods described in Chapter 5. In the present context it is appropriate to concentrate on the method described in Section 5.16. Some salesmen find it difficult to think in terms of probabilities. In that event, it is better to ask them to forecast how many orders they expect to contest, and to estimate the percentage they expect to gain. Each salesman should be able to use this revised method to identify the sales volume he expects to obtain from each of the customer categories shown below:

	Firm orders	Orders to be contested	% orders gained
Existing customers	£V000 (cat 1*)	£W000 (cat 2*)	P
Prospective customers			
Already contacted		£X000 (cat 3A*)	P'
Identified but not			
contacted		£Y000 (cat 3B*)	P''
Not yet identified		£Z000 (cat 4*)	P'''

Total expected sales £V000 + £W000 × P + £X000 × P' + £Y000 × P'' + £Z000 × P'''

To achieve these sales each salesman has to contest orders to the value of £$(V + W + X + Y + Z)$000. Past experience indicates that V should be adjusted to allow for those few apparently firm orders which inevitably will be cancelled.

It has been suggested that it is asking a lot to expect salesmen to think even in term of percentages. Although this may be true of people selling consumer products, those who are employed to sell technical products do not seem to have much difficulty with the concept after the first two or three attempts. For those salesmen dealing with a relatively small number of customers, or who are operating in a well established territory, most of the potential sales will fall in the V, W and X categories, and in that case it is relatively easy to apply past experience to estimate the percentage of orders which will be contested successfully. As suggested in Section 5.16 these 'bottom up' forecasts will normally be compared with 'top down' forecasts, and after some form of negotiation, agreement will be reached upon a single sales forecast; some compromise between the bottom up and top down value. The value of sales to be obtained from customers who have yet to be identified, that is, the £Z000, is the value which is most open to abuse and to unjustified change during this negotiation process.

14.3.2 Number of sales visits required
Calculation of the number of sales visits needed to service each customer category (see also Section 15.6) should take into account the nature of the products, company policy with regard to applications advice and follow-up service, and records of what has been achieved in the past.

---

* From Section 5.16.

(a) *Existing customers*

An estimate of the number of sales visits needed to contest £W000 of new orders can be prepared based on direct experience with each customer. Probably salesmen will tend to overestimate, and their forecast can be tempered by comparing it with what has been achieved, companywide, in the past, and by comparing what they forecast last year with what they actually achieved. In practice, such a detailed analysis may not be sensible except for very large customers. Other customers might be slotted into perhaps one of three categories, for example major, medium and marginal customers, each category being associated with an average number of sales visits per year. When determining call frequency the 80/20 rule should not be forgotten, namely that 80% of the profits are likely to be obtained from sales to 20% of the customers. Call frequency should clearly concentrate on the more profitable customers.

(b) *Prospective customers already contacted*

The requirements of these prospective customers are known in some detail. Evaluation of the selling effort needed to convert each into a customer will be based on a combination of the impression gained during previous visits and experience of dealing with similar types of customer (see (c) below). The number of sales visits required as follow-up once initial orders have been obtained will have to be estimated in a similar way and added to the number of sales visits needed to obtain the first orders. Where the number of prospects is large it may be more sensible to group them into categories as suggested above.

(c) *Prospective customers identified but not contacted*

Estimation of the number of sales visits needed to reach the target sales volume will have to be almost entirely based on past performance as there will be no first hand experience to utilise. The estimating task will be made easier if a record has been kept of what I have termed the 'new business sales ratio', that is, the number of sales visits required to obtain £1000 worth of new orders. The ratio will normally be calculated as an average value for the past 1 to 3 years.

Obviously this ratio can be calculated for customers of different size and in different industries or market segments. Thus if over the past 2 years 150 sales visits have been needed to a particular category of prospective customer in order to obtain orders worth £N000 for product A, then the relevant new business sales ratio is $150/N$. With today's ease of information processing it is probably best to start by recording sales data so that new business sales ratios can be calculated for a large number of categories of customers, and only simplifying when it has been proved that such detail is not useful. This is the opposite to the traditional approach of not entering into more detail until the generalised approach has been shown to be unsatisfactory.

The number of sales visits needed to achieve the sales target is simply the sum of the product of the sales target × new business sales ratio, for each customer category or market segment. It is quite legitimate to modify historic new business sales ratios in the light of forecast business conditions and forecast company competitive advantage. Thus if it is considered that next year will be 20% tougher than the last 2 years, and that the company is not so competitive as it was, say only 95% as good as it used to be, then the new business sales ratio becomes equal to $150 \times 1 \cdot 2 / 0 \cdot 95 \times N$. The temptation to modify this ratio downwards in blind hope or in desperation, in order to reduce on paper the number of sales visits associated with a given sales target, must be resisted.

(d) *Prospective customers not yet identified*

The number of sales visits needed to reach the sales target for this category can be estimated by multiplying an average new business sales ratio for the whole market by the sales target.

14.3.3 Call capacity and journey planning

Once the number of sales visits has been agreed, the number of man selling days needed to undertake them can be calculated. In the case of existing customers or customer categories the average call duration will be known. Given that there is no contrary information, this average duration can be transferred forward to the following year. Similarly, records should have been kept of the average duration of new business calls.

The next step is to calculate how many visits can be fitted into the normal selling week, having made allowance for the time needed to identify new prospects, to make appointments, to fill in report forms and to travel between calls. Although salesmen obviously attempt to arrange a succession of appointments with customers who are located close to each other, difficulties of arranging appointments with busy purchasers, combined with the fact that customers of industrial products tend to be few in number and hence are unlikely to be geographically concentrated, means that much of an industrial salesman's time, often 30–50%, can be spent travelling, and only 20–30% in front of customers.

The number of effective calls per day for individual salesmen varies between one and six, depending on the industry, the type of product and the distance between calls. An activity analysis of a typical selling day can be used to establish a realistic standard call rate for any product/service and market under consideration. For example, most industrial sales require at least two or three visits before an order can be obtained. Second and third appointments are usually relatively firm – the second call in particular is often the longest because it has become necessary to enter into considerable detail about how the product will be applied and about deliveries and prices. It makes sense to treat such calls as major calls, organising the rest of the week around them. It should by now go without saying that any numbers arrived at by this type of analysis need to be cross-checked with what has been achieved in the past, (presupposing that such records exist!).

14.3.4 Calculation of sales force size

It is now straightforward, based on average or standard call rates, to calculate the number of man weeks work needed and hence the number of salesmen required, namely:

$$\text{number of man weeks} = \frac{\text{number of calls}}{\text{expected number of calls per week}}$$

number of salesmen required =

$$\frac{\text{number of man weeks}}{\text{number of effective working weeks per annum}}$$

The number of effective working weeks is simply 52 less statutory and company holidays and an allowance for sickness.

14.3.5 Can this sales force size be afforded

The sales force size calculated in the above manner is unlikely to be accepted without further review, because it assumes that existing efficiencies are adequate, whereas the average cost of obtaining and retaining each £1000 order may need to be reduced if adequate profits are to be made. If so, then the cause of the problem should be sought by looking at the complete marketing strategy and not just at improved sales planning or improved sales organisation. The cause might be a decline in the company's competitive position as a result of an old product, lost distribution, less promotion or a decline in the business climate. If instead of examining these fundamentals salesmen are simply exalted to work harder, this may well create a sense of frustration and cause the better salesmen to leave — making the situation even worse.

The simplest method of review is to look at current practice. If this year's turnover is £5m and seven salesmen are employed, and if next year's sales target is £5·5m, then the result of the above calculation should produce an answer in the range 7—8. Should the answer be eight, it will be necessary to calculate whether the profit from the additional £0·5m turnover will exceed the cost of an additonal salesman. Should the answer arrived at from the above calculation exceed eight, then it is likely that salesmen have been allowed to overestimate the number of sales visits they need and the time required per call (see also Section 14.6) and the calculation process should be repeated under closer supervision.

A second method of reviewing the size of the sales force is to compare its effectiveness with that of two or three of the company's more successful competitors (see Fig. 14.1). Differences in efficiency revealed should not be accepted without further analysis. Competitor A may be achieving a higher sales per salesman because they are concentrating on particular customers or customer categories, or because they have a higher national market share, whereas competitor C may be achieving higher sales per salesman simply because they have fewer salemen (see Section 14.4.3.). Unless strategy is changed to take account of these differences, and providing that otherwise the proposed sales per salesman is of the right order, then any reduction in sales force size will inevitably lead to a reduction in turnover (and probably profit), and any idea that it will not will be wishful thinking.

Many companies would consider the above methodology unnecessary and

Factor	Units of measurement	Company	Competitor A	Competitor B	Competitor C	Competitor D
Turnover	£					
Size of sales force	Number					
Salesman productivity	Sales per salesman					
Basis of compensation	Salary levels and commission rates					
Concentration of sales force effort	+ = more efficient − = less efficient					
Competitor visit frequency vs company visit frequency (i) to major customers (ii) to other customers	+ = more frequent − = less frequent					

Fig. 14.1 *Analysis of sales forces*

wasteful, believing instead that it is not neccessary to go beyond a simple extrapolation of past performance. Although this approach seems logical and time saving, it does not provide each salesman with a clear indication of how many sales visits he should be making each week in order to undertake enough sales visits to each category of customer to contest a sufficient number of orders to make the achievement of his sales target possible. Knowledge of these parameters not only makes the salesman's job easier (particularly for new salesmen) but provides detailed targets for the sales manager to use for control purposes. The existence of a detail plan helps management encourage detail feedback and thereby helps them exercise better control: control which is needed not just because of the high cost of employing technical salesmen, but because the viability of companies is so obviously dependent on their effectiveness.

14.4 Sales force structure

Once the sales force size has been determined consideration should be given to alternative methods of dividing the sales force. The more usual methods of division are by customer type, by product, by territory, or by some combination of all 3 (see Figs. 14.2 and 14.3).

14.4.1 Division by customer type

This method of division is adopted in two distinct circumstances. First where salesmen need detail knowledge of the user industry in order to sell effectively, and that knowledge is difficult to obtain or at least takes a long time to obtain. Without industry knowledge salesmen will be unable to fully appreciate the nuances of the problems faced by prospective customers, and are less likely to be able to present a solution in terms that customers can appreciate. The second circumstance is where the size of individual customers is sufficient to justify a special account approach, with each salesman being allocated individual customers so that they can establish strong personal links with key customer personnel, and grow to understand how each customer operates, and their special problems and needs. Customers in this category may well include agents and distributors as well as end users and government departments. Different sales approaches will probably be required for different parts of each customer company and salesmen need to know whom to approach in order to attain a given objective.

14.4.2 Division by product type

This method tends to be adopted where the product is technically complex and it takes considerable training and experience to be able to demonstrate and sell its capabilities, and to be able to advise how it can best be utilised in a given situation. Product specialisation usually means that salesmen have to travel relatively long distances to visit customers, and therefore, if individual order levels are low, this will not be economic and some sort of combination approach will be more appropriate (see Section 14.4.4). Apart from duplication of travel patterns, care must be taken to avoid customers becoming irritated with having several salesmen from the same company call on them in succession. It helps if each salesman makes it clear that he is in effect representing a separate company to his counterpart selling a different product range. An alternative approach is for salesmen from each specialist division or product range to carry literature and to have a general knowledge of their sister products. Whenever a customer expresses interest in one of those sister products the lead can be passed on.

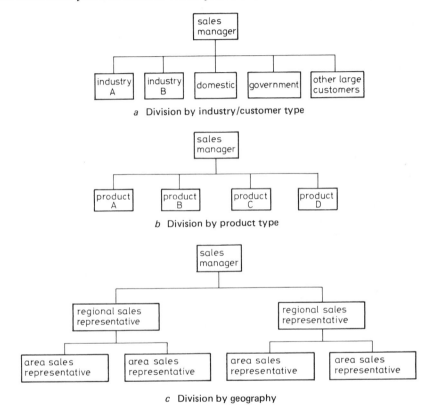

a Division by industry/customer type

b Division by product type

c Division by geography

Fig. 14.2 *Sales organisation*

Division of the sales force by product type inevitably leads to some clashes where different groups may claim that a particular (usually new) product should or should not become their responsibility. Such conflict can only be resolved by identifying not only potential customer companies, but also who within those companies is likely to be responsible for the buying decisions for the product in question, and allocating the new product to whichever product group is most used to dealing with that category of buyer. For example, a company introducing a novel conveyor fitting may decide that this equipment is normally bought by maintenance engineers rather than by works management. Rather than allocating the fitting to the conveyor product group, it may instead be allocated to a group responsible for selling, say, pipe fittings, who normally sell to maintenance engineers.

In multi-product companies the division or product group with the most appropriate production capacity may not be the same division which has the most appropriate selling capability. In such cases the producing division would do well to consider acting as a supplier to the part of the sales organisation which is in the best position to sell the product. Each to his own expertise. Where it is felt that split responsibility would be demotivating it is frequently more straightforward to hand over the production know-how than the sales know-how, and if that is the case, product responsibility should be allocated on that basis.

14.4.3 Division by geography

Geographic territories are particularly appropraite where:

1   The value of individual orders is relatively low and in order to achieve a given sales target it is necessary for salesmen to undertake a substantial number of calls each day. Clearly this is only likely to be practical if travelling distances are short.
2   There is a need to provide rapid response to sales enquiries, to after-sales queries, and requests for spares.
3   The nature of the product is sufficiently straightforward to enable one man to sell a broad range of products.
4   The number of customers is sufficient to justify dividing the country into separate areas.

The physical size of a geographic territory will depend on the density of potential customers, the average number of calls per day achievable, and the call frequency needed. Clearly the smaller the territory, the higher the market share that salesmen should be able to achieve, because they will be able to call on a higher percentage of the potential customers in that territory, and call on them more frequently. Sales per call tend to increase proportionately to the call frequency up to some point where a more frequent call rate makes no further sense. Equally, as the territory becomes smaller the number of cold calls available will gradually decrease in number, or the likelihood of success will rapidly be reduced as the most likely prospects are systematically visited.

Eventually the average sales per call will decrease to the point where it is no longer economic to reduce the size of a territory further, and in that case other ways of increasing sales volume will have to be sought. Ideally territories would be evenly allocated in the sense that the amount of effort needed to achieve the sales target in each territory is the same, but this ideal state rarely exists (see Section 14.5.2).

14.4.4 Division by a combination of criteria

The density of potential customers in a particular geographic area for a company selling, say, two product ranges may justify one salesman for each range, whereas in another area where there are relatively few customers, it may only be economic to appoint one salesman, and he will have to handle both ranges as best he can. Generalising this idea, companies may divide their sales force by a combination of the three criteria mentioned above, leading to the type of structures illustrated in Fig. 14.3*a*. The exact structure adopted will depend on the relative importance of product type, versus geography, versus customer type, and hence, for example, it could be equally valid to divide the organisation primarily by area and secondarily by product as to use the structure illustrated.

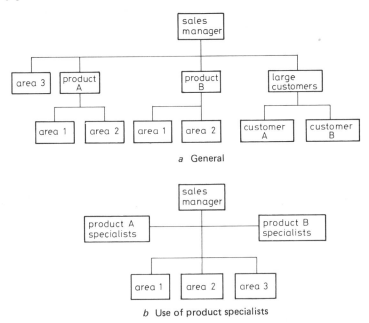

a General

b Use of product specialists

Fig. 14.3   *Sales organisation: division by a combination of criteria*

Where companies sell a broad range of technically complex products requiring specialist knowledge, it is not sensible for specialist salesmen to make special approaches to every potential customer. It can be more economic to employ general salesmen who will serve as an introduction to the company and act as a guide to its services. Once the services required have been identified and a genuine requirement established, a general salesman can pass on the lead to the relevant product specialist and the appropriate organisation in this case is illustrated in Fig. 14.3*b*.

The change of personnel involved can be irritating to customers and frequently they will tend to try to deal direct with the specialist salesman on future occasions, leaving the territory salesman a diet of cold calls. Not only can this be discouraging to the general salesman but the specialist is often not able to sell the rest of the product range correctly. Although it may appear to duplicate effort, both salesmen should continue to call on the customer, with the territory salesman remaining the main link between customer and supplier.

The split of manpower between general and specialist salesmen will depend on the complexity and variation of product, on average order size, and on the expected level of routine repeat orders which will not require specialist selling time.

14.5 Territories and sales quotas

Having calculated the number of sales personnel required and determined how to structure the sales force, it is possible to establish territories and to set sales quotas for individual salesmen. In the case of sales forces structured around the type of customer or type of product it is possible that there will be only one salesman for each category. In all other cases some sort of geographical division of the country will be necessary. If the type of analysis set out in Section 14.3 has been built up on a geographic basis, it is a relatively simple task to form a number of similarly sized territories, similar that is, in terms of the number of standard man-weeks work. The sales quota for each salesman would be the expected sales from each territory, and although numerically different, would be based on comparable work loads (see also Talley [92]).

A particularly convenient way of dividing the country into regions is to utilise the post code system. The first two letters of the post code divide the country into about 120 areas. The number of customers and potential customers within each post area can be identified and sales territories built up from a number of post code areas. This system has the advantage that it is fairly flexible and individual post code areas can be re-allocated to different sales territories as the size of the sales force changes, as customers relocate, and to reflect individual sales capabilities. As established salesmen leave, their replacements will not initially be able to handle such a large work load, and in the interim some of that work load can be off loaded to other territories. Using post codes as the unit of division confers other advantages. First, customer records which are computerised can be referenced quickly by post code because most businesses have a unique post code, and secondly, direct mail can be presented to the post office suitably batched into post coded groups. Not only does the post office offer discounts for mail presented in this way, but the mail timing can be organised to suit the requirements of the salesman within whose territory the post codes fall.

14.5.1 Calculation of territory sales potential

Although it is pleasant from the salesman's viewpoint to be directly involved in the sales volume and salesforce size forecasting process, management needs, in addition to checks on the overall results (Sections 14.3.1 and 14.3.5), a method of assessing the validity of the numbers suggested by individual salesmen. In other words, are the territories being worked efficiently? Two territories may yield equal sales volumes, but one of them may be capable of yielding much higher sales were it worked efficiently. Other than swapping salesmen and territories the answer can only be obtained by calculating the number of potential customers within each territory and estimating their average order value. Two possible methods of achieving this are suggested.

The first is simpler in theory and more comprehensive, but often cannot be used because of lack of customer data. Suppose total national product sales, that is for all competitors, is forecast to be $£A$. In many industrial markets or market segments it is possible to individually identify those cutomers who are responsible for as much as 40% and sometimes 80% of total demand. It should be possible to identify the post codes of each of these customers and in that way calculate the proportion of the 40% or 80% of total demand which eminates from each post code area. These results can be extrapolated to include total market demand. Using these post code area results it is possible to estimate total market demand in each geographic territory, and by multiplying the figure arrived at by the company's national market share, to obtain a reasonable estimate of the immediate sales potential for each territory. Hopefully it will correspond more or less with the value which was calculated in Section 14.3.1. If it is greater then that is a sign of a poorly worked territory, and vice versa. Of course, in the long term the immediate potential could be increased by improving the company's market share.

The second method estimates immediate sales potential by dividing the market up into segments or customer categories. Various ways of dividing industry into groups of a similar nature have been devised. One widely applied system is the standard industrial classification (SIC) which divides industry into over 300 groups. For most suppliers no more than 20 codes are likely to be significant. The next step is to examine sales records (for at least 1 year and perhaps for 2 or 3 years where the sales pattern has changed little) and to estimate the value of sales to companies within each code category. The immediate sales potential in each territory can then be calculated by multiplying for each code category the number of customer companies located in that territory by the average order value within that code category, and summing across all SIC codes. The method is illustrated below:

Code category	Value of product bought nationally	Numbers of category in companies	
		Nationally	Within one territory
1	V^1	N^1	n^1
2	V^2	N^2	n^2
3	V^3	N^3	n^3
4	V^4	N^4	n^4
5	V^5	N^5	n^5
6	V^6	N^6	n^6

$$\text{Territory sales potential} = \frac{n^1 V^1}{N^1} + \frac{n^2 V^2}{N^2} + \frac{n^3 V^3}{N^3} + \frac{n^4 V^4}{N^4} + \frac{n^5 V^5}{N^5} + \frac{n^6 V^6}{N^6}$$

In all businesses there will be a small number of customers who have an exceptionally high level of demand, and to prevent the averages being distorted the figures for these companies should be extracted and treated separately. This method is obviously more accurate for companies with significant market shares.

14.5.2 Practical problems

We now have a system for dividing the sales load equitably between the sales force and for checking whether territories are being worked effectively. It has been necessary to analyse:

1 Who should be visited.
2 How often.
3 The total time commitment per visit.
4 The average order value.

However, practice is never that simple. Salesmen are normally set targets somewhat in excess of their forecasts. New business activity forms most of the difference between what salesmen claim it is possible to achieve and the target which they are set. Inevitably there is a strong temptation for management to increase sales value in this category somewhat arbitrarily — especially as there is little actual data — in order to demonstrate sales forecast growth. However, not only will this lead to false expectations from senior management but it can be strongly demotivating to salesmen. Targets only motivate if they are considered to be within the bounds of possibility.

Problems also arise as salesmen come and go, and as the number of salesmen employed changes. Suppose one year ago the country was conveniently divided into four territories, but as a result of growth it is now sensible to employ five salesmen. Not only will the established salesmen wish to cling on to established accounts, but customers often prefer to deal with the man that they know. Hence any changeover has to handled carefully and by the time that handover is completed it may be appropriate to employ six salesmen. This sort of problem is more acute where the number of salesmen is being reduced, because obviously the handover has got to be much more rapid. A similar problem occurs when customers physically move and/or change the nature of their business.

It will also be apparent that in practice some salesmen are capable of handling a larger workload than the standard set, and if they are to be kept fully occupied they will need to be allocated a larger territory. Thus at any moment in time sales territories are not likely to be equal in terms of standard workload, but a record of variations can be maintained and rewards adjusted accordingly.

Individual sales quotas are not meaningful where most of a company's sales are gained from a small number of large contracts. It has been shown that customers are influenced by the scale of the effort mounted by suppliers to try to obtain an order, and so once a promising lead is obtained it is likely to be necessary for several members of the sales force to combine, and to work as a team, with their own lead gathering activities relegated to second priority. It is no good coming second ten times out of ten — it is better to come first once.

14.6 Sales force control

Control is dealt with in more depth and generality in Chapter 17. Control requires actual results to be compared with some predetermined target, such that any variation between them will initiate appropriate remedial actions. Control also implies longer term efforts to ensure performance improves over time.

The first step towards sales force control is to systematically gather information about current performance. A standard report form of the type shown in Fig. 14.4, if filled in after every sales visit, not only provides the means of gathering information about individual performance, but also can form a basic input to a company information system (see Section 4.18). The exact layout and information included on such a report form will depend on the nature of a company's business and it may be extended to two A4 sheets, but in essence the following information is required for sales control purposes:

1 Assessment of business potential of company visited, product by product.
2 Assessment of which competitor products are currently bought.
3 Assessment of what benefits will have to be provided to change the current buying pattern or to protect existing sales.
4 Assessment of other factors (see Chapter 12) which will affect the buying pattern.
5 Record of action taken with respect to items 3 and 4.
6 Record of reasons given by customers, plus the salesman's own assessment, of why a sale was/was not achieved (naturally this latter assessment will be dominated by product/price/delivery reasons rather than by the capability of the salesman, his call frequency or his ability to see decision makers).
7 Proposed date and objective of next visit (this should also be entered into the salesman's diary).

If a computerised marketing information system is being used, then once salesmen have filled in such a form for every customer, there will be no need for them to repeat the process after each subsequent sales visit. When salesmen inform the sales office of their call plan for the following week (based on the call frequency as calculated in Section 14.3.2, but regularly updated) copies of the forms can be issued to them with the previously recorded data printed on each line, making it necessary only to make amendments and to write in additional data after each visit. No more than 5 minutes should be needed after each customer visit. When orders are received and delivered, section 2 can be updated by the sales office; all other data would be updated as salesmen file new reports. 'The purpose of the visit' line should concentrate on how the buying criteria are being influenced, and how competitor claims are being countered. The actual reasons for previous orders being gained/delayed/lost can be preprinted and referred to when deciding on action needed. If a computerised information system is not being used then it will probably be necessary to make do with a simpler version of the form.

SALESMAN: ....   DATE: ....

Section 1

COMPANY ....
ADDRESS ....
....
CONTACTS (names and titles) ....
(* those already seen) ....
....
No. of EMPLOYEES .... TURNOVER ....
INDUSTRY (S I C code) ....
LEVEL OF ACTIVITY Ex Good F. Good Fair Poor
PRODUCTS OF INTEREST (enter potential in £000)

A .... [ ]   B .... [ ]   C .... [ ]
D .... [ ]   E .... [ ]   F .... [ ]

Section 2

DATE FIRST VISITED .... DATE FIRST ORDER ....
FIRST CONTACT MADE VIA ....
EST. ANNUAL SALES .... SALES YEAR TO DATE ....
SALES LAST YEAR ....
LAST ORDER: DATE .... VALUE ....
OUTSTANDING DELIVERIES BY CUSTOMER ORDER No.
(and est. delivery) ....

Section 3

PURPOSE OF THIS VISIT ....
OUTCOME OF VISIT (tick who seen) ....
....
ACTION NEEDED (and dates) ....
....
DATE OF NEXT VISIT ....
PURPOSE OF NEXT VISIT ....
....

Section 4

COMPETITOR PRODUCTS USED
    NAME   MODEL   VOLUME | WHY
                                           |

COMPETITORS WHO VISITED RECENTLY ....
....

STATED SELECTION CRITERIA (rate 1–5):
Price [ ]   Durability [ ]   Availability [ ]
Reputation [ ]   Finish [ ]   Compatability [ ]
Technical Back up [ ]
Other ....
ACTUAL REASON WHY ORDER GAINED/DELAYED/LOST
              GIVEN BY CUSTOMER | OWN ASSESSMENT
                                   |

Fig. 14.4 Customer sales report form

WEEK NO . . . .

CO. NAME	CONTACT NAME AND TELEPHONE NO.	SALESMAN	PRODUCT	EXPECTED ORDER VALUE	ORDER PROBABILITY	ACTION NEEDED (DATE)

Fig. 14.5 *Weekly summary of outstanding enquiries*

Although it is important to have detail information available for use by salesmen when preplanning their calls on individual customers, and for use whenever a problem arises, a weekly summary form is usually sufficient for routine control purposes. Such a form might be headed 'outstanding enquiries' (see Fig. 14.5). The data may be extracted by computer or manually from the sales report forms filed by salesmen during the previous week. The outstanding enquiries form should be examined by management at the beginning of each week to help ensure that every enquiry is properly followed up. Actions which had not been completed during the previous week would naturally be carried over to the following week. Ideally the list would start with the most urgently needed follow-up actions, rather than being presented in alphabetical order or in the order in which the data was first recorded.

On a slightly longer time scale, the value of orders gained by each salesman could be summarised on a simple monthly report form, see Fig. 14.6 (the monthly report could subsequently serve as a database for a summary report on the performance of each territory product group, division or whole company). Inclusion of figures for the percentage profit margin for each product keeps all concerned aware of where the effort should be concentrated. The target value of sales per visit should correspond to the figure used earlier (in Section 14.3.2) to evaluate the overall number of visits required. In accordance with normal practice on report forms of this nature, space is allowed for salesmen and their direct supervisors to note the main causes of variances and to propose remedial action. Provision of columns for revised targets is essential and provides a clear indication that the company is prepared to revise its targets if circumstances beyond the control of individual salesmen change. This can be a considerable motivational aid; although it is difficult to make such alterations on an individual basis without upsetting other members of the sales force, especially if a commission system is in operation, because targets are normally revised downwards and very rarely upwards.

Although a monthly report form begins to pinpoint a salesman's capability for selling one product rather than another, and his ability to convert prospects into new customers, if effective action is to be taken to correct any persistent variances between target and actual, then more analysis will be required. For example, it is possible to record time per call and sales per call and it might be possible to build up a picture as shown in Fig. 14.7.

Fig. 14.7 shows that there are clear points of diminishing returns. If a poorly performing salesman had the call pattern shown by the crosses this might explain his poor performance. Too much time is being spent with some customers, probably old established ones, and this has left insufficient time to sell efficiently to other customers. If controls are to be fully effective it must be made clear to all concerned that the prime objective of the controls is to try to improve operating efficiency, by using forms to highlight factors which influence the number of orders gained. To achieve this objective it is essential to have regular face to face reviews with each salesman, so that difficulties can be clarified and actions taken to

SALESMAN .... MONTH ....

	SALES THIS MONTH			SALES LAST MONTH			YEAR TO DATE			
	Target	Actual	Variance	Target	Actual	Variance	Target	Revised target	Actual	Variance
PRODUCT A: Repeat orders (% margin) New orders										
PRODUCT B: Repeat orders (% margin) New orders										
PRODUCT C: Repeat orders (% margin) New orders										
TOTAL: ALL PRODUCTS Repeat orders New orders										
No. of visits to existing customers % Visits producing orders Sales per visit										
No. of visits to new prospects % visits producing orders Sales per visit										

Cause of variances ....
....
....
....
....

Proposed remedies ....
....
....
....

Fig. 14.6 *Monthly report form*

overcome them, probably using the list of outstanding enquiries and the monthly report forms as the initial agenda.

However, the manner in which these reviews are undertaken and the control system applied, has to be managed quite carefully if a 'big brother' image is to be avoided. Most technical salesmen like to feel they are free and able to manage their time and their sales approach for themselves; that is usually a major attraction of the job. Control systems must be used as a means of guiding salesmen towards improved performance and not as a strait-jacket.

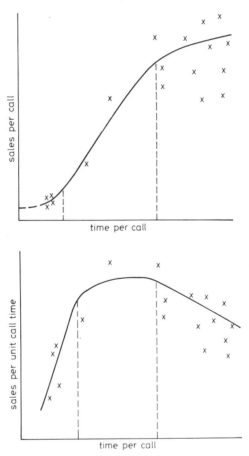

Fig. 14.7   *An analysis of sales call effectiveness*

Sometimes the reviews will bring to light problems of a broader nature and a detailed investigation into the causes of persistent variances may reveal deficiencies in the company's marketing mix, or the information base on which the targets were originally set. For example, sales forces often become aware of shifts in the pattern of customer demand, or the need for new products, well before this can be picked up by routine analysis or marketing research. Only when proposed remedial action is not undertaken efficiently and targets consistently missed, would the reporting system be used as a basis for sanctions. Finally, no control system would be complete without some cross-reference (see Fig. 14.1) to the standards of performance being achieved by the sales forces of competitors.

Like everything else in business, the relevance of particular parts of control systems will change over time and hence the systems themselves must be regularly reviewed to ensure that they are still appropriate to the operating circumstances, and in particular that they are not adding more to costs than they are to profits.

14.7 Recruitment

Realisation of the key role played by salesmen in industrial marketing and an appreciation of the time commitment involved in training a new man — a commitment that inevitably will hinder other duties being properly carried out — will rightly cause sales managers to be very critical when recruiting.

Reference has already been made to the importance of technical and industry know-how to effective industrial selling. Many people hold the view that such experience and know-how takes longer to acquire than selling skills, and for this reason they concentrate on recruiting staff from other departments or from competitor companies. In many cases direct contact is made with competitors' salesmen, especially where an existing member of staff is aware that the said salesman is not entirely happy in his current employment.

Much has been written in specialist publications about recruitment and it is not appropriate to repeat it in detail here. However it is worth emphasising the importance of preparing a detail job specification, because not only is it a valuable recruitment tool, but it also provides a useful framework for determining training needs and for later appraisals. The job specification should include a precise statement of the objectives of the employment in terms of sales performance and growth, of the responsibilities, authority and expected methods of operation, and of the criteria by which performance will be appraised. From the job specification it is possible to draw up a profile of characteristics such as age, education, work experience, training, interests, enthusiasm, appearance, persuasiveness, reliability, determination and the like. Clearly an acceptable range for each factor must be set and care must be taken over terms used to describe characteristics that can only be assessed qualitatively.

Having framed an advertisement based on the job specification and the personal profile, all respondents should be sent a form specifically designed to help fill in the profile, rather than a standard form. Money spent preparing a suitable form will be more than repaid by saving time when comparing applications at the later stages of the recruitment process. Candidates selected for interview on their fit with the profile should be sent a job description and general data about the company — perhaps even a list of items they should consider before deciding to accept the employment. Such a list will provide a useful supplementary agenda for the interview.

Interviews have three main purposes: first to confirm one's belief that what has been written on the application form is true and to fill in any missing details; secondly to enable personality factors to be assessed, and thirdly to enable the candidate to assess the company and raise any queries.

As with marketing research interviews, it is essential to have worked out in advance the ground to be covered, with the level of structuring being inversely related to the complexity of the job. It is also essential to record one's impressions so that critical items are not accidently overlooked, and so that there is additional data available for when the final comparison is made. An example of a typically easy to use form is shown in Fig. 14.8. It could be extended to whatever level of detail was considered to be appropriate. Popular criteria include factors such as enthusiasm, intelligence, reliability, loyalty, learning ability, tact, leadership, administrative capability, management potential.

Ideally one should end up with a complete set of profiles which can be compared with the range set initially, and with each other.

	Scale	
	1 2 3 4 5	
General		
Good appearance		Poor appearance
Relaxed manner		Very tense
Fluent speech		Cannot express self clearly
Self-confident		Nervous
Good health		Poor health
Experience		
Knows product well		Little product knowledge
Knows industry well		Little industry knowledge
(has many contacts)		
Excellent sales record		Little sales experience
Could he sell me?		
Taken trouble to find out about the company and job		Shows little knowledge of company or job
Good listener		Poor listener
Relevance of replies to questions		Does not properly answer questions (rambles)
Consistency of answers		Answers leave doubts as to their truth
Determined		Easily discouraged

Fig. 14.8   *Typical assessment form (based on Smallbone [93])*

14.8 Training

The purpose of training* is to enable salesmen currently achieving sales of, say, £100 000 per year to sell £120 000 next year. Not only will such an outcome improve the level of job satisfaction, but it will clearly help reduce the company's

*Several of the ideas in this section are explained in more detail in Brown [94].

unit selling costs. Training is aimed at improved product knowledge, sales technique and motivation. Product knowledge is essential for effective industrial selling. There is nothing more efficient at losing the interest of customers than not being able to answer what seems to them to be straightforward questions about the construction of a product, how it works, where it has been used, with what results, and how exactly it can be best applied to the situation under discussion.

Selling is a practical skill and is therefore best learned by doing, that is, on the job. The usual approach to on the job training is for salesmen to be accompanied by their immediate superior on their sales visits for a day. The first step to effective selling is to preplan the calls. This habit can be installed by asking salesmen, prior to entering each customer's premises, to explain the object of the call, who is being seen, how he knows that is the right person (hopefully recorded as on Fig. 14.4), what are the expected problems, how they will be overcome, and what reasons will be offered to justify the next sales visit. If it is expected that an order will be obtained, how does the salesman plan to close the sale.

During the sales visit the supervisor should be introduced as an observer and he should not get involved in the sales conversation unless he is directly asked by the customer and even then he should hand back to the salesman as quickly as possible. In this way he has maximum opportunity to observe the salesmen at work and he does not undermine their confidence by taking over – even if he can see a sale being lost because of a wrong tactic. The supervisor's job in this situation is training not selling.

After each visit salesmen should be encouraged to complete their paperwork prior to driving on to the next customer. First, it is more likely to be accurate, and secondly at the end of the day the salesmen will have finished work and will not have an hour's paperwork hanging over their heads. At the end of the training day, and only at the end, the various training points should be discussed, so as to avoid building up tensions and inferiority complexes which could affect the sales performance during the day itself.

On the other hand, if salesmen are to be introduced to new material or to a new product – whether this be at head office or in the field – this is probably best undertaken at the beginning of the day when the learner is freshest. On the face of it such one to one introductions to new products seem inefficient, but the rate of learning will be higher than in large groups. The other end of the spectrum is the national sales conference where the speakers often appear as actors on a stage, and hence the audience settle back to enjoy the performance rather than make a serious attempt to take in what is said.

Even the top sales engineer should be subject to training days; it is like a coach with a top player who is more skilled than the coach; the coach can still help the player find ways of improving. Equally important, the coach can observe and learn himself and pass on what he learns to other members of the sales force. New or junior sales engineers can often be best trained by an initial assignment to an established salesman. In this way the new man receives more attention than he would if he were simply allocated to a small territory under the sales manager, and it enables the management potential of the senior man to be assessed.

From time to time more formal classroom sessions will be needed to supplement on the job training. Typical topics are objectives of selling, the role of the salesman, information systems, call planning, choosing new prospects, identifying and meeting customer needs, the initial approach to customers, the feasibility study, negotiations, closing, presales assistance, after-sales back up/reassurance.

14.9 Motivation

Perhaps the most important quality of a salesman is his persistence in the face of much lack of interest and many 'no thank you's'. The level of persistence is dependent on individual motivations. Motivation of people can only be achieved face to face, not by memo or on the telephone. It sounds trite to say that for one man to motivate another, he first must gain the other's respect, but it is nevertheless true. In the case of sales organisations, frankness, trustworthiness, fairness and backing when dealing with problems (be they internal or external to the organisation) are especially important. There is also evidence to indicate that personal motivation is reinforced if predetermined standards or targets exist against which performance can be appraised, especially when there has been direct involvement with the target setting process. This involvement can be achieved by the bottom up forecasting process already described. Where the final targets set do not agree with those initially put forward, there will be some loss of motivation unless the reasons for the differences are fully explained.

Artificial means of motivation should not be necessary. For example, sales competitions are generally not appropriate to industrial sales organisations. Carefully worked out plans of action are likely to be abandoned in order to boost short term sales, causing a loss of continuity when the plan has to be reimplanted once the contest is over. In any case, short term sales surges are normally followed by a slump as people have to remotivate themselves once the stimulus is removed. Similarly, regular monthly contests are either ignored because the same two or three people win them every month, or even if based on percentage improvement over the previous month, may be subject to abuse.

Finally it is pertinent to recall that the net motivational effect on people equals the incentives applied to them less the disincentives. Much attention is paid to the incentives and often much less attention is paid to removing disincentives, such as lack of training, lack of feedback, lack of back-up and not being told what is going on.

14.10 Payment schemes

Views on this subject seem to be as wide as the number of people involved in sales management. Some companies strongly believe that the only way to motivate their sales team — including sales managers and/or sales directors — is to include commission in their remuneration. The logical extension of this line of reasoning is that to obtain maximum effort from all employees, they should all be paid by results. There are various possible reasons that can be put forward for treating sales personnel differently, namely:

(a) Paying non-sales personnel by results is not practical as their performance cannot be individually assessed, because it is dependent on too many factors outside their personal control (a group bonus scheme does of course satisfy this criteria).
(b) The continual negative pressure placed on salesmen by buyers needs to be countered by direct financial motivation.
(c) Tradition.

The extreme version of the payment by results approach is to employ commission-only salesmen or self-employed sales agents who sell a range of non-competing products. Although this method of payment by results reduces overheads and at the same time provides plenty of sales incentive, it stands the most chance of misfiring, with products being sold with insufficient technical backing and with little incentive to spend time dealing with post sales complaints.

The efficacy of a commission system probably depends as much on product complexity as anything else. Selling complex products is very much a team effort, often involving design engineers, estimators, application engineers, internal sales personnel as well as sales engineers in the field. It is a long term process of gradually convincing prospective purchasers that the company being represented is worthy of a trial, and building on that trial to obtain the status of a regular supplier. The convincing process revolves round being able to demonstrate that the supplier understands the nature of the needs of the purchaser, and that the needs will be exactly and reliably fulfilled at an economic price. Pressures applied by a commission system may encourage sales personnel to oversell and place personal short term commission considerations in front of the long term satisfaction of customer needs.

The necessity to avoid this happening, and to avoid the motivation problems which arise if members of sales teams are rewarded differently, causes many companies to argue that industrial salesmen should not be paid commission. These companies believe that they can sufficiently motivate their staff to strive to achieve sales targets by a desire to see the company do well, and to ensure their own and their colleagues' job security. For example, recognition of the 'mentioned in despatches' variety is a very valuable motivation which is too rarely used. No commission also means that sales forces will be more flexible with regard to training, attending exhibitions or demonstrations, or undertaking important sales visits when other members of the sales force are ill or have other priorities.

Some companies operate some form of bonus scheme, based on profit achievement, in the belief that this provides the best of both worlds by motivating everyone to help ensure that targets are achieved, but without singling the salesmen out for special treatment or sacrificing flexibility. Depending on the ease with which different activities can be separated, the bonus might be companywide or awarded to individual divisions or product groups.

In the case of less complex products, such as certain production equipment and consumables (e.g. soldering irons or industrial vacuum cleaners or drills) and certain office equipment, where the cost and the importance of the purchase is not high, and especially where it is difficult (or considered not to be worth spending the time) to truly differentiate between alternative products, then the role played by individual salesmen increases in importance. The final choice between products is likely to be very largely influenced by the impression the salesman makes on purchasers, because any other clear decision variables are lacking. In this situation the case for operating a commission system seems stronger.

There are no general rules for determining the exact nature of a commission system. It is generally considered that the base salary should be sufficient to provide a living wage and that the commission rate should be such as to provide a fair return for normal effort and yet leave clear incentive for exceptional effort. There is no logical reason why there should be an upper limit. The more dependent the salesman is on the efforts of others in order to close a sale, the lower the commission element should be. A normal rate in the engineering industry is for commission to represent about 15% of total salary rising in some cases as high as 33%. Depending on the commission level, consideration should be given to agreeing a fall back rate for holidays and illness. With many products, especially where order values are large, there can be considerable monthly fluctuation in sales volume and in such cases commission is usually based on some form of moving average – possibly a quarterly average – in order to smooth out the fluctuations.

In an attempt to overcome some of the problems outlined above, commission systems can become very complicated. For example, a company selling capital goods requiring a high level of support activity may divide the commission: say two-thirds to the field representative and one-third spread among the support group (remember they will support more than one representative). To prevent salesmen selling products into applications where they are not suitable and to encourage proper follow up, some companies pay commission in stages, say 25% on receipt of order, 25% on installation, 25% after one year and 25% after two years. If these sorts of systems are combined with differential commission rates for new products or new customers, and a commission proportional to the gross margin on each product, one can begin to see why some companies consider it impractical to implement a fair system.

14.11 Appraisal

Appraisal should be a continuous process and appraisal forms used to record what has been observed on a routine basis. Like interviewing forms, they do ensure that the obvious is not overlooked. Annual appraisals are usually linked to salary reviews, and if proper training and help has been provided throughout the year, they should not, involve detail discussion of sales technique, but instead deal with good and bad points which have been persistent throughout the year. The appraisal criteria should clearly relate to the job specification and the achievement of specified objectives: for example, achievement of target sales over the product range, number of new accounts opened, on time completion of paper work, or response to training sessions. Training, motivation and appraisals are all closely linked, and a good response to training may well balance a below target performance. It is easy for people to become over-critical during appraisal interviews and this can be destructive. It is preferable to encourage people to believe that they have the will and capability to perform better in the future. Thus all appraisals should be positive in the sense that any faults pointed out should be accompanied by a proposal to help eradicate them.

14.12 Expenses

There is an obvious need, for cash reporting and tax reasons, to keep clear records and receipts of expenses. However, it often seems that many companies become obsessed with the need to justify every penny of expenses spent. It would be better if company management set a general level of acceptable expenditure and as long as personnel kept close to that level there would be little point querying every detail, if for no other reason than that genuine hard-working salesmen find it irritating and dismotivating. In general the expenses of the good salesman will not be high. He will not be prepared to waste time over long lunches and coffee breaks (especially when paid on some incentive basis). Occasionally there will be the justified exception where a considerable amount of money has been spent.

14.13 Key accounts

Sometimes senior management assign personal responsibility for key accounts to the sales manager. In that case the importance of these accounts *vis-à-vis* the overall performance of the sales force must be made clear so that the manager can plan his time methodically. Otherwise the obvious clashes, where the manager has to decide whether to abandon a days planning or a days training, to respond to a call from one of the key customers, are not likely to be resolved in a way which fosters the best overall results. The situation is different if the manager makes the decision himself, he is then in charge of his own priorities.

If each salesman has a few key accounts, special planning attention should be paid to them and the manager should ensure he visits these customers from time to time so that his input to the planning will be based on individual knowledge rather than general know-how. Such visits also ensure that should salesmen suddenly leave, there is a personal basis upon which the company relationship can be continued. However, the sales manager must be careful not to undermine the status of his sales staff, as, of course, buyers will have a natural preference to deal as far up the organisational tree as possible.

14.14 Technical applications advice

Technical applications advice is intended to help customers solve their problems, whatever they may be, in the most efficient manner. It is closely linked to demonstrations and to customer training. The spread and complexity of technology is such that very often buyers will not understand how a particular product works, and more important, how it can be applied in their company to provide the claimed benefits. At the very least, technical applications advice involves helping customers to select the most appropriate product from the range available. However, it can extend to explaining how to undertake appropriate trials, and in the case of components or materials, how to design the rest of the product to take best advantage of the particular features offered. An obvious example is the use of an adhesive rather than welding, rivets, or nuts and bolts. Explaining these matters is part of the sales process, but is often better undertaken by someone who not only is technically expert and experienced in the customer industry but who is also less obviously a sales person.

For this reason responsibility for applications engineers is often allocated to technical departments rather than to marketing or sales departments. In companies which sell made to order equipment, applications engineers, once an order has been gained, often assume responsibility for ensuring that the completed product meets customer requirements, and in this project engineering role have as much responsibility to works management as to the technical manager or the sales manager. In other companies, application engineers spend only a small proportion of their time dealing directly with customer problems, rather than with development or production related problems, and in that case they form a natural part of the technical department. However, where dealing with customers forms a major part of their work, applications engineers clearly become part of the mainstream selling effort, and while they obviously need to keep up-to-date technically, their day to day activity needs to be controlled by sales management.

14.15 Customer training

An extension of technical applications advice which is relevant in the case of capital equipment, is customer training: training in how to use the equipment in the most efficient manner. Being able to offer such a service is not only a valuable tool when selling, but it also helps ensure that subsequent user experience is satisfactory, thereby increasing the probability of obtaining repeat and referral orders. Direct involvement with the practical use of equipment can also help bring to light areas for potential improvement and avoid unnecessary calls by service personnel. For these reasons customer training is best carried out at the customers' premises and on the actual equipment which has been purchased by the customer. It also helps establish an ongoing company to company relationship. It is the establishment of such an ongoing relationship which lies at the heart of successful industrial selling.

Chapter 15

Selling

15.1 Sales Role

The salesman or the sales engineer is the crucial end link in the marketing process, and the quality of the sales effort can make or break all the rest of the marketing effort which has preceded it. It is particularly crucial (as indicated in Section 12.10.6) in industries where customers are not able to readily differentiate between competitive offerings.

Industrial selling is not primarily concerned with selling by one's personality (i.e. implying elements of trickery) but by proving applicability. Salesmen have to convince potential customers that the product or service that they are selling will confer greater benefits on the customer's business should they decide to buy it, than would competitive offerings. These benefits may take the form of direct cost reductions (e.g. production costs, information costs, transportation costs), of enabling cost reductions to be made in other areas (e.g. using a reliable accurate process temperature controller may allow the use of cheaper material elsewhere in the manufacturing process), or of improvements in product performance. It is often necessary to gain an in-depth understanding of how companies operate, and to become involved in trials before being able to persuade prospective customers that these benefits can be obtained.

This means that selling many engineering products can be a protracted and expensive process. It is therefore vital that effort is concentrated where it is likely to reap most reward. To do this, the importance of each potential purchaser must be assessed, their methods of selecting products, systems and components must be understood, and an awareness developed of when they are most likely to buy. This is generally achieved by maintaining routine contact direct with potential customers and with others in the industry. Enquiries about how company XYZ or company ABC are getting along, while visiting one of their competitors, is not idle gossip, it is helping develop awareness.

Having identified the most likely potential customers it is still necessary for salesmen to be sure that the product they are selling really will be of benefit to these potential customers, before they commit company resources to an extensive sales effort. They reach that certainty first by research into the nature of potential customer's businesses prior to initial sales visits, and secondly by learning more about those businesses during visits. This means that salesmen have not only to explain in general terms what their products or services can do, but also, by discussing with prospective customers the nature of their businesses, to identify with them potential applications which can be investigated in more depth.

If salesmen can demonstrate that they can see the purchase from the customers viewpoint, their proposals are likely to carry much more weight. In order to understand the customer's viewpoint about products which require engineering skills in their evaluation, selection, installation, application and service, salesmen need to have some basic engineering knowledge. In the case of technically complex products that knowledge has to have some depth, and in the case of products which are sold across wide sectors of industry, the knowledge has to be broad.

The sales role can also be related to the buying stages referred to in Section 12.9. The lengthy selling process just described relates most obviously to a new buy. In the case of a straight rebuy customers already have a high level of understanding about their requirements. It has been shown that in these circumstances it is usually buyers who initiate decisions to change suppliers, and hence efforts have to be focused on gaining their attention by concentrating on commercial matters such as price, delivery guarantees, quality guarantees and ease of ordering. To make an impact in these areas it is necessary, as explained above, to understand buyers' decision criteria. It is rare to break into a rebuy situation on technical grounds unless there is a quality deficiency in what is already being bought (thereby creating a modified rebuy situation), or unless a very significant product plus is offered. Product plus usually means less cost, perhaps via quicker assembly, reduction of finishing, better quality, or reduced price, but sometimes means higher added value, perhaps, for example, enabling the end product to be serviced less often or more cheaply. In either case considerable knowledge about what is being currently used has to be obtained — somehow.

Where customers have decided to modify a rebuy on their own initiative, because they will be actively reassessing a limited number of competing products, it is a little easier to displace the existing supplier. However, it is necessary to get in early, and to do that, salesmen need to know when a reassessment is being undertaken. Industry knowledge is paramount. Getting in early may enable the revised buying criteria to be influenced, even though customers will normally be fairly well aware of their requirements. Hence the degree of influence and the length of the sales process is likely to be shorter than for a new buy.

The sales role not only involves obtaining orders but also obtaining information about new and changing customer needs and about competitive and potentially competitive offerings (an offering is the product, plus the whole range of services and expectations offered to buyers of that product). Much apparently casual conversation can pay dividends. A chat with a customer's fitter on the shop floor may lead to mention of a problem installing the product in some situations, often accompanied by a proposed solution. If the problem is reported back, investigated, and found to be widespread, a small design change may be proposed which will solve the problem and further enhance sales. Equally such a chat may lead to mention of why the fitter prefers the product over the competition and again this knowledge may prove to be a valuable sales aid.

Salesmen also have a role to play in finding new uses for products and proposing extensions to product ranges. They can do this by observing users' problems and thinking innovatively about solutions to them.

To summarise, the salesman's role involves:

1 identifying potential customers;
2 deciding which customers and potential customers to concentrate on;
3 identifying who to deal with in each company;
4 preplanning sales visits;
5 selling, by convincing customers that what is being offered represents better value in the specific circumstances under consideration than what is being offered by anyone else;
6 planning his time effectively,
7 gathering information.

Although selling may be the most crucial part of this role, it is unlikely to be accomplished efficiently unless the other six parts are also carried out. Gathering information was dealt with in Section 14.6. Each of the other areas will be dealt with in turn, the second and third being taken together under 'assessment of customer'. Consideration will subsequently be given to specific types of sales activity.

15.2 Identification of potential customers

Methods of identification have been dealt with in other chapters but will be summarised here. There are two aspects of the problem:

1 Identifying companies who may have a need for the product.
2 Identifying when that need is likely to arise.

Many leads come with no direct effort from salesmen, from advertisements, direct mail and press releases, as enquiries at an exhibition, or as referrals from satisfied customers. Others will come as a result of formally commissioned marketing research or from informal research by salesmen among friends and acquaintances or from non-competing salesmen (at the hotel bar!). However, it is unlikely that such sources alone will provide a sufficient number of contacts to satisfy the planned new business sales target. Consequently it is important for salesmen to undertake their own systematic research.

Often the most effective source of leads are the buyers and engineers who salesmen meet day to day. Regardless of whether a particular sales interview is with an existing customer or a potential customer, or is likely or not to produce an order, it does no harm to ask, especially now they know more about the product range, whether they are aware of other potential users. Rarely is such a request refused, and it very often yields useful suggestions. If the premises of one of the suggested users is local, it may be feasible to visit them immediately. They can be telephoned by the salesman there and then, mentioning that he is at J. Smiths and Mr Smith thought they may have a use for the product. If convenient the salesman can call immediately: if not a date can be fixed. (Telephone calls should also be used to arrange extra visits at short notice, whenever prearranged visits turn out to be abortive or to last much less time than expected, or in contrast, to apologise for being delayed.)

Published information is a less effective source of leads. Obviously it is possible to work through local and/or trade directories, covering each business category which may have some requirement for the product range. Unfortunately this is not a very efficient process. Business categories in directories tend to be very broad and hence the initial follow-up process (see Section 15.3) will bring to light many companies who will never be prospective customers.

Other published sources often used are reports of new contracts awarded, of factory extensions, or of new products being developed. Unfortunately, by the time the news is published most of the buying decisions will already have been made, but that does not mean that following up such leads is not worthwhile. There is always next time, the possibility of second sourcing, or of a redesign.

Some enterprising salesmen study the situations vacant advertisements, and not only for a new job. If a potential customer is recruiting designers or production personnel, that is an early warning that a buying decision may be imminent. An advertisement for a new buyer or chief engineer may mean that a previously locked door can now be opened. However, the main source of information about the imminence of a buying decision will be daily news gathering of the type referred to above.

15.3 Assessment of customers and prospective customers

Having identified new prospects, the next step is to determine whether they have a definite need for the product(s) on offer, usually by outlining to these prospective customers typical uses of the product and exploring with them whether similar requirements exist in their businesses. A telephone call can eliminate companies who clearly do not have a need. It is amazing the number of people who send for literature who have no buying requirement; perhaps they are assembling a library of catalogues, or wish to generally keep up-to-date in the field, or they are undertaking a project (often marketing research), or have circled the wrong number on the reply paid card. A telephone call will also establish those who have a remote need and who are worth periodically re-telephoning in case the need becomes less remote. In spite of the fact that at this stage salesmen often do not know the name of the 'right' person to talk to in a company, and finding them is a certain way to boost the revenue of British Telecommunications, using the telephone is undoubtedly more cost effective than speculative cold calls, especially if the telephone calls, within reason, are saved up until salesmen are in the locality and between sales visits. This uses salesmen's time more effectively, cuts down the need to spend half a day every week at base telephoning around, reduces telephone bills, and sometimes enables initial visits to new prospects to be fitted in as suggested above.

That leaves the more hopeful prospects who appear as if they could have a need for the product(s) on offer. Before arranging an appointment some attempt should be made to ascertain how closely they are tied in with competitors and whether it is worth (in terms of potential order value) trying to gain their business. If it is decided that it is, the purpose of the initial telephone call becomes more specific, namely to arrange a first appointment with as many members of the buying team as it is possible to see initially. It is normally not possible to sell technical products to new customers over the telephone and so this should not be attempted. It will very often confuse and partially put off whoever is on the other end of the line. Salesmen have been known to talk themselves out of an appointment agreed earlier in the telephone call.

Unfortunately it is often not very clear from a telephone call whether or not it is worth making an immediate preliminary visit. The nature of some products is such that prospective customers do not fully understand how they can be used with benefit, and therefore they are unlikely to react positively to salesmen's outline descriptions of products and their typical uses. In these cases salesmen have to visit each prospect to see for themselves. Very often a general discussion will lead to other potential applications being unearthed.

In other cases, even though the need has been identified as remote, it is still worthwhile undertaking a visit so that product awareness can be reinforced and hopefully some product enthusiasm generated, because that may just make the need less remote. As different circumstances arise, prospects may remember the benefits promised, and consider that they may prove desirable in the new circumstances. This is often the case with materials and components which have to be designed into products. Development personnel have to be aware of what is available at an early stage, sometimes as early as the idea conception. Sometimes development personnel shy away from salesmen because they do not wish to waste their time when the proposed use is very tenuous and uncertain. However, it is at this preliminary design stage where good applications advice can pay dividends and ensure the component or product on offer is adopted later. In order to obtain that initial appointment it may be necessary to make it clear that no hard sell will be attempted and that the tenuous nature of the enquiry is appreciated, and to explain that a general exploration of potential new applications can be as beneficial to the supplier as to the prospective customer. There are no rules for deciding whether it is worth making a visit, and so if there is any doubt, it is best to make a visit, fitting it in around other less speculative appointments.

The discussion so far has been in terms of new prospects, but obviously it is also necessary to assess when to visit existing customers. This can be achieved by maintaining regular telephone contact to obtain early warning of new requirements or of any dissatisfaction with the service being provided, or of any vigorous competitor activity. In this way visit frequency can be changed to meet circumstances; sometimes visiting every week and at other times not visiting for six months. Should regular telephone calls not yield any reason to arrange a visit after a period of several months, this may be a sign of a satisfied customer regularly ordering, but it may also be a sign of some dissatisfaction or of loss of interest. Accordingly a sales visit should in any case be arranged periodically, either simply to reassure and reinforce, or to find out what is causing the customer to reassess his requirements.

15.4 Preplanning sales visits

It is rare in the case of technical industrial products for it to pay to cold call. It is usually more effective to have made an appointment and to have found out something about the current situation in order to preplan each sales visit. Calling

---

1   Is this visit worth the time and effort — to me and the customer, why?
2   Why is it necessary to make this visit next week?
3   Why should it have priority over other visits that could be made next week?
4   Who should be seen? Is the current contact the right person? Can he make the decision to buy? Who else needs to be seen and how is this to be achieved?
5   How should the sales approach be adapted to suit the interests of different decision makers, emphasizing, for example, product performance, reliability, ease of operation, maintenance, overall cost, as appropriate? Overall, what is considered to be the most important selection factor?
6   In what way will this sales visit lead to additional sales, immediately or in the future?
7   Is the objective of the visit to secure an order? Is that realistic?
8   If the objective is not an order, what is it and is it worthwhile (see 1, 2 and 3 again)?
9   What percentage of customer purchases do we currently obtain? Even if 100% why is the volume not greater, why is it not less? How can it be changed?
10 What obstacles are likely to be met and how will they be overcome?
11 What can be done during the visit to prepare the way for future sales? With whom? What sales aids, brochures, slides, samples, offers of demonstration are needed?

and more specifically for new prospects

12 Who can decide to change the source of supply? Who will influence the decision?
13 Who does the company buy from now and in what way is that satisfactory or unsatisfactory to them?
14 Are there any really good reasons why they should change and buy from us?
15 How are these reasons to be put across — demonstration, referrals, films, samples, free trial?

Fig. 15.1   *Factors to consider when pre-planning a sales visit (modified from Brown [94])*

without an appointment is time wasting and it does not give the impression of efficiency or respect. If a salesman calls on a company without an appointment he may be told to come back when he has an appointment, asked to arrange an appointment for another day, be kept waiting because the relevant person is busy, or be seen by the office junior. In every case the salesman's time is not being used very efficiently.

Basic data gained about the nature of a prospects business, about the size of the business, and about the types of problems which could be solved by the product(s) being sold, gained during the abovementioned 'screening process', can be used to preplan the first visit. Obviously subsequent visits can be planned in more detail as more information will be available. The purpose of preplanning is to make sure that time − both salesman's and customer's − is not wasted by irrelevant discussions. It is essential to determine beforehand what outcome is being sought as a result of a sales visit, what the likely obstacles to that outcome are, and to have an idea of how they are to be overcome. Examples of the types of question a salesman should be asking himself are listed in Fig. 15.1. Several of the questions deliberately overlap to ensure that the issues are fully considered.

15.5 Selling

Until the first sales visit, prospective customers have to rely on second or third hand information about suppliers, gained from reading advertisments and brochures, or from talking to peers. However, they will have tentatively formed definite views and will expect those views to be confirmed by the salesman, both during the initial telephone conversation and during the initial sales visit. If these views are not immediately confirmed this creates uncertainty in the prospective customers' minds about whether they have properly interpreted the information previously presented to them, and that makes them sceptical about what salesmen say. Accordingly, the initial selling effort should be strongly linked to the advertising and brochures that have preceded it. In fact in many cases a good starting point is to ask what motivated the customer to request or agree to a sales call.

It is also essential that salesmen quickly convey to prospective customers that they are not simply interested in making a sale but in helping solve the customer's problem, whatever that may be. Customers are only interested in their own problems and possible solutions to those problems. The problem may be the design of a new product, reduction of noise in a machine shop, more accurate weighing of material, holding given temperature limits in an oven or whatever. In accordance with the marketing concept the salesman must offer solutions to these problems via the product or service that he is selling. The first step towards that state of affairs is for the salesman to listen to what the customer is saying, to observe what is happening and to ask relevant questions. Good relevant questions are taken as a sign of a professional approach and can be used to gain customer confidence, because they indicate that the salesman has a broad understanding of the sorts of problems the prospective customer faces. The purpose of the questions is to find out what are the specific problems faced by the customer at the present time, to understand their importance to the customer, and to begin to understand the potential difficulties involved in overcoming them.

Salesmen who are able to persuade customers to show them exactly where and how a problem has arisen are presented with a wonderful opportunity to find out more information as they walk through the premises – about other applications, about the overall health of the company, as well as more detail about the application in hand. It is also important to find out what the customer's level of technical knowledge is, so that the discussion can start off at the right point. It is only just less bad to bore someone with what they already know, than it is to lose them because of their lack of knowledge. If customers cannot understand the significance of what is being said, they certainly are not going to be influenced by what is said.

Often it is necessary to undertake more than one visit before the nature of the requirement becomes clear – sometimes to the potential customer as well as to the supplier. Only when the nature of the need is clear to both parties can relevant product benefits begin to be demonstrated. However, before time is spent on demonstrations it is important to try to be sure that the prospect really intends to make a purchase. In the case of capital equipment it is necessary to check whether there are likely to be funds available for the purchase. This is not the same thing as the lack of a financial sanction, because preliminary enquiries are often made in order to help the prospective user build up a case for funding, and help at this stage will often, but not necessarily, predispose the user towards the helpful supplier. Alternatively the prospective customer may merely intend to use information culled from the first sales visit to apply pressure to his existing supplier, or possibly the prospect may be genuinely only interested in a general way and have no immediate or definite application in mind. This of course is less likely if the buyer becomes involved in the discussions.

The next part of the process often sorts the successful salesman from the less successful. During the discussion of ways and means of solving the customer's problems, and during any necessary demonstrations of the proposed solution (i.e. product or system), there is an opportunity to gradually redefine the problem, diminishing the importance of factors which the salesman's product cannot meet and introducing a string of new needs which the product can satisfy – preferably ones that are unique to the product. In this way the benefits being offered will gradually come to closely fit what is now thought to be needed and hopefully at the same time will gradually become less close to what is being offered by the competition. Depending on the complexity of the problem and its solution, various steps in the selling process may well involve technical staff, demonstrators, applications experts, service staff, marketing support staff and senior management. Once it is apparent that a decision is imminent, particularly in the case of high value equipment, it can be of considerable advantage for senior management of the vendor to meet with senior management of the potential buyer, first to establish their credibility as a reliable knowledgeable supplier, and second to present their case direct rather than secondhand via the other staff involved in the buying decision. It is up to the salesman to establish who the final decision maker will be and to gauge jointly with management the method and timing of a senior level approach. It is vital not to give the impression that anyone is being short circuited; rather the visit should be seen as an attempt to support the sales activities already undertaken and to offer reassurance that the potential business will be given priority and that high level follow up is assured if there should be any unresolved problems or uncertainties.

In spite of the emphasis in industrial selling on proving applicability (Section 15.1), it is nevertheless necessary, before a salesman can persuade a prospective customer to buy, for the prospect to come to trust the salesman and the company he represents. Much of the groundwork is laid by careful promotion and a good track record, but it has to be reinforced by the salesman's own efforts. It has been suggested (Brown [94]) that this process involves five stages:

1　The customer comes to like the salesman and considers it a pleasure and worth while to talk to him.
2　The customer comes to trust the salesman because he does not appear to oversell or make false promises, and he tries hard to iron out problems.
3　The customer concludes the salesman knows his business and knows his products.
4　The customer concludes the salesman understands the customer's business and can help solve one or more of his problems.
5　The customer realises the salesman is backed by an efficient company, a good product and good service.

Thus the customer has to reach stage 4 before he really begins to pay attention to what the salesman says about applicability.

The method of achieving these five aims will vary — industry to industry, company to company — and it is not within the scope of this text to teach people how to do it, although many of the relevant factors are dealt with in this chapter. For those who need or wish to read more, reference should be made to the many excellent books on the subject. Some understanding of how to undertake persuasive communication, how to deal with receptionists and secretaries, how to make appointments, is of considerable value in business life in general, and should not be dismissed by those who do not expect ever to get out on the road selling.

By combining the ideas in various texts on selling it is possible to form some basic rules, and these are briefly set out in Fig. 15.2. What cannot be achieved at one interview becomes part of the objective for the next one. Salesmen leaving companies after a visit should always be clear about the potential product application(s), whether there really is an order in the offing, the approximate value of any order to be placed, the time-scale leading up to a decision, the names of any personnel involved in the decision other than those seen, the probability of being seriously considered as a supplier, and the next action to take. In some cases

1   *Know your product* — how it can be applied, its limitations, where it has been successful. The greater the product knowledge the more likely it is that it will be possible to find a way to demonstrate how the product can help solve the customer's problem. Certainly start by explaining how the product works in general, and its benefits in general, but it is essential to quite quickly begin to relate those benefits to the customer's problem.

2   *Know your customer* — his problems, his values, his needs. If you do not understand his problem you cannot begin to help him solve it. Maybe he does not understand it either so ask leading questions and try to define it together. Listen to the answers.

3   *Know your competitors* — your customers are his prospects, your prospects are his customers. In presenting a particular product feature and pushing its importance you may be unwittingly pushing your competitor's strongest point. You have just lost a sale. Ask the buyer where he thinks you are strongest.

4   *Do not knock the competition* — by saying they are bad. The customer may have respect for their product and you are making him feel foolish or antagonising him. (He is losing respect for your views). If buyers mention the competition the response should be along the lines 'they are good but we are better'. Any factual comparison undertaken should ideally be related to user experience.

5   *A planned pitch* must never appear to be that to the customer. Ideally it should sound like a response to his questions and his problems.

6   *Do not block objections or leave them unstated.* Bring them out and deal with them. Objections based on fact are easily dealt with. Emotional objections are more difficult because the basis of these emotions may be deep rooted and hard to get at.

7   *Closing* — sum up to ensure that both parties are agreed about the decision criteria and how they are to be met. Is the value of the benefit from your product greater than its price? Help make it seem so, reduce the tension of the decision (one week's free trial etc.). Often the customer is logically convinced but not strongly enough to overcome the fear of a wrong decision (emphasis on guarantee, back-up service and referrals help in this respect).

8   *Put existing customers before prospects* — you have something to lose.

9   *Avoid battles or win—lose situations.* Go for win—win problem solving. Do not lie, the customer may be asking you questions he already knows the answers to, to test your integrity or he may check your answers later. Do not promise what the product cannot deliver. You may achieve a sale this time but you have sold for the competition next time. If your product cannot solve the customer's problem recommend the best alternative product that can — you will be remembered.

10 *Follow up* — post-purchase dissonance will be made worse by trivial problems in initial use but the customer may not complain he may simply buy elsewhere next time. So follow up, make sure everything is OK and reassure him he has bought the best. Ideally the customer will have convinced himself that his buying decision is basically right so that even if things go wrong in some way thereafter he will tend to back the supplier and be tolerant providing he can see efforts being made to put things right. The sales interview will have established the requirement that the product can realistically be expected to meet and as such when it does, repeat sales may be expected. Much of the skill of selling is getting the buyer to agree that the fulfillable needs are the ones he, the buyer wants fulfilling.

Fig. 15.2   *Basic selling rules (based on various texts)*

the next action may be to do nothing for six months. If answers to these questions have not been obtained naturally during the course of the visit, then prior to departure they should be ascertained politely but straightforwardly.

Finally, it must be remembered that, particularly in industrial markets, repeat orders can be more important to sales success than new orders. It is therefore necessary for salesmen to follow up to try to ensure that orders are delivered on time, to discover whether ordered products are performing in the manner promised, and whether the commercial service being provided is satisfactory, and if not, to initiate action to attempt to put the matter right. In other words the aim is to minimise post-purchase dissonance (see Section 12.10.7) and to keep the customers sold.

15.6 Time planning

Consideration was given in Chapter 14 to methods of determining the number of sales visits needed to existing customers, to identified prospects and to new prospects in order to achieve a given sales target. Although this information should be developed in conjunction with each salesman, it may well be beneficial for each salesman to individually pursue the approach a little further, step by step, after he has been allocated a definite annual sales target.

Suppose that the sales target is £500 000 and that target business from existing customers represents £400 000. The first step is to divide existing customers into two categories in accordance with the 80/20 rule, or if it is appropriate into three categories (the top 10%, the next 30% and the remaining 60%). The next step is to calculate, based on past performance, the number of sales visits that ideally should be made to each of these categories of customer, and hence the time commitment required to achieve the sales targets. To this has to be added the time needed to undertake sufficient sales visits to meet the new business targets, taking into account that while many new prospects will be identified for salesmen, they will have to find many others themselves. The third step is to try to fit the time commitment into a working year; in other words to organise an annual call plan.

Suppose the outcome of an initial attempt to organise an annual call plan produces the numbers shown in Table 15.1. The task appears impossible until it is examined in more depth. First consider existing customers. Analysis of the small customers indicates an average order value of only £666 each, which means that the bottom 30% average only some £300 each. Some of these customers do not merit any visits at all, the bottom 30 perhaps are worth an average of one visit a year and the next 30 perhaps two visits a year, supplemented by quarterly telephone calls to show that they are not forgotten. It will be obvious from the conversation during these telephone calls whether a sales visit is in order and this will often ensure that visits to customers are not just made because their number has come up, but instead because there is some change in their circumstances or buying requirements. Sales visits should never be made just as routine. Salesmen must be in sufficiently close contact either as a result of links forged during previous visits or as a result of interim telephone calls, to know when to arrange the next visit. It is no good arriving three days after the buying decision has been made. The current order level is, of course, not the only criterion to be used when

Table 15.1   *Draft annual call plan*

(Note: The actual numbers are illustrative averages and the actual number of visits and order values for individual customers would of course vary quite considerably).

Visit potential

Assume 230 selling days per year, and allowing for time to identify new prospects, an average of $3\frac{1}{2}$ visits per day, making 805 visits per year.

Visits to be made *Existing customers*	No. of customers	No. of visits per year	Annual order value
Top 10% 1 visit per month	10	120	£240 000
Next 30%: 1 visit every $1\frac{1}{2}$ months	30	240	£120 000
Last 60%: 1 visit every 3 months	60	240	£ 40 000
	100	600	£400 000

New customers

(a) *Identified prospects*. Suppose 24 have been identified and that the historic success rate of converting such prospects into customers is 1 in 4. Assume failures require an average of $1\frac{1}{2}$ calls and successes an average of 3 visits. Ideally successes would be followed up by 1 visit per month for 3 months and then 1 visit every $1\frac{1}{2}$ months, to give 8 visits for a customer gained half way through the year. If the average order value is £4000 we have:

Successful sales	6	48	£ 24 000
Unsuccessful visits	18	27	—
	24	75	£ 24 000

(b) *Unidentified prospects*. Suppose the success rate is 1 in 7 and that failures require on average 2 visits and successes require on average 7 visits during the year. If the average order value is £3000 we have:

Successful sales	25	175	£ 75 000
Unsuccessful sales	175	350	—
	200	525	£ 75 000
Annual total	324	1200	£499 000

judging the number of sales visits it is worth making to a particular customer; the prospects for increased business must be taken into account and hence some of the bottom 60 customers may be worth more than one or two visits a year. Similar reasoning can be applied to other existing customers and could result in a revised plan of the type shown in the top half of Table 15.2. The value of

Table 15.2   *Modified annual sales plan*

Existing customers		No. of customers	No. of visits per year	Annual order value
Top 10%	possible increased business: 18 visits per year	6	108	£155 000
	static business: 8 visits per year	4	32	£ 96 000
				£251 000*
Next 30%	possible increased business: 12 visits per year	10	120	£ 50 000
	static business: 4 visits per year	20	80	£ 80 000
				£130 000*
Next 30%	possible increased business: 6 visits per year	10	60	£ 15 000
	static business: 1/2 visits per year	20	30	£ 13 000
Bottom 30%	possible increased business: 4 visits per year	10	40	£ 7500
	static business: 1 visit per year	20	20	£ 6500
		100*	490*	£ 42 000*
Identified prospects				
Successful sales		6	48	£ 24 000
Unsuccessful sales		18	22	–
		24*	70*	
Unidentified prospects				
Successful sales		18	126	£ 54 000
Unsuccessful sales		108	130	–
		126*	256*	
Annual total		260	816	£501 000

* Sub-totals included for comparison with Table 15.1.

increased business has deliberately been kept to very moderate levels for purposes of illustration.

Next consider new customers. Perhaps many of the first calls to new prospects need not be made at all if the companies were approached initially via a well prepared telephone call. Similarly, many second and third visits could be avoided, if during the first sales visits, salesmen realistically assessed whether an order was likely to be forthcoming. Such a systematic approach might reduce the average number of calls per unsuccessful effort nearer to one. If the maxim of concentrating effort were followed, that is concentrating on the more hopeful of the prospects, the success rate for previously unidentified prospects could well be marginally improved to 1 in 6. No change is suggested for previously identified prospects because presumably these already fall into the category of 'more hopeful'. If the salesman is achieving $3\frac{1}{2}$ visits per day he is probaby fitting visits to minor customers around visits to major customers and hence no improvements have been suggested in this direction.

Clearly we are now near a realistic plan, and one which concentrates effort where it is most likely to be rewarded — actually spending more time than previously with some existing customers. However no allowance has been made for contingencies such as unexpected loss of business from existing customers or sickness. On the other hand, increased use of the telephone might reduce the number of follow-up sales visits needed.

The purpose of this fictitious exercise has been to demonstrate how methodical planning can lead to significant improvements in performance by redirecting the efforts being made. Sustained improved performance is usually a result of improved method and not merely increased effort.

15.7 Selling high value items

High value items include contracts to build and/or install either individual items of plant and equipment, or complete systems of items such as high voltage links or factory conveyor systems. Selling high value items usually requires a very protracted and expensive sales effort and very often an overseas sales effort. Suppliers of high value items often have established a strong reputation and therefore prospective customers frequently make the first contact. Even so it is necessary to visit the would be purchaser to find out more about what is required, to establish the company as a serious contender for a particular order, and to find out who should be contacted so that a detail specification of what is required can be built up. It is dangerous to rely on paper specifications unless there has been recent previous contact or contracts with the prospect, or unless there are strong reasons to believe that the company is not being considered as a serious contender for the order and is being asked to tender as a matter of good form. The initial visit may be followed up by one or more visits by technical staff, so that an outline system design can be prepared and agreed with the potential customer as a basis for preparing an estimate or tender. Even where a standard specification has been/or is subsequently to be issued to competitors, these efforts may either bias the specification towards the company's strengths, or provide insights which will enable a more competitive tender to be prepared. During this process it is essential for salesmen to try to establish their company as the preferred contender (see Section 11.12), the one which people get on with, the one which really knows what it is doing, and the one which is clearly going to go to a lot of trouble to get the tender and the contract right, and to provide a good service. Some competitive advantage must be generated during the sales process.

Most companies cannot afford to incur such expensive efforts on every prospect, and therefore some preliminary intelligence as to the chances of success, based on political, commercial and technical grounds — and particularly on the names of likely competitors — is needed before mounting a full campaign. As stated previously it is better to win one out of five tenders rather than come second five times out of five. Out of every 20 initial visits it may be wise to withdraw from 12 or to put in a minimum effort covering bid and to concentrate on the other eight, perhaps thereby obtaining three orders, rather than spreading the effort over all 20 and obtaining perhaps only one order. For such efforts to be really effective a multi-disciplinary team taken from management, sales, engineering, production, finance, customer training and service departments often has to be assembled. Each member makes contact with the appropriate people in the customer organisation so as to ensure that all aspects of what is required are fully understood and to ensure that everyone involved in the buying decision can be encouraged to form the right view of the eventual bid or proposal. If it is possible to gain preferred supplier status, even if the initial bid price is high, buyers often allow a second chance — either to reduce the price or to further justify the higher bid price in terms of service, quality, efficient design and the like. The general rule is to influence the engineers first and the commercial people second, to avoid losing out to lower priced but lower value competitor bids.

Many companies underprice contracts simply because they have not investigated what is required in sufficient depth, and they are subsequently forced to come back to the customer for extras or to provide a cut price system. Very often it is possible to educate customers into rejecting such bids from competitors by explaining the extent of what is involved, how various costs arise and what would be the effect of taking short cuts. That is not to say that it is automatically a good idea to go for a higher price solution. The idea is to explain what alternatives are available and what they mean to the user in terms of performance, reliability and cost. Let the customer build up what he wants from the building blocks you provide. That is the way to become the preferred supplier.

Where contracts are very large and/or involve the use of several technologies, individual companies are often unable to provide the breadth of services sought. If one technology is dominant it is usually acceptable for companies operating in that technology to appoint subcontractors for the elements of the contract where they do not have relevant skills. Very often the prospective purchaser will wish to 'examine' the subcontractors, and in that case a strong liaison has to be established between the sales forces of the main contractor and the subcontractors. For the subcontractors, the sales effort involves two clear stages; first selling to the main contractor, and secondly to the final customer. Occasionally these stages become intertwined, with subcontractors selling themselves first (or simultaneously) to the final customer in order to help gain acceptance with the main contractor.

If there is no dominant technology, the desired breadth of service can be provided by a number of companies joining together as equal partners in a voluntary consortium. Each consortium member takes responsibility for part of the total package offered to the customer. Obviously the problems involved are greater than just a co-operative selling and pricing stance. As a result should the voluntary consortium prove successful, it is often kept in being, and members' sales teams are briefed to look for contracts where all or part of the consortium skills can be utilised.

15.8 Selling to large organisations

Many large buyers of industrial products are increasingly beginning to organise their buying on similar lines to the public sector. Thus while selling to these organisations may still be considered a special case, it is an increasingly common and important one. In the case of less complex or technically well understood items a purchase specification is normally issued, and the lowest bid from those companies who have been able to prove that their products meet the specification, and that they are able to deliver in the required quantities and on time, is accepted. In other words while the ultimate decision is price based, much earlier effort is needed to gain inclusion on the list of acceptable suppliers (this is the two-stage analysis of alternative offerings referred to in Section 12.10.2). Often the purchasing agency will wish to visit the prospective supplier's factory to look over production and quality control capabilities, as well as undertaking a formal product trial.

The selling process may also involve making efforts to influence the wording of purchase specifications towards what the supplier is best able to offer. With very large customers this can involve making contact with their standards departments. Over a period of time it may be possible to introduce company thinking· into the specifications, and, equally important, to receive advance warning of the likely requirements of new specifications before they are issued, so that development effort can be channelled accordingly. Inasmuch as many public sector specifications are based on British Standards, membership of the relevant BSI committees can be an essential part of this process.

For companies involved with high technology, not only is the government the largest customer but it is also a major source of development funds, particularly for large projects which could not realistically be funded by a single commercial enterprise. Many companies try to obtain these development contracts in the hope of using the acquired expertise in their commercial products. In some industries government contracts are the only way by which companies can afford to employ a sufficient number of high quality personnel to keep up with the latest technology. Companies intending to follow this path have to sell themselves in a very special way. They have to sell at the highest levels as well as further down the tree, in order to establish credibility as an organisation which can be trusted to successfully undertake complex projects. They have to be prepared to become involved in many meetings and factory visits and very often to reveal design, costing, inspection, testing and production control procedures.

15.9 In conclusion

Selling is a practical skill but one where effectiveness can be considerably improved by planning. The exact nature of the selling process varies widely from industry to industry but always involves the following essentials:

1 Identifying and making contact with potential customers.
2 Establishing their requirements.
3 Evaluating their level of interest.
4 Increasing their level of interest by offering to satisfy their requirements effectively.
5 Demonstrating how their requirements will be satisfied, that is convincing the customer of the credibility of the offer and that the product and company will perform as promised.
6 Creating a preference over competitive offers by reiterating points 4 and 5.

	Repeat industrial goods	Capital equipment
Explores and understands the needs of the customer	1st	2nd
Product knowledge	2nd	1st
Ability to clinch the order	3rd	3rd
Contacts in the industry	4th	4th
Knowledge of the market	5th	5th
Call preparation	6th	6th
Knowledge of own company and the service it could give	7th	7th
Answers questions/objections better	8th	9th
Number of new customers gained	9th	11th
Better presentation	10th	7th
Better at making initial contacts	11th	10th

The first two factors stood well ahead of the remainder, being mentioned nearly three times as often as the 3rd and 4th factors.

Fig. 15.3 *Sales success factors (from Dunkeld and Cashin [95])*

7 Closing the sale: that is ensuring that all points or objections have been raised and overcome and that there remain no more factors hidden which could prevent a favourable decision. All too often it is discovered that a sale has been lost for reasons which no one on the sales team has been aware of and therefore has not dealt with.

8 Keeping the customer sold for repeat orders by following up and maintaining good customer—supplier relationships, for example by pre-warning the customer of price increases and explaining why they are unavoidable, and by ensuring that complaints are quickly and effectively dealt with.

In 1979 a survey undertaken by the Institute of Marketing (see Dunkeld and Cashin [95]) asked sales managers to list the factors which they considered most important in determining the difference in sales performance between their best salesmen and their average salesmen. The factors are listed in order in Fig. 15.3. There is no reason to believe that they have changed. If there were to be a final message it is that knowledge is power. Knowledge of the product, of the customer and of the competition.

Chapter 16

Distribution

16.1 Why distribution is important

There are two main reasons why distribution is important to engineering companies: increased competitive advantage and reduced costs.

Increased competitive advantage is achieved by improving product availability. In the case of frequently bought goods, such as raw materials, components or consumables, customers prefer to deal with suppliers who offer frequent, quick and reliable delivery, because that enables them to reduce their own stockholdings. The cost savings are such that many customers are prepared to pay a price premium to obtain this level of service. As an extreme example, a small subcontractor was contacted by a major vehicle manufacturer late one Friday afternoon to establish whether they could supply a batch of bushes. The normal supplier had not only not delivered to schedule but had closed for the weekend. Without the bushes a vehicle production line would have to be stopped and therefore the price premium the manufacturer was prepared to pay was very considerable. In addition, manufacturers often require both frequently and infrequently bought goods urgently, and of necessity orders are placed with whoever is able to meet the urgent delivery requirements, rather than with the supplier who otherwise offers best value for money. Finally, in the case of low value items or products which require regular servicing, customers often prefer to deal with local suppliers, and therefore will only buy products which are available through local distribution outlets.

Reduced costs as a result of efficient distribution management, can make a significant impact on profits. It is not uncommon for distribution costs to represent 15% of total costs, or 30% of all overhead costs, and hence the profit impact of any cost saving will be considerable.

16.2 Influence of the type of product

Obviously different types of products have to be distributed in different ways. It is necessary to have some idea what these differences are, in order to properly understand the rest of this chapter.

The first type of product are those which are built to customer order. In this situation distribution involves arranging on-time delivery of the finished product, from the manufacturer's factory to the user's premises, by the most economical means. The main influence on delivery reliability will be the manufacturer's scheduling of design, production and product testing. For that reason delivery or distribution is very often included within the job responsibilities of the manufacturer's works manager. Usually he is anxious to move completed products out of his factory as quickly as possible to make room for the next order, and any delays at this stage are most likely to arise because the customer does not wish to take delivery immediately. If this is because the customer has put back his delivery requirements, the question of who bears the storage costs is usually negotiated, bearing in mind the need to avoid losing customer goodwill. A frequent compromise is that the customer is immediately invoiced for the product but the cost of physical storage rests with the producer. On the other hand, if it is obvious that the producer has no space available the customer can usually be persuaded to bear the storage costs himself.

Some made to order products (usually capital plant) are finally assembled at the users premises and in that case the delivery problem is one of scheduling material, components and subassemblies to arrive on site in the right order and at the right time. Usually economical transportation takes second place to keeping the assembly process moving. Made to order products represent the simplest distribution situation.

The second type of products are those which are offered with a number of options. These products are usually built up by the producer to a stage just short of final assembly. Final assembly is undertaken only when an order is received. The finished products are usually delivered direct from supplier factory to user, whether or not they have actually been sold by an intermediary. In this situation, effecting rapid delivery is a matter of ensuring that part assembled products and components are readily available for completion, and of ensuring that there is efficient control of the final assembly operations. Determination of the interim stock levels required will follow the principles described in Section 16.4.4 for finished goods. As before, the products normally will be despatched as soon as they are completed, subject only to the speed with which the despatch paperwork can be prepared, the product packed and transport made available.

Where some of the options offered prove particularly popular, they become more or less standard and therefore it is possible to consider holding stocks of these more popular options, either at the manufacturing plant or at intermediate locations. The cost effectiveness of this choice will be determined by the principles set out later in this chapter.

The third and most complex distribution situation occurs when products are built for stock. Not only will there be decisions to take about stock levels, the location of stock and economical transportation, but these decisions will have to be linked into the choice of distribution and sales channels.

16.3 Elements of physical distribution systems

Let us first look at the physical movement of products. The term business logistics has been coined to cover the task of moving material, from where it is first obtained to the final customer. Physical distribution is part of this process, being concerned with the efficient movement of finished products to the final user, so that they arrive at the time users wish to receive them and in usable condition.

In its simplest form physical distribution involves a series of steps as follows:

> stocking − loading − transport − unloading − stocking − loading −
> tranport − unloading − stocking

The number of times the sequence is repeated is a measure of the complexity of the system. Normally the largest number of cycles required for industrial products is four; when, for example, low value products such as pulley belts are moved from production line to factory storage, factory storage to main distributor, main distributor to local stockist and local stockist to consumer. At the other extreme, made to order products such as machining centres may only be moved through one cycle, that is from production despatch area to user factory. More cycles will be involved for products which are exported, especially if the main overseas agency acts as a central stockist prior to onwards transportation to other distributors in his country.

As distribution chains become longer, fluctuations in demand experienced by the factory can be considerable (see Section 2.6) and the size of stockholdings will increase. Even where distributors have paid for that stock, its management often falls back onto the manufacturer. Large stocks also increase the difficulties associated with outofdate stock whenever a new model is introduced. Complexity and control of the system is further increased by the number of times ownership of the product changes hands.Regardless of the number of cycles involved, control of physical distribution requires consideration to be given to the following activities:

(a) *Order processing*: involves keeping track of each order as it moves through various stages of design, production, test and distribution. Often the efficiency of this 'paperwork' system has a major influence on delivery promptness and costs.

(b) *Materials handling*: involves efficiently moving stock from the production centre to storage points and subsequently from the storage points for packaging and onward transportation, and if appropriate, back again to new storage points. The layout of storage centres and the capabilities of materials-handling equipment are crucial to the process.

(c) *Stocking*: involves selecting the location of storage points and the method of physically storing the product within them.

(d) *Packaging*: involves protecting the product and facilitating materials handling. Palletisation and containerisation are important factors in this category but clear labelling also has a major impact. Packaging does not tend to be used as a sales aid, other than to demonstrate that the product is well protected from damage during transportation and storage.

(e) *Stock control*: involves selecting the appropriate level of stocks to be maintained, bearing in mind sales forecasts, normally accepted delivery delays, the costs of holding stocks and the most efficient volumes of production.

(f) *Transportation*: involves selecting the most appropriate mode of transport and controlling its cost and performance. If a company uses its own fleet of vehicles this has to be routed efficiently and maintained at optimum size.

Although all these parts of the physical distribution system are vitally important, detailed discussion of many of them is more appropriate to specialised texts, than to a general marketing text. The discussion in this chapter will cover only the basic principles, with special emphasis on where physical distribution impinges on marketing strategy; that is the balance between costs and making the product readily available. It is also recognised that the choice between different transportation modes (road, rail, air, water, pipeline, conveyor) can have a substantial effect on performance, but the significance of these choices is normally readily apparent in a given situation. For the sake of simplicity, road transport (which carries over 80% of freight tonnage in the UK) will be referred to throughout.

16.4 Some basic concepts pertinent to physical distribution

16.4.1 Customer service level

The term customer service level relates to the averaged ability of a company to supply an order rapidly, usually from stock. Thus if a company receives orders for 500 items during a week and can supply only 450 immediately, it is operating at a customer service level of 90%. Normally customer service levels are not measured in terms of immediately meeting orders but in terms of meeting them within a defined time-scale, such as 24 hours, or 3 days, or 10 days. Consequently, customer service level may be defined as, 'the percentage of orders which are met within a specified time period following order placement.' The time element is important; clearly a company need not hold as much stock to achieve a 95% customer service level within 7 days as it would need to achieve a 95% customer service level within 3 days.

The time period which is accepted as normal varies from industry to industry. In order to determine what is appropriate (see also Section 17.3.2) it is necessary to look at the situation from the customer's viewpoint. What will they consider to be bad, fair or good delivery; what will they consider unnecessary icing on the cake (i.e. will not pay a premium for)? An extreme example is a blood bank. If one was bleeding to death it would not be very helpful to be told that delivery could not be made until the next day. There are many industrial equivalents, for example, raw materials, components and subassemblies whose non-delivery within the specified time period would cause customers' production to stop. Other examples are spares for critical items of plant and equipment, such as oil supply hose, electronic process controllers or production conveyor parts. Even where users hold vital spares themselves they still expect a 24 hour or better service in case a second breakdown occurs – and they often do. In the case of made to order products, customers do not expect deliveries to be immediate and a 4 to 6 week delivery period is often accepted as normal.

Sometimes it is possible by efficient organisation to improve on what is achieved by competitors at little extra cost, and in that case the extra service provided can be promoted into a powerful sales aid. However there is no point in providing greater service than customers will value; that is, than will influence the purchase decision. (The results of any customer survey in this connection, must be interpreted with care, as customers will inevitably state delivery requirements much more stringent than are really necessary). Usually there will be some spread around an industry 'norm' within which differences will have relatively insignificant affects on sales volume. For example, if the norm is 6 weeks, 5 or 7 weeks delivery may not concern customers, whereas offering only 9 weeks will: and offering 3 weeks may make them take notice, even if 6 weeks is quite adequate for their needs. Sometimes offering an unnecessarily short delivery can lead customers to believe that the supplier is trying to cover up some other deficiency: why otherwise would he offer 3 weeks delivery when everyone knows that 6 weeks is quite adequate? On the other hand if the industry norm is 3 days, offering 4 days could result in some loss of business and offering 5 days certainly would. Offering 2 days may well increase business.

Whatever customer service level is set, there will be some loss of sales whenever specific customer requirements cannot be met. Some of these customers will transfer their business elsewhere rather than wait for delivery. The aim then is to balance the loss of profit associated with this loss of custom, against the level of expenditure needed to avoid losing it. For every company there will be some customer service level above which the costs of providing a better service will be higher than the profits that the higher level of service would earn. Even though it is difficult to measure the effect, because so many other factors influence sales volume, the only way to find out for sure is to experiment: to actually change the customer service level offered. A simple substitute measure may be to monitor the number of complaints and progressing telephone calls received, at different customer service levels (see also Section 17.3.2). Companies which can meet all orders immediately are almost certainly holding too much stock.

16.4.2 Influence of order processing delays
There is little point holding substantial stocks if the remainder of the order processing system is not organised to ensure a rapid response to orders. For example, if a 3 day delivery is quoted, but order processing and order preparation take 2 days, little flexibility is left to optimise transportation.

The components of delivery lead time, that is the time which elapses between order placement and order delivery are as follows:

1 *Order transmission* – from customer to supplier. It can be speeded up by accepting telephone or preferably telex orders in advance of written confirmation.

2 *Order processing* – that is the interpretation of a customer's order into an authorisation to the despatch department to deliver, and in the case of made to order products into an authorisation for manufacture to be completed. The time can be reduced by an efficient 'paperwork' and stock record system. An additional benefit in this respect is the capability to keep customers informed about the progress of their order. A little courtesy in this area can do as much for repeat business as extensive advertising and sales efforts.

3 *Order preparation* – that is the time needed to withdraw the necessary products from stock, assemble and pack them, ready to be loaded into a delivery vehicle. It is reduced by efficient materials handling and packing.

4 *Distribution* – that is the time elapsing between despatch and receipt of goods by the customer. Methods of reducing it are dealt with in Section 16.5.

The aim is to achieve a target customer service level at minimum total system cost, and that may mean spending more on one element, if thereby, a greater reduction in the costs of the other elements can be achieved.

16.4.3 Delivery reliability

Very often it is more important to customers for delivery to be reliable rather than rapid. For example, many companies purchasing components, consumables or raw materials for their production facility will normally be able to estimate when they will require delivery, somewhat in advance of the required delivery date, and so, when they compare otherwise compatible suppliers, they are more likely to favour the ones who quote a delivery of, say, 6 weeks and who can be relied upon to deliver on the specified day, than suppliers who quote 4 weeks but sometimes deliver a week early and sometimes a week or two late. In the former case they can place the order well in advance, and can plan their production knowing exactly when the delivery will be made. In the latter case they will be forced to take account of the possible late delivery and order 5 weeks in advance. If the delivery is subsequently made in only 3 or 4 weeks, that could create substantial stock holding problems. Other companies, especially those who make products to order, are not able to plan their purchasing requirements well in advance and in that case reliable speed of delivery will be paramount. although many would still favour a supplier who quotes 7 days and is known to be reliable, rather than a supplier who unreliably quotes 3 days. There is the overriding suspicion that the short delivery promise will have been made in order to obtain the order, in the full knowledge that it cannot be met. This represents poor marketing and poor sales practice. Over a period of time it is possible for a customer to build up a record of supplier performance. This record can be summarised into a readily usable form as shown below. For each delivery the reliability of the delivery promise (R) can be recorded as a ratio:

$$R = \frac{\text{actual delivery period}}{\text{promised delivery period}}$$

When a substantial number of values for R have been recorded the average value and standard deviation can be calculated*, enabling a delivery promise of, say, 6 weeks to be interpreted as $5-7\frac{1}{2}$ weeks. A small standard deviation is more important than an average value which approaches unity.

16.4.4 Cost effective stock levels

It is now relevant to consider the costs involved in stockholding. First there are the costs of capital (C) tied up, both in the stocks themselves and in the facilities needed to store and handle them. Obviously the greater the stocks held the greater will be the investment required. The capital tied up in this manner could otherwise be invested in other parts of the company's operation or used to reduce its overdraft. In practice the annual investment cost is calculated as the product of the total investment and the current bank lending rate.

Secondly, there are the running costs (R) of heating buildings, of operating and maintaining materials handling and storage systems, and of operating an efficient record system. Thirdly, it is necessary to consider the economies of production. Suppose a company operates batch production, then, given its production facilities, there will be some batch size which is more economic than other batch sizes. From the point of view of production economy it would be logical to replenish stocks at intervals which corresponded to the optimum batch size. For example, if the optimum batch size were 1000 units and average sales were 50 units per day, stocks would be replenished every 20 days. Unfortunately demand is not steady, and on occasions stock will be sold before the planned replenishment date. Based on normal demand variations it is possible to predict how often these 'stockouts' will occur. If the answer indicates that the target customer service level cannot be met, it becomes necessary to consider holding safety stocks, that is equivalent to 2, 3 or even 10 days normal demand, depending on demand variations. The higher the safety stocks the higher will be the stock holding costs outlined above. Sometimes it will be more economic to change the size of production batches away from what is most economic, and replenish stocks more (and sometimes less) frequently, rather than hold substantial safety stocks. Similarly, when production is continuous it is sometimes judged to be more sensible to reduce or increase the rate of production away from the most economic rate, rather than increase stocks or reduce customer service. If the costs of such uneconomic production (P) are considered with the other cost parameters, and if S represents the profits earned from product sales, it can be seen that the most efficient level of stocking will correspond to the situation

$$\Delta C + \Delta R + \Delta P > \Delta S$$

that is where any increases in stocking or production costs will be greater than the additional profit thereby earned, and any decreases in costs will be less than the profit thereby lost. Thus in an optimum situation where, say:

$$C + R + P = 1000 \quad \text{and} \quad S = 2000$$

* An even simpler approach would be to record two average values, one for all values of R greater than 1 and one for all values of R less than 1.

then if $C + R + P$ were increased to 1010, S would increase to 2005 and if $C + R + P$ were reduced to 990, S would decrease to 1985

In practice it is extremely difficult to calculate where this point lies, partly because of the large number of interrelating variables on which C, R, P and S depend, and partly because the value of many of the variables (such as S) are forecast rather than defined. As a result, many companies forgo an integrated approach for the conceptually easier task of separately minimising the costs of each of these aspects of the operation. The chances of the outcome representing an overall cost minimisation are slim and the effort required to obtain a working approximation to the minimum will usually be worthwhile, particularly for the more popular product lines. Normally 80% of the sales volume will come from 20% of products and therefore the stock levels of those 20% have to be particularly closely controlled. From a marketing viewpoint it is necessary to decide whether it is worth deviating from this optimum point, usually with a view to improving customer service levels, in order to enhance the company's reputation and hopefully gradually increase sales volume.

16.5 Factors influencing the choice of physical distribution method

The objective of an efficient physical distribution system is to reduce the costs of providing a given customer service level. Companies essentially have three choices, namely:

(a) to deliver direct to customers (or allow them to collect);
(b) to deliver via company owned distribution depots;
(c) to deliver via outside distributors.

The choice comes down to a trade-off between long distance haulage costs, local redelivery costs, stock holding and stockout costs, depot running costs, and communication costs (factory to depot and depot to depot). The size of each of these costs, and hence the most economic choice depends on a number of factors, namely:

1 the value and physical size of orders;
2 the number and geographic spread of customers;
3 delivery frequency;
4 the technical complexity of the product;
5 the level of installation and service help required.

Each of these factors will be considered in turn

16.5.1 Value and physical size of orders
Some products are of sufficient value to justify individual delivery to customers regardless of their physical size, perhaps for reasons of security or product fragility, or rapid delivery. In these cases the costs of individual delivery form only a small

part of the total price that the customer pays and therefore delivery economics tend to be a secondary consideration.

Some products are physically large and heavy, sufficiently large or heavy that individual items have to be delivered on separate vehicles. More often it is the size of the individual orders rather than single products which fill vehicles. On other occasions three or four or even 12 or 15 orders may be needed to fill a vehicle, but providing sufficient orders are received within the promised delivery period from customers located acceptably close to each other, it may still be sensible to deliver them consecutively, with each vehicle following some sort of circular route.

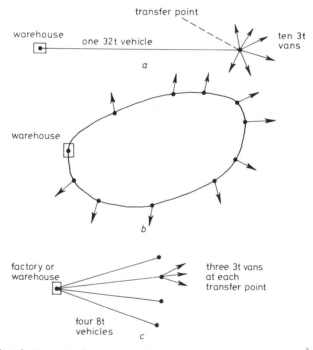

Fig. 16.1   *Transferring orders from a large vehicle to several smaller vehicles*

16.5.2 Number and geographic spread of customers

We have already introduced a geographic proviso and this proviso becomes more important as the physical size of orders becomes less and the number of orders needed to fill vehicles increases. As the number of orders needed to fill a large vehicle grows, say to more than can be delivered by a single vehicle in a single day, it can be more economic to offload orders into smaller vehicles at local transfer points (Fig. 16.1a) whose location will be chosen, so that they are readily accessible from the main trunk road network and yet are reasonably central to known delivery addresses in the surrounding area. In some cases a single large vehicle can offload at several transfer points (Fig. 16.1b) before returning to base. Alternatively, if the total volume of orders in a given geographic area is low, or because of traffic conditions, it may be more economical to deliver by a series of smaller vehicles, either to transfer points (Fig. 16.1.c) or direct to customers. There are a number of permutations and usually the choice is based on a comparison of the cost of each alternative, calculated over an extended time period.

16.5.3 Delivery frequency

The above sorts of approaches are all very well providing there is a sufficient volume of orders to keep all the vehicles, both long distance and local, busy on every day of the week. In practice, the number of orders to be delivered on a given day or in a given week can fluctuate very widely, and therefore in some weeks there may be a need for, say, 3 large vehicles and $10\frac{1}{2}$ small ones, and in other weeks a need for $5\frac{1}{4}$ large vehicles and only $7\frac{3}{4}$ small ones. These problems are more likely to occur if customers are geographically widespread and if it is only necessary to deliver to them infrequently. The diseconomies of such a fluctuating workload will be worse for companies that only own a small vehicle fleet. Indeed many companies have an insufficient physical volume of deliveries to keep even one vehicle fully occupied.

Fluctuating workloads can be overcome in two main ways. First, by using the services of outside carriers such as National Carriers, TNT, Securicor or whoever. Manufacturers often choose to use outside carriers to perform a complete factory to customer delivery service. Sometimes they may consider using their own vehicles to deliver to the local distribution centres of external carriers, leaving them only with the responsibility for onward transmission to customers on smaller vehicles. However, unless the delivery frequency to each distribution centre is fairly regular, the problem of storing batches of orders to make up a vehicle load and of pacifying customers who have to wait for delivery until other customers place a sufficient number of orders, are likely to far outweigh any transportation economies gained. Occasionally manufacturers hire external carriers to undertake only the long haul portion of the delivery.

A second solution to the variability problem is to turn the transfer points into stocking points. They need not to be totally owned warehouses: renting part of a warehouse may be sufficient. This is an appropriate solution when demand is sufficient to keep one or more vehicles fully occupied with local deliveries, but insufficient to require regular trips by a larger vehicle, which instead would travel from the manufacturer's factory to the stocking point, as and when stocks needed replacing. Setting up stocking points will increase stock levels and the costs of materials handling, communication and warehousing. On the other hand, having intermediate stocking points very often means that a faster delivery of (small) orders can be achieved than when individual orders have to be despatched from the factory.

The stocking points need not be owned by the manufacturer but instead by appointed distributors, in which case they would undertake the cost of local delivery and stocking — as well, of course, as the cost of local selling — in return for a mark up on the selling price. However, the decision to use distributors is rarely taken purely because of physical distribution considerations (see Section 16.7).

16.5.4 Technical complexity of the product

The more complex the product, the less likely it is that the manufacturer will be able to find distributors with sufficiently knowledgable sales forces to sell that product properly (see Section 16.7). Once a manufacturer has had to stand the burden of selling direct to end users, it tends to make little sense to use distributors purely to handle physical delivery. In addition, orders for complex products tend to be high value and infrequent, and therefore direct delivery can often be justified. A special case of technical complexity is where the product is hazardous, such as chemicals; or delicate, such as instruments, and in that case companies have to rely on their own transportation because few other companies will take the responsiblity.

At the other extreme, are companies which offer a very wide range of straight-forward products. Rather than use distributors they may set up their own regional sales centres — sometimes supplementing their own range with those of other suppliers (often imported products). This is a form of vertical integration and the decision will be based on the potential return on investment offered by extending company activities in this way. A decision whether to set up regional stocking centres in parallel to the sales centres will depend on the distribution economies already discussed. In general, where local sales offices can be justified, local stocking centres can also be justified, but if, for example, the selling cycle is a long one or delivery frequency low then delivery direct from the factory may still be the best proposition. A special case is where companies hire rather than sell their equipment. Customers who hire equipment expect delivery to be virtually on the same day that the order is placed, and this makes local outlets more or less essential. The choice of whether to set up a company owned centre or to use intermediaries will again depend on whether the total volume of business is sufficient to make the former option economic.

16.5.5 Installation and service help required

Some products require specialist factory support during their installation. Depending on the duration of the installation work, it may be sensible to employ local installation technicians, or to send technicians direct from the factory. For some products, such as heating and ventilating equipment, an established installation trade exists. In these cases manufacturers tend to appoint a number of 'preferred installers' to whom all installation work is handed over (see Section 16.7).

Where products need regular servicing, the volume of service business, at least in terms of numbers of visits to customers, is likely to exceed the volume of sales. After all, each product will require servicing more than once during its life, and therefore, even if the sales volume in a given area does not justify setting up a regional service centre, it may well justify the cost of setting up a regional stocking centre. The decision will be influenced by the speed of response which is expected by customers.

Once a service centre is established, the additional costs to turn that service centre — which in any case will have to hold some stocks — into a distribution stocking centre are relatively more easily justified.

16.6 Types of industrial distribution channels

Many products are not sold by manufacturers direct to the final user. Instead they are sold via intermediaries. In the case of industrial products there are three main types of intermediary:

1   Agents: that is individuals or organisations who sell on behalf of a manufacturer in return for a commission. At no stage do they take title to the goods themselves, although sometimes they hold stocks. Goods are often delivered in bulk to agents premises prior to onward transportation to individual customers.
2   Distributors: that is organisations who actually buy products from manufacturers for the purpose of reselling. Sometimes there are several links in the chain between manufacturer and user, with larger distributors selling to smaller distributors, who in turn sell to users.
3   Installers: that is organisations who install the manufacturer's product at the user's premises. Usually the installer has to visit the customer with the manufacturer's salesman in order to quote for the installation work. It is rare for the manufacturer's sales force to have the authority to determine installation prices. Sometimes installers also act as distributors or as agents, selling the product as well as the installation service to customers. Installers are normally appointed by manufacturers but they can also be appointed by agents or distributors.

A fourth type of intermediary is beginning to gain importance in industrial markets, namely voluntary groups. Voluntary groups started in the retailing area, with groups of small retailers combining together so that they could place sufficiently large orders with suppliers to enable them to buy at the price levels offered to the large retail chains. Part of the deal often involved delivery to a single location. The price advantages offered to members of voluntary groups has caused a number to begin to be formed in industrial markets – normally to buy lower value items. In order to do this effectively, groups often form a co-operatively owned company to buy and distribute products to group members. Once established, these ventures could supply non-members, but this is not normally the aim. To suppliers, a voluntary group could either be considered as a distributor with a defined number of customers which require little separate sales attention, or as a single large customer. For suppliers who normally sell via distributors, the establishment of a voluntary group within a territory could well sour existing channel goodwill, and that has to be offset against possible loss of business to competitors, before deciding whether or not to compete for group custom. It remains to be seen whether voluntary groups grow to become a major distribution channel in industrial markets.

16.7 Choice of distribution channel and channel members

Choice of distribution channel is a major part of company marketing strategy. The prime choice is between selling entirely via one's own salesforce, selling entirely via distributors, agents or installlers, or selling using some combination of these. As with physical distribution the choice will be significantly influenced by the value of individual orders and by the complexity of the product.

In the case of complex products it is normally sensible for manufacturers to sell direct because of the difficulties involved in training outside sales forces to be effective. It is not so much the cost of the initial training which is the problem, or even the need to continually update that training, but it is the need for distributors' sales forces to accumulate sufficient technical applications experience to understand and help solve customers' applications problems successfully. Very often distributors' sales forces never achieve that level of know-how because of their time commitment to the various other products that their employers distribute.

Where individual order levels are lower, salesmen need to gain more orders per week to justify their employment costs, and this will normally only be possible if customers are located geographically close to each other. This being the case, companies often employ their own sales staff in areas where customer density is high, but sell via distributors or agents where customer density is low.

For other products the value of individual orders is so low that the cost of a visit to individual customers cannot be justified by the value of a single order. This problem is solved by using distributors, whose salesmen will visit customers to sell not one product, but the whole range of products that the distributor handles. Distributors are actually selling the reliability and range of their services rather than individual products. Even then, very often, only infrequent visits to each customer can be justified, and in that case the customer is usually given a catalogue, in which the whole range of products that are on offer are laid out. When the customer wishes to buy a particular product, all he has to do is to look up the relevant part number in the catalogue, telephone the distributor and ask what the current price and delivery are, and then confirm the order in writing. Incidently, in these cases advertising tends to assume as much importance as with consumer products, as its relative influence on the buying decision will be increased, simply because there is less direct contact with individual salesmen.

Distributors also tend to be adopted where it is necessary to offer a rapid delivery service, and hence to hold stocks at regional centres, but where the sales volume is insufficient to justify company owned centres. Agents, on the other hand, tend to be chosen in preference to distributors for products which can be economically delivered direct from manufacturer to customer, without any intermediate stocking. Agents are very often ex-salesmen from the relevant industry who have decided to work for themselves, and if chosen with care they can provide an adequate level of technical applications know-how.

When companies begin serious attempts to make inroads into a given export market, very often their first step is to appoint a national 'agent'. In this context the term 'agent' is sometimes used to describe a well established organisation which will take on responsibility for all sales, service and delivery within the designated territory. In other words the word 'agent' is used to describe a distributor with a national or multinational territory, and who will often sell via other distributors, each with a smaller territory of their own. In the case of high value products (or projects) the term '(export) agent' tends to be used to describe an individual or organisation whose role is to generate initial interest within the territory, to the point when it becomes worthwhile for the supplier's own sales team to follow up and provide the technical expertise. Very often the commercial agreement is nego-tiated direct with the supplier rather than through the agent.

Something of a special case are products which require specialist installation. In order to provide a satisfactory installation service, manufacturers either have to set up their own installation service, or appoint a chain of approved or preferred installers.For complex equipment such as capital plant, where successful installation is highly dependent on product knowledge, and where the number of installations is relatively low, manufacturers tend to undertake installation themselves. However, for other less complex and usually higher volume products, the decision will be largely influenced by the number of outlets needed to provide the level of service that customers expect. Even large manufacturers, when they divide their total sales by the number of outlets needed, may find that the sales volume at each outlet is insufficient to support a viable enterprise. In that case manufacturers either have to deal with other manufacturers' products, and in effect diversify away from their core manufacturing business, or have to accept the need to deal through specialised installers. Where the decision is marginal, the balance may be tipped by whether or not it is possible to adequately control the quality of workmanship of specialist installers, by whether the manufacturer wishes to spread management effort into non-manufacturing enterprise, and by whether or not the manufacturer's product will be installed as part of a system. Obviously where a system is involved it becomes necessary to stock a wide range of products, and the resulting installation business can no longer validly be considered as a simple extension of a manu-facturing business. In these cases, a specialist installation and service trade tends to grow up, because they are able to provide a local service more efficiently than manufacturers. Where an established installation trade exists, many customers will approach a number of installers local to them for quotes, rather than approach competing manufacturers.

Where the cost of the product forms a relatively small part of the total installed costs, customers will be more concerned with selecting the best installer rather than the best product brand, and in that case, most customers will pay little attention to the installers brand choice for individual components of a system, except perhaps for the major components; but even then the installer's recommendations are normally accepted, if he can point out that the chosen brand is well known and well reputed. Thus it is essential to ensure that one is broadly represented, but, and here is the catch, only by good quality installers. If the product proves unreliable in service, even if that unreliability is a result of poor installation, it will be the manu-facturer who is blamed. Similarly, if the installation service is poor, that paucity will tarnish the manufacturer's image.

If it is decided to sell through intermediaries then a further broad choice has to be made between:

(a) *Intensive distribution.* That is selling through as many distributors, agents and installers as possible.
(b) *Specialist distribution.* That is only selling via outlets which specialise in the type of product being supplied.
(c) *Selective distribution.* That is selling via those outlets which are most efficient, provide the desired back-up service, or create an image compatible with the product and its producer.

Ideally one would wish to be selective and yet make products available wherever and whenever customers wished to inspect them, purchase them or see them demonstrated; but since distributors will not handle a product unless they foresee a sufficient sales volume and mark-up to more than cover themselves, the number of outlets which will handle a given product will be limited by the total sales value of that product.

Because the number of specialist outlets is limited, manufacturers moving into new market areas are rarely immediately able to be selective and deal with the most efficient outlets, or indeed any of the larger better established ones. Distributors of engineering products are normally required by manufacturers to sign contracts preventing them from handling directly competitive products and therefore the better established distributors will not be free to deal with newcomers. On the other hand it will not be appropriate for newcomers to make do with the also rans. The distributors to link with are those who are trying very hard to build up a business in the distribution field. Not only will they sell more energetically but they are more likely to respond favourably to help with their efforts. Newcomers also have to take care to avoid signing up with distributors who take on new products with no intention of actively selling them, simply to prevent competitor distributors from gaining the opportunity. Even if manufacturers are subsequently able to extract themselves from such an agreement, perhaps via a minimum sales volume safeguard, they will have lost valuable market impact.

Once a significant market share has been achieved this can then be used to persuade some of the established distributors to relinquish their existing contracts with other companies, and thereby fill the gaps in the network - but not to supersede the earlier members of the network who are still operating efficiently.

Because many specialist engineering products sell only in limited volume, customers have become accustomed to the fact that they will only be available through a limited number of outlets, and they accept the inconveniences (within limits) that that involves.

For less complex products, where customers do not differentiate highly between makes and choose almost entirely on price and delivery, the level of inconvenience and uncompetitiveness tolerated is low. Customers normally ring up whichever distributor they normally deal with for the class of product to be bought, and find out what the current price and delivery is. If the customer is not happy with what he hears, he will probably ring two or three other distributors he has dealt with before and repeat the question. While the distributor who was contacted initially may handle 'our' products, the one who offers the best price – delivery combination may not, and a sale will have been lost. While this is in part a stock control and distribution problem, it also indicates that where products are not highly differentiable, fairly intensive distribution can pay dividends. In general, the aim is to appoint enough distributors to provide a competitive service to customers, but few enough to make the retention of the manufacturers business important to each of them (see Section 16.8).

Some products only sell well if cusomers can buy them locally (especially if there will eventually be a need to buy spare parts, or if the products need to be installed), or if a same day delivery service can be offered, or if applicable, a same day repair service. In these cases the number of distributors is not governed so much by sales volume considerations as by the need to provide a localised service, and therefore distributors have to be offered a high mark-up to compensate for a lower turnover. Alternatively, some manufacturers provide their distributors with consignment stocks, that is free of charge, so that they can meet customer requirements quickly and yet not have to bear the cash burden of high stock levels. Very often in these cases, arrangements are made to enable distributors to obtain urgently required items from neighbouring distributors who are holding them on consignment.

To summarise the discussion so far, the choice of channel depends on product complexity and the ability of intermediaries to sell it properly, on average order value, on the need for specialist installation and after-sales service, and on the ability of manufacturers to persuade intermediaries to stock their product. All these factors can be reduced to cost effectiveness, with the overall objective of obtaining a planned level of competitive advantage in terms of sales and service coverage and delivery effectiveness, at minimum cost. The main choices are summarised in Table 16.1.

Whatever channel is chosen, the situation must be closely monitored so that appropriate changes can be undertaken when necessary. However, it should be remembered that distribution is possibly the least easy element of the marketing mix to change quickly and effectively. For example, a company which has been successful and enjoyed considerable sales growth might foresee economies in setting up its own distribution network. However, abandoning the existing distributors will involve considerable loss of goodwill which it will have taken years to build up, and will vacate sales capacity that competitors will be only too anxious to fill. Should sales subsequently turn down again there will be no easy path back. Although it may gradually be possible to build up a new network, the loss of sales and profits during the interim period would be very considerable. In other words once a decision has been made to sell via distributors it is very costly to change back to direct selling, and vice versa.

However, cost effectiveness is not the sole criterion. When deciding whether or not to use distributors, it should be borne in mind that it can be quite difficult to control the way they operate (see Section 16.8), and that if they have a disagreement over terms of payment, or over credits for faulty goods or old stock, or over deliveries, they are quite likely to start talking to competitors. They can also

Table 16.1   *Choice of distribution methods for products made for stock*

Distribution method	Choice parameters
Factory to factory direct (deliveries to individual customers or a small number of customers in a given area)	High value or large physical size (weight) of product or individual orders enabling customers to be serviced by full or part loads
Factory to factory via own distribution points	Small/medium, value /size, products. Large number of orders in locality of distribution point. Local delivery volume fairly stable
Factory to factory, via own stocking points and/or via external carriers	As above but local delivery volume unstable and/or rapid delivery required
Stocking points located with sales/service centres	High level of technical advice, installation and/or service required. Own wide and high volume product range
Outside distributor	Small/medium value products with low individual order level
Outside installer	Products which are installed as part of a system and where total system costs tend to be much greater than individual product costs

Note: External carriers will be used if regular delivery volumes are insufficient to fully and economically occupy company-owned vehicles, although some account has to be taken of the advertising value of having smart vehicles with the company name on their side.

Agents tend to be used wherever it is uneconomic to employ an additional member of the sales team to cover a given geographic territory, but where it is economic for the manufacturer to deliver direct to customers either using his own transport or external carriers. This then falls midway between manufacturers using their own sales force and arranging delivery themselves, and using distributors.

frequently (if sometimes unwittingly) be sources of leaks of fairly confidential information (essential visits for marketing researchers!).

16.8 Controlling a channel

In order to make sensible decisions about costs it is important to isolate each element of the distribution activity, and to calculate the costs involved. Having calculated the costs and made channel choices, it is then possible to allocate standard costs for each element and to control against these standards. From time to time changes in technology or to user requirements will make it necessary to revise the standards. In some cases changes will be so significant that changes to the channel structure may have to be considered. In this connection, consideration has to be given to whether to allocate a given geographic area exclusively to one distributor or whether to allow different distributors to fight it out. It is normal with industrial products to try to persuade distributors not to handle competitive products, ideally as part of a signed agreement, but unless the supplier is very firmly established in the market this is only possible in exchange for a commitment not to appoint another distributor within the immediate vicinity. It is not legal to actually stop one distributor selling in another's territory, but of course the manufacturer can withhold his full support from such incursions. Rather than risking 'border feuds' it is probably best not to allocate defined geographic territories, but instead simply to locate distributors at strategic points around the country (relative to the geographic location of major customers), such that none necessarily has to operate on another's doorstep. Some companies, for example, simply guarantee not to appoint another distributor within 10 miles or 20 miles, or whatever is the appropriate distance.

However, setting appropriate standards (cost and service) is only a starting point. Much more important is the need to persuade channel members to work to the standards. One of the most effective methods of persuasion is for manufacturers to make the retention of their business important to channel members, because the more important it is, the harder they will try on his behalf. Although ultimately there is no substitute for market share and steady sales at each outlet, it is possible to generate loyalty in other ways, such as help with local promotion and advertising, rapid exchange of faulty products, guaranteed deliveries of product and spares, sales leads and occasional direct sales help. Active sales help is especially important for new distributors to help them establish a reasonable sales volume, and to convince them that the products will sell well given a reasonable level of effort. On the other hand, initial help does not mean that the supplier needs to dictate how distributors should go about promoting and selling, nor indeed does it mean that distributors should be left entirely free to act as they please. Some mutually agreed compromise is necessary; the extent of the influence tending to increase with the degree of installation help, selection advice, and after-sales service that has to be provided by distributors – as the quality of these services will influence the manufacturer's reputation as much as the quality of the products themselves.

Another sensible approach is to gather all channel members together over an extended lunch or for an evening. Such an occasion offers the opportunity to promote the supplier's products (especially the new ones), to generate product enthusiasm, to reinforce what the supplier believes to be good business behaviour, to find out common niggles before they become major barriers to sales effort, and to enable distributors to exchange experiences in order to find better ways of promoting and selling.

Certainly it is vital to have a good quality product and a good quality service, because distributors do not like handling products which cause a lot of problems, partly because no one likes continuous hassle and partly because it will begin to have an adverse effect on the distributor's own reputation. Obviously occasionally things will go wrong, and it is part of the suppliers job to have tied distributors in closely enough that they will be reasonably tolerant. One of the methods used is to offer distributors help with running their business, either free or at minimal cost. For example, a supplier may help a distributor to install a new stock control system, or a computerised ordering system, or a management accounting system. Small distributors are usually very proud of their independence and if there is any hint that using such services will reduce their independence they will shy away. The services must be offered in the hope that loyalty will follow. On the other hand, larger distributors will be growth and profit oriented and on occasions suppliers may be in a position to loan them money at favourable rates in order that they can update their facilities. Once accepted, such loans tie the supplier–distributor knot very closely indeed.

In spite of the 'carrotlike' affect of these sorts of efforts, some element of 'stick' should be in the background. Normally distribution agreements specify a minimum sales volume achievement and a minimum stock holding. The minimum stock holding provides a financial incentive to achieve the sales volume target; but what is a reasonable sales volume for each territory? All too often no real attempt is made to work this out (see Section 14.5.1 for possible methods). As a result minimum sales volume requirements are usuallly too low to be useful, other than in extreme cases.

In a well run channel, termination is likely to occur well before the minimum sales volume is reached. Normally a distributor's sales performance falls gradually, or his dissatisfaction with an agreement increases gradually, and therefore, by regularly monitoring performance parameters such as sales volume, share of total company sales, stock turn, number of new customers, number of lost sales and so on, early warning of failing performance can be obtained. Other measures which can be used are the level of complaints from customers about individual distributors, and the extent to which neighbouring distributors are able to poach. Once warning signs are picked up, attempts will normally be made to rectify the situation, and only if those attempts fail is consideration given to terminating an agreement.

Finally, if distribution is to be handled and controlled efficiently, it is essential that the responsibility for setting distribution policy be allocated to an individual manager or director. The title of that person is not important and may be the marketing manager, the distribution manager or the works manager depending on the structure of the company. Individual segments of the activity may be managed by separate departments, but there must be only one person responsible for co-ordinating and evaluating the profit impact of all aspects of the system.

16.9 Influence of computers

The distribution and stocking of many products has been and will continue to be radically reformed by the increased use of computers. Products which are regularly ordered, for production or by distributors, will increasingly be ordered direct to suppliers' computers from customers' computers, as soon as customer stocks have reduced to a specified reorder level. The necessary 'paperwork' will be raised by computer and transmitted to the relevant departments within supplier and customer companies, either to a line printer or on to a VDU. The advent of such systems may substantially reduce order transmission and order processing delays and costs, and reduce the proportion of urgent deliveries demanded, but it will not alter the fundamental distribution policy decision, that is, the type of system to be adopted to achieve the greatest overall competitive advantage at an acceptable cost.

Perhaps more far reaching, particularly in the case of simpler and/or less expensive products, would be the advent of transmittable catalogues, price lists and sales videos (Section 13.9). If customers were able to adequately select between brands in this way and subsequently easily place orders direct with manufacturers, then the local sales role of distributors could become redundant, and the economic balance would tip towards direct delivery. While the impact of this change would not be so significant for products which required localised installation and service backing, it would nevertheless necessitate a fundamental re-examination of existing distribution channels.

Chapter 17

Marketing Control and Audit

17.1 Defining marketing control

This chapter examines marketing control in a general way rather than examining its application to specific parts of marketing operations. Control is often defined as a process of comparing what is actually achieved (results) with what was planned to be achieved (objectives), and taking steps to bring the actual nearer to the planned. The assumption is that the plan is correct, but it may not be; changed circumstances may have made the plan, and/or the objectives, unattainable or inappropriate. Although it is right on a day to day basis to proceed as if the plan is correct, it would be foolish to take that for granted, and hence reviews must be undertaken – perhaps formally every month – to check.

This means that the control process consists of two parts; first, keeping on the chosen course, and second, checking that the course itself is correct. On this basis marketing control could be defined as the process of (i) comparing what is actually achieved with what was planned to be achieved, and taking steps to bring the actual nearer to plan, and (ii) of examining the assumptions on which the plan was based, in the light of the current situation, to ascertain whether those assumptions are still valid, and if not to modify them appropriately to serve as a basis for a revised plan and/or revised objectives.

Another way of looking at this idea is that effective control systems help people to learn how to improve their performance by progressively identifying and removing or reducing the effect of causes of poor performance. However, if the cause is big and unyielding, it is necessary to step back a stage further, and to reconsider how the desired objectives are to be achieved. If no revised plan can be devised then the objectives themselves will have to be reconsidered. Once a revised plan has been agreed, hopefully there will follow an analysis of why such a large 'problem' was not foreseen, with a view to improving forecasting methods in the future.

These concepts are normally incorporated into a sequential control process, as follows:

1 set objectives – sales levels and cost budgets;
2 measure performance – regular reporting procedures;

3 analyse deviations – via regular reviews to isolate causes;
4 initiate corrective action – with target dates, either to achieve the original objectives or to determine reasonable new objectives.

Each of these stages will be considered in more detail in the sections below.

However, first a word of caution. Control systems cost money to set up and to operate, and there is no point developing a control system which controls in such detail that the operating costs outweigh the potential profit gain. For example, it is common not to accurately count every minor item of stock, or to chase every small unpaid bill, or indeed to service every small customer. On the other hand, major problems often cannot be solved without breaking them down into detail, and if a control system is not set up to provide that detail, then problem solving can become rather a hit or miss affair. Some engineering companies may believe that they do not have the resources needed to control in the detail implied by this chapter, and in that case they should identify the parameters which will exert most influence on the success of their businesses and monitor and control those. The problem is where to draw the line. Luckily the cost of operating control systems is steadily decreasing and nowadays most companies – even small ones – can afford to control in quite considerable detail. However, many companies have yet to take full advantage of these reduced costs, and as a result many readers may find a large gap between the principles of control described here and what actually takes place in their organisations.

17.2 Setting objectives: measurable parameters

Regardless of the generality with which they are originally stated, if they are to be useful for control purposes, objectives must be set out in terms that can be measured. An objective such as 'increased market share' is of little practical value. What is required is a precise statement such as 'increase market share from 8% to 10% by 30th November'. This objective can then be broken down into sales volume objectives for different products and different salesmen, month by month. In other words a hierarchy of control parameters can be introduced, each appropriate to the action or effect which is to be controlled. Control parameters need to be appropriate in two senses. Appropriate first of all in the sense that the parameters which are controlled are the ones which will actually influence achievement of the objective; hence, for example, all the argument about whether control of money supply will improve the economic situation. There is no point in simply controlling expenditure on advertising and on the sales force, if the parameter which will affect profits is the cost per order received.

The second sense is that the control parameters must be chosen to be appropriate to the type of decision that can be taken. Thus a marketing director will be more concerned about parameters such as the ratio of direct selling costs to turnover, or promotional costs to turnover, rather than the monthly expenses total of an individual salesman. On the other hand, an area sales manager will be directly concerned with the expenses, and interested in the former only insofar as they refer to his area, because the wider decisions and actions which will affect their value are outside his span of control. In general the level of detail decreases as one progresses up the hierarchy, with, for example, directors being concerned with total and product group sales volume, and salesmen concerned with orders for particular product variations from individual customers.

A wide range of objectives (or standards) are normally required to control properly all aspects of marketing activity (see Miller [96]). They can be specified in terms of numerical, time based, and non-numerical parameters.

17.2.1 Numerical parameters

Numerical parameters are many; for example, sales volumes, growth rates, market shares, prices, costs – a whole hierarchy of parameters which if appropriately chosen can be used to control and improve marketing decisions. Rather than simply using single parameters, combining them into ratios can often reveal more useful control information. For example, the ratios sales costs/turnover and number of new orders/number of enquiries, provide several pointers towards possible corrective action which bare figures for sales costs, number of new enquiries or number of new orders, would not. Suppose that while sales have been increasing, sales costs as a percentage of sales have also been increasing. This is a sign that the product is becoming more difficult to sell. Possible reasons for this difficulty are (a) less effective promotion, (b) the product is ageing, (c) market growth is less than expected, (d) a natural upper limit of market share is being approached or (e) inefficient selling. The cause of any change can be pinpointed further by examining the percentage of enquiries converted into orders. If this has been increased or maintained this tends to confirm that the sales force is having to work harder and longer to maintain the conversion ratio. If the number of enquiries being converted has fallen, this might be a sign that inappropriate promotion is generating too many enquiries from people with no real need; or that the sales force is not large enough to handle the volume of enquiries (ie promotional and sales force spending is out of balance). On the other hand, if sales volume has decreased and costs as a percentage of sales have also decreased, then this may be a sign of false economy, or a sign that resources have been directed away from a less profitable product group to a more profitable product group.

Purely financial parameters are the province of management accounting. Although it is important that marketing executives understand how financial data is gathered, processed and summarised, if they are to be able to detect obvious errors which would otherwise lead them down the wrong path, and if they are to be able to influence the choice of financial control parameters which are reported to them and used to control their performance, explanations of management accounting methods are not appropriate in the present context. Reference should be made to specialist texts. Unfortunately many accounting systems fail to record the result of individual investment decisions (see also Ramo [43]). This makes control very difficult. Results are usually lumped together for reporting purposes, and requests to provide information with respect to a narrower section of activity tend to be met with the response that it is not practical to allocate separate costs to every minor item. Although this is true as a generality, the extent of the truth is steadily decreasing in proportion to decreasing information processing costs. A typical example of this dichotomy could be the establishment of a demonstration centre. In order to obtain approval to set up a demonstration centre most marketing departments would have to provide a cashflow analysis, a usage pattern, and a forecast of increased sales. However, once the centre was established, the rent/rates/ heating/power/maintenance costs would normally be amalgamated with those for the rest of the site. Time spent by individuals in the centre might be recorded spasmodically, but it is extremely unlikely that individual orders will be associated with that time. Lack of accurate records makes it very difficult to judge the accuracy of the initial forecasts on which the investments decision was based.

17.2.2 *Time parameters*
Time parameters are concerned with the dates by which specific actions are planned to be completed or financial targets reached. Their measurement and recording poses no special problems, but that does not mean that they should not be given equal prominence to the numerical parameters outlined above.

17.2.3 *Non-numerical parameters*
Non-numerical parameters are more difficult. In the marketing world these are the measurements of selling effectiveness, advertising effectiveness, sales force organisation, customer service levels, product attractiveness and so on. These are the numerous items which in the end can only be judged subjectively, but which nevertheless require to be judged. There is little doubt that the quality of that subjective judgement will be improved by isolating and recording as much relevant numerical data as possible. The process itself will improve the understanding of cause and effect, even if it does not provide definite answers.

17.3 Setting objectives: typical examples

Setting appropriate and measurable objectives is not easy. Some of the difficulties are illustrated in the two examples described in the following sections.

17.3.1 *Sales mix*
Production departments are normally only able to vary the proportion of different products that they produce to a limited extent before severe cost penalties are incurred. It is therefore incumbent on the sales force to sell all the various products; in volumes which are within these limits, and not to simply achieve a sales target by concentrating on the easiest to sell products. The division of sales between different products is termed the sales mix. Each product will contribute to profits at a different rate, and hence ideally the sales mix will only be chosen after analysis of the profit to be earned by producing and selling different mixes; possibly to the extent of considering dropping some products entirely in favour of others.

It is very unlikely that market conditions will allow sales mix targets to be exactly met, with shortfalls for one or two products hopefully being made good by other products. Hence, rather than trying to calculate a 'most profitable' mix, it is much more sensible to take the most profitable product first and establish a target sales volume for it (hopefully taking account of the law of diminishing returns; that is once a given sales volume has been reached, the effort to increase the volume further will become disproportionate and will be better spent on other products). The volume chosen may exceed capacity, and in that case consideration needs to be given to extending capacity by investment, or by subcontracting parts of the manufacturing process. The next most profitable product will be considered next and so on, until the production capacity has been filled. In fact the total arrived at should be in excess of capacity, as it is rare for all targets to be achieved — rather like overbooking on aircraft.

Unfortunately there may still be pockets of production undercapacity. The sales volume chosen for some products may not be as great as the relevant production capacity and that capacity may be insufficiently flexible to be used for other products. Pressures from works oriented and number oriented personnel to increase sales volume to capacity should be resisted, as attempts to reach the higher volume would absorb a disproportionate amount of general management and marketing effort.

Finally, the sales mix must take account of future plans. Effort should be directed towards some new products at the expense of more profitable established products, in the hope that these new products will become the profit earners of tomorrow. As a result, at the beginning of the year the target mix of products will be chosen subjectively, based on an interpretation of the capabilities of the company and the forecast marketing environment.

17.3.2 Customer service level

Companies finding themselves in what many would consider the enviable position of attaining orders in excess of capacity, have to undertake a balancing act. If these orders are accepted, their delivery and indeed the delivery of other orders will be delayed. There will be a loss of a customer goodwill. On the other hand if orders are turned away, those customers may not try again and in 3 or 6 months time their orders may be needed to fill production capacity. Most companies do not turn away orders, preferring to try to extend capacity by overtime and by subcontracting, and by trying to offset any loss of goodwill by increased promotional and sales effort. This is undoubtedly because few companies feel sufficiently certain about future order levels to risk the loss of a given customer's business. Goodwill, like many other things, follows the S-curve (see Williams [97]) and beyond a certain point, further delivery delays can cause little further loss of goodwill — it is beyond the point of no return.

In order to set a standard, it is first of all necessary to establish some relationship between loss of goodwill (or orders) and delivery delays. If records have been kept systematically this should be straightforward, but otherwise reliance will have to be placed on a subjective impression, by thinking about past experience, talking to existing and past customers, and by examining what competitors offer (see also Section 16.4.1).

If the fictitious relationship between loss of goodwill and delivery delay shown in Fig. 17.1 applied, a company might decide to set its standard delivery delay at two weeks. A two week delay is on the flat part of the curve and will incur little loss of goodwill. Suppose sufficient orders are gained to extend the delay to four weeks, then spreading the delay over all the customers would represent a major loss of goodwill. It may be better to risk losing some less profitable customers and concentrate the loss on them: for example, the four week average delay could be met by extending delivery to 12 weeks for the 15% least profitable customers, enabling the other 85% to be offered $2\frac{1}{2}$ weeks $(4 = 0.85 \times 2.5 + 0.15 \times 12)$. In this way the under-capacity problem will be self-righting and the profit mix will have improved in the process.

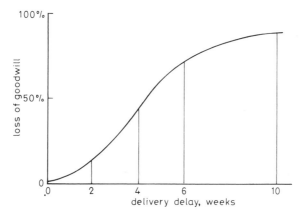

Fig. 17.1   *Loss of goodwill following delivery delays*

Of course in practice the spread of the delay will be considerably influenced by feedback from the sales force as to which customers need rapid delivery, and which could manage with an extended delivery, and which of these, if approached nicely, would accept four weeks delay without loss of goodwill. Therefore, out of the above 85%, maybe 20% could be persuaded to accept four weeks, and that would provide some slack to meet the needs of other customers who may not be prepared to accept more than, say, a one week delay.

17.4 Reporting procedures

Once the measures to be used for control purposes have been agreed, the next step is to organise regular reports on what is actually being achieved, in terms of the measures set. Wherever possible, data should be gathered on a continuous basis, first to ensure that reports are timely, and secondly to minimise the possibility of errors in sporadic reports from directing efforts in entirely the wrong direction. As indicated earlier, this is one of the hazards faced by companies who rely on sporadic marketing research reports rather than using them to supplement their own continuous information collection activities. Regular information, however simple, is better at revealing trends.

The type of weekly report needed from the sales force has already been dealt with (Section 14.6). Of particular importance are details of any large orders or major customers lost or gained. Similar reports from other individuals in the marketing department are required, detailing what has been achieved, how much has been spent and why, and indicating the extent of deviations from plan and the steps which have been initiated to correct those deviations. Such reports are obviously too numerous and too detailed for the head of a large marketing department and hence they should be progressively summarised.

Like objectives, reports must be appropriate to the type of decisions that can be taken. Section heads will require a detail weekly report of the activities in their departments so that they can quickly initiate any corrective action required. These actions and the results achieved will be summarised and summed into a monthly report covering the whole marketing department. The monthly report may include, for example, summary statements of discounts and credits costs, sales force costs, promotional costs, distribution costs, information costs (marketing research, forecasting, record keeping and information processing), planning costs, installation and service costs, and administrative costs. The reports at each stage should be presented in an easy assimilated way which will facilitate decision making. They should highlight trends which may require action, and only include those numbers which are relevant to the report reader. Inclusion of other numbers will be time wasting and confusing.

In general, the higher up the hierarchy that a control meeting occurs, the less frequently it is likely to be held. In that case only broader issues which do not have to be dealt with immediately should be considered. At the other extreme, items which require to be put right tomorrow by action today will be communicated by word of mouth or telex and it is the average outcome of a large number of such control actions which finds its way on to weekly, monthly and quarterly reports.

17.4.1 Reporting numeric data

It is helpful to supplement numerical reports with graphs. For example, sales volume or sales calls per day could be presented in a manner similar to that adopted for product quality control, see Fig. 17.2.

Selection of permitted deviation will become more accurate as experience of recording results and of operating a control system is gained. In general the shorter the time horizon the larger the percentage deviation which can be permitted. Suppose a salesman who has a target of 60 sales calls every 4 weeks, that is 15 calls per week or 3 calls per day, only achieves 1 sales call on a given day. That is a quite acceptable deviation provided it is not repeated. A deviation to as few as 10 calls in one week would just be acceptable, providing that as before it is not repeated, and there seems to be some attempt to fit in 4 sales per day in order to get back to the monthly target. A call rate of 55–65 in a 4 week period is also likely to be acceptable, and in a quarter of 12 weeks a call rate of 170–190 would be permitted. The reason for the higher permitted deviation is that in the short term, unexpected events can make plan achievement impossible, but over the long term the well known 'swings and roundabouts' effect will exert its influence and opportunities should occur to make good at least some of the shortfalls. In other words the longer the time period the less 'chance' should influence results.

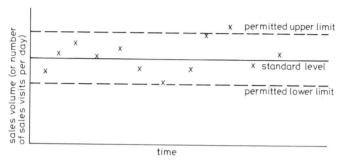

Fig. 17.2   *An example of using graphs to promote control*

17.5 Tracing the cause of deviations from plan

Wherever a significant deviation (or variance) is recorded, its cause should be established. To find the linking factors it is necessary to sift through much information. In addition to reports about internal activities, regular inflows of information should be being received about the market and about changes in the company's competitive position (see Chapter 4). Informal reports of extra efforts being made by competitors, of decreased buying activity by customers, and rumours of new products about to be launched, have to be considered alongside published data. If the cause is not clear, but seems to be in particular direction, then it will be necessary to work progressively through increasing levels of detail. For example, a revenue variance may be traced to a service cost variance, which might be traced to a particular component which is below normal quality because a disagreement with the preferred supplier led to orders being quickly placed with other suppliers before a full quality check could be undertaken. Or sales volume variance could be progressively traced back to delivery difficulties within a particular geographic area. Causes may be broken down into four categories:

(a) Poor plan implementation; as a result of inefficiencies such as the sales force being too large, individual spending levels being too high, inefficient use of time, poor sales technique, too much advertising, poorly directed advertising, poor delivery, poor product quality, new product introductions delayed and so on.

(b) Incorrect forecasting; of the economic cycle, of business confidence, of market growth, of competitive position.

(c) Totally unexpected events; competitor introduces revolutionary new product or exceptionally effective advertising, or purchasing manager of very large customer dies and replacement strongly favours competitors.

(d) Unrealistic plan; either objectives, strategy or action programmes.

Obviously the correct causal category must be identified before any appropriate corrective action can be initiated.

17.6 Control response time

The right action too late can be as bad as the wrong action at the right time. It is no good deciding to wait another month in the hope that the effect will go away of its own accord. Even if it does, the company will be no further forward, because it will be unaware of the cause, and the effect may reappear in a month or two but this time more permanently.

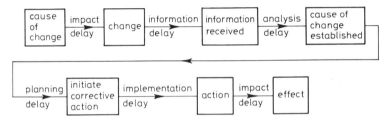

Fig. 17.3   *Control system delays*

There are a number of inevitable delays between the initiation of a variance and its correction. These delays are illustrated in Fig. 17.3. It is desirable to reduce these delays as much as possible. Computer based systems are enabling information processing and analysis delays to be reduced from as much as one working week to half a day. However, perhaps the most significant time saving can be achieved by looking for causes of change, rather than waiting for those causes to create an impact. If it is known that a competitor is to launch a new product in about three months, it makes sense to try to evaluate the impact of that launch on the market and to decide in advance what counter measures should be taken. This allows those measures to be considered at relative leisure and for their introduction to be timed to coincide or even to just precede the competitive launch. Whereas if the launch is allowed to go ahead, by the time the impact has been assessed and counter-action effected, considerable erosion of market share could occur.

Time lags between cause and effect mean that it is not possible to reach equilibrium; to permanently keep on target, other than by coincidence. It is like trying to steer a car whose wheels do not turn in direct response to the steering wheel, but only after, say, 20 or 30 seconds. As adjustments are made for feedback received from the market, there will be a tendency to overreact in the opposite direction in an attempt to get back on course as quickly as possible (see also Williams [97]). By the time the extent of this overreaction is appreciated, the effect will be much greater than planned, and a further correction will be required. Nevertheless, it seems fair to suggest that with experience each subsequent correction should become more accurate and a dampening effect achieved, see Fig. 17.4.

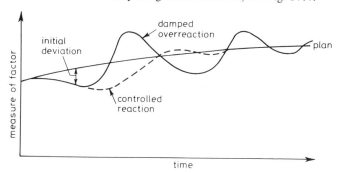

Fig. 17.4 *Typical oscillating control*

In addition, if the same cause reappears at some later date, the previous experience may enable a more controlled and cost effective reaction to be undertaken. However, this usually does not occur, for a number of reasons. First, in marketing, variables do not change one at a time or very predictably, and therefore the learning process must be applied with caution. The ideal response of 12 months ago is unlikely to be exactly right today. Secondly, managers prefer to err on the side of overreaction, so that they can demonstrate to their superiors that they are taking 'positive action'. Thirdly, to minimise the cost of overcorrections, countervailing forces (because of implementation and impact delays), would have to be applied as soon as the previous correction is detected to be beginning to have some effect. It would take a brave man to take such a step. As a result, corrective forces tend to be over applied, and fairly inefficiently over applied. The cost balance to be worked out is not simple and not static; the values will change over time. The ideal reaction would be one which would minimise the value of:

> (Loss of profit resulting from deviations from plan) − (cost of corrective reaction, including any loss of profits in other areas resulting from diversion of attention and effort).

The situation is further complicated because in some cases, such as sales volume falling below target, overreaction to get sales back on target may not need any correction. Most companies operate below capacity and hence a greater than planned sales volume can be readily accommodated.

17.7 Link between control and motivation

Individuals can be motivated to strive to achieve targets and to complete action programmes assigned to them if they are aware of the overall targets for the business, of how they were set, of why it is important to the ongoing health of the business that they be achieved, and of how the achievement of individual targets will contribute to the achievement of the overall target.

Inevitably some programmes fall behind, but if the control procedures are generally seen to be aimed at getting programmes back on target rather than aimed at assigning blame, individuals are more likely to be open and to co-operate with them. It has been said that the ideal manager is one who absorbs all blame from above for his department's failings, while at the same time encouraging his subordinates to find solutions to their problems. Unfortunately this is not a recipe for job security in many companies and in most cases some sort of blame will be passed on to individuals. Even so, this can be done in a positive way which will encourage further co-operation, rather than in a repressive dismotivating manner. Co-operation is essential if the links between effect and cause are to be made. The reporting system, however good, can only report a condensed version of all the facts, the complexities and the interrelationships. Many of these can be understood only by being in direct contact with the situation over an extended period of time. In many cases the decision maker will be sufficiently removed from the situation that he has to rely on the information provided by those who are in day to day touch. Unfortunately, these are precisely the people whose views of the situation will be biased because, inevitably, they will be trying to champion one point of view or another, or they will be providing excuses rather than facts, or they will be deliberately distorting the facts to try to hide the real cause. Many an apparently intractable problem has been solved when the decision maker finally makes time to get into direct contact with the real action, as it takes place. The cause and thence the solution becomes obvious.

A positive co-operative approach should help ensure that control systems are respected and used by managers. However, being positive and seeking co-operation does not mean readily accepting excuses for missed targets and being readily persuaded to amend targets – downwards. Being positive involves seeking new ways of achieving existing targets, and only revising them if the competitive environment has changed so substantially that they can no longer be justified. If targets are amended too readily every time they are missed, little heed will be paid to them in the future and their value as standards of performance and as motivators will be lost (see Smallbone [93]). Performance will be no different than if there had been no targets in the first place. This sort of effect is illustrated on the graphs shown in Fig. 17.5 and they unfortunately correspond all too closely with the reality in many companies.

Control systems must focus on those things that operating managers perceive to be important and not on trivia if they are not to be regarded simply as yet another hurdle to be surmounted or circumvented. Very often it appears that disproportionate amounts of time are spent on relatively minor matters, perhaps because their relative simplicity makes accurate reporting and control possible, and thereby helps create a fantasy that the whole business is under tight control, whereas major problems may be being ignored because they are complex, and difficult to report on and to control. To be effective, control systems must focus on the key criteria for success and failure in each business area, and if necessary apply different criteria to each, rather than stifling them with inappropriate 'general' requirements. These criteria are best established by discussions with relevant operating managers — which takes us back to the first paragraph of this section. Even then these key criteria will be ignored if they are not given priority at control meetings. Regardless of what is written down, if top management place more emphasis on, say, reduced distribution costs, than on planned customer service levels, middle management will soon adopt similar priorities. If the emphasis changes from month to month they will become confused, resentful and demotivated.

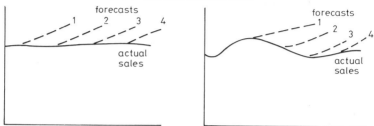

Fig. 17.5   *Unheeded sales forecasts*

Finally, if they are not to be demotivating, control systems must emphasise mutually compatible targets. It is no good setting high sales targets if at the same time promotional and selling costs are cut, and plans to introduce new competitive products or to revitalise the distribution channel are postponed.

To summarise, control systems will be motivating if:

(a) Managers who are responsible for the achievement of targets are involved in the target setting process.

(b) There is fast accurate feedback of results to managers who are able to take some action to correct deviations as they occur.

(c) The control system concentrates on key criteria for success, and is used to try to improve performance rather than only to allocate blame.

(d) Key control parameters are actually used regularly by senior managers — to control.

(e) If circumstances change beyond the range where compensating action within the agreed strategy can enable targets to be met, strategies should be changed. In some cases even revised strategies will not make the targets achievable, and in those extreme circumstances the targets themselves should be changed to reflect the new environment.

(f) The targets must be mutually compatible.

17.8 Marketing audit

Control systems are targeted at operational marketing performance, e.g. advertising effectiveness or sales force effectiveness. Audits are concerned with the methods adopted to formulate marketing objectives, strategies, and action plans. A marketing audit involves an independent assessment of the evidence from which a given plan, proposal or forecast has been derived, and of the system used to interpret the evidence into action programmes. In other words, is the plan based on a true and fair view of the situation and is it logically derived?

The objective of an audit is to recommend how the reliability and effectiveness of planning and forecasting processes can be improved: is the present system appropriate to the specific circumstances of the company? In order to achieve this audit objective a marketing audit may involve:

1 The independent preparation of a separate plan or forecast in order to compare points of difference and thence propose an improved planning/forecasting system.
2 The examination of the system which is in use, testing it for accuracy and effectiveness.

These approaches are dealt with in more detail in Sections 17.9 and 17.10.

It is not the main purpose of an audit to comment on whether correct conclusions have been drawn from the evidence, but to comment on the effectiveness with which the evidence has been gathered, analysed and interpreted. However, the audit process will inevitably throw up answers which may be at variance with the established position, and defence of the existing plan can lead to suggestions for improved systems being rejected without real thought being given to the validity of the proposals themselves. To avoid personnel blocking the audit investigation it must be made clear from the start that the main purpose is to improve the performance of the marketing function, and that no one will be blamed, demoted or sacked for deficiencies revealed, but they may well be if they do not implement changes to procedures subsequently agreed – although of course, failure to implement is very often caused by failure to communicate and to train, rather than by individual inability or unwillingness to cope. If the prime function of improving the system is to be achieved, the audit must concentrate on explaining the causes of differences rather than concentrating on the differences themselves.

There are various opinions about when an audit should be held. Some believe that it should be undertaken immediately after a plan has been completed, when memories are still fresh and there is still time to modify the plan if that seems appropriate; but this runs the definite danger that the audit will come to be considered as part of the plan preparation process, rather than as a review of the process. It is probably better to undertake audits midway through the planning process, thereby providing time for system modifications to be thoroughly thought out before they need to be implemented.

Companies automatically accept the need for an independent audit of their accounting systems. In contrast, marketing systems and sales forecasts, which are the foundation of other company planning and decision making, are infrequently subject to the same scrutiny. This is unfortunate, because in general, the certainty of being subject to audit ensures a more thorough and systematic approach. Success can often breed complacency, and hence successful companies can benefit from an audit as much as the less successful. It can be regarded as preventative maintenance. It might be argued that marketing plans are already subject to a series of stringent scrutinies, but that would be to miss the point; such reviews are themselves part of the system which produces the plan and not events free from bias. In many cases those involved are simply too deeply involved to be able to see the wood from the trees. In order to introduce more rigour into the programme, the complete system needs to be subject to an independent audit, rather like customer audits of vendor quality control procedures.

Table 17.1 *Checklist of key activities in developing successful marketing strategy (from Sasson [13])*

	Yes	No
Market research		
Is the effect adequate, and showing a return?	☐	☐
Are the results used by senior management?	☐	☐
Is demand forecasting undertaken?	☐	☐
Are overseas markets researched?	☐	☐
Is performance assessed against customer requirements?	☐	☐
Is performance assessed against competitor's performance?	☐	☐
Product planning		
Is product policy clearly defined?	☐	☐
Are product designs in line with what the customer wants, particularly overseas?	☐	☐
Do design briefs for R & D include data on user needs and price—volume needs?	☐	☐
Are R & D costs controlled to establish R & D cost effectiveness?	☐	☐
Is the approach to pricing flexible?	☐	☐
Is close attention paid to the profit mix of the product range?	☐	☐
Market planning		
Is the market policy clearly defined?	☐	☐
Are alternative distribution methods reviewed in terms of effect on sales and profits, as well as on costs?	☐	☐
Is sales forecasting undertaken, and for overseas markets?	☐	☐
Are overseas agents adequately motivated through personal contact, pricing freedom, market feedback, and being welcomed?	☐	☐
Are markets carefully selected and is the market mix periodically reviewed?	☐	☐
Are market resources planned as part of long term business planning?	☐	☐

Table 17.1   *continued*

	Yes	No
Selling		
Do sales engineers have specialised product knowledge and is this made available to customers?	☐	☐
Does senior management participate in selling?	☐	☐
Is multi-level selling aimed at all customer decision making units?	☐	☐
Are sales force activities planned and controlled in detail?	☐	☐
Is outside recruitment of sales staff used as a means of avoiding an inbred inward-looking approach?	☐	☐
Is the sales force motivated with appropriate individual incentives?	☐	☐
Sales promotion		
Are records of promotional expenditure kept and analysed?	☐	☐
Are shared promotions used, in preference to none?	☐	☐
Are catalogues regularly updated, and for overseas are they printed in local languages?	☐	☐
Are films and direct mail used as well as exhibitions and advertising?	☐	☐
Is as much use as possible made of public relations and technical press editorials?	☐	☐
Are demonstrations used as a convincing form of promotion?	☐	☐
Sales service		
Are there standards for product servicing, including breakdowns and repairs, and is performance monitored?	☐	☐
Are there standards for customer servicing, including training, installation and demonstrations and is performance monitored?	☐	☐
Are service engineers decentralised, and does sales service report to sales or marketing?	☐	☐
Do users know whom to contact when in difficulty?	☐	☐
Is stock policy appropriate, particularly for spares availability and delivery?	☐	☐
Are overseas agents self-sufficient for stocks, spares and trained staff, and are their manuals in local languages?	☐	☐

17.9 Independent Plan

The methodology of producing a marketing plan has already been dealt with in Chapters 8 and 9. It can be useful to use one of the numerous check lists which have been published (see for example, Fig. 17.6) as a guide, but of course the whole point of an audit is to comment on whether the system in use is appropriate to the unique circumstances of the company being audited, and therefore care must be taken to avoid recommending some universal all-embracing, and hence inefficient, system.

It is much more difficult to actually obtain data of the desired reliability than to tabulate parameters. Whatever the individual difficulties to be overcome before a considered profit and loss forecast and action plan can be produced, its prime purpose in our context is to serve as a comparator. Where there are differences, the audit must assess whether these are a result of (a) poor original data, or (b) poor interpretation of data.

Errors in original data can result from:

(a) wrong sources;
(b) bad wording of questions and bad rapport with sources;
(c) insufficient number of sources;
(d) a few key sources not being approached;
(e) insufficient cross-checking and rechecking between different sources.

The use of insufficient sources may be typified by a company relying on information provided by the buying department of customer XYZ, who may know that they have bought 300 straight winders so far this year; 500 last year and about 600 the year before; that on average they last 5 years, that is they should have between 2500 and 3000 in use. Whereas the head of the maintenance department may have records showing that there are 1787 straight winders in XYZ company and that reliability problems have led to an enhanced rate of replacement, although of course the new process just coming on the stream next year will halve the number of straight winders needed.

Potential errors in interpretation of data are as numerous as there are people. The essence in both cases is to agree upon a method or approach, which if followed, will reduce the probability of error.

17.10 Auditing the system

The second form of audit involves testing the existing planning system to check for accuracy and effectiveness. Table 17.1 lists some useful guidelines.

17.10.1 Objectives
It is essential to start at the beginning and to examine how objectives are set. Ask about ten people at various levels within the company what they think the overall company objectives are, and ten completely different answers will probably be

Table 17.2   *Market planning guidelines*

(a) all employees clear about objectives of the company

(b) regular meetings of board/management committee to review, set and communicate objectives

(c) marketing personnel clear about department objectives, their basis and who sets them

(d) information gathering systemised, documented and evaluated to provide reliable bases for forecasts and strategy

(e) marketing personnel given a basic understanding of how the marketing plan is prepared

(f) a good plan format is available which can be used as a guide

(g) marketing personnel clear about marketing strategy, detail action programmes and who does what in order to achieve the objectives

(h) results are regularly monitored against forecast and corrective action initiated and communicated. Changes as a result of external and internal factors should be separated.

obtained, rather than ten answers which essentially say the same thing. Therefore the first step is to ensure that company objectives are agreed at top level, formalised, and then communicated throughout the organisation. Without clearly stated objectives it is not possible to start to produce a sensible marketing plan. The second step is to try to ensure that these objectives are realistically based upon the resources of the company and reflect the environment in which it operates. For example, a 20 strong UK company could not realistically expect to build sales of, say, solar panels from 0 to 300 in one year, but if the same company operated in Israel, 300 may be an attainable target. The third step is to repeat the medicine but for the marketing department only.

17.10.2 Information

In order to produce a good plan it is essential to have reliable and wide ranging information. It is necessary to check whether all the obvious sources are being used; newspapers, magazines, market surveys, company reports, analysts reports, customers, suppliers, even competitors. Although titbits are fed back from most of these sources from time to time, it is rare to find them properly recorded so that a complete picture can be formed. Using several sources enables the accuracy of each to be checked, one against the other. When previously made assumptions do not hold, the sources of information for those assumptions should be checked, to see if there is a trend of inaccuracy, so that information from those sources can either be discarded or treated with caution in the future. It is also important to record a wide spectrum of information; for example, economic, social and technical trends, the health and strategy of competitors, the health and strategy of customers.

In order to avoid scarce resources being wasted gathering and analysing unnecessary data, auditors should check that the parameters which are essential to the planning and control process have been identified, and the accuracy to which they have to be known determined. Each parameter that is to be used in the planning process must be assessed individually. For example, many companies having recognised the importance of segmentation for planning purposes, and having taken the trouble to define segments, persist in recording sales by product group and not by market segment, thereby losing a valuable link in the learning process. There is little point in preparing a plan if performance is not monitored against that plan — at all levels and not just at the final profit and loss level.

17.10.3 Preparation

A comprehensive plan format is a valuable aid to the preparation of good plans. A good format will stimulate thought and serve as a check list to ensure that no factor remains unconsidered by default. A good format will ensure that plans are easily compared; between products, between divisions and between years. It is important to establish what, if any, planning concepts are in use — product life cycle, cumulative experience, risk matrix, market share, economies of scale and so on — and whether they are applied wisely. Are there other concepts which would be more useful or would increase understanding?

The next area to consider is who prepares the plan, who helps and why? Is this sensible? Do those involved truly take a marketing system view; that is, consider suppliers, customers, competitors, channels, environment, development, production, stocking and profit. Is all the carefully gathered information used, and is a concensus interpretation obtained, or at least alternative interpretations allowed and recorded? At the early stage of setting down the base position and the base assumptions, top management should have reviewed and input their opinion in order to minimise later changes, reduce wasted detail work, and allow modifications to occur before positions become polarised. Also at this stage, there should be an attempt to broadly set down in outline two or three real alternative strategies, clearly showing their basis, their strategic implications, and an approximation of their turnover/profit/ resource implications. Top management, in conjunction with operating management, should select one of the alternative strategies and communicate their reasons for doing so to everyone involved. Only then should more detail work begin, preparing action programmes and financial statements. If this approach is followed, subsequently negotiated revisions to the plan should involve matters of detail rather than of principle, and as a result any changes should not require the plan to be completely reworked.

17.10.4 Using the plan

It is now possible to move on to look at how the annual and the long term (3/5 year) plans are used. Who has copies? On what basis are copies restricted, and do all personnel have copies of the parts which affect them directly? On the assumption that personnel expected to contribute to the implementation of a plan may well try harder if they are able to identify with the plan and to follow the thinking behind it, it may be wise to make copies more widely available.

The two step approach applied in Section 17.10.1 to objectives should now be extended to cover strategy and action programmes. Experience indicates that not only will there be a wide diversity of answers, but also that there will be large areas of no knowledge at all. At this point one might reasonably wonder what, if any, point there is in expending much time and effort in producing a plan, if many personnel cannot remember, or have never been made aware of, its content. The second problem is relatively easily put right. Ensuring memory is only slightly more difficult if the contents of plans are regularly used by senior management for control purposes – and that brings us back to the operating control system. Audits can legitimately examine the efficacy of control systems, but that has not been considered here, as a description of the process would repeat much of what was discussed in the earlier sections of this chapter.

17.11 In conclusion

This book has attempted to provide a systematic approach to the problems of choosing the right products and the right markets to operate in, and having chosen; of operating as effectively as circumstances will allow. However, unless strategy formulation is frequently audited, and operations continuously controlled, the desired results are unlikely to be obtained.

References

1   LEAVITT, T.: 'Marketing myopia', *Harvard Business Review*, July/August 1960
2   KOTLER, P.: 'Marketing management: analysis planning and control' (Prentice Hall: 3rd edn. 1976 and 5th edn. 1984)
3   FREY, A. W.: 'Advertising' (Renold Press Company, 1961)
4   McCARTHY, E. J.: 'Basic marketing: a managerial approach' (Irwin, 1964)
5   KOTLER, P.: 'From sales obsession to marketing effectiveness', *Harvard Business Review*, Nov/Dec 1977
6   RODGER, L. W.: 'The coming age of marketing maturity' *in* RODGER, L. W.: 'Marketing concepts and strategies in the next decade' (Associated Business Programmes, 1973)
7   MICHEL, K. O.: 'Design of an intrafirm management developed programme for strategic management' *in* ANSOFF, H. I., DECLERK, R. P. and HAYES, R. L. 'From strategic planning to strategic management' (John Wiley & Son, 1976)
8   HISE, R. T. and KELLY, J. P.: 'Product management on trial', *Journal of Marketing*, Oct 1978
9   WILLS, G.: 'Sources of UK marketing information' (Thomas Nelson & Sons, 1969)
10 WILSON, A.: 'Assessment of industrial markets' (Associated Business Programmes, 1973)
11 ACKOFF, R. L.: 'A concept of corporate planning' (Wiley, 1970)
12 CHAMBERS, J. C., MULLICK, S. K. and SMITH, D. D.: 'How to choose the right forecasting techniques', *Harvard Business Review*, July/August 1971
13 SASSON, H.: 'Marketing strategies for technology based enterprise' *in* RODGER, L. W. 'Marketing concepts and strategies in the next decade' (Associated Business Programmes, 1973)
14 KOTLER, P. and COX, K. K.: 'Readings in marketing management' (Prentice Hall, 1972)
15 WILLS, G.: 'Technological forecasting' (Pelican, 1972)
16 AYRES, R. U.: 'Technological forecasting and long range planning' (McGraw Hill, 1969)
17 FISHER, J. C. and PRY, R. H.: 'A simple substitutional model of technological change' *in* CETRON, M. J. and RALPH, C. A.: 'Industrial applications of technological forecasting: its utilisation in R & D management' (Wiley Interscience, 1971)
18 'Perspectives on experience' (Boston Consulting Group, 1972)
19 ABELL, D. F. and HAMMOND, J. S.: 'Strategic market planning' (Prentice Hall, 1979)
20 'UK machine tool industry forecasts: 1981–1986' (Henley Centre for Forecasting, Nov 1981)
21 SCHOEFFLER, S., BUZZELL, R. D. and HEANY, D. F.: 'Impact of strategic planning on profit performance', *Harvard Business Review*, March/April 1974
22 BUZZELL, R. D. and WIERSEMA, F. D.: 'Successful sharebuilding strategies', *Harvard Business Review*, Jan/Feb 1981

23   SKINNER, R. S.: 'Launching new products in competitive markets' (Associated Business Programmes, 1973)
24   MARKIN, R. L.: 'Marketing: strategy and management' (Wiley, 1982)
25   FORD, D. and RYAN, C.: 'Taking technology to market', *Harvard Business Review*, March/April 1981
26   SCHEUBLE, P. A.: 'R.O.I. for new product planning', *Harvard Business Review*, Nov/ Dec 1964
27   KLAW, S. K.: 'The soap wars: a strategic analysis' *in* KOTLER, P. and COX, K. K.: 'Readings in marketing management' (Prentice Hall, 1972)
28   CHISNALL, P. M.: 'Effective industrial marketing' (Longman, 1977)
29   CORDOZO, R. N. and SMITH, D. K.: 'Applying financial portfolio theory to product portfolio decisions: an empirical study', *Journal of Marketing*, Spring 1983
30   'The product portfolio', Perspective No 66 (Boston Consulting Group, 1973)
31   BUZZELL, R. D., GALE, B. T. and SUTTON, R. G. M.: 'Market share – a key to profitability', *Harvard Business Review*, Jan/Feb 1975
32   WOO, C. W. and COOPER, A. C.: 'The surprising case for low market share', *Harvard Business Review*, Nov/Dec 1982
33   LORENZ, C.: 'Why Boston Theory is on trial', *Financial Times*, 1981, Nov 11
34   (a) GOOLD, M.: 'How dogs can be given more bite', *Financial Times*, 1981, Nov 13
     (b) GOOLD, M.: 'Why dicey definitions are so dangerous', *Financial Times*, 1981, Nov 16
35   WENSLEY, R.: 'Strategic marketing: betas, boxes or basics' *Journal of Marketing*, Summer 1981
36   WIND, Y. and MAHAJAN, V.: 'Designing product and business portfolios', *Harvard Business Review*, Jan/Feb 1981
37   KARNANI, A.: 'Equilibrium market share: a measure of competitive strength', *Strategic Management Journal*, 1982, **3**
38   KAMI, M. K.: 'Gap analysis: key to super growth', *Long Range Planning*, 1969, **1**
39   ELIASSON, G.: 'Business economic planning' (Wiley, 1976)
40   ANSOFF, H. I.: 'Corporate strategy' (McGraw Hill, 1968: Pelican, 1976)
41   LORANGE, P. and VANCIL, R. F.: 'Strategic planning systems' (Prentice Hall, 1977)
42   WINER, L.: 'Are you really planning your marketing', *Journal of Marketing*, American Marketing Association, Jan 1965
43   RAMO, S.: 'The management of innovative technological corporations' (Wiley Interscience, 1980)
44   TROWBRIDGE, M. E. O. K.: 'Market research and forecasting as applied to the chemical plant industry: objectives, advantages and procedures', *Chemical Engineer*, Nov 1969, **CE 402**
45   ANSOFF, H. I.: 'A model for diversification', *Management Science*, 1958, **4**, No. 4
46   MARQUIS, D. G.: 'The anatomy of successful innovations' *in* 'Managing advancing technology, Vol. 1: Strategies and tactics of product innovation' (American Management Association, Inc., 1972)
47   SEVERIENS, J. J.: 'Product innovation, organisational change and risk' *Society for Advancement of Management, Advanced Management Journal*, Fall 1977
48   JOHNSON, S. C. and JONES, C.: 'How to organise for new products', *Harvard Business Review*, May/June 1957
49   HILL, R.W.: 'Marketing technological products to industry' (Pergamon Press, 1973)
50   MILLER, D. and FRIESEN, P.: 'Innovation in conservative and entrepreneurial firms', *Strategic Management Journal*, Jan/Mar 1982
51   'Success and failure in industrial innovation' (Project SAPPHO), The Science Policy Research Unit, University of Sussex, Mantell Building, Brighton, East Sussex BN1 9RF, 1972
52   PEREL, M.: 'Managing corporate new venture programs', SRI International Business Intelligence Programme, Guidelines No 1964, 1981

53 RADOSEVICH, H. R.: 'Strategic implications for organisation design' *in* ANSOFF, H. I., DECLERK, P. R. and HAYES, R. L.: 'From strategic planning to strategic management' (John Wiley & Son, 1976)

54 ANSOFF, H. I. and STEWART, J. H.: 'Strategies for technology based business', *Harvard Business Review*, Nov/Dec 1967

55 DAVIDSON, J. H.: 'Offensive marketing' (Cassell, 1972)

56 CARSON, J. W. and RICKARDS, T.: 'Industrial new product development: a manual for the 1980s' (Gower Press, 1979)

57 'The management of new products' (Booz, Allen & Hamilton, 1965)

58 TOLL, A. R.: 'New techniques in product planning' *in* CORAM, T. C. and HILL, R. W.: 'New ideas in industrial marketing' (Staples Press, 1970)

59 ANGELUS, T. L.: 'Why most new products fail', *Advertising Age*, 24 March 1969

60 OXENFELDT, A. R., MILLAR, D., SCHUCHMAN, A. and WINICK, C.: 'Insights into pricing from operations research and behavioural science' (Wadsworth Publishing Company, 1961)

61 GABOR, A. and GRANGER, C. W. J.: 'A systematic approach to effective pricing' *in* RODGER, L. W.: 'Marketing concepts and strategies in the next decade' (Associated Business Programmes, 1973)

62 STAPLETON, J.: 'How to prepare a marketing plan' (Gower Press, 1982)

63 BAIN, J. S.: 'Essays on price theory and industrial organisation' (Little Brown and Company, 1972)

64 DUNCAN REEKIE, W.: 'Advertising and price' (The Advertising Association, 1979)

65 SCHERER, F. M.: 'Industrial pricing: theory and evidence' (Rand McNally College Publishing Co., 1970)

66 DEAN, J.: 'Pricing policies for new products', *Harvard Business Review*, Nov/Dec 1950

67 ATKIN, B. and SKINNER, R.: 'How British industry prices' (Industrial Market Research Ltd., 1976)

68 MARKIN, R.: 'Marketing: strategy and management' (Wiley, 1982)

69 HOWARD, J. A. and SHETH, J. N.: 'The theory of buyer behaviour' (Wiley, 1969)

70 WEBSTER, F. and WIND, Y.: 'Organisational buying behaviour' (Prentice Hall, 1972)

71 HILL, R. W. and HILLIER, T. J.: 'Organisational buying behaviour' (Macmillan, 1977)

72 CYERT, R. M. and MARSH, J. G.: 'A behavioural theory of the firm' (Prentice Hall, 1963)

73 ROBINSON, P. J., FARIS, C. W. and WIND, Y.: 'Industrial buying and creative marketing' (Allyn and Bacon, 1967)

74 LEHMANN, D. R. and O'SHAUGHNESSY, J.: 'Difference in attribute importance for different industrial products', *Journal of Marketing*, April 1974

75 BRAND, G. T.: 'The industrial buying decision' (Associated Business Programmes, 1972)

76 BELLIZZI, J. A. and McVEY, P.: 'How valid is the buy-grid model', *Industrial Marketing Management*, 1983, **12**

77 JOHNSTON, W. I. and BONOMA, T. U.: 'The buying centre: structure and interaction patterns', *Journal of Marketing*, Summer 1981

78 HAKANSSON, H.: 'International marketing and purchasing of industrial goods: an interaction approach' (Wiley, 1982)

79 BUCKNER, H.: 'How British industry buys' (Hutchinson Marketing Library, 1967)

80 WILSON, A. and FOWLER, J.: 'Marketing of non-differentiated industrial products' *in* RODGER, L. W.: 'Marketing concepts and strategies in the next decade' (Associated Business Programmes, 1973)

81 FESTINGER, L. A.: 'A theory of cognitive dissonance' (Stamford University Press, 1962)

82 HART, N. A.: 'Industrial advertising and publicity' (Associated Business Programmes, 1978)

83 LEAVITT, T.: 'Communications and industrial selling', *Journal of Marketing*, April 1967
84 LEAVITT, T.: 'The morality of advertising', *Harvard Business Review*, July/Aug 1970
85 CHORAFAS, D. N.: 'Sales engineering: the marketing of technological products' (Cassell, 1967)
86 STRONG, E. K.: 'The psychology of selling' (McGraw Hill, 1925)
87 BROADBENT, S.: 'Spending advertising money' (Business Books, 1979)
88 GENTRY, S. and RODGER, L.: 'How British industry promotes' (Industrial Market Research Assn. Ltd., 1978)
89 FARIS, P. W. and BUZZELL, R. D.: 'Why advertising and promotional costs vary: some cross sectional analyses', *Journal of Marketing*, Fall 1979
90 LILIEN, G. L.: 'ADVISOR 2: Modelling the marketing mix decision for industrial products', *Management Science*, February 1979
91 KINNARD, R. W.: 'Measuring the profitability of industrial advertising' (Business Books, 1981)
92 TALLEY, W. J.: 'How to design sales territories', *Journal of Marketing*, January 1961
93 SMALLBONE, D. W.: 'The practice of marketing' (Staples Press, 1972)
94 BROWN, R.: 'From selling to managing' (American Management Association, 1968)
95 DUNKELD, S. B. and CASHIN, M. R.: 'Sales force practice today' (Institute of Marketing, 1979)
96 MILLER, E. C.: 'Objectives and standards of performance in marketing management' (American Management Association, 1967)
97 WILLIAMS, L. A.: 'Industrial marketing management and controls' (Longmans, 1967)

Bibliography

Chapter 1 The Marketing Concept

FAYERWEATHER J.: 'International marketing' (Prentice Hall, 1970)

Chapter 4 Information

RAWNSLEY, A.: 'Manual of industrial market research' (Wiley, 1978)

Chapter 5 Forecasting

ABERNATHY W. J. and WAYNE, K.: 'Limits of the learning curve', *Harvard Business Review*,
  Sept/Oct 1974
BRIGHT, J. R.: 'Evaluating signals of technological change', *Harvard Business Review*, Jan/
  Feb 1970
CHAMBERS, J. C., MULLICK, S. K., SMITH, D. D.: 'An executive guide to forecasting'
  (Wiley Interscience, 1974)
MORONEY, H. J.: 'Facts from figures' (Pelican, 1974)
SMITH, D. N.: 'Delphi forecasts for manufacturing technology' (S M E, University of Michigan,
  1979)
TWISS, B. C.: 'Social forecasting for company planning' (Macmillan, 1982)

Chapter 6 Market Structure and Segmentation

DEVINE, P. J., JONES, R. M., LEE, N., TYSON, W. J.: 'An introduction to industrial eco-
  nomics' (George Allan & Unwin, 1974)
NEEDHAM, D.: 'Economic analysis and industrial structure' (Holt Rinehart & Winston, 1972)
PRATTEN, C.: 'Economies of scale in UK manufacturing industry', Department of Applied
  Economics Occasional Papers No. 28, Cambridge University Press, 1972
PRAIS, G. J.: 'The evolution of giant firms in Britain' (Cambridge University Press, 1976)

Chapter 7 Product Analysis

CATRY, B. and CHEVALIER, M.: 'Market share strategy and the product life cycle', *Journal
  of Marketing*, Oct 1974

HEDLEY, B.: 'Strategy and the business portfolio', *Long Range Planning*, Feb 1977

HUSSEY, D.E.: 'Portfolio analysis: practical experience with the directional policy matrix', *Long Range Planning*, Aug 1978

THORELLI, H. B. and BURNETT, S. C.: 'Nature of the product life cycle for industrial goods businesses', *Journal of Marketing*, 1981, No. 4

Chapter 8 Planning

DOBSON, S. M., BAILEY, J. C. and SHORROCK, J. E. T.: 'Planning the strategy for troubled times', *Management Today*, Sept 1981

WEBSTER, F. E.: 'Industrial marketing strategy' (Wiley, 1979)

Chapter 9 Product Market Planning

WIND, Y. J.: 'Product policy: concepts methods and strategy' (Addison-Wesley Publishing Company Inc, 1982)

Chapter 10 Introducing New Products

BAKER, M. J.: 'Industrial innovation, technology, policy, diffusion' (Macmillan, 1979)

BARNES, D.: 'Discussion groups as an aid to new product development', *Industrial Marketing Digest*, 1980, **5**, No. 3

BUGGIE, F. D.: 'How to innovate', *Management Today*, Sept 1981

BUIJS, J.: 'Strategic planning and product innovation, some systematic approaches', *Long Range Planning*, Oct 1979, **12**

COOPER, R. G. and LITTLE, B.: 'Dimensions of industrial new product success and failure', *Journal of Marketing*, July 1979, **43**

SHINGLETON, J.: 'The customer as a source of new product ideas', *Industrial Marketing Digest*, 1981, **6**, No. 1

Chapter 11 Pricing

FOGG, C. D. and KOHNKEN, K. H.: Price cost planning', *Journal of Marketing*, April 1978

RYAN, W. J. L. and PEARCE, D. W.: 'Price theory' (Macmillan, 1977)

Chapter 12 Industrial buying

WIND, Y. and WEBSTER, F. E.: 'A general model for understanding organisational buyer behaviour' *Journal of Marketing*, April 1972

Chapter 13 Promotion

COLLEY, R.: 'Defining advertising goals' (Association of National Advertisers, 1962)

WEINBURG, C.: 'Advertising management' (Harper Row Ltd., 1974)

DHALLA, N.K.: 'Assessing the long term value of advertising', *Harvard Business Review*, Jan/Feb 1978

Chapter 14 Sales force decisions

JEFFRIES, A. A. and DUXFIELD, T. S.: 'Management and training of technical salesmen' (Gower Press, 1969)
WILSON, H. T.: 'Management of a sales force' (Gower Press, 1970)

Chapter 15 Selling

BLAKE, R. R. and MOUTON, J. S.: 'The grid for sales excellence' (McGraw Hill, 1970)
MILLER, G. A. and BORGEN, C. W.: 'Professional selling: inside and out' (Von Nostrand Reinhold Co., 1979)
BRAND, G. and SUNTOOK, F.: 'How British industry sells' *Industrial Market Research Ltd.,* 1977
FENTON, J.: 'The A–Z of industrial salesmanship' (Heineman, 1977)

Chapter 16 Distribution

BOWERSOX, D. J.: 'Logistical management' (Macmillan, 1978)
GATTORNA, J.: 'Handbook of physical distribution management' (Gower Publishing Co. Ltd., 1983)
BUXTON, G.: 'Marketing logistics' (Macmillan, 1975)

Chapter 17 Marketing control and Audit

WILSON, R. M. S.: 'Management controls and marketing planning' (Heineman, 1979)
WILSON, R. M. S.: 'Financial dimensions of marketing (Vol. 1)' (Macmillan, 1981)

Industrial marketing
Case histories of UK practice[*]

Contents summary

These case histories provide an opportunity to study marketing problems which have been faced by UK companies. All of them have previously been used on management courses. Working through the problems in the manner described in the series introduction should guide practitioners and students of marketing towards a greater understanding of how marketing theory[†] can help resolve real-life problems. The breadth of products and technologies covered should also help to broaden their awareness and their thinking. However, each case is complete in its own right and therefore it is not essential to work through the complete series. Instead it may be preferable for individuals to concentrate on those cases which seem most relevant to their situation.

Case History 1 – W.J.T.:
The Launch of a Packaged High Temperature Heat Recovery Unit
Describes the attempt of a small company to move from made-to-order systems towards a standard product, by filling an apparent market gap. Draws attention to issues such as acceptable levels of financial and technical risk, and practical product launch strategies.

[*] These case Histories are available from the University of Aston in Birmingham at £7.95 including postage, cash with order. Cheques should be made payable to the University of Aston and sent to:

Publications Officer
IHD Office
University of Aston in Birmingham
Gosta Green
Birmingham
B4 7ET
UK

[†] These cases were specifically written to fit chapter by chapter with this book.

Case History 2 — British Coldforming Company:
Responding to Change
Describes how a single technology components manufacturer was affected by political, economic and technical change outside its control. Focusses attention on whether such changes can reasonably be forecast, and how they can be dealt with.

Case History 4 — Canfield Electronics:
Learning from Marketing Research
Compares two marketing research studies commissioned by a manufacturer of communication and control equipment for use in hazardous areas. It draws attention to the problems of choosing competent researchers, preparing an adequate brief, maintaining control (so that research results will actively help decision making), and learning from previous mistakes.

Case History 5 — Dunlop:
Forecasting UK Demand for Car Tyres
Describes the forecasting methods adopted by Dunlop. Raises issues such as the accuracy and breadth needed for forecasts, and the extent of their contribution to improved decision making.

Case History 6 — Simplex Lighting:
Developing a Segmentation Strategy
Describes an attempt to segment the market for industrial lighting equipment and to develop suitable segmentation strategies. Draws attention to the segmentation process, the extent to which different segments should be concentrated upon, and the problems of developing compatible but differentiated segment strategies.

Case History 7 — Bigmill Limited:
Deciding Where to Concentrate Product Development Resources
Describes the product development alternatives facing a manufacturer of milling machines. Focusses on how product life cycles and portfolio theory can help put the alternatives into perspective.

Case History 8 — Inco Electochemical Division:
Planning in Practice
Describes the planning process followed by Inco to help choose and develop a new business venture. Draws attention to the difficulties of diversification and new venturing, and to the limits of planning's contribution to success.

Case History 9 — The Mainline Control Terminal:
A Product Market Mismatch?
Describes how apparently logical technical developments can fail to meet market requirements. Draws attention to the problems created by rapidly advancing

technology and of matching available technology to market needs, as well as to the problems of choosing suitable methods of promotion for new products with a defined but limited market appeal.

Case History 10 – Wilmotts:
The Development of a Timber Grading Machine
Describes the problems faced by an individual in his attempts to develop and market an innovative product. Draws attention to the problems arising from long development cycles, meeting statutory requirements, and from limited funds; for example, lack of adequate market information and analysis, and the need to obtain financial, marketing and technical help.

Case History 11 – Geest Materials Handling:
Strategies for Standard and Non-standard Products
Contrasts the pricing, distributing and promotional strategies adopted for different ranges of products. Raises issues about the breadth of product ranges, market based pricing, loss leaders and selling via mail order.

Case History 12 – Ashton and Moore Limited:
Handling Ongoing Contracts
Describes how a potentially very large metal finishing contract was obtained and why that led to the purchase of expensive new plant. Sets out the alternatives facing the company when the contract was unexpectedly cancelled. Raises issues such as acceptable levels of commitment to a single customer, the amount of money and effort to be expended to gain a new customer, and how much confidential manufacturing information should be released to enquirers in order to gain their confidence.

Case History 13 – Linvar:
The Launch and Promotion of Linspace 21
Describes the launch and promotional strategy adopted by Linvar. Focusses attention on the problems of deciding how much to spend and how to divide the expenditure between the various forms of promotion.

Case History 14 – Marwin Cutting Tools:
Managing a Technical Sales Force
Describes how the sales force was organised and controlled. Raises issues about setting sales priorities, allocation of sales territories, incentive systems, control systems, and combining selling direct with selling via distributors.

Case History 15 – Unimation:
Selling Industrial Robots
Describes the methods adopted by the company to follow up enquiries. Draws attention to the need to continually evolve procedures as the market situation changes.

Case History 16 — Anton Products:
The Distribution of Rubber Conveyor Belts
Describes the choices facing Anton Products when it decided to streamline its distribution practices. Focusses particularly on the choice between minimum cost and maximum impact, as well as on the methods used by large companies to reach investment decisions.

Case History 17 — The Hydrovane Compressor Company:
An Example of Marketing Control
Describes how the company plans, controls and motivates its sales and distribution channel. Raises issues about the extent, accuracy and methodology of sales forecasting, budgetary control, operational control, and distribution control.

Index

action plans, 140, 146, 147, 359
advertisement placement, timing and frequency, 268–273
advertisement presentation, 267–268
advertising agencies, 267
advertising awareness, 260
advertising conflicts, 271–273
advertising effectiveness, 282–284
advertising expenditure, 113
advertising image, 257–259
advertising messages, 264
advertising process, 263–273
advertising recall, 282
advertising role, 259–263
after sales service, 220, 346
agents, 313, 347, 348–349
AIDA, 268
appraisal interviews, 306–308, 314–315
attributes analysis, 179

barriers to entry, 98, 153–154, 209, 258–259
Bayesian analysis, 86–89
bid teams, 33
bidding, 32, 215–220, 331–333
Boston portfolio matrix, 123–127
bottom up forecasts, 92, 291
brainstorming, 179
brands, 265
break even, 121, 139, 154
brochures, 278–279
budgets, 140–141
business analysis, 186–187
business definition, 138
business objectives, 139
business strategy, 13, 140
buy response curve, 200–201, 208, 211

buyers risk premium, 159–162
buyers role, 232
buying criteria, 242–243, 245–246, 248, 251, 264, 325
buying decision reinforcement, 263
buying different products, 242–246, 248–251
buying models, 227–231
buying power, 49
buying stages, 227–228, 230, 237–239, 242–244, 249, 319
buying teams, 231, 234, 247–248, 249

capital goods, 220–221, 244, 246, 250–251, 331–333
case studies, 382
cash cows, 124
cash flow, 120–122, 124, 146
catalogues, 278–279, 348
central services, 25
channel choice, 347–352
choice of forecasting method, 65–68
cluster sampling, 48
commission, 312–314
communications, 25
company image, 166, 260, 266–268
company purpose, 138
competitive advantage, 5, 9, 96, 100, 105, 163, 168, 186, 197, 264, 336
competitive basis, 95
competitive position, 123
competitive strength, 127–128, 134
competitor scrutiny, 198
competitor size and numbers, 95
complementary pricing, 196
computer lists, 60
computer systems, 62

concentrated marketing strategy, 105
conferences, 280–281
consignment stocks, 351
consortiums, 333
consumer buying behaviour, 225–231
contract pricing, 215–220
control, 132, 173, 303–309, 356–367
control and motivation, 365–367
control of distribution, 352–354
control response time, 364–365
convenience goods, 226
correlation, 82–83
cost plus pricing, 204–207, 214
credibility, 261, 266
customer based organisation, 33–34
customer categories, 50
customer enquiries, 262–263
customer evaluation, 303–304, 318–319,
    321–323, 324, 325
customer lists, 60
customer loyalty, 114, 154
customer records, 42, 300, 303–304
customer service level, 339–340, 360–
    361
customer size, 16, 48–49
customer training, 316–317
customer trends, 42

data sources, 42–45, 47–50
decision trees, 86–89
definition of marketing, 1–2
delivery delays, 340, 361
delivery frequency, 345
delivery reliability, 341–342
delivery systems, 343–346
Delphi forecasting, 71–73
demand forecasts, 19, 21
demand security, 95
demand variables, 4
derived demand, 18–21
design capability, 18
desk research, 46
destocking, 20
deviations from plan, 363–364
differential advantage, 100
differentiated marketing strategy, 105,
    265
direct mail, 277–278
discounts, 113, 115, 194, 197, 203, 212
distress purchases, 16
distribution, 334–355
distribution chains, 99

distribution channels, 347
distribution control, 352–354
distribution importance, 336
distribution of different types of product,
    336–337
distribution systems, 100–101
distributor agreements, 354–355
distributor enthusiasm, 261–262
distributor territories, 353
distributors, 100–101, 261–262, 347–
    354
diversification, 157–158, 160, 165
dog products, 124–125

economic cycle, 13–14, 118, 210–211
economies of scale, 96–97
efficiency of organisations, 25
eighty-twenty rule, 17
elasticity of demand, 199
enquiries, 262
enquiries converted into orders, 42
environment, macro, 13–15
environment, marketing, 12, 15, 21–23
exchange value, 194
exhibitions, 192, 273–277
expected values, 83–89, 160
expenses, 315
experience curve, 80–81, 206
exponential smoothing, 79
exporting, 34, 96

fashion, 95
feedback, 39
field data sources, 47–50
field trials, 188–189
follower companies, 176
forecasting, 64–93
forecasting method choice, 65–68
forecasting problems, 72, 75, 79, 81, 83
forecasts, bottom up, 92, 291
forecasts, demand, 19, 21
forecasts, top down, 92
four P's, 4
free trials, 281
frequency of purchase, 226
functional organisation, 26–29

gap analysis, 128–130
GEC/McKinsey portfolio matrix, 127–
    128
geographic based organisations, 35–36
goodwill, 115, 167, 235, 361

government intervention, 167, 209
government policy, 14
government subsidy, 118–119
growth, 139
guarantees, 161

horizontal integration, 101

idea generation, 178–180
identifying potential customers, 320–321
image, advertising, 257–259
image, company, 166, 260, 266–268
image, product, 114, 212
implementation of marketing principles,
    10
incentives, 197
incorrect data, 56–57, 371
industrial buyers, 231–233
industrial market environment, 16–18
industrial purchasing process, 233–246
information, 36–63, 372–373
information bias, 56, 366
information sources, 42–46, 47–50, 57,
    63
information systems, 58–63, 303–304
information time horizons, 37–39
information usage, 62–63
information, common errors, 43, 56–57
innovation, 157–160, 163, 169–180
innovation success, 173–174
installation, 346, 349
installers, 347
intensive distribution, 350
intermediaries, 347
interviews, appraisal, 306–308, 314–315
interviews, marketing research, 53–55
interviews, recruitment, 309–310
interviews, structured/unstructured, 54
interviews, telephone, 55
items for resale, 245–246

joint ventures, 169–172
journey planning, 293

key accounts, 315–316

learning costs, 162
learning curve, 80–81, 206
leasing, 221
licences, 169–172
life cycles, 66, 107–120
loss leaders, 196

machine tool demand, 82
macro environment, 13–15
made to order products, 18, 179–180,
    220–221, 250–251, 331–333, 337
mail order, 279, 348
mail shots, 277–278
management attitudes, 145–146
marginal pricing, 196–197
market definition, 2, 102, 123–124
market evaluation, 153–155
market growth, 124–125, 154
market leadership, 176, 208–210
market planning guidelines, 372
market potential, 40, 75–76, 155, 163
market related risk, 156–160
market saturation, 155
market segmentation, 102–106
market segments, 160, 265, 266
market share, 78, 84–86, 96, 118, 124
market share expansion, 125–126
market size, 15, 38
market structure, 38, 48–49, 94–103,
    208–210
market trends, 38
marketing audit, 367–374
marketing concept, 2
marketing cycle, 1–3
marketing department authority, 28
marketing department tasks, 26–28
marketing environment, 12, 15, 21–23
marketing management, 3
marketing mix, 4
marketing orientation, 8
marketing research, 45–58, 179, 185,
    189
marketing research brief, 46
marketing research evaluation, 87–88
marketing research interviews, 53–55
marketing strategy, 110–116, 140
marketing strategy checklist, 369–370
matching the competition, 207–208
matrix organisation, 31–32
media, 265–267
media schedules, 272
models, 83–86
monopolies, 210
morphological analysis, 74
motivation, 312, 365–367
multiplier effect, 19

new business sales ratio, 292
new product analysis, 186–187

new product pricing, 81
new product screening, 180–185
new product testing, 187–190
new products, 38, 168–193
new technology, 37, 82, 157–160, 162, 176, 221
new ventures, 174–175
normative relevance analysis, 73–74
numerical data, 358–359, 362–363

objectives, 139–140, 357–361, 371–372
off peak pricing, 196
oligopoly, 208–209
operational marketing, 5
opportunity costs, 166
order processing, 340–341
organisation culture, 15–16, 24–35
organisation principles, 24–26
organising for innovation, 173–175
organising for marketing, 24–35
outside carriers, 345

P.I.M.S., (profit impact of marketing strategy), 84–86
package of benefits, 5, 8
packaging, 282, 338
parallel technology, 40, 95
penetration pricing, 195
pent up demand, 112
perceived value, 6, 213, 220, 233–234
performance reviews, 306–308
personal marketing research interviews, 53–55
persuasive communication, 259
physical distribution, 338–346
pioneer companies, 176
pioneer products, 176
pipe market segmentation, 104–105
plan implementation, 148–149
plan negotiation, 144
plan preparation, 373
plan use, 373–374
planning, 131–167
planning benefits, 132
planning guidelines, 372
planning hierarchy, 135–136, 149–150
planning horizons, 131–132, 143
planning in practice, 141–145
planning incentives, 147–148
planning manuals, 135
planning process, 133–138, 141–142, 144–148, 150

planning purpose, 131–133
post codes, 300
post purchase dissonance, 254, 263
postal questionnaires, 50–53
posters, 281
preferred bidder status, 218–219, 250
preferred customer, 252
press releases, 279–280
prestige pricing, 195
price, 194–224
price bands, 202–203
price elasticity of demand, 199–200
price leadership, 208–210
price premium, 212
price reduction, 210–211, 212
price skimming, 212
price value barometer, 210
price–volume profit relationship, 203–204
price–volume relationship, 199–203
pricing capital goods, 220–221
pricing complementary products, 196
pricing contracts, 215–220
pricing goals, 195–197
pricing methods used by British industry, 222–223
pricing products, 99–100, 211–214
probabilities, 86–89
probabilities, posterior, 87
probabilities, prior, 86
product abandonment, 115–116, 165–167
product and market risk, 156–160
product appeal, 11
product appraisal, 180–185
product awareness, 260
product benefits, 11, 318
product conception, 178–180
product decline, 115
product depth, 163
product development, 116–117, 122, 171–172, 177–190
product development costs, 121–122
product development risk, 177–178
product differentiation, 99–100, 106, 198
product extension, 113, 157
product group organisation, 29–31
product growth, 112–113
product image, 114, 212
product improvements, 114, 115
product introduction, 110–112
product launch, 110, 191–193
product launch rate, 175–177, 179

product life cycle, 66, 107–119
product life cycle expenditure and income, 120–122
product life cycle prediction, 108
product lives, 9, 97, 119–120
product management, 29–31
product market, 152–167
product market matrices, 156–160
product market strategy, 152–153, 162–165
product maturity, 113–114
product orientation, 7, 8–10
product package, 5
product portfolios, 122–128
product positioning, 103, 115
product pricing, 211–215
product range, 163, 165–166, 202, 214
product range pricing, 214–215
product replacement, 111, 116–119, 156–165
product saturation, 114–115
product screening, 180–185
product specialisation, 296
product specification, 6, 152, 169, 181–182, 187–188
product strategy, 109
product succession, 116–119
product systems, 18
product testing, 187–189
product width, 163
profit, 6, 203–204, 206
profit over product lives, 121–122
project management structures, 32–33
promotion, 192–193, 256–288
promotional budgets, 111, 282–288
prospects, 292, 320–323
prototypes, 188
public policy, 14
public relations, 279–280
purchase specification, 219, 245, 250, 325, 331, 333
purchaser-supplier links, 252–253
purchasing process, 233–246

question mark products, 125–126
questionnaires, postal, 50–53
quota sampling, 48

rapid skimming, 212
ratchet effect, 21
recall tests, 282
reciprocal purchases, 194
recruitment interviews, 309–310

regional sales centres, 346
reporting procedures, 303–307, 361–363
reputation, 189, 195–196, 198, 203, 236, 253, 261
research and development capability, 96, 168–169, 175–177
resistance to marketing, 10–11
resource allocation, 132
return on investment, 140, 162, 164, 183
return over product life cycle, 120–122
risk, 123, 125, 139–140, 153, 156–164, 166, 176–178, 235–237, 251

sales agents, 313
sales authority, 29
sales call rates, 293, 362–363
sales force, 42, 289–335
sales force appraisal, 314–315
sales force control, 303–309
sales force economies, 294–296
sales force motivation, 312
sales force recruitment, 309–310
sales force role, 289–290
sales force size, 290–296
sales force structure, 296–300
sales force training, 192, 310–312
sales forecast security, 139
sales forecasts, 76–80, 290–291
sales forecasts using probabilities, 89–92
sales gap forecasts, 128–129
sales leads, 320–321
sales management, 27–34
sales mix, 359–360
sales organisation structure, 296–300
sales per call, 298
sales planning, 296, 328–331
sales potential, 75–76, 155, 300–302
sales presentations, 276–277
sales quotas, 300–302
sales reports, 303–308
sales role, 318–320
sales schedules, 60
sales spending, 113
sales targets, 24, 191
sales territories, 298, 300–302
sales trends, 76–80
sales visit planning, 323–324
sales visit reports, 59–60
sampling, cluster, 48
sampling, quota, 48
scenarios, 69–71

second sourcing, 252
security of demand, 95
selective distribution, 350
selling, 7, 324–328, 334–335
selling costs, 294
selling efficiency, 294
selling high value items, 331–333
selling ideas, 183
selling team, 332
selling to large organisations, 333–334
selling vs. marketing, 7–8
seminars, 276–277
service costs, 80
service engineers, 42
shopping goods, 226
skimming the cream, 212
sources of information, 42–46, 47–50, 57, 63
special accounts, 296
specialisation, 24
specialist salesmen, 296–297, 299
specialist distribution, 350
specialist exhibitions, 275–276
speciality goods, 226
sponsorship, 281
staff and boss relationship, 25–26
standard deviation, 77
standard industrial classification (SIC), 301
star products, 126
statistics, 43–45, 48, 76–80
stock control, 339
stock levels, 112, 116
stocking costs, 342–343
strategic marketing, 4
strategy, 140
strategy, business, 13, 140
strategy, product, 109
structured/unstructured interviews, 54
sub contractors, 97, 259, 332, 337
subjective forecasting, 92
substitute products, 153
substitution forecasting, 74–75
suggestion schemes, 178–179
supplier credibility, 261
suppliers search process, 237–241, 253
systematic planning, 133–134

takeovers, 169–172
technical applications advice, 250, 316
technical applications engineer, 42
technical articles, 280–281
technical change, 8–9, 14, 22–23, 98, 119–120
technical parameters, 17
technological forecasting, 67–69
technological substitution, 40, 74–75, 95
technology life cycle, 119–120
technology push, 179
technology's influence on market structure, 97–98
telephone interviews, 55
telephone marketing research interviews, 55–56
television advertising, 266
territory sales potential, 300–302
time value of money, 183
topdown forecasts, 92
trend extension, 76–80
trials, 187–189, 281
types of information, 39–41

ultimate market potential, 40
undifferentiated marketing strategy, 105
undifferentiated products, 99, 198, 240, 245, 253–254, 350–351
unit cost forecasts, 80–82
unit costs, 99, 204
unnecessary innovation, 172–173
uses of promotion, 256–257

value added, 6
value added in sales chain, 101
value of purchases, 17
value perception, 6, 213, 220, 233–234
value price ratio, 208, 211, 214, 224
venture teams, 174–175
vertical integration, 94, 101–102
voluntary consortiums, 333, 347

warehouses, 345
warning of change, 36, 132–133